OUR THOMPSON FAMILY IN MAINE,

NEW HAMPSHIRE AND THE WEST

BY

REV. CHARLES N. SINNETT

CONCORD, N. H.

RUMFORD PRINTING CO.

1907

OUR THOMPSONS IN MAINE, NEW HAMP-
SHIRE AND THE WEST.

PREFACE.

This is the story of a sturdy, honest, witty, patriotic and talented family. It is like that of many others of the name who have starred the history of Great Britain and America with noble achievements along many lines. And hosts of other Thompsons, as sturdy and gifted as these, have devoted their time and talents to the possession of lands— of which they have taken the best of care. Hence this book is largely the story of family migrations to the shaggy forests of Maine, to the fair fields of the West, and the sunny slopes of the Pacific, that broad acres might be theirs. It is a magnificent record that, though the author of this book has carefully studied the history of many of these acquisitions, he has found no slightest trace of any Thompson using unfair means in his quest. And at his country's call these precious acres and the homes upon them have always been left behind. When James Thompson moved to New Meadows, near Brunswick, Me., he made that whole region glow with patriotism when the news of the battle of Bunker Hill reached him in the field by the river. This is the story of all neighborhoods where these Thompsons have lived. Not till the last note of war had died away did they go back to the fields and forests which had such a charm for them. Find any Thompson who is a brilliant scholar, successful in the law, or along any line of work, and he is holding firmly to some island, or plot of "God's green earth." Let his country need him tomorrow and in the gray dawn his steps will ring down the pathway of duty. An old Thompson coat-of-arms lies before me. It shows that through long generations the family has been what it is today.

This book holds much about the noble Thompson women and of those who wisely chose Thompsons for husbands. Read the chapter on the descendants of Lieut. Hugh Mulloy and his wife and you have a picture of what these women have ever been, and what a precious heritage they gave to all the generations after them; and where a Thompson woman has not chosen to marry, the neighborhood where she has dwelt has arisen to call her blessed because of her unfailing charity. The brilliant career of Emma Eames is sketched as showing the talents of this race from which she sprang.

The author of this book has carefully examined every Thompson record and legend and has given the story of the ancestry as clearly as he could. He is still searching in Great Britain for more light on this matter. The results will be given in due time. He has gathered many other Thompson records, which may be printed later on.

This book, on which so much time has been spent in the last eight years, is nov published with many grateful thanks to the hosts of friends who have helped upon its pages.

Of that which has ever piloted the family Alonzo Thompson of Denver, Col., has well written:

"The guidance of Hope is a star on our way,
A beacon of light which points to the day
Whose curtain ne'er falls in the gloom of the night,
We follow it still, and the pathway is Right!"

EDMORE, N. D., November 22, 1906.

CHARLES N. SINNETT.

CHAPTER I.

THE THOMPSON ANCESTRY.

After reading with the greatest care every story of the Thompson ancestry which has been handed down among the descendants, and searching many other papers along these historical lines, we give, by the author's kind permission, the summary of Rev. Dr. E. S. Stackpole in his "Old Kittery, Me., and Her Families." He carefully searched all old documents which could throw any light on this matter.

There is a tradition that Robert Thompson was the emigrant ancestor of the Thompsons of Durham, N. H. He may have been the one who witnessed a deed in 1652. Thompson's Point, just south of the Cocheco River, was so called as early as 1644, and probably in 1635. Thompson's Point House was taxed in Dover, N. H., in 1648. The name of the owner is not given. Perhaps he was deceased.

(1) William Thompson appears in the records soon after this. Mr. John Scales of Dover, N. H., says he came from England in 1633. He received a grant of land in Dover, N. H., in 1656. This was laid out, March 17, 1658/'59 "beyond Cocheco Logg Swamp." Nov. 8, 1715, John Thompson, Sr., of Dover, conveyed to John Tuttle fifty acres of land which "were granted to my father, William Thompson, by the town of Dover." It lay beyond Cocheco Log Swamp, "bounded on the south by Bellamy Bank River." There is no evidence that William Thompson ever lived on this grant. On Oct. 15, 1656, a grant made to John White in 1651, was assigned to William Thompson. It was in Kittery, a short way below Sturgeon Creek. Several indications suggest that he had married the daughter of John White. In 1659 William Thompson was presented at York Court "for rebellion against his father and mother-in-law." He bound himself to the court in a bond of £20 "that hee will be of good behavior towards all men, especially towards his father and mother." (State copy of Court

Records, Vol. I, page 331.) William Thompson died in 1676, and his estate was appraised, June 22 of that year, at £52 and 18s. He left twenty-three acres of land, a house and orchard in Kittery, Me., and fifty acres in Dover, N. H., which he gave to his sons, William and Robert, and to John White. His wife had probably died before 1676. He left children, whose ages were given in 1677 as follows:

(2) John Thompson, aged 18; m. Sarah Woodman.

(2) William Thompson, aged 16; probably m. Mary Lovering.

(2) Robert Thompson, aged 13; "living with Toby Hanson in Dover."

(2) James Thompson, aged 11; m. Elizabeth Frye.

(2) Alexander Thompson, aged 6; m. Anna Curtis.

(2) Judith Thompson, aged 2.

Rev. Dr. Stackpole's sketch of the above children is also given here, as it shows some items of interest.

(2) John Thompson, the first child mentioned above, m., between 1678 and 1680, Sarah, daughter of Capt. John Woodman of Oyster River, Durham, N. H. He gave a bond in 1684 for the proper administration of his father's estate and to provide for "James his lame, impotent brother." March 30, 1708, John and James Thompson, "sons of William Thompson late of Kittery," conveyed the homestead at Cold Harbor to Francis Allen. The deed was witnessed by Jonathan Woodman, Robert Huckins and Daniel Kincaid, all residents at Oyster River. John Thompson's will was probated July 24, 1734. Wife, Sarah, survived him.

(3) John, m. Mary Davis, daughter of Ensign John Davis of Durham, N. H.

(4) Sarah Thompson, m. Abraham Scales.

(3) Jonathan, m., Jan. 23, 1717/18, Sarah Burnham of Durham, N. H.

(3) Robert, m. Abigail Emerson of Durham, N. H.

(3) Sarah, m. Samuel Hill of Durham, June 12, 1718.

(3) Hannah, m. Moses Stevens of Somersworth, N. H.

(3) Elizabeth, m., July 6, 1727, Eleazar Clark of Wells, Me.

(3) Mary, m. Hubbard Stevens.

(2) William Thompson, "living with Richard Otis of Dover in 1677," probably m., on the 4th of Sept., 1682, Mary Lovering, supposed to be the daughter of John Lovering of Dover. He lived in what is now Somersworth, N. H.

He had a son, William, who sold to Samuel Alley, Aug. 30, 1735, land that belonged to his father, William Thompson, deceased. This son, William, d. before Dec. 8, 1749, when Samuel Alley conveyed twenty acres in Rochester, N. H., to Elizabeth, widow of William Thompson, and her children.

(2) Alexander Thompson m. Anna Curtis, daughter of Thomas Curtis of York, Me. He had a grant of land in Kittery, Me., 1694; d. July 13, 1720. Widow, Anna, administratrix of estate, Oct. 4, 1720.

  (3) Elizabeth, m. John Allen of York, Me.

    (4) Elizabeth Allen, b. Oct. 2, 1718; m. David Avery in 1742.

  (3) Abigail Thompson, m. John Garry, or Geary; published Oct. 21, 1720.

    (4) Nine children recorded in York, Me.

  (3) Benjamin Thompson, b. Oct. 14, 1702; published Nov. 27, 1726, to Hannah Smith, daughter of Joseph Smith of York, Me.

    (4) Benjamin Thompson, b. Sept. 7, 1727; lived in Kennebunk, Me.; m. (first), Dec. 31, 1752, Eunice Lord, daughter of Nathaniel Lord, Jr.; m. (second), Mary Foster.

Children of first wife:

    (5) Benjamin Thompson, d. Feb., 1839 (85y.); Revolutionary soldier; m. (first), Elizabeth Lord; m. (second), Mrs. Hannah Luques.

    (5) Alexander Thompson, b. Arundel, Me., Aug. 27, 1757; d. Topsham, Me., Feb. 23, 1820; moved to Topsham, Me., 1785; m., April 8, 1784, Lydia Wildes or Arundel, Me., b. 1764; d. April 17, 1858. (See full records, Chapter VII.)

    (5) Stephen Thompson, m. Lois Taylor.

    (5) James Thompson m. Anna Walker.

    (5) Eunice Thompson, m. Daniel Perkins.

    (5) Lemuel Thompson m. Susanna Haley. (See full records, Chapter VIII.)

    (5) Isaac Thompson, d. at sea.

    (5) Hannah Thompson, m. Abner Littlefield.

    (5) Ezra Thompson, m. May Merrill.

Children of second wife:

    (5) Moses Thompson, unm.

    (5) May Thompson, d. young.

    (5) Lydia Thompson, m. Israel Burnham.

(4) Hannah Thompson, m. Jeremiah Linscot.

(4) Alexander Thompson b. Feb. 20, 1733/'34; m., 1772, Abigail Emery.

(4) Daniel Thompson, m., 1764, Sarah Linscot.

(4) Joseph Thompson, m., 1788, Olive Junkins, daughter of Capt. John Junkins. A large family. (See Rev. Dr. Stackpole's records.)

(4) Abel Thompson, m., 1767, Eleanor Staples and had several children.

(4) Ebenezer Thompson m., 1772, Mercy Staples.

(4) Meribah Thompson, m., 1760, Thomas Moulton.

(4) Mary Thompson, m., 1767, Daniel Linscot.

(3) John Thompson, b. Dec. 30, 1704; he settled in Sanford, Me.; published, Dec. 7, 1728, to Priscilla Davis of Haverhill, Mass., daughter of Stephen Davis and Mary Tucker.

The six children born in York, Me., were:

(4) Anna Thompson, b. Jan. 7, 1731/'32.

(4) John Thompson, b. Oct. 26, 1733.

(4) Jesse.

(4) Priscilla.

(4) Naomi.

(4) Olive, b. March 17, 1747/'48.

(3) Samuel Thompson, b. April 6, 1707; published Nov., 1730, to Hannah Bracket of Berwick, Me.

(3) Joseph Thompson, b. May 13, 1711; published Nov. 20, 1733, to Mary Welch of York, daughter of Philip Welch.

(4) Joseph Thompson, b. July 10, 1734; published, March 19, 1757, to Olive Harmon.

(4) Thomas Thompson, d. young.

(4) James Thompson, b. Oct. 6, 1739.

(4) Mary Thompson, b. June, 1746; m. Joseph Nowell.

(3) Jonathan Thompson, b. May 1, 1713; published, Oct. 1, 1737, to his cousin, Dinah Thompson, daughter of James Thompson.

(4) Elizabeth Thompson, b. May 14, 1739; m. James Gilpatrick.

(4) Abigail, m. Nathan Littlefield.

(4) Judith, m., 1770, Daniel Smith of York, Me.

(4) Esther Thompson, m. John Day.

(4) Jonathan Thompson, unm.

(4) Anna, m., 1804, Nathaniel Coffin of Shapleigh, Me.

(3) Curtis Thompson, b. June 2, 1715; published, Feb. 13,

1740, to Sarah Jenkins of York, Me., daughter of Daniel Jenkins.

(4) Sarah Thompson, b. Feb. 5, 1741; m. (second wife),
Nathaniel Lewis of Kittery, Me.

(4) Huldah Thompson, b. Dec. 29, 1744; m., 1767, Jacob
Emery.

(4) Dodavah Curtis Thompson, b. March 31, 1746.

(4) Jonathan Thompson, b. May 31, 1748; m. Lucy Mc-
Intire.

(4) Esther Thompson, b. June 1, 1751; m. Nicholas Fer-
nald.

(3) James Thompson, d. Oct. 22, 1724.

(2) James Thompson. We now come to this son of the Thompson ancestor in whom we are most interested. He was
born in 1666, according to the clear statement in his
father's deed that he was 11 years old in 1677. As is
noted in the statement of his brother John, "he was lame
and impotent." But it seems clear that he grew from
this early weakness into a manhood of the sturdiest type,
The bond which his brother gave to provide for him was
carried out in the same faithful and loving manner in
which many Thompsons in the long years since then
have fulfilled such pledges to their kin and neighbors.
James Thompson was a tailor by trade. Land was
granted him in Kittery, Me., in 1694 and 1696, for the
records state that James Thompson, on Feb. 1, 1709/'10,
late of Kittery, but now of York, sold these lands. It is
said that land was granted to him in York, Me., in 1701,
and that he removed thither prior to 1719. The York,
Me., records have the following, "York, Oct. 23, 1717, laid
out and bounded to James Thompson a tract of land
whereon he now liveth, being on both sides of the high-
way that leads towards Barwick from York Bridge, which
said James Thompson purchased of his brother Alexander Thompson, for forty acres, Jan. 4, 1713/'14." In
1727, James Thompson moved with his family to New
Meadows, Brunswick, Me. James Thompson was married
in Dover, N. H., by Rev. John Pike, March 3, 1700/'01, to
Elizabeth Frye, daughter of Adrian Frye, one of the
early, sturdy settlers at Frye's Point, Kittery, Me. She
was evidently a woman of great strength and ability.

List of the children of James Thompson furnished by Miss
Sarah A. Thompson of Topsham, Me., with this note: "I
send this copy of the records from the family Bible of my

grandfather, Ezekiel Thompson. It differs, in the number of children of his father, Capt. James Thompson, from all other records found of that family, but you can verify it from the list of the names of these children in the own handwriting of Captain James, which you have already copied." Help with this list was also furnished from the records which were gathered, March 5, 1838, by Gen. Jedediah Herrick from the town clerk of York, Me., and from Mr. Joseph Thompson, who was the only one of the Thompson name living at York in 1838:

(3) Judith Thompson, m., July 1, 1724, John Smith of York, Me., and had a large family.

       *   *   *   *   *

       *   *   *   *   *

(3) Alexander Thompson, b. at Kittery, Me. Ezekiel Thompson in his Day Book says: "He lived in Brunswick, Me., before the Indian wars. He lived to be over 80 years old. He had ño learning, but he was a hardy, honest, industrious man. He had several daughters, but only one son, James Thompson." Owned at New Meadows, Me., lot 40, 100 acres. M., May 20, 1731, Sarah Grover of York, Me., daughter of Matthew Grover.

       *   *   *   *   *

(4) James Thompson, b. York, Me., Dec. 9, 1735. Ezekiel Thompson says, "He died in Wales, Me., leaving sons, Alexander and William, and several daughters." M. —— Anderson, who m. (second), John Arno of Monmouth, Me.

  (5) Alexander Thompson.

  (5) William Thompson.

  (5) Several daughters.

(4) Sarah Thompson, b. April 7, 1738; m. Thomas Gray and moved to Wales, Me.

(4) Hannah Thompson, b. New Meadows, Me.; m. "a Dr. John Nevers and moved to St. John, in the British Dominion."—Ezekiel Thompson.

  (5) Daughter, m. Ebenezer Crosby of Hampden, Me.

  (5) Daughter, m. Timothy Crosby.

(4) Tamsin, m. "Philip Jenkins and moved to Wales, Me., near Monmouth. The son of David Jenkins and Mercy Thompson."—Ezekiel Thompson.

(4) Elizabeth Thompson. Ezekiel Thompson says, "She died an old maid."

(4) Mercy Thompson and Mary Thompson. These two are added to the list of children by the Rev. Dr. E. S. Stackpole.

* * * * *
* * * * *

(3) Capt. James Thompson, called Jr. in some old records; b. Kittery, Me., Feb. 22, 1707; d. at Topsham, Me., Sept. 22, 1791; m. Reliance Hinkley, Mrs. Lydia (Brown) Harris and Mary Higgins. (Full records of his family on pages 16 to 43, Chapter II.)

* * * * *
* * * * *

(3) Cornelius Thompson, b. York, Me., Oct. 14, 1709; d. 1792; m. Hannah Smith of York, Me.

Ezekiel Thompson says: "My Uncle Cornelius had six sons:

"(4) Thomas, who moved to Plattsburg, N. Y.

"(4) Amos Thompson, who moved to Bowdoin, Me.

"(4) Joel Thompson, who moved to Lewiston, Me.

"(4) Richard Thompson, who moved to Wales, Me.

"(4) Robert Thompson, who d. at New Meadows.

"(4) Phineas, lost at sea on ship-of-war." (See full records of the family, pages 44 to 148, Chapters III and IV.)

* * * * *
* * * * *

(3) Sarah Thompson, b. April 17, 1711; "died in twenty days after her birth."

* * * * *
* * * * *

(3) Mercy Thompson, called Marcia and Marciel in some old records, b. April 1, 1712; m. (first), Mr. Austin of Brunswick, Me.; m. (second), David Junkins (some say Jackson) and settled in Brunswick, Me.

Children of first husband:

(4) David Austin, a celebrated Indian killer.

(4) Benoni, twin with the above.

(4) Shadrack Austin; lived in Greene, Me.

Children of second husband:

(4) Philip Jenkins; lived in Wales, Me.; m. Tamsin Thompson, daughter of Alexander Thompson and Mary Grover.

(4) David Jenkins.

* * * * *
* * * * *

(3) Joseph Thompson, b. March 23, 1713/'14; d. before 1759, as his deed shows. Lived at New Meadows and Sebascodegan Island, Harpswell, Me. He was in the latter place in 1756. Ezekiel Thompson says: "My Uncle Joseph lived and died on Sebascodegan Island. It is said that he was as strong as two stalwart men. He had four sons." M. Mary Hinckley, daughter of Dea. Samuel Hinckley of Brunswick, Me. It was perhaps his widow who m., Feb. 14, 1765, Isaiah Webber. He had lot 49 at New Meadows, 78½ acres.

(4) William Thompson, m. as his first or second wife, Miss Robbins of Dover, Me. It is probably the earmarks of his cattle which were recorded at Harpswell, Me., May 30, 1774.

(4) Joseph Thompson, Jr. Earmarks of his cattle recorded at Harpswell, Me., June 27, 1774; m., April 23. 1774, Sara Webber. Rev. Dr. E. S. Stackpole: "On April 16, 1773, Joseph Thompson and his wife, Sarah, gave a deed of 18 acres of land to James Stackpole, 'said land being a majority of the Lot No. 15, in the first division, and being a part of the real estate of my late honored father, and falling to my share as set off to me by men chosen by the Judge of Probate.' This land bordered on the New Meadows River, on Sebascodegan Island."

(4) John Thompson, d. at Bowdoin, Me.; perhaps m., Dec. 27, 1781, Lydia Small.

(4) Capt. Cornelius Thompson. "He was very active in the Revolutionary War. He first served as a private in the army for awhile until his term of enlistment expired. Then he went on board a privateer, and, some time before peace was declared, he commanded a fine armed brig, and proved himself to be a prudent, courageous commander. After the Revolutionary War closed he moved to Salem, Mass., and from thence to Mount Desert, Me., where he carried on navigation."

(5) Daughter, m. Mr. Robbins of Dover, Me.

(4) Judith Thompson, b. Brunswick, before her father moved to Sebascodegan Island, Feb. 8, 1743; d. Thomaston, Me., April 13, 1797; m., May 18, 1767, James Stackpole, who moved to Thomaston, Me. There were many and sturdy descendants, who are widely scattered over the country." These rec-

ords will be found in the "Genealogy of the Stackpole family," by Rev. E. S. Stackpole.

(4) Margaret Thompson, m. Mr. Toothaker.

* * * * *
* * * * *

(3) Dinah Thompson, b. May 6, 1716; m. her cousin, Jonathan Thompson, son of Alexander Thompson and Anna
Curtis; publishment of marriage, Oct. 1, 1737.

(4) Sarah Thompson, b. Feb. 5, 1741/'42; m. Nathaniel
Lewis of Kittery, Me.

(4) Huldah Thompson, b. Dec. 20, 1744; m., 1767, Jacob
Emery.

(4) Dodavah Curtis Thompson, b. March 31, 1746.

(4) Jonathan Thompson, b. May 31, 1748; m. Lucy Mc-
Intire.

(4) Esther Thompson, b. June 1, 1751; m. Nicholas Fer-
nald.

* * * * *
* * * * *

(3) Benjamin Thompson, b. York, Me., Sept. 9, 1717; d. 1765;
m., Oct. 17, 1744, Abigail Philbrook. (See full records,
pages 149–189, Chapter V.)

* * * * *
* * * * *

(3) Sarah Thompson, b. Nov. 8, 1719; m. ——— Scammon of
York, Me. Rev. Dr. E. S. Stackpole says he was of
Saco, Me.

* * * * *
* * * * *

(3) Mary Thompson, others call her Mercy, Marcial, etc., b.
Dec. 10, 1722.

* * * * *
* * * * *

(3) Richard Thompson, b. June 11, 1724. Ezekiel Thompson,
"Uncle Richard Thompson lived and died at Kennebunk, Me., a respected farmer; he left a large family
of sons and daughters." M. (first), Elizabeth Maddox,
a sister of John Maddox of Arundel Me.

(4) Caleb Thompson, m. ——— Clark of Wells, Me.

(5) David Thompson, m. ——— Clark of Wells, Me.

(6) Lucy, Mehitable, Ruth, Miriam, Elizabeth, Jane,

    Hannah and Theodore, who were in Kennebunk, Me., in 1841.

 (5) Joshua Thompson.

 (5) Elizabeth Thompson.

 (5) Richard Thompson.

 (5) Polly Thompson.

 (5) Caleb Thompson.

(4) Richard Thompson, m. (first), Abigail Page, daughter of Col. David Page of North Conway, N. H.; m. (second), Mary Smith of Wells, Me., daughter of James Smith.

Children of first wife:

 (5) Robert Page Thompson, m. Elizabeth Stowers of Prospect, Me.; settled in Freeport, Me., and lived also in Lewiston, Harmony and Eddington, Me.

 (6) David Page Thompson, m. Elvira Savage Follett.

 (7) Justine Thompson.

 (6) Upham Thompson.

 (6) Barnard Newall Thompson.

 (6) Elizabeth Lois Thompson.

 (6) Samuel Stowers Thompson.

 (6) Richard Thompson.

Children of second wife:

 (5) Samuel Thompson.

 (5) James Thompson.

 (5) Abigail Thompson.

 (5) Joseph Thompson.

(4) Mercy Thompson, m. Jonathan Littlefield.

 (5) Nathaniel Littlefield.

 (5) Daniel Littlefield.

 (5) Huldah Littlefield.

 (5) Polly Littlefield.

 (5) John Littlefield.

(4) Hannah Thompson, m. Samuel Smith, brother of the wife of Richard Thompson.

 (5) Stephen Smith.

 (5) Joseph Smith.

 (5) Hannah Smith.

 (5) Robert Smith.

 (5) Abigail Smith.

(4) Joseph Thompson, m ——— Wakefield.

 (5) Caleb Thompson.

 (5) Lyman Thompson.

(4) David Thompson, m. (first), Lydia Perkins of Kennebunk, Me.; m. (second), ——— Cousins.

Child of first wife:

> (5) Lydia Thompson, m. Isaac Littlefield of Kennebunk, Me.

>> (6) Ephraim Littlefield.

>> (6) Mary Jane Littlefield.

>> (6) Isaac Littlefield.

Children of second wife:

> (5) Seth Thompson; lived at Hermon, Me.

> (5) Mehitable Thompson.

> (5) Thomas Thompson.

> (5) Betsy Thompson.

> (4) Abigail Thompson, m. Stephen Smith of Wells Me.

*   *   *   *   *
*   *   *   *   *

(3) Elizabeth Thompson, b. April 19, 1726; d. Dec. 22, 1726.

CHAPTER II.

Capt. James Thompson of New Meadows, Brunswick, Me., and his descendants.

His line: (1) William Thompson; (2) James Thompson of Kittery, Me.

(3) Capt. James Thompson, b. Kittery, Me., Feb. 22, 1707; d. Topsham, Me., Sept. 22, 1791. Wheeler, in his "History of Brunswick, Topsham and Harpswell, Me.," says of him, "He came to Brunswick from Biddeford, Me., about 1739, and settled on the New Meadows River."

In 1757 he was in Capt. John Getchell's company, with his brothers, Cornelius and Alexander, and with Samuel Thompson. He was selectman at Brunswick, Me., 1748, 1752, 1753, 1754 and 1757. He was a dealer in general merchandise, and some of his account books are in the possession of his great-great-grandson, Mr. Charles Sproull Thompson of Milwaukee, Wis. A few records of sales are herewith given from this ancient book:

"1737. 8 bushels of meal at 13 shillings, 5 pounds & 4 shillings.

"1738. Sold two dozen buttons at 15 shillings. A jacket and breeches at 4 pounds & 10 shillings. A cow at 11 pounds. Fifteen pounds of beef at 7 shillings & 6 pence. Half a load of hay at 2 pounds. For making a jacket one pound. A pair of leather breeches at 3 pounds and 5 shillings. One ton of oak timber at 33 shillings. A calf at 2 pounds and 11 shillings. One grindstone at 2 pounds and 3 shillings.

"1739. One half a load of hay at 1 pound and 5 shillings. Two bushels of white meal at 1 pound and 6 shillings. Two bushels of rye meal at 1 pound and 2 shillings. One bushel of Indian meal at 1 pound and 7 shillings. A hat at 3 pounds and 18 shillings. One thousand pens and one ounce of thread at 9 shillings. Twelve yards of bed ticking at 6 pounds. One cake of gingerbread at 1 shilling. One half a kentle of fish at 15 shillings. Wharf timber at 7 shillings.

"1740. Two bushels of apples at 10 shillings. One pair of cards at 11 shillings. One axe at 1 pound. Two calves at 2 pounds and 8 shillings. Two quarts of rum at 2 pounds and 8 shillings.

"1741. A pair of knee breeches at 3 pounds and 5 shillings. A swine at 3 pounds and 6 pence. Four gallons of cider at 8 shillings. 6 pounds of butter at 18 shillings. Twenty days' work by brother Benjamin at 10 pounds.

"1742. One quart of oil at 2 shillings. 8 pounds of sheep's wool at 1 pound, and 17 shillings. Half a barrel of flour at 3 pounds and 13 shillings. One quarter of a barrel of meal at 3 pounds and 12 shillings.

"1743. One bushel of salt at 14 shillings. To use of gondola for two days, 10 shillings.

"1744. One bushel of peas at 12 shillings and 6 pence. 6 bushels of meal at 3 pounds and 2 shillings Feb. 18, 1744. To one day's work of myself and oxen, 1 pound and 6 shillings. To one yoke of oxen for one day, 8 shillings. To mending fence two days, 1 shilling. One bushel of potatoes 7 shillings.

"1745. Half a bushel of peas at 12 shillings. To use of grindstone, 16 shillings.

"1749, Sept. One barrel of rum, 30 pounds. One barrel of flour, 15 pounds. Five bushels of meal, 8 pounds and 5 shillings. Two pounds of candles, 12 shillings. Ten pounds of flax, 2 pounds. 8 pounds of Sheeps wool, 4 pounds.

"1749. Three handkerchiefs, 30 shillings."

Mr. Charles Sproull Thompson says: "From the old account book it seems that James Thompson was a cobbler, did some farming, and had scows on the New Meadows River. He prospered well, and became a man of much importance. He was distributing colonial gunpowder to his scattered neighbors about the time when these entries close. I have his commission as ensign in Revolutionary Army, which is signed by Gov. Shirley of Massachusetts."

In 1741 he owned at New Meadows, Me., Lot 34, 100 acres.

Capt. James Thompson m. (first), April 13, 1732, Reliance Hinckley, who d. May 23, 1751; she was the daughter of Dea. Samuel Hinckley, who traced his ancestry to Governor Hinckley of Massachusetts, who came with the early settlers to Plymouth. The line is thus given: (1) Samuel Hinckley; (2) Samuel Hinckley; (3) Gov. Thomas Hinckley; there were ten children of this first marriage; m. (second), Dec., 1751, Mrs. Lydia (Brown) Harris, who d. Feb. 10, 1764; she was of Ipswich, Mass.,

2

and was a sister of Lieut. Benjamin Brown; there were six children of this second marriage; m. (third), March 22, 1764, Mary Higgins, who d. May 23, 1790; there were no children of this third marriage.

Children of Capt. James Thompson and Reliance Hinckley:

(4) Elizabeth Thompson, b. March 13, 1733; d. July 21, 1766; m., Aug. 8, 1752, Daniel Weed of Newbury, Mass. "They were both buried on Great Island, Harpswell, Me., where they had made their home after their marriage; these parents d. within a year of each other, and their six children were thus doubly orphaned and they were adopted by their uncles and aunts; Mrs. Reliance Edgecombe of Saco, took Patience Weed."

(5) James Weed, b. New Meadows, Me., July 17, 1753.

(5) Relyance Weed, b. Oct. 7, 1754, m., Nov. 21, 1771, George Brown of Georgetown, Me.

(5) Patience Weed, b. Sebascodegan or Great Island, Harpswell, Me., Aug. 3, 1756; m. Thomas Chamberlain.

(6) The daughter, Reliance Chamberlain, came on a visit to her mother's aunt, Jemima Ham, and she married her eldest son, John Ham.

(7) Reliance T. Ham.

(5) Lydia Weed, b. June 23, 1758; m. Samuel Welch.

(A Thomas Weed of Thomaston, Me., m., July 16, 1777, Annie Williams. He may have been of this family.)

(4) Brig.-Gen. Samuel Thompson, b. New Meadows, Brunswick, Me., March 22, 1735; d. Topsham, Me., May 16, 1798; (63 y.). He was buried in the old cemetery at Ferry Point, Topsham, Me. When he had laid out this graveyard he said, "It is where I can go by land and water." But when the railroad bridge was placed across the river all those who had been interred in this quiet place were removed to River View Cemetery in Topsham. The general's remains were easily identified, as he had been buried in a coffin bound in brass and adorned with a brass plate. His bones were placed in the same grave as those of his son, Humphrey. In 1903 a Revolutionary soldier's marker was placed on his grave by the Sons of the American Revolution. He is said to have moved to Topsham, Me., in 1784.

He was licensed to sell tea in 1763, as a retailer in 1772 and 1774 and as an innholder in 1773. He was very successful in business and is said to have been worth $35,000 when he died. A little less than one half of this amount was in real estate, of which he owned the most in Topsham, though he possessed considerable in Bowdoin, and some in Bath and Brunswick. We shall get a still clearer idea of his business ability if we consider the troublous times in which he lived, and that in the tax list of 1758 his real estate was valued at but four pounds and his personal property at ten pounds and eighteen shillings. In 1763 his taxable property was, real estate seven pounds, two oxen, one horse, one cow, two swine, thirty-nine vessel tonnage and three pounds income on trade. What he gained from these humble beginnings was done by the strictest honesty, as, in the midst of the many abusive stories flung against him by his political enemies, there is but one that lays a finger on his business fidelity.

In the days in which General Thompson lived it was impossible to obtain much education at school, though the people of New Meadows sent to Boston when they could for the best instructors of those times. Yet no one ever saw him give one mournful look over this, or heard him tell what he might have done if his early environment had been better. He pored eagerly over the few books which he could secure, and was ever ready to learn of all whom he met and from every changing scene of his life. Once he heard a person say, "What a pity that man never had a better education!" He turned quickly and replied, with his brightest smile, "If I have no education, perhaps I can furnish a few ideas to those who have been in the schools."

While attending the General Court one of the law-yers handed him back a paper which he had written, requesting him to read it. "I wrote it for you to read, not to read myself," he said. One of the members of that same Court said to him, "If your education had been good you would have been a great man." But this earnest plea could not lead him to shed one tear over his past. He answered, with his face radiant with fun and hope, "If I had your education, I could put you in my pocket." And this noble man, like many others who have borne his name, made of all deficiencies in his early training an inspiration to help every boy and girl he could to the best and fullest education. His mind was so full of this that one day when he was walking

in Brunswick with some gentlemen who were absorbed
in other things, he pointed enthusiastically to a piece
of land which they were passing, and said, "That was
intended by the God of nature for an institution of
learning." That same spot became the location of Bowdoin College, to which he gladly donated land. He was
also a member of its first board of overseers. And
when ne died the board of the college attended his
funeral in an earnest, grateful body, for well they knew
what a friend this famous school had known in him.

Judge Freeman wrote of Samuel Thompson, "He was
a portly man, not of very tall stature, but somewhat cor-
pulant, and apparently of a robust constitution."

Illustrations of his ready wit have already been given;
and every occasion of his life served as a background
on which these brilliant flashes shone out in the most
kindly manner. When he was in the House of Representatives he often excited the mirth of his fellow members. In the most strenuous days of the Revolutionary
War he lifted many a burden from the hearts of his
fellow patriots by his bright sayings. Amidst the peals
of laughter which followed, these dark clouds were
rolled away which the most powerful arguments could
not have robbed of their ominous knells of the down-
fall of America.

And he was never the man who wished to say the
bright things himself. Much that he said was only for
the sake of waking up the latent powers of merriment
and hope in others. And when any keen shaft was
aimed at him no one was more ready than he to see all
its force. Once, when a member of the General Court,
he was crossing a toll bridge leading into Boston, when
the bridge-keeper demanded toll of him. Toll was not
required of the members of the. Legislature and the
brigadier replied, with some dignity, "I belong to the
House, sir." The toll man made answer: "Belong to the
House! I should think you belonged to the barn." Then
the brigadier's merry laughter rang out as he nodded
his head. After that his favorite suit was one of gray
broadcloth, brushed in the neatest manner.

Nathan Goold of Portland, Me., has well said in his
most interesting pamphlet on Brigadier Samuel Thompson: "His long service to our country, much of it
without compensation, renders us under obligations

to his memory. Recognizing his services, the war department has recently named one of the batteries that comprise Fort McKinley on Great Diamond Island in Portland Harbor, 'the Thompson battery.' The armament consists of three eight-inch and two six-inch guns, mounted on disappearing carriages. When Samuel Thompson was but sixteen years old he appears in local history as a 'centinel' in Capt. John Getchell's company, from Aug. 14 to Sept. 14, 1751. He had a service of over four weeks of faithful scouting and guard duty. In 1757 he was a member of the train band, under the same Captain. At a Town meeting held in Brunswick, Me., Nov. 17, 1774, Samuel Thompson was chosen moderator. At that same meeting he was elected Captain of the town military Company with Robert Dunning as Lt. and Thomas Thompson as ensign. He was a member from Brunswick of the three Mass. Provincial Congresses and participated at Concord when men and means were voted to make the beginning of the Revolutionary war. He was also at the head of the Committee of Safety for his District. The records all clearly show that he occupied a position of prominence with his associates at these Congresses. On Oct. 13, 1774, he was appointed one of the committee to wait on Gen. Gage on the disturbed condition of the Province. Oct. 21, 1774, he was made one of the committee to obtain the names of those accepting appointments under Parliament, and the same day was appointed on a committee on the non-consumption agreement. Dec. 7, 1774, he was appointed a committee to represent Harpswell, Me., to prepare a paper on the number of that town's inhabitants, and the extent of the commerce of the colony. Dec. 10, 1774, he was appointed on a committee for Lincoln County to ascertain the state of the militia. Mch. 29, 1775, he was on a committee to bring in resolves in regard to accepting appointments under Parliament and in publishing their names. The Provincial Congress on Apr. 11, 1775, ordered that Col. Thompson be desired to immediately repair to Brunswick, Casco Bay, Woolwich, Georgetown, and other places of interest, to intercept the work of one Edard .Parry who was supplying the enemy with masts, spars and timber. He at once went with twenty resolute men and seized Parry and compelled him to give bonds with the penalty of two thousand pounds to abide in the town until the pleasure of Congress was known. They also made the enemy pay for their refreshment—which cost 42 shillings in legal money. This was before the Revolutionary war had actually begun. And the terror which spread among the Tories was increased by many other sturdy deeds.

"Ten days after the battle of Lexington Colonel Thompson wrote a letter from Brunswick to the Committee of Safety at Cambridge which is still preserved in the Mass. Archives. The penmanship is fair and his autograph is creditable. He had then been a selectman of Brunswick from 1768 to and including 1771. He was a delegate to the Cumberland County Convention of Sept. 21, 1774, at Falmouth Neck, now Portland, to consider the alarming state of public affairs and was one of the committee who drew up the resolutions that expressed the people's sentiments, of which it has been said that they compared favorably with any resolutions of that time. He had been the moderator of their town meetings, had just been appointed on the committee of inspection, and had been added to the committee to petition the General Court. The letter is as follows:

" 'I this minute have an opportunity to inform you of the State of our affairs to the Eastward; that we are all Stanch for our country, Except three men and one of them is Deserted, the other two are in Irons; as to the vessels which attempted to Convey Stuff to our enemies are stopt, and I am about to move two hundred of white pine masts and other Stuff got for our Enemies' use. Sir, having heard of the Cruill murders they have done in our Province (At Lexington and Concord) makes us more Resolute than ever, and finding that the Sword is drawn out first on their side, that we shall be animated with that noble Spirit that wise men ought to be, until our Just Rights and Libertys are Secured to us. Sir, my heart is with every true Son of America, though my Person can be in but one place at once, tho very soon I hope to be with you on the spot. If any of my Friends inquire after me, Inform them that I make it my whole business to pursue those measures Recommended by Congreses, we being upon the Sea Coast and in danger of being invaded by Piriats—as the 27th of inst there was a boat or barge came into our harbor and river, and sounding as they went up the river.

" 'Sir, as guns and powder is much wanted in this Eastern Parts and also Provisions, Pray, Sir, have your thoughts something in this matter against I arrive, which will be as soon as business will admit. Sir, I am, with the greatest regard to the Country, at heart, your Ready friend and Humble Servt.

" 'Samuel Thampson.

" 'Brunswick, Apr ye 29, 1775.'

"The effect of this letter is clearly seen from the fact than on the 9th of the following May the Council and House of Representatives ordered that a barrel of gunpowder be delivered to Col. Thompson from the commissary stores at Falmouth for the towns of Harpswell and Brunswick, he to account to them for the same. He carried the powder to the captains before May 31st and they were ordered to deliver it to the men when necessary.

"The British vessels then cruising along our coast were a constant menace to the peace of the fishermen and farmers who dwelt near the seashore and on the islands. They impressed men into their service, appropriated stores and resented remonstrance by burning buildings. The insolence of the British officers was almost unbearable and they were sincerely hated, none more so than Capt. Henry Mowatt of the *Canceau*, who in Apr., 1775, was at Falmouth protecting Capt. Thomas Coulson in the rigging of his mast ship, much to the annoyance of the inhabitants."

Dr. G. A. Wheeler in his fine History of Brunswick, Topsham and Harpswell, Me., gives the following account of the plan to break up this oppression of the enemy: "In May, 1775, occurred what is locally known as 'Thompson's War.' For some weeks previously, Col. Samuel Thompson, Col. Purington, Capt. John Simmons, Aaron Hinkley, Esq., John Merrill, Esq., Thomas Thompson and James Potter, had been holding secret meetings at the house of Aaron Hinkley, and had concocted a plan, first suggested by Col. Thompson, of seizing the British warship *Canceau*. Samuel Thompson was chosen Colonel, and John Merrill and Thomas Thompson were chosen Captains. Capt. John Simmons was appointed commodore. To prevent a premature disclosure of their plans, all the roads leading to Portland were closely guarded and none allowed to pass un-

less sworn to secrecy. Notwithstanding this, some inti-
mations of their designs reached the ears of Mowatt.
The original plan was to procure a vessel of suitable
size to carry a company of about seventy men; to dis-
guise the vessel as a wood coaster; to conceal the men
in the hold; sail for Portland in the night, go alongside
the *Canceau* and board her immediately. The rendez-
vous was to be New Meadows. The disclosure of the
plot somewhat altered their arrangements. They
sailed from New Meadows on the night of May 8th, and
landed on the morning of the 9th in a grove of thick
trees at a place called Sandy Point. There were about
fifty armed men, each wearing in his hat a small bough
of spruce. Their standard was a spruce pole with the
green top left on."

Mr. Nathan Gould, in his excellent history of Brigadier-General Thompson, which should be in the hands
of all members of the Thompson family, continues this
story: "Their camp, on the back side of Munjoy Hill,
was between Tukey's and the railroad bridge, in a thick
grove of pine trees where the men were concealed from
view. Sentinels were posted and Peletiah Haley was
sent into the town for information. Those who passed
that way were taken care of for a time. About one
o'clock, as Capt. John Merrill and two of his sentinels
were walking near the shore, they saw Capt. Mowatt,
Rev. Mr. Wiswell of St. Paul's Church, and the ship's
surgeon, land and walk up the hill. They seized and
carried them to Col. Thompson, who received Capt.
Mowatt's sword, which he immediately returned. The
news of all this soon reached the town's people and
caused consternation. The camp was visited by prominent citizens who strongly urged the release of the prisoners. Col. Thompson and his men refused to do so,
they contending that the war had already begun and
that Providence had put the captives into their hands.
As night was approaching it was decided to take the
prisoners to Marston's Tavern, which was done under
the escort of Col. Thompson's men and the Falmouth
Neck Co. The tavern stood in what is now Monument
Square, where the Am. Express office now is, but back
from the street. The two companies were drawn up before the door, where they remained. The excitement was
at it height. Lt. Hogg, the sailing master of the *Canceau,*

threatened to burn the town if Capt. Mowatt was not
released within two hours. It is said that Col. Thompson, having a slight impediment in his speech, replied,
'F—f—fire away. For every gun you fire I will cut off a
joint of Mowatt.' Gen. Jedediah Preble said that two
guns were fired without shot and that they frightened
the women and children to such a degree that some
crawled under the wharves, some ran down cellar and
some out of town. Such a shrieking scene was never
presented to view here.

"Evidently by a previous understanding or by the
alarm, Col. Edmund Phinney's regiment assembled in
town and there was so much talk of rescuing the prisoners that two or three companies were put under arms
to prevent its being accomplished. The fact was the
people of Falmouth Neck, at that time, were not ready
for the rebellion against the British government. The
timid property owners and the Tory element were the
prominent people of the town and not until they felt the
iron hand of British tyranny the next Oct., when their
town was burned by Capt. Mowatt, did the people of all
classes have a common cause. Then there was no hesi-
tancy, and old Falmouth made a proud record of her
people to the end of the war.

"Col. Thompson, of course, was considered the cause
of the tumult and many of the leading citizens appealed
to him to release Mowatt, and every argument was used
to effect it. The most convincing one, no doubt, was
that there was a great scarcity of corn in town and, if
the harbor was closed at that time, there must be great
suffering. Capt. Mowatt was in favor with the leading
town's people and they of course thought a gentleman
had been outraged. About 9 o'clock that night the prisoners were released on parole to return the next morning, Gen. Preble and Col. Enoch Freeman pledging
themselves for them. Capt. Mowatt did not return the
next morning at nine as promised, and the sponsors were
confined. The reason Mowatt gave for not fulfilling
his agreement was the fear of his own life. Col.
Thompson and his men were much disappointed by this
turn of affairs and called upon Gen. Preble and Col.
Freeman for refreshment for the soldiers, which they
provided at the cost of about fourteen pounds. Where-
upon they were released, the next day but one. Thomp-

son called upon them to pay for the time and expense of the men, amounting to 158 pounds and 18 shillings, which they refused to do. All this enraged Col. Thompson and his associates, who seized all the goods they could find belonging to Capt. Coulson and Sheriff Tyng, and levied on Capt. Jeremiah Pote, all notorious Tories. Enoch Illsley contributed refreshments but we find no complaint from him. The soldiers carried off one of Coulson's boats and another belonging to Capt. Mowatt from under his guns and hauled them nearly over to Back Cove.

"They neither returned anything nor gave up Calvin Lombard of Gorham, who fired a brace of balls at Mowatt's vessel, although demanded by that officer. All this has come down to us as 'Thompson's War,' and properly so. Gen. Preble said then, 'Mowatt never will fire upon the town in any case whatever.'

"After the release of Mowatt the officers who had resolved themselves into a board of war voted that Mowatt's vessel ought to be destroyed, and a committee was appointed to consider in what manner it should be done. By the most strenuous efforts of the people of Falmouth Neck they were prevented from carrying out their purpose. After the burning of the town the next Oct. the people were no doubt aware of their mistake. If they had destroyed the vessels in May the town would have been saved. The history of Brunswick well says, 'A year later the plan would have been a success.'

"The goods which were 'sacked' in Falmouth were accounted for formally to the General Court, Oct. 21, 1776, and instruction asked for the disposition of the same. It was not a case of plunder. None suffered but the Tories. There were about 600 soldiers in the town at the time, and most of them had gone before the night of the third day, having feelings of great indignation against the inhabitants of Falmouth Neck. They said the town ought to be laid in ashes and spoke sneeringly of the 'Falmouth gentry.' If the capture could have been carried out, Casco Bay would have been the scene of one of the most brilliant events of the Revolutionary War. Soon after the soldiers left the town Mowatt weigned anchor, and with Coulson went to Portsmouth, N. H. But he did not forget to return and burn Falmouth. Col. Thompson and his men were greatly disappointed, but they bravely turned their energies to other noble work for the country which they loved so well."

It has been well said of Bridgdier Samuel Thompson: "He was a leader among men throughout his life, and one of great integrity. He possessed no mean power of debate and could express himself tersely and vigorously. His manner was outspoken and vehement but he was a grand leader, and running over with zeal and patriotism. After the Revolutionary War he filled many minor offices and served on committees of importance and was ever a faithful public servant whose integrity was never questioned in any history of his time."

Brig.-Gen. Samuel Thompson married Abial Purinton, b. Truro, Mass., May 23, 1738; baptized Truro, Mass., July 23, 1738; the marriage intention was dated Georgetown, Me., Dece. 1, 1757; daughter of Dea. Humphrey Purinton[2] and Thankful Harding. She is said to have been a very handsome woman.

The children of Brig.-Gen. Samuel Thompson:

(5) Reliance Thompson, b. March 31, 1758; m. (say family), June 12, 1779, John Mallet as his second wife.

(6) Samuel Thompson Mallet, lived Lisbon, Me.

(5) Rachel Thompson, b. Feb. 19, 1761; d. young.

(5) Rachel Thompson, b. July 9, 1763, alive in 1843; m., March 10, 1783, John Wilson.

(5) James Thompson, b. June 15, 1765; m., Dec. 3, 1790, Mary Wilson.

(6) Dorcas Thompson, b. Sunday, Sept. 4, 1791.

(6) Rebecca Thompson, b. Feb. 12, 1793; m. Charles E. White.

(6) Samuel Thompson, b. Oct. 9, 1794.

(6) Mary Thompson, b. Sept. 13, 1796; m., May 15, 1814, William Mustard.

(6) Ezekiel Thompson, b. Sept. 30, 1798.

(6) James Thompson, b. Sunday, March 22, 1801.

(6) Ruth Thompson, b. April 19, 1803; unm.

(5) Humphrey Thompson, b. Dec. 11, 1767; d., Topsham, Me., May 29, 1804; m. Mary, probably Mary Strout, who d. Sept. 25, 1835 (66 y.); marriage intention, Oct. 10, 1798.

(6) Harry Thompson.

(7) C. H. Thompson, b. Dec. 5, 1841; m. Mary C. Colby, b. Jan. 5, 1841; d. June 5, 1886.

(8) Luella May Thompson, b. Jan. 1, 1867; d. March 18, 1897.

(8) Charles Edgecomb Thompson, b. April 18, 1869.

(8) John Albert Thompson, b. Feb. 23, 1872.

(8) Annie Maud Thompson, b. Sept. 4, 1874.

(7) Sarah Jane Thompson Lessure, b. June, 1835; d. Dec. 25, 1892.

(5) Aaron Thompson, b. Oct. 18, 1769; d. Oct. 25, 1769.

(5) Aaron Thompson, b. Nov. 16, 1770; marriage intention, 1828, to Mary Cushing of Cape Elizabeth.

(5) Thomas Cheney Thompson, b. July 14, 1774; d. ———; unm.

(5) Samuel Thompson, Jr., b. Oct., 1780; d. March 2, 1858. Drowned. A schoolmaster.

(5) Thankful Thompson, m., 1803, William Wise of Sacarappa, Me.

(5) Elizabeth Thompson. Nathan Goold of Portland, Me., says the m. John Mallet.

(5) According to Miss Sarah A. Thompson of Topsham, Me., daughter, who d. in July, aged about 18 years.

* * * * *

(4) James Thompson, b. Feb. 22, 1737; d. June 14, 1757.

* * * * *

(4) Reliance Thompson, b. June 27, 1738; d. about 1810; m. (first), Nov., 1756, James Edgecombe, who d. Jan. 25, after they had lived together about twenty years. They resided in Saco, Me. There were 12 children. M. (second), June 6, Capt. Joseph Woodman and they lived together 13 years. M. (third), Lieut. Benjamin Brown, with whom she lived eight years.

Children of first husband:

(5) James Edgecombe.

(5) Thomas Edgecombe.

(5) Reliance Edgecombe.

(5) Sarah Edgecombe.

(5) Lydia Edgecombe.

(5) John Edgecombe.

(5) Aaron Edgecombe, b. Saco, Me., May 9, 1767; d. about 1809; m. Elizabeth Hewey, b. Brunswick, Me., Oct. 2, 1768; d. 1849. They lived in Topsham, Me., on the direct road to Bowdoin and Litchfield, Me., the third house from the Bowdoin line. Their son, Arthur Edgecombe, lived and died in this same house. The grandson, Charles P. Edgecombe, now occupies the place and sent these records.

(6) Mary Elizabeth Edgecombe, b. Topsham, Me., March

12, 1792; d. Aug. 30, 1847; m., 1810, Isaac Cotton Pennell, b. Topsham, Me., March 27, 1784; d. June 14, 1861. Butcher. Moved to Machias, Me. He was the son of Stephen Pennell and Mary Cotton; grandson of Thomas Pennell and Mary Riggs.

(7) Stephen Pennell, b. Nov. 12, 1811. Lumberman at Machias, Me.

  (8) Nine children.

(7) Aaron Edgecombe Pennell, b. Feb. 4, 1813; d. Feb. 21, 1847. Lived Machias, Me. Carpenter.

  (8) Six children.

(7) William Eaton Pennell, b. Dec. 7, 1814; d. June 10, 1868. Lumberman at Machias, Me.

  (8) Ten children.

(7) Charles Jameson Pennell.

(7) Mary Elizabeth Pennell, b. Sept. 13, 1823; d. Dec. 29, 1877.

  (8) Five children.

(7) Charles Jameson Pennell, b. Sept. 7, 1826. Painter at Machias, Me.

  (8) Twelve children.

(7) Sarah Brown Pennell, b. Jan. 8, 1829; d. June 22, 1863.

  (8) Child; d. young.

(7) Emeline Hall Pennell, b. Feb. 22, 1838.

  (8) Two children.

(6) Reliance Edgecombe, b. Topsham, Me., Feb. 10, 1794; m. John Hewey of Lisbon Falls, Me.

(7) Arthur Edgecombe Hewey, b. May 3, 1826; d., Auburn, Me., Jan. 1, 1899.

  (8) John Hewey, lived Lewiston, Me. Machinist. M., Nov. 28, 1876, Laura A. M. Buker, b. Jan. 9, 1852, daughter of Isaac W. Buker and granddaughter of James Buker and Jane White.

    (9) Lizzie P. Hewey, b. Nov. 28, 1877; d. Jan. 8, 1888.

    (9) Arthur B. Hewey, b. Jan. 9, 1887. Machinist in Lewiston, Me.

    (9) Florence Hewey, b. Feb. 5, 1889. Resides in Lewiston, Me.

  (8) Joanna Hewey, b. May 9, 1828; d. Nov. 3, 1850.

(6) Hewey Edgecombe, b. Sept. 23, 1796; d. March 2, 1846. Lived at Machias, Me.

(7) Eliza Hewey Edgecombe; went West after her parents died.

(6) Aaron Edgecombe, b. April 9, 1799; d. April 15, 1855; m. and lived in Norway, Me., and some of his descendants are there now.

(6) Arthur Edgecombe, b. Oct. 16, 1804; d. Feb., 1880; m. (first), 1834, Julia Ann Graves, b. Topsham, Me., and d. Topsham, Me., Oct. 10, 1841.

(7) Gilbert Longfellow Edgecombe, b. March 25, 1837; d. July 27, 1865. Died from exposure in the Civil War; m. Sarah Ann Mosely, b. Brunswick, Me., April 10, 1817; d. Oct. 3, 1883.

(7) Pembrooke Somerset Edgecombe, b. Topsham, Me.; d. Machias, Me., Oct. 19, 1867. Single.

(7) Charles Pennell Edgecombe, b. Topsham, Me., March 8, 1848; farmer; m., Feb. 28, 1877, Lizzie Sarah Booker, b. Bowdoin, Me., Jan. 28, 1839, daughter of Joseph Warren Booker and Zelora Coombs.

(8) Betsy Coombs Edgecombe, b. Topsham, Me., Feb. 24, 1878. Graduate nurse of Maine General Training School of Portland, Me.

(8) Arthur Caroll Edgecombe, b. Nov. 5, 1879.

(8) Harold Charles Edgecombe, b. Nov. 29, 1881.

(8) Lillian Edgecombe, b. Nov. 12, 1883.

(8) Pembrooke Edgecombe, b. Nov. 3, 1885.

(8) Gilbet Edgecombe, b. May 22, 1887.

(8) Velzora Booker Edgecombe, b. Dec. 14, 1889.

(8) John Coombs Edgecombe, b. Dec. 25, 1892.

(8) Sarah Card Edgecombe, b. April 30, 1896.

(5) Pemberton Edgecombe. Lived Bath, Me.

(6) Samuel Edgecombe.

(5) Ezekiel Edgecombe.

(5) Daniel Edgecombe.

(5) Samuel Thompson Edgecombe.

Child of second husband:

(5) Sarah Woodman.

*   *   *   *   *

(4) Adrian Thompson, b. March 9, 1740; d. June 16, 1740.

*   *   *   *   *

(4) Rachel Thompson, b. Jan. 3, 1741; d. Dec. 27 (Feb. 28), 1762; m. Dec. 11, 1759, James Curtis of Falmouth or New Meadows, Me.; b. May, 1735; d. Webster, Me., April 6, 1824. (89 y.) He was in the war of 1756 and was in Fort William Henry when it capitulated to the French. He was a captain in active service in the Revolutionary

War. He was a decon of the church of Brunswick, Me., of which Rev. Jesse Appleton was pastor. After living more than fifty years in Brunswick, he went to the home of his daughter, Mrs. Hannah Davis, in Roxbury, Mass., where he died. He m. (second), Polly Bosworth.

(5) Hannah Curtis, b. Sept. 14, 1760; d. Dec. 29, 1843; m. Jesse Davis of Roxbury, Mass., and settled in Lisbon, Me.; had considerable property invested in lands and mills.

(6) Rachel Davis, m. Benjamin Bryant, Esq., of Lisbon, Me.

(7) Pauline Bryant.

(7) James Bryant; a trader at Webster, Me.

(7) Ann Smith Bryant; m. Daniel Weymouth.

  (8) Daniel Weymouth; d. young.

  (8) John Weymouth; resides Tacoma, Wash.

(7) Benjamin Dole Bryant; lawyer.

(7) Mary Dole Bryant; d. young.

(7) Walter Bryant, probably d. at sea.

(7) John Curtis Bryant, d. at Webster, Me., June 18, 1884.

(7) Christopher Columbus Bryant.

(7) Hannah Curtis Bryant.

(7) Eliphalet Bryant.

(7) Elizabeth Smith Bryant.

(7) Daniel Curtis Bryant.

(6) William Davis, b. Feb. 29, 1762; d. at sea.

*   *   *   *   *

(4) Ruth Thompson, b. May 27, 1743; d. Dec. 21, 1803; m. Daniel Curtis; no children.

*   *   *   *   *

(4) Aaron Thompson, b. May 29, 1745; d. about 1763. "He sailed from Ireland and was never heard from. He wrote a letter from Philadelphia, which is still preserved."

*   *   *   *   *

(4) Isaiah Thompson, b. April 17, 1747; d. young.

*   *   *   *   *

(4) James Thompson, b. May 22, 1750; d. June 7, 1751.

Children of the second marriage of Capt. James Thompson with Mrs. Lydia (Brown) Harris.

(4) Benjamin Thompson, b. Oct. 26, 1753; d. Oct. 9, 1793; m. Rhoda Ham.

(5) "One son and four daughters."

(4) Jemima Thompson, b. Oct. 18, 1755; m. (first), John Ham, b. Sept. 1, 1744, and settled in Bath, Me. He was the son of Tobias Ham and Annie Smith; m. (second), Thomas Smith. No children.

Children of first husband:

(5) Five or six sons and four or five daughters.

*   *   *   *   *

(4) Ezekiel Thompson, b. New Meadows, Me., Sept. 16, 1757; d. March 25, 1832. "Ezekiel Thompson, Esq., deceased Mch 21, 1832 at ten minutes past 2 o'clock in the morning. He had his senses to the last and dropped off easy." He was collector of the internal revenue and postmaster at Lisbon, Me. He also settled many estates. He was a very prominent and useful man. In the day book which was kept by him were found many things of historical interest relating to the Thompson and Purinton families. This is in the possession of Miss Sarah A. Thompson of Topsham, Me., to whom and her cousin, Miss Hattie A. Purinton, are due many thanks for their long and careful searching of old records and for the copies which they made of these.

In the day book mentioned above Mr. Thompson gives the following sketch: "Ezekiel Thompson was born in that part of Brunswick which is called New Meadows, in the County of Cumberland, State of Maine, on the 16th day of Sept., A. D. 1757, and was the son of Capt. James Thompson who was born in Kittery, in the County of York, in sd. State, on the 22nd day of Feb., 1707, who having had three wives in the thirty-two years; by the first two he was blessed with nine sons and nine daughters and he deceased in Topsham on the 22nd day of Sept., 1791. The said James Thompson was the son of James Thompson who was born in the County of York (in the town of old York). Lydia Thompson, wife of said Capt. James Thompson, and mother of said Ezekiel, was born in old Ipswich, in the County of Essex, and was the daughter of Benjamin Brown of the said Ipswich. Said Ezekiel Thompson was married by Rev. Samuel Eaton, 15th of Feb., 1781., to Priscilla Purinton, who was born in the said New Meadows on the 29th day of October, 1759, and was the daughter of Col. Nathaniel Purinton who was born in Cumberland, and deceased in Topsham in 1788. Said Nathaniel Purinton was the son of Deacon Humphrey Purington who lived in Georgetown, now Bath, near the turnpike and New Meadows River, and was born Truro, Cape Cod, and was deceased (drowned) at Gorham, Mass. Priscilla Purinton, wife of said Nathaniel, and mother of said Priscilla, was born in Cape Elizabeth in the County of Cumberland, in said State and deceased at Harpswell. She was the daughter of Mr. Thomas Woodbury and Priscilla his wife of Cape Elizabeth and formerly from Beverly, Mass."

The following is also taken from the day book: "1827, Sept. 16. Sunday. This day I am seventy years of age. I lived of my time about 24 years at New Meadows, Brunwick, Cumberland Co.—about 16 years in Topsham, in County of Lincoln—23 years in the village of Little River and about 7 years where I now live, about three quarters of a mile northerly of said Little River Village. Hezekiah B. Thompson and Joanna now lives with me. Charles and John Holman now live in Topsham. Lydia Herrick at Lewiston. Reliance Tebbetts at Little River. Priscilla at Lisbon, near the Factory. My wife is about 68 years of age. We have lived together about 45 years."

Much help was found in an old Bible published in 1780, found among the papers of Ezekiel Thompson. Miss Sarah A. Thompson found an old paper from this, carefully wrapped up and marked, "Children's ages." The birth of the first child of Ezekiel Thompson was found in another record. Charles Sproull Thompson of Milwaukee, Wis., has his old family Bibles. Ezekiel Thompson m., Jan. 4, 1781, Priscilla Purinton, b. Oct. 27, 1759; d. at about ten o'clock in the morning, Sept. 7, 1835; daughter of Col. Nathaniel Purinton and Priscilla Woodbury.

(5) Abner Purinton Thompson, b. to them on the 6th day of Oct., 1781, at New Meadows. On the 3d day of May, 1782, Abner, deceased at Topsham.

(5) Lydia Thompson, b. Topsham, Me., March 15, 1783, on Saturday at 10 o'clock a. m.; d. March 13, 1830. Ezekiel Thompson says: "Lydia Herrick, wife of

Capt. Oliver Herrick, of Lewiston, departed this
life on the 15th day of March, in the year of our
Lord, 1830, of a short illness of about 5 or 6 days.
She died with her senses and without a groan or
struggle, aged 47 years and 18 hours. She died on
her birthday, lacking four hours." M., Dec. 24,
1809, Capt. Oliver Herrick of Lewiston, Me., b.
July 21, 1782; d. June 4, 1852. He was captain in
the U. S. army in the 1812 war. Miss Sarah A.
Thompson has a letter written by him when he
was a prisoner in Halifax Harbor. He was representative and senator to the Legislature, etc.; the
son of John Herrick of Lewiston, Me., b. July 9,
1752; d. May 9, 1834, and who was for many years a
representative in the Maine Legislature. His father
m., March 14, 1780, Lydia Griffin of Falmouth, Me.
The grandfather of Capt. Oliver Herrick was Maj.
Israel Herrick of the line of Joseph Herrick of
Salem, Mass. (Capt. Oliver Herrick m. [third],
May 22, 1831, widow May Davis of Poland, Me., who
d. Dec. 23, 1861. No children.)

Lydia Herrick Thompson and Capt. Oliver Herrick had eight
children, but only the following records are given in the Herrick genealogy:

    (6) Ezekiel Thompson Herrick, b. Jan. 13, 1811; d.
         Feb. 5, 1861.

    (6) Elvira Herrick, b. May 4, 1813; d. Oct. 16, 1815.

    (6) Hannah Herrick, b. May 25, 1815; d. Jan. 20, 1851.

    (6) John Herrick, b. July 23, 1816; d. July 9, 1856;
         resided at Auburn, Me.; m., Oct. 21, 1840, Maria
         Little, b. Feb. 11, 1821; d. Dec. 25, 1867, daugh-
         ter of Thomas Little.

      (7) There were nine children, but only these records
           are given: Maria Augusta Herrick, b. Aug. 1,
           1841; d. Aug. 7, 1870; m., Aug. 25, 1864, John
           S. Adams, son of Rev. Aaron Adams and Har-
           riet.

        (8) Kate Leland Adams, b. Jan. 21, 1867.

        (8) Nellie Little Adams, b. April 10, 1869; d. May
            10, 1889.

        (8) Maria Herrick Adams, b. July 23, 1870; d. Aug.
            17, 1870.

      (7) Lydia Thompson Herrick, b. Feb. 10, 1845; m.,
           Dec. 7, 1870, Capt. Lewis Dwinal, b. April 19,

1840. In the Civil War he was captain in the
Fifteenth Maine Volunteer Infantry, from Oct.,
1861, to July, 1868. Afterwards resided at
Bangor, Me. Son of Amos Dwinal and Sarah
Sherburn Small. No children.

(7) Eunice Thompson Herrick, b. March 21, 1854; d.
March 23, 1855.

(7) John Little Herrick, b. Jan. 3, 1854; d. March 23,
1855.

(6) Oliver Herrick, b. Sept. 15, 1821; d. Nov. 18, 1878;
served in the Civil War, Company H, Tenth
Maine Vols.; d. of disease contracted while he
was in the army; m., Jan. 1, 1857, Sarah Piper;
no children.

(5) Reliance Thompson, b. Topsham, Me., May 23, 1785,
on Sunday at half past eleven in the afternoon; d.
at Topsham, Me., Jan. 11, 1856; m. in Lisbon, Me.,
September, 1802, Isaac Tebbetts, b. Somersworth,
N. H., Jan. 1, 1773; drowned in the Androscoggin
River May 6, 1816. "He came to Maine when a
young man, and finally met with business at Lisbon Falls, which was then known as Little River
Village. He opened a store such as was kept in
country villages at that time. He also became an
owner in mills, etc. It was supposed that he went
down to the river to examine a water privilege
which he was intending to purchase and that he
stepped on a rock which stood out a little from the
shore and slipped from it into the water, which
was very deep there and which had a swift current, which quickly carried him down stream. He
was a good swimmer, and had divested himself of
his clothing, but evidently became exhausted and
perished. This was a great sorrow for his home
and was a calamity which was widely felt outside
of his family. Though not a church member, he
was brought up in one of the finest old Congrega-
tional families. He was commonly called " 'Squire
Tebbetts,' though it is not known that he held any
public offices."

(6) Charles Tebbetts, b. Oct. 8, 1803; d. April 16, 1806.

(6) Albert Tebbetts, b. Dec. 12, 1805; d., Dallas, Ore.,
Oct. 27, 1863. He was in business at Dallas several years; unm.

(6) Harriet Tebbetts, b. Oct. 30, 1807; d., Brunswick, Me., July 4, 1884; unm.

(6) Octavia Tebbetts, b. Oct. 30, 1809; d., Brunswick, Me., Oct. 15, 1884; unm.

(6) Priscilla Elizabeth Tebbetts, b. Dec. 11, 1811; d., Bangor, Me., July 13, 1835; m. in Lisbon, Me., Jan. 1, 1833, Luther Dwinal, a merchant of Bangor, Me.

(7) Sarah Octavia Dwinal, b. Nov. 21, 1833; d. Feb. 16, 1895; m. in Topsham, Me., Aug. 9, 1859, by Rev. A. D. Wheeler, Charles Carroll Everett, D. D., who was b. in Brunswick, Me., June 19, 1829; d. Oct. 16, 1900. He graduated at Bowdoin College in 1850; studied at Harvard Divinity School and at the University of Berlin. He was librarian, tutor and professor of modern languages at Bowdoin College from 1853 to 1857. After graduating at Harvard Divinity School in 1859, he settled over a Unitarian Church at Bangor, Me., occupying this position with great ability and endearing himself to everybody by his sweet character and white life for a period of ten years. In 1869 he became professor of theology at Harvard College, and in 1878 became dean of the divinity school. He published "The Science of Thought" (Boston, 1869); "Religions Before Christianity." (Boston, 1883); "Fichte's Science of Knowledge" (Chicago, 1884); "Poetry, Comedy and Duty" (Boston, 1888); "Ethics for Young People" (Boston, 1891); "The Gospel of Paul" (1892). His philosophy is deeply tinged with that of Hegel, but without sacrifice of his individual quality, and is much enforced and illustrated from his scientific studies.

(8) Mildred Everett, b. June 3, 1860; d., Florence, Italy, March 26, 1903 (42y.). "The last of her line on both sides of the house."

(7) Charles Tebbetts Dwinal, b. June 30, 1835; d. in infancy.

(6) Charles Carr Tebbetts, b. Feb. 24, 1814; d., Charleston, S. C., May 22, 1834. At the time of his death he was on his return from St. Augustine, Fla., where he went for his health. He was a young man of great promise.

(6) Sarah Richardson Tebbetts, b. Aug. 18, 1816; m. in Topsham, Me., by Rev. A. D. Wheeler, Aug. 22, 1844, Dr. Hall Chase of Waterville, Me., who d. July 20, 1851.

(5) Nathaniel Thompson, b. Tuesday, Jan. 30, 1787, at about seven o'clock in the evening.

(5) Charles Thompson, b. Topsham, Me., the 30th of Nov., 1789, about half past six o'clock Monday evening; d. Topsham, Me., Oct. 4, 1866. "He was a banker and merchant and president of the Androscoggin Bank from its foundation in 1834 until the expiration of its charter." Miss Sarah A. Thompson, his daughter, sends the following sketch: "When he was about nine years of age his father moved to Lisbon, Me., where he remained until he was twenty-one years of age. He then returned to Topsham, entering the store of Porter and King as clerk. The following letter written to his father by Dr. Benjamin James Porter when Charles Thompson was about to sever his partnership with him gives a good picture of this noble man in his early years. It is needless to say that he always lived up to the reputation throughout his long and eventful life:

"'Topsham, Me., Nov. 6, 1811.

"'Ezekiel Thompson, Esq.:

"'I have this morning been advised that your son, Charles Thompson, has recently been appointed Deputy Sheriff. If I had been consulted I doubt if I should have advised the acceptance of that office. You may perhaps think that I should have been influenced by selfish motives, in the case of the advice which I should have given. It is true that I feel a deep regret in parting with him, as I have for some time felt him almost essential for my domestic trade. But I have other reasons which I think are not selfish. Among which are his talents for trade, which, in my opinion, are by few equalled. If he should engage in mercantile pursuits by himself, or with a partner, a few years would insure him a fine fortune. His integrity is of the highest stamp, and his industry and application are almost without parallel in so young a

man. Sir, in whatever employment Mr. Thompson
shall find himself I am confident that he will suc-
ceed to your expectations, and even to the most
sanguine expectations of his friends. I am con-
vinced that if he accepts this appointment I shall
sustain a great loss. My esteem for him, and my
desire to promote his interests, will induce me to
acquiesce in any system which you and Mr. Thompson shall deem most interesting, reserving to myself the liberty of friendly interference whenever
occasion may arise. With best wishes for your
family prosperity I am, dear sir, Respectfully Your
obedient servant,

"'BENJAMIN J. PORTER.'

"His early earnings were invested in navigation
with such success that he made it the chief business of his life in connection with his banking.

"He was an ardent patriot and was adjutant of
the Third Regiment, First Brigade, and Eleventh
Division, of the State Militia from 1812 to 1820.
His commission was signed by Elbridge Gerry. It
is in the possession of Mr. Charles Sproull Thompson of Milwaukee, Wis. He was considered so
worthy of confidence in 1818 that the Circuit Court
of Common Pleas placed the entire charge of the
court house of Topsham, Me., in his hands, with
authority to grant the use of it to any purpose
which he considered proper. He never sought office, though capable of filling with honor to himself and advantage to the public any office which
the community could bestow. He accepted no
office but that of representative to the Legislature
for a short period, and also a few minor offices
which he did not feel at liberty to decline. Public
life had no charm for him. His happiness was
found in his home, where he was a devoted husband, a kind father, and such a lover of hospitality
that his 'latch string was always out.' He was a
good neighbor and a valued friend. He was deeply
interested in the cause of education, not only for
his own family, but he was a liberal contributor to
it because of the large benefits which it would
bring to others. He was one of the chief support-
ers of the Topsham Academy. Two of his sons

were graduates of Bowdoin College with the highest honors, one of them spending two years in Europe for study and travel. Death claimed the other son in one short month after his graduation. He was a liberal supporter of religion and a decided Unitarian in his views. He was a man of the strictest moral integrity, one whose word was always to be relied upon, and he expected and inspired the same thing in others. His character was without a stain. He was shrewd, penetrating and calculating in his opinions in regard to men and things, and these always deserved and received the consideration of others. His advice in regard to matters of business was often sought and always deemed valuable.

" 'A voice at midnight came, he started up to hear,
    A mortal arrow pierced his frame; he fell, but
      felt no fear;
    His spirit with a bound burst its encumbering
      clay,
    His tent at sunrise, on the ground, a darkened
      ruin lay.' "

Charles Thompson m., May 14, 1821, Ann Emery Purinton, b. Topsham, Me., May 7, 1802; d. Jan. 1, 1873, the daughter of Humphrey Purinton and Sarah Emery, one of the noblest of women.

(6) Emery P. Thompson, b. Feb. 26, 1822; d. April 13, 1826.

(6) Charles Woodbury Thompson, b. Topsham, Me., Jan. 14, 1824; d. June 5, 1880; resided in Topsham, Me.; bookkeeper, trader and ship owner; m., Oct. 3, 1849, Jane Hunter Whitney, b. Topsham, Me., March 16, 1828; d. Aug. 8, 1866, daughter of Joseph Whitney and Nancy Hunter.

(7) Annie Eugenia Thompson, b. Sept. 1, 1853; m., Aug. 18, 1880, Edwin A. Scribner, b. Topsham, Me., 1856; d., Bordentown, N. J., May 22, 1898, son of Charles E. Scribner and Sarah Ann Hall. He graduated at Bowdoin College in 1877.

(8) Jessie Harward Scribner, b. Boonetown, N. Y., Dec. 30, 1882.

(8) Charles E. Scribner, b. July 6, 1884; won the gold star medal at Paterson (N. J.) Military

School and entered Columbia College in 1901.

(8) George R. Scribner, b. Dec. 18, 1891.

(7) Jennie Thompson, b. Aug. 5, 1866; buried with her mother, Aug. 8, 1866.

(6) Sarah A. Thompson, b. April 5, 1826. A noble woman of great intellectual power.

(6) Eugene Thompson, b. May 8, 1828; d. of consumption, Oct. 1, 1850, one month after graduating from Bowdoin College. A young man of fine promise.

(6) Emery Purinton Thompson, b. Aug. 10, 1831; d. Aug. 11, 1875; graduated from Bowdoin College in 1854. He travelled and studied in Europe for two years, but was too much of an invalid to take up an occupation. Of him and his brother Eugene it was truly said, "Two more promising young men never graduated from the halls of Bowdoin College."

(6) Humphrey Purinton Thompson, b. Topsham, Me., June 13, 1838; d. Feb. 24, 1903; graduated from Phillips Academy, Andover, Mass.; lived in Topsham, New York City and Alma, Col.; merchant; m., Oct. 7, 1863, Annie Matilda Stag Sproull, b. New York City Aug. 21, 1844; resides 827 West Macon Street, Decatur, Ill.; has resided in New York City, Topsham, Me., and Providence, R. I.; graduated from the New Brunswick Female Institute April 14, 1861; daughter of John Jeremiah Sproull, b. New York City Feb. 25, 1819; d. May 31, 1890; resided in New York City; he was the general eastern agent of the Illinois Central Railroad from 1854 till his death; he m., Oct. 16, 1843, Mary Augusta Earl, b. New York City Feb. 10, 1824; d. Nov. 4, 1899.

(7) Charles Sproull Thompson, b. New York City Oct. 29, 1864; present address, Commercial agent of the Illinois Central Railroad, Milwaukee, Wis.; moved there from Dallas, Tex., in May, 1906; graduated from Phillips Academy, Andover, Mass., in 1883; A. B. from Harvard College in 1887; A. M. from the University of Chicago, 1891; has lived in New York City, Topsham, Me., Chicago, etc.; m., April 20,

1901, Mrs. Ruth (Gage) Frost, b. Arlington, Mass., Nov. 18, 1873; educated in private schools in Boston, Mass., and in Dresden, Germany; daughter of Charles Otis Gage and Charlotte Lapham Reed.

(8) Priscilla Abbott Thompson, b. March 12, 1902.

(8) Barbara Thompson, b. July 31, 1904.

(7) Isabella Dunning Thompson, b. Nov. 29, 1866; resides 827 West Macon Street, Decatur, Ill.; graduated from Franklin Family School, Maine, 1880, Brunswick (Me.) High School, 1883, Wellesley College with A. B., 1887, and A. M. in 1905, Columbia College Summer School, 1902; now teaching ancient languages in James Milliken University, Decatur, Ill.; m., Sept. 29, 1898, Dr. George Stover Machan, b. Augusta, Ill., July 21, 1867; d. April 6, 1901; graduated from Bowdoin College in 1893, Maine Medical School, 1896; son of Robert M. Machan and Sarah Wintrode.

(8) Helen Whitman Machan, b. Providence, R. I., Oct. 4, 1900.

(7) Dora Mollor Thompson, b. Feb. 6, 1869; d. Dec. 8, 1893. "She was an invalid and received instruction at home. She was well known and beloved by all."

(7) Dr. John Budd Thompson, b. Nov. 5, 1874; graduated at Brunswick (Me.) High School, 1892, Bowdoin College, 1896, Maine Medical School, 1899; resides 63 Hammond Street, Bangor, Me.

(7) Le Grand Mitchell Thompson, b. Topsham, Me., March 18, 1876; resides 310 Boston Street, Lynn, Mass.; attended Franklin Family School; in Brunswick (Me.) High School, but did not graduate; employed by an electrical company; m., Nov. 18, 1879, Sarah Alice Wilson, b. Charlestown, Mass., May 13, 1871; graduated from Charles G. Pope School, Somerville, Mass., June 26, 1893; daughter of Thomas J. J. Wilson and Ellen Augusta Thomas.

(8) Edith Fairfax Thompson, b. June 28, 1901; d. April 26, 1902.

(8) Ralph Burton Thompson, b. Oct. 18, 1902.

(8) George Raynard Thompson, b. June 10, 1904.

(6) Henry Hersey Thompson, b. June 30, 1841; resided

in New York City, now with sister, Sarah A.; unm.

(5) Priscilla Thompson, b. Topsham, Me., Aug. 6, 1792, Thursday morning at sunrise; d. Topsham, Me., Nov. 7, 1864, at nine o'clock; m., Nov. 26, 1815, Paul C. Tebbetts of Lisbon, Me., b. March 4, 1871; d. Sept. 9, 1861; he came from Somersworth, N. H., and was connected with the old Tebbetts family of Dover, N. H.

  (6) Susan T. Tebbetts, b. Sept. 16, 1816; d. Oct. 25, 1892; m., Oct. 3, 1837, Francis T. Purinton. (See Purinton genealogy.)

  (6) Priscilla T. Tebebtts, b. Jan. 5, 1818; d. April 29, 1864; m. Philip Briggs.

  (6) Joanna H. Tebbetts, b. March 19, 1820; d. Aug. 16, 1845.

  (6) John Green Tebbetts, b. July 12, 1823; d. May 26, 1892; m., July 13, 1846, Clara Burnham, who d. Dec. 13, 1898.

  (6) Gilbert Carr Tebbetts, b. Aug. 11, 1827; d. July 20, 1867.

(5) John Holman Thompson, b. Friday, at sunset, in Topsham, Me., June 5, 1795; d. Aug. 25, 1860, at ten and one half o'clock; registrar of deeds, postmaster and trader for many years at Topsham, Me.; m. (first), Rebecca Snow, b. Aug. 25, 1798; d. twenty-two minutes to eight o'clock, May 3, 1843; daughter of Samuel Snow and Mary Purinton.

  (6) Albert T. Thompson, b. Topsham, Me., Oct. 24, 1824; d. Bangor, Me., June 19, 1895; resided in Topsham, Bath and Bangor, Me.; for many years he was assistant treasurer of the B. & R. R. R.; then was treasurer of the E. & N. E. R. R.; m. (first), Mrs. John Byron of Bath, Me., b. Jan. 25, 1824; d. Yarmouthville, Me., Jan. 30, 1898; no children; m. (second), Harriet Snow, b. March 29, 1800; d. Oct. 24, 1873; daughter of Samuel Snow and Mary Purinton; no children.

(5) Hezekiah Bryant Thompson, b. Saturday, Jan. 30, 1798, at Little River Plantation, near Little River Falls on the Androscoggin, about seven miles from Brunswick Falls; d. Presque Isle, parish of Linwood, County of Carleton, N. B., June 7, 1858; he d. in the presence of the postmaster, Thomas John-

ston; unm.; he assisted his father as a collector of the internal revenue; taught school; buried on the Johnston farm, Presque Isle, N. B.

(5) Joanna Bryant Thompson, b. plantation of Little River, Me., Tuesday, May 3, 1803, in the afternoon; d. at Topsham at 8.40 a. m., March 25, 1885 (81y., 10m., 12d.); unm.

* * * * *

(4) Sarah Thompson, b. Sept. 16, 1760; m. in Brunswick, Me., March 4, 1782, Theophilus Hinkley.

(5) Four sons and four daughters.

* * * * *

(4) Rachel, twin with Ruth, Thompson, b. Dec. 29, 1763; d. Jan. 14, 1794.

* * * * *

(4) Ruth Thompson, b. Dec. 29, 1763; d. Feb. 17, 1839; m. (first), May 23, 1783, Robert Thompson, b. New Meadows, Me., Sept. 11, 1757; d. 1808; her cousin and son of Cornelius Thompson; m. (second), Col. William Stanwood. No children of this second marriage. (See full records, pp. 69–77.)

CHAPTER III.

Cornelius Thompson of New Meadows, Brunswick, Me., and his descendants.

His line: (1) William Thompson; (2) James Thompson of Kittery, Me.

(3) Cornelius Thompson, b. York, Me., Oct. 14, 1709; d. about 1792. Ezekiel Thompson says of him in his day book: "He had no learning, but was hardy, honest and industrious. He served in the Indian wars, 1757, in Capt. John Getchell's Company with Alexander, James and Samuel Thompson. He owned, at New Meadows, Me., in 1741, lots 37 and 38, 200 acres of land."

Wheeler, in his "History of Brunswick, Topsham and Harpswell, Me.," gives a picture of the house of Cornelius Thompson and furnishes the following description of it: "Probably the oldest house now (1877) standing in Brunswick is what is known as the Robert Thompson house. It is on the south side of the road to Harding's Station, and is the first house to the east after passing Cook's Corner. It was erected by Cornelius Thompson and was owned in the Thompson family until 1869. Cornelius Thompson owned the lot in 1738/9, and his first child was born in 1741. If, as is probable, the house was erected before the birth of this child, the house is not less than 136 years old. The chimney of this house is about four feet square at the top. The bricks are laid in clay. The flooring boards are from sixteen to eighteen inches wide, and are trenailed instead of being nailed. The west room, or parlor, is panelled on the sides and ends up to the windows, and is plastered above. The sides of the building on the north and east are bricked between the studs as high as the ceiling of the lower story. This was done for warmth. In the center of the parlor is a buffet, with shelves, etc., elaborately moulded by hand. The frame of the house is of massive timber. The door hinges are of wrought iron, large, clumsy, and of curious construction. The house faces the south. The present road north of the house was not made when the house was built. The occupants had a private road leading southeasterly to the New Meadows River Road, which was a short distance off."

Mrs. Medora Small of Oakland, Me., writes: "Wheeler gives a good picture of the old Cornelius Thompson house. I slept in it many times when I was a child. It was very quaint inside, with its big fireplace, winding stairs, 'buffet' in the parlor, etc. There used to be the framed silhouettes of all my grandmother's brothers and sisters. These may still be at the home of Miles Purinton at Harding's Station, near the bridge between New Meadows and West Bath. He may have other relics, as his grandfather, Robert Thompson, died in that house." This house was burned a few years ago.

Miss Sarah A. Thompson of Topsham, Me., says: "Thomas Grows of New Meadows, now deceased, helped to transfer the bones of Cornelius Thompson, with bones of his relatives, from the old graveyard on his farm to the cemetery. He said that he stood still in wonder when he saw the large size of the spine of Cornelius and mused, 'Many others of the family were built on this same pattern—and I wonder not that this sturdy race is famed for its "backbone" in every good cause of liberty and truth.'"

Mr. Weston Thompson of Brunswick, Me., writes: "A deed from Alexander Thompson to Cornelius Thompson appearing in the registry of York Co., Me., book 19, page 16, describes the grantee as of Biddeford, Me., and calls him a tanner. That deed must have been taken when Cornelius was a young man, after he left Kittery, Me., where I suppose he was born, and before he arrived in New Meadows, where he was in 1739. This deed was shown me by Charles E. White of Topsham, Me., whose mother was a Thompson, and who obtained the deed from the archives of Brigadier Samuel Thompson."

Cornelius Thompson m. Hannah Smith. Dr. E. S. Stackpole feels sure that she was the daughter of Nicholas Smith and Hannah Hadden, who were m. June 25, 1695, and that she was b. at York, Me.

Ezekiel Thompson, nephew of Cornelius, writes in the old account book of his father, Capt. James Thompson, which is now in the possession of Mr. Charles S. Thompson of Milwaukee, Wis., "The old gentlemen (Cornelius) and lady died about 1792." From this same account book are taken many of the records which follow, and which were most carefully written down by this same Ezekiel Thompson.

(4) Thomas Thompson, b. New Meadows, Me., Oct. 20, 1741; d. at Norway, Me., about 1825, aged 70 years. He lived in New Meadows until about 1810 and then moved to Platts-ᴜurg, N. Y. He m. his cousin, Mehetable Hinkley, the only child of Thomas Hinkley, who was killed by the Indians at New Meadows, Me., in July, 1751. Her mother was Agnes Smith, who m. as her second husband, Thomas Cotton. Mehetable (Hinkley) Thompson d. 1842.

(5) Cornelius Thompson, d. at Plattsburg, N. Y.; m. Phœbe Hinkley, daughter of Shubal Hinkley of Hallowell, Me.

(6) Tnomas Thompson.

(6) Shubal Thompson.

(6) Harlow Thompson.

(6) Maria Thompson.

(5) Lois Thompson, m., Nov. 1, 1792, Elijah Hall of Brunswick, Me., and moved to Norway, Me., where she d. July, 1836, and her husband d. December, 1836.

(6) Thompson Hall.

(6) William Hall.

(6) Isaac Hall.

(6) Mrs. Hall.

(6) Mrs. Hobbs.

(6) Mrs. Cobb.

(5) Hannah Thompson, d. about 1840; m. (first), Samuel Brackett of Falmouth, Me.; m. (second), Mr. Guile, about 1840.

Children of first husband:

(6) Dr. Cornelius Brackett.

(6) Stephen Brackett.

* * * * *

(4) Olive Thompson (called Esther in some old records), b. July 25, 1743; d. 1829; m. Joseph Allen, b. York, Me., 1742; d. Monmouth, Me., June 14, 1828; moved from New Meadows, Me., to "Bashford Place" in south part of Monmouth, Me.

(5) Aaron Allen, m. —— Jewell, and moved to western New York.

(5) Esther Allen, m. Robert Niles.

(5) Mehetable Allen, m. Samuel Thompson, son of Richard Thompson and Elizabeth Ricker. (See page 68.)

(5) Patty Allen, b. 1779; m. John Gilman.

(5) Olive Allen, m. Reuben Bashford.

(5) Mary Allen, unm.

THOMPSON GENEALOGY. 47

(5) Joseph D. Allen, b. May 27, 1784; d. Jan. 23, 1868; settled
on the farm now owned by his grandson, Almon J.
Chick; m., 1808, Susannah Roberts, b. Durham, Me.,
1785; d. Feb. 13, 1849.

(6) Sally F. Allen, b. May 17, 1808; d. Oct. 4, 1808.

(6) Cordelia F. Allen, b. March 31, 1810; d. April, 1891; m.
Levi J. Chick.

(7) Four children.

(6) Sally J. Allen, b. Jan. 26, 1813; d. Nov. 19, 1838.

(6) Alvin A. Allen, b. April 12, 1816; m. Almira H. Frost;
resided in Everett, Mass.

(6) Joseph O. Allen, b. May 10, 1818; d. Lake Village,
N. H., June 15, 1886; m. (first), Miss Hall; m. (second), Mary Chick.

(6) Olive T. Allen, March 15, 1820; m. Albert Truesdale;
resided in Somersworth, N. H.

(6) Sylvanus S. Allen, b. May 27, 1824; d. Oct. 19, 1824.

(5) Philena Allen, b. 1792; d. July 8, 1826; lived at Monmouth, Me.; m. (first wife), John Sawyer, Jr., b. Feb.
13, 1791; d. May 5, 1870; farmer.

(6) Mary Sawyer, b. Sept. 13, 1817; d. Aug. 12, 1818.

(6) Allen B. Sawyer, b. May 21, 1819; d. Jan. 19, 1842.

(6) Harlow H. Sawyer, b. Aug. 26, 1821; d. June 15, 1869;
lived at Monmouth, Me.; m. Margaret Atwood of
North Wayne, Me.

(7) Dr. Alton Sawyer, b. Sept. 23, 1848; m. Lizzie
Leavitt; resides at Gardiner, Me.

(7) Augusta Sawyer, b. Dec. 20, 1850; resides at Monmouth, Me.; m. June 1, 1876, Frank Rideout.

(7) Albert A. Sawyer, b. Feb. 21, 1853; resides Monmouth, Me.; m. (first), May 23, 1879, Ada Trask;
m. (second), Addie Brown.

(7) Mary A. Sawyer, b. June 21, 1856; m., Oct. 21, 1879,
John Hinkly.

(7) Ida M. Sawyer, b. July 21, 1859; d. Aug. 9, 1867.

(7) Ruth A. W. Sawyer, b. Nov. 4, 1861; resides Monmouth, Me.; m., Nov. 23, 1892, Smith Emerson.

(6) Joseph Augustus Sawyer, b. March 12, 1823; d. July,
1894; unm.

(6) John Sawyer, b. June 29, 1826; d. Oct. 15, 1826.

*   *   *   *   *

(4) Eunice Thompson, b. Oct. 16, 1747; d. Nov. 12, 1841; resided at Litchfield, Me.; m., Aug. 21, 1774, Abijah Richardson, b. Woburn, Mass., Feb. 22, 1749; d. March 15,

1822; farmer; town treasurer; for several years he was
a member of the Massachusetts Legislature from Litchfield, Me., before 1820.

He was the son of Hezekiah Richardson, b. Billerica,
Mass., May 8, 1715; d. June 17, 1795, aged 80 years, and
who m., Sept. 20, 1740, Elizabeth Walker, who was b.
Feb. 28, 1717; d. July 12, 1792, aged 75 years. Abijah
Richardson was the grandson of Nathaniel Richardson
and Mary Peacock. He was descended from Thomas
Richardson, the youngest of the three brothers, Ezekiel,
Samuel and Thomas, who settled in Woburn, Mass., and
helped in the formation of the church there, in 1641.

(5) Amos Richardson, b., Litchfield, Me., Jan. 7, 1775; lived
near his father for several years on the farm which is
now occupied by Mr. Earle; he moved to Ohio in 1817;
m., Sept. 15, 1796, Sarah McFarland, who d., Aug. 14,
1820.

  (6) Sally Richardson, b. June 2, 1797; m. John Bailey and
  lived in Hartland, Me.

  (6) Abijah Richardson, b. Dec. 1, 1799; d. young.

  (6) Jedediah Richardson, b. May 12, 1801; d. young.

  (6) Amos Richardson, b. March 9, 1805; d. Gardiner, Me.,
  Aug. 5, 1890; m. Miranda Bassford.

  (6) Jennie Richardson, b. Oct. 25, 1806; m. Luke Taylor.

  (6) Lyman Richardson, b. April 19, 1810; d. in infancy.

  (6) David Richardson, b. Aug. 15, 1812; m. Betsy
  Trenchard and lived in Canaan, Me.

  (6) Wesley Richardson, b. Oct. 12, 1815; d. Nov. 15, 1889;
  lived in Lowell, Mass.; m. Phœbe Moses.

(5) Jesse Richardson, b. Oct. 29, 1777; d. July 2, 1854;
lived near Litchfield Me; an active, successful business
man; captain of a military company; m. (first), Experience Higgins; m. (second), Hannah Starbird.

Children of the first wife:

  (6) Sarah S. Richardson, b. July 14, 1800; d. 1889; m.
  Uriah Nason and lived in Litchfield, Me.

  (6) Jesse Richardson, b. Jan. 18, 1802; d. at sea.

  (6) Augustine Richardson, b. March 7, 1804; m. Abigail
  Savage.

  (6) Columbus Richardson, b. June 4, 1806.

  (6) Patty Richardson, b. Oct. 14, 1808; d. Jan. 18, 1857;
  m., 1830, Caleb S. Wilson.

  (6) Mary Baker Richardson, b. Feb. 19, 1811; m. Jacob
  Wilson and lived in Augusta, Me.

(6) Eunice Thompson Richardson, b. July 2, 1813; d. 1872; m. Madison Sayles.

(6) Aaron Richardson, b. Sept. 6, 1815; lived at Otisfield, Me.

(6) William Richardson, b. April 22, 1818; d. Feb. 10, 1821.

(6) Laura Richardson, b. June 5, 1820; m. Orrin Smith and lived at Augusta, Me.

(6) William M. Richardson, b. May 8, 1822; d. Dec. 27, 1857; m., Aug. 31, 1843, Priscilla Coombs and lived at Litchfield Corner, Me.

  (7) Kirkwood Richardson, b. Aug. 31, 1853; d. Sept., 1854.

  (7) Martha Richardson; d. young.

  (7) Henry Coombs Richardson; resides at Providence, R. I.

Children of second wife:

(6) Celia A. Richardson, b. Oct. 6, 1843; m. Mr. Flint; resides at Carlisle, Ark.

(6) Prince W. Richardson, b. July 5, 1845; served in the Civil War.

(6) Nancy Ann Richardson, b. Oct. 5, 1847; m. William Randall and resides at West Springfield, Mass.

(6) Correctus Richardson, b. May 10, 1849; killed at the battle of the Wilderness, May 16, 1864. "He was only six days past 15 years old when he was shot in the neck and stood up hanging on a tree until he bled to death."

(5) Lois Richardson, b. March 1, 1779; d. April 23, 1827; m. Levi Robinson, who d. at Moscow, Me., Feb. 25, 1866; he lived at Litchfield Corner and Plains for several years and then moved to the Million Acre Tract in Moscow, Me.; son of Jabez Robinson.

(6) Mattie Robinson, b. July 11, 1804; m. Thomas Kellett.

(6) Lorinza Robinson, b. Dec. 10, 1805.

(6) Daniel Robinson, b. Nov. 6, 1806; d. June 2, 1817.

(6) Hannah Robinson, b. Jan. 26, 1809.

(6) Caleb C. Robinson, b. May 14, 1811; d. Dec. 25, 1892; lived at Skowhegan, Me.; m. Lucy B. Johnson, who d. Dec. 15, 1886. (69 y., 11 d.)

(6) Mary Robinson, b. Sept. 16, 1814; m. John Gorman.

(6) Seth Robinson, b. March 7, 1817; d. Nov. 13, 1869; m. (first), Mary Dunlap; m. (second), Catherine ———, who d Dec. 16, 1878. (62 y., 11 d.)

(6) Nahum Robinson; d. Minneapolis, Minn., 1895.

(6) Sarah Ann Robinson.

(6) Margaret Robinson; d. Great Falls, N. H.

(5) Abijah Richardson, b. Aug. 26, 1781; d., Bath, Me., Aug.
       24, 1868; lived on Oak Hill; m., May 12, 1805, Betsy
       Johnson, who d. March 19, 1858.

(6) Clarissa Richardson, b. June 23, 1805; m. Josiah Smith.

(6) Orrin Richardson, b. Sept. 4, 1807; d. 1832.

(6) Robert Richardson, b. Jan. 29, 1809; m. Betsy Towle;
       lived at Gardiner, Me.

(6) Almira Richardson, b. Dec. 31, 1811; m. Alfred War-
       ren and lived at Ipswich, Mass.

(6) Ambrose Richardson, b. May 20, 1814; m., May 2,
       1846, Alma J. Libby.

(6) Harriet Richardson, b. Oct. 4, 1819; d. 1837.

(6) Emily Richardson, b. 1822; m. Albion K. Buker, b.
       May 22, 1824; d. April 26, 1842.

(6) Guy Carleton Richardson, b. Aug. 7, 1826; resides at
       West Gardiner, Me., R. F. D. No. 14. "He is an old
       school teacher." M. (first), May, 1850, Cordelia
       Day; m. (second), Feb. 2, 1853, Mary Ann Elwell;
       m. (third), Feb. 20, 1886, Elizabeth Lewis.

(5) Eunice Richardson, b. Nov. 2, 1783; d. July 27, 1848; m.,
       Jan. 7, 1808, Jeremiah Winslow, b. Lewiston, Me., Jan.
       15, 1783; d. at Bath, Me., May 18 ,1836. He moved to
       Litchfield, Me., in 1807; after his marriage he lived be-
       yond the Corner, towards Oak Hill; in 1824 he moved
       to Brunswick, Me., and then to Bath, Me.; son of
       Kenelmn Winslow and Elizabeth Cole.

(6) Cornelius Thompson Winslow, b. Feb. 7, 1809; lost at
       sea.

(6) Horatio N. Winslow, b. Aug. 22, 1810; d. at Bath, Me.,
       March 30, 1878; m. (first), Mary F. Brimijohn; m.
       (second), Mary L. Marston.

(6) Phœbe R. Winslow, b. June 8, 1812; lived at Gardiner
       and Bath, Me.; m. Levi Huntington.

(6) Mary Ann Winslow, b. March 25, 1814; resides at Taun-
       ton, Mass.; m. Rufus Geary.

(6) Kenelmn Winslow, b. March 14, 1816; d., Lowell,
       Me., 1875; m. Hannah Cotton.

(6) Sarah R. Winslow, b. July 1, 1818; d. Aug. 17, 1864;
       lived at Cornville, Me.; m. Samuel Longfellow.

(6) Jesse Winslow, b. June 25, 1823; d. at sea, June, 1842.

(6) Eunice Caroline Winslow, b. Dec. 21, 1825; d., Boston,
       Mass.; m. Levi Oliver.

(6) Jeremiah Winslow, b. Sept. 17, 1829; d. Dec. 30, 1881;
     lived at South Abington, Mass.; m. Lydia Cook.

(5) Phineas Richardson, b. Feb. 3, 1786; d. ———; m. and
     settled in New Brunswick.

(5) Hannah Smith Richardson, b. July 11, 1788; school
     teacher.

(5) Cornelius Thompson Richardson, Esq., b. Jan. 3, 1792;
     d. April 27, 1875; buried at North Turner, Me.; settled
     in Turner, Me., about 1818. "He was bound to learn
     the blacksmith's trade, and served seven years of his
     boyhood in this work. He then had his trade, a suit
     of clothes, and a few dollars. His work was often six
     miles from his home, and he walked that distance night
     and morning with a cheerfulness and energy which
     followed him all his life and is seen in many of his
     descendants." Some say he lived at Livermore, Me.,
     before he moved to Turner. A tanner and stone cut-
     ter; m., in Livermore, Me., March 25, 1813, Sarah Rol-
     lins Lovejoy, b. Fayette, Me., Oct. 8, 1792; d. May 17,
     1881; daughter of Jacob Lovejoy and Sally Rollins.

(6) Phineas Robinson Richardson, b. Litchfield, Me., Feb.
     21, 1814; d. Keene's Mills, Me., June 27, 1901, at the
     home of his daughter, Mrs. Charles Willard. "Be-
     fore he was twenty-one years old he went to Massa-
     chusetts, which was a long journey in those days.
     After working there awhile he shipped in a whaler
     at New Bedford, and made two voyages, which oc-
     cupied four years, and which took him to the Indian
     Ocean, Madagascar, St. Helena, Africa, South
     America, and to the East and West Indies. Later he
     became an engineer on boats plying between Maine
     ports and Boston, Mass., which position he filled for
     many seasons. He finally settled on a farm in North
     Turner, Me. Before this he had lived at Bangor,
     Me., for a number of years. During the Civil War
     he was an engineer on a mail packet and transport,
     which took him to the Gulf of Mexico and to several
     Southern ports. In politics he was a staunch Re-
     publican from the first formation of that party. He
     was an uncompromising advocate of temperance.
     His marked characteristics through life were fidelity,
     industry, perseverence and opposition to shams in
     all forms. He had always been hardy and vigorous,
     never employing a doctor until he had a slight par-

alytic shock about two years before his death. This sickness injured his sight so that he could not read, which was a great drawback to his enjoyment, as he had always been a great reader. Still, he was very cheerful and courageous." M., in Bangor, Me., Sept. 23, 1845, Prudence G. Page, b. Freeport, Me., Nov. 5, 1823; d. May 12, 1879; lived in Turner, Me., from 1857 till her death; daughter of Philemon Page and Prudence Grant.

(7) Hester Ann Rogers Richardson, b. Jan. 17, 1847; d. Sept, 23, 1883; studied in Turner (Me.) public schools; lived at Bangor and Turner, Me.; m., May, 1871, Orren Henry Leavitt, b. Turner, Me., March 6, 1841; resides in Manchester, N. H.; newspaper editor; son of Aaron Leavitt and Abigail Bates.

(8) Lunette Faustina Leavitt, b. May 19, 1877; d. April 19, 1882. (4 y., 11 m.)

(7) Cornelius Thompson Richardson, b. Turner, Me., Oct. 20, 1848; resides at Rangeley, Me.; he and his brother Phineas are proprietors of the Kennebago Lake House; he was a little over three years old when his parents moved to Bangor, Me.; lived much in Turner, Me.; moved to Rangeley, Me., 1870; studied in Bangor and Turner (Me.) schools; m. (first), Nov. 1, 1884, Cora E. Hewey, who d. Aug. 7, 1901; m. (second), Aug. 19, 1903, Mrs. Annie B. (Emery) Hewey of Rangeley, Me; no children.

(7) Phineas Richardson, b. Turner, Me., Oct. 15, 1851; studied in Turner schools; moved to Rangeley, Me., 1871; proprietor with his brother of the Kennebago Lake House; m., Dec. 6, 1880, Addie Pillsbury, b. Rangeley, Me., March 28, 1859; studied in schools of Rangeley and New Vineyard, Me.; daughter of Charles H. Pillsbury and Mary T. Quimby.

(8) Prudence May Richardson, b. Rangeley, Me., Oct. 7, 1881; graduated at Hebron (Me.) Academy, 1900; stenographer and bank clerk in Rangeley, Me.

(7) Sarah Maria Richardson, b. Bangor, Me., June 28, 1854; resides at Keene's Mills, Me.; studied in Turner (Me.) schools; m., Sept. 28, 1878, Charles Farwell Willard, b. Skowhegan, Me., Sept 6, 1847; lumberman; son of Charles Morse Willard and Mary Russ.

(8) Randilla Willard, b. Turner, Me., May 16, 1885; graduated at Leavitt Institute, Turner, Me., 1902; studied in Bliss Business College, Lewiston, Me.

(8) Max Farwell Willard, b. May 18, 1889.

(7) Edward Page Richardson, b. Bangor, Me., Jan. 10, 1856; resides in North Turner, Me.; graduated at Turner schools, 1875; has lived in Bangor, Turner and Hartford, Me.; farmer; m., Oct. 11, 1879, Lizzie G. Ellis, b. Hartford, Me., May 5, 1856; daughter of Benjamin F. Ellis and Lucia G. Pratt; no children.

(7) Dora Amanda Richardson, b. Feb. 12, 1858; resides in North Turner, Me.; studied in Turner schools; has lived for awhile in Cambridgeporft, Mass.; m., in Turner, Me., March 11, 1880, Frank Leslie Kilbreth, b. Boston, Mass., Aug. 2, 1853; studied in schools of Lawrence, Mass., and Winthrop, Me.; carpenter; son of James Kilbreth and Alice Griffin.

(8) Burt Walden Kilbreth, b. Cambridgeport, Mass., Dec. 10, 1880; resides in Dixfield, Me.; graduated at Leavitt Institute, Turner, Me., June 20, 1901; mill man; m., Nov. 25, 1905, Jessie Mason Dillingham, b. Turner, Me., May 21, 1881.

(8) Alice Maude Kilbreth, b. North Turner, Me., Oct. 5, 1885; resides in North Turner; graduated at Leavitt Institute, Turner, Me., June 18, 1903; teacher at Turner Village, Me.

(8) Gertrude Louise Kilbreth, b. North Turner, Me., March 15, 1892; studied in Turner public schools.

(7) Mary Page Richardson, b. April 1, 1862; d. Jan. 1, 1865.

(7) Frederick S. Richardson, b. May 14, 1867; resides in Dixfield, Me.; employed in a spool mill; m., in the fall of 1896, Helen A. De Costa of Hartford, Me.

(6) Hester Ann Rogers Richardson, b. Nov. 4, 1815; m., in Turner, Me., Aug., 1840, Ezekiel B. House.

(7) Lois A. House, b. Sept. 13, 1842; m. Henry C. Drake.

(7) Alice House, b. Aug. 2, 1848; m. Charles Hines.

(6) Atwell Richardson, b. Livermore, Me., Oct. 29, 1817; m. Lois Dillingham.

(6) Cornelius Thompson Richardson, b. Livermore, Me., Oct. 6, 1819; resides in Newton Center, Mass.; m., Oct., 1859, Ruth Rollins, b. June, 1830, in Belgrade,

Me.; daughter of Josiah Rollins and Theodate Taylor.

(7) Rolla Thompson Richardson, b. Feb. 13, 1861; studied in Hallowell (Me.) public schools and Dirigo Business College, Augusta, Me.; resides in Rangeley, Me.; builder; m., in Pennsylvania, about 1890, and wife d. Dec. 15, 1901.

  (8) Rachel Richardson, b. ——; d. 1900.

(7) Cora Frances Richardson, b. Oct. 15, 1864; studied in Dearborn School, Boston, Mass., Hallowell (Me.) public schools, Maine Central Institute; m., June 17, 1886, Howard Pike, b. Feb. 21, 1891.

  (8) Ruth Abigail Pike, b. Sept. 23, 1887; d. Jan. 18, 1894.

(6) Abijah Richardson, b. Turner, Me., June 6, 1823; d. Feb. 20, 1874; lawyer in Boston, Mass.; m. (first), Jan. 1, 1848, Caroline Williams, who d. in April, 1853; m. (second), 1855, Fannie L. Bent, b. Cambridge, Mass.

Child of first wife:

  (7) George C. Richardson, b. Oct. 18, 1852; graduated at Harvard College, 1874.

Children of second wife:

  (7) Edith M. Richardson, b. July, 1867.

  (7) William Bent Richardson, b. July, 1869.

(6) William Henry Richardson, b. Turner, Me., Aug. 13, 1826; d. April 6, 1861; steamboat engineer; m. (first), Jan. 1, 1852, Amanda Friend of Sedgwick, Me.; no children; m. (second), Lucy R. Harrison, b. Bangor, Me.; d. Turner, Me., Aug. 6, 1861.

  (7) Children d. young.

(6) Sarah Rollins Richardson, b. Turner, Me., July 9, 1829; resides in North Turner, Me.; m., Jan. 1, 1862, Elisha Lovejoy, b. Turner, Me., Sept. 29, 1838; d. Nov. 6, 1903; station agent and postmaster at East Livermore, Me.; son of Jonathan Lovejoy and Ruth Benjamin.

  (7) William Henry Lovejoy, b. April 10, 1862; d. Altoona, Fla., Jan. 13, 1886.

*   *   *   *   *

(4) Amos Thompson, b. New Meadows, Brunswick, Me., Sept. 3, 1749; d. Bowdoin, Me., June 6, 1835. (86 y.) Settled in Bowdoin, Me.; m. Hannah Wooster, b. Falmouth, Me.,

1741; d. Bowdoin, Me., Jan. 25, 1835; they lived together
sixty years.   (See full records, Chapter IV.)

*   *   *   *   *

(4) Martha Thompson, b. New Meadows, Me., Aug. 16, 1751; d.
    1849; m. her cousin, Jonathan Thompson, b. Georgetown,
    Me., July 1, 1748; son of Benjamin Thompson[3] and
    Abigail Philbrook; this family resided at Monmouth, Me.
  (5) Jonathan Thompson; m. ——— Jewell.
  (5) Benjamin Thompson; m. ——— Jewell.
  (5) Phineas Thompson; m. ——— Allen.
  (5) Aaron Thompson.
  (5) Jonathan Thompson,
  (5) Abigail Thompson.
  (5) Priscilla Thompson; m. ——— Jewell.
  (5) Martha Thompson.
  (5) Emily Thompson.

*   *   *   *   *

(4) Col. Joel Thompson, b. New Meadows Me., Oct. 23, 1753; d.
    Lewiston, Me., May 1, 1841. (88 y.) Mrs. Carrie T.
    Healey: "He was in a Harpswell (Me.) company in the
    Revolutionary War. A certificate of the Massachusetts
    war service says: 'Joel Thompson appears with the rank
    of Sergeant on the muster rolls, Capt James Curtis' Co.,
    dated Aug. 1, 1775. Time of enlistment May 15, 1775,
    service 3 months & 2 days. He belonged to Brunswick,
    Me.' Not long after the Revolutionary War he moved to
    Lewiston, Me., where he made his home for the rest of
    his days, being there 66 years. The place was called
    'Pond Town, a Plantation adjoining Winthrop, Me.' He
    represented Lewiston, Me., in the General Court of
    Massachusetts."
        D. F. T., "He was representative in the State Legisla-
    ture for many years." M., Feb. 18, 1780, Martha Cotton,
    b. Brunswick, Me., May 18, 1762; d. July 16, 1828; daugh-
    ter of Rev. Thomas Cotton and Agnes Smith.
  (5) Mehetable Thompson, b. May 10, 1782; d. March 22,
      1839; m. as his first wife, Feb. 8, 1802, Gen. Jedediah
      Herrick, b. Jan. 9, 1780; d. Hampden, Me., Oct. 10,
      1847. He was the son of Joseph Herrick, Esq., who
      moved from Milton, Mass., to Lewiston, Me., 1772, and
      then resided in Greene, Me.
        "Gen. Jedediah Herrick was educated in Boston,

Mass. By profession he was a civil engineer. He was captain and major in the 1812 war. He distinguished himself in action at the time of the burning of the corvette *John Adams*. Penobscot County, Me., was formed in 1806 and General Herrick was appointed its first high sheriff by Governor Story of Massachusetts. He was major-general of the Tenth Division of the Massachusetts Militia, Maine then being a part of Massachusetts, Dec. 17, 1816, and he resigned his commission in 1828. In politics he was a Federalist. He spent his last years as a man of leisure, devoting a great deal of his time to the study of geology and metallurgy. He assisted men of science. He was a man of unusual culture, and was widely known among the scientific and literary men of his day. The *New England Historical Geneological Register* of January, 1850, says of him: 'He was the author and publisher of an extended genealogical history of the Herrick Family, full of loving and patient research and laborious investigation. He was also engaged upon the histories of the families of Preston, Haywood, Leach, Scales & Kilburn, from which he was also descended.' "

(6) Sophronia Preston Herrick b. Jan. 1, 1803, d. of consumption April 8, 1841; m., Aug. 14, 1825, Charles Buck of Hampden, Me., who d. in 1863; merchant.

   (7) Son, b. and d. May 22, 1826.

   (7) Charlotte Frances Buck, b. Feb. 19, 1828; m. B. F. Brooks and resided at 15 Joy Street, Boston, Mass.

      (8) Esther Brooks.

      (8) Clara Brooks.

      (8) Flora Brooks, etc.

   (7) Charles Herrick Buck b. Jan. 9, 1830; d. May 28, 1830.

   (7) Mary Mehetable Buck, b. Aug. 17, 1831; d. South Natick, Mass., April 22, 1858; m. at Jamaica Plain, Mass., Oct. 4, 1856, Dr. George J. Townsend of Natick, Mass., brother of Adjutant-General Townsend and a grandson of Elbridge Gerry of historic fame.

   (7) Rev. Charles Wentworth Buck, b. Aug. 19, 1833; A. B. at Amherst College in 1855; studied law in Boston; practiced law in St. Louis, Mo.; graduated from the Theological School of Meadville, Pa., and settled at Fall River, Mass., as a Unitarian minis-

ter; in 1868 he was settled over the Park Street
Church, Portland, Me., and remained there until
1879, when he moved to Cambridge, Mass.; m.,
Dec. 29, 1863, Mary Ellen Stevens, daughter of
Oliver Stevens and Mary Blood.

(8) Charles Buck, b. Oct. 16, 1865; d. July 27, 1866.

(8) Oliver Stevens Buck, b. Sept. 15, 1867.

(8) Philip Welch Buck, b. Jan. 3, 1869.

(8) Theodore Buck, b. April 20, 1870; d. Sept. 14, 1870.

(8) Charlotte Frances Buck, b. Sept. 14, 1871.

(8) Frona May Buck, b. Sept. 2, 1876.

(7) Robert Herrick Buck, Esq., b. Aug. 21, 1835; resided
at Denver, Col., 1835; went from Boston to Colorado in 1869; attorney-at-law and United States
commissioner; served in the United States Volunteers in the Civil War, captain of the Sixth Missouri Infantry; m., in Boston, Mass., Oct. 4, 1865,
Julia Webster.

(8) Robert Fletcher Buck, b. Aug. 4, 1866.

(8) Arthur Buck, b. April 10, 1868.

(8) Sally Fletcher Buck, b. March 13, 1870.

(8) Philip Gordon Buck, b. Oct. 31, 1871; d. July 6,
1876.

(8) Alice C. Buck, b. March 27, 1873.

(8) Russell Buck, b. July 9, 1876; d. Nov. 28, 1878.

(7) Sopnronia Porter Buck, b. Aug. 21, 1835.

(7) Jonathan Frederick Buck, b. April, 1839; d. Dec.
1839.

(6) Clara Cotton Herrick, b. Sept. 15, 1804; d. Nov. 13,
1839; m., June 28, 1835, Rev. Josiah Hayden Janes.

(7) A large family.

(6) Charles Thompson Herrick, b. May 28, 1806; d. Jan.
16, 1852; m., Dec. 11, 1835, Reuben H. Stetson of
Hampden, Me., merchant, who d. July 7, 1864.

(7) Reuben Kidder Stetson, b. Dec. 4, 1837; m., Dec. 13,
1865, Clara A. Hopkins.

(8) Reuben Kidder Stetson, b. March 11, 1867.

(8) Frank Bowler Stetson, b. July 18, 1868.

(8) Charlotte Herrick Stetson, b. June 7, 1872.

(7) Charlotte Herrick Stetson, b. Nov. 22, 1839; unm.

(7) Elizabeth Kidder Stetson; m., Aug. 10, 1867, Dr.
Lewis Edwin Norris of Hampden, Me.

(8) Elizabeth Stetson Norris, b. Nov. 10, 1867.

(8) Annie Burleigh Norris, b. Jan. 20, 1869.

(8) Caroline Cole Norris, b. Aug. 15, 1871.

(7) Henry Stetson, b. 1845; d. 1846.

(6) May Tyler Herrick, b. May 25, 1807; d. May 20, 1829; m., Sept. 5, 1824, Maj. Jesse Wentworth, merchant, of Hampden, Me.

(7) Frances Elizabeth Wentworth, b. May 26, 1826; d. June 17, 1873; m., Sept. 16, 1855, Reuben Cutler of Farmington, Me.

(8) Charlotte Cutler, b. Dec. 18, 1859.

(8) Nellie Cutler, b. June 17, 1863; d. April 30, 1864.

(8) Isaac Moore Cutler, b. July 16, 1866; d. Sept. 26, 1867.

(7) Jedediah Herrick Wentworth, b. April 14, 1828.

(6) Alfred Herrick, Esq., b. Feb. 17, 1810; resided in Toledo, Ill.; m. (first), Sept. 3, 1838, Mary Ann Lane of Prescott, Me., who d. March 9, 1840; daughter of Josiah Lane, Esq.; m. (second), Oct., 1846, Eliza Davis Lane, sister of the first wife, who d. June 12, 1858.

Child of first wife:

(7) Alfred Henry Herrick, b. June 16, 1839; merchant in San Francisco, Cal.

Children of second wife:

(7) Mary Ann Herrick, b. Nov. 14, 1849; m., in Hampden, Me., June 4, 1873, Albert A. Mayo, who resided in Cameron, Penn., of the firm of Mayo Brothers, merchants and manufacturers of lumber.

(8) Large family; one of whom Frederick Mayo, was b. March 29, 1874.

(7) Clara Ella Herrick, b. June 6, 1853.

(6) George Rupert Herrick, b. May 10, 1812; civil engineer; moved to Illinois about 1854, and on the journey met with a steamboat accident in which he lost all his household goods, among which was the family Bible, with records; m., June 14, 1835, Mary Childs Nichols, b. May 8, 1814; native of Nobleboro, Me.

(7) Caroline Eliza Herrick, b. April 13, 1836.

(7) Daughter, b. and d. 1838.

(7) Helen Maria Herrick, b. 1840; d. 1843.

(7) Mary Frances Herrick, b. 1842; d, 1843.

(7) George Albert Herrick, b. June 22, 1844; banker in Chicago, Ill.

(7) Hannah Ella Herrick, b. May, 1846; m., Oct., 1868,

Maj. Benjamin L. Ullen of Ullen, Pulaski County, Ill.; attorney by profession; lieutenant in the Union Army in the Civil War, and wounded at Fort Donaldson; in 1874 was at Mound City, Ill., where he was circuit clerk of the county.

(8) Florence Edith Ullen, b. July, 1868.

(8) George A. Ullen, b. Oct. 18, 1871.

(6) Sarah Thompson Herrick, b. July 10, 1814; d. Boston, Mass., Nov. 26, 1881; for over 30 years she was a resident of Baltimore, Md., and was well known to the Union-loving people during the Civil War; treasurer of the Ladies' Union Relief Association; m., Oct. 16, 1834, Camilius Kidder, Esq., a merchant of Bangor, Me., who moved to Baltimore, Md.

(7) Elizabeth Kidder, b. Sept. 6, 1835; m., April 18, 1860, John Truslow of New York City, for several years on the board of assessors of Brooklyn.

(8) Robert Truslow, b. July 9, 1861.

(8) Sarah Truslow, b. June 26, 1863.

(8) John Kidder Truslow, b. Nov. 26, 1865; resided in Peekskill, N. Y.

(8) Arthur Truslow, b. Feb. 2, 1868.

(8) Walter Truslow, b. Feb. 28, 1871.

(8) Mary Truslow, b. May 2, 1873.

(7) Dr. Jerome Henry Kidder, b. Oct. 26, 1842; A. B., Harvard College; A. M., 1865; private and non-commissioned officer in the Tenth Maryland Volunteer Infantry, June 16, 1863, to Jan. 31, 1864; attached to the United States Army General Hospital, Patterson Park and Hicks, as medical cadet, 1864-'66; M. D. from the University of Maryland, 1866; appointed *Caviliero de Real Orden Militari Portuguesse du Noss Senhor Jesus Christi*, by the king of Portugal, Dec. 17, 1869; the reception of the decoration ordered by joint Congress, May 26, 1870; promoted to past assistant surgeon, March 10, 1871; served in Japan, 1868-'70; March, 1874, was sent on the *Swanton* as surgeon and naturalist for the observation of the transit of Venus; promoted to full surgeon in the United States Navy, and then was mostly engaged upon a scientific work in Washington, D. C., at the Smithsonian Institute and the naval library; m., Sept., 1878, Anne May

Maynard, daughter of the late Hon. Horace Maynard of Tennessee.

(8) Ann Maynard Kidder, b. Aug. 14, 1880.

(8) Henry Maynard Kidder, b. Oct. 30, 1882.

(7) Camilius Gage Kidder, b. July 6, 1850; fitted for Harvard College at Phillips Exeter Academy; A. B., Harvard, 1872; in 1885 was a member of the law firm of Emmett, Burnett & Kidder, New York City; m., Dec. 3, 1881, Matilda Cushman Taber, daughter of Gustavus Taber and Angelie B.

(8) Jerome Taber Kidder, b. Feb. 10, 1883.

(6) Caroline Freeman Herrick, b. Aug. 25, 1817; d. May 2, 1818.

(6) Caroline Freeman Herrick, b. Oct. 27, 1819; m., Sept. 13, 1839, Joshua Hill, a lawyer of Hampden, Me.

(7) George Rupert Hill, b. Nov. 14, 1840; d. Sept. 28, 1841.

(7) Fannie Wentworth Hill, b. April 28, 1843; d. Sept. 3, 1845.

(7) Clara Caroline Hill, b. Nov. 17, 1846; m., Dec. 31, 1866, Wilbur Brown, a lumber merchant of Portland, Me.

(8) Caroline Hill Brown, b. Aug. 1, 1868.

(8) Emily Hunter Brown, b. March 9, 1871.

(7) Charlotte Herrick Hill, b. Oct. 17, 1851; m., June 28, 1871, Marshall H. Dutch, a dry goods merchant of Portland, Me.

(7) Anna Cora Hill, b. Nov. 21, 1854; d. same day.

(5) Joel Thompson, b. Lewiston, Me., July 26, 1784; d., Wayne, Me., Sept., 1851; moved to Wayne in 1848; he came to Litchfield, Me., in 1809, and taught school in the vicinity of Oak Hill; he lived in Litchfield several years, and was on the Committee of Safety in the 1812 war; a man of decided ability; m. (first), Ruth Dwinal, daughter of Aaron Dwinal of Lewiston, Me.; she d. before 1811; m. (second), Rachel Wilson of Topsham, Me., b. Dec. 12, 1813; d. Jan. 1, 1853; daughter of William Wilson and Mary Patten.

Child of first marriage:

(6) Joel Dwinal Thompson, b. Dec. 24, 1809; d. at Bangor, Me., Feb. 21, 1853; he taught school in early life and later was in business at Bangor, Me.; m., Feb. 17, 1842, Hariet Newell French of Auburn, Me., b. April

11, 1818; d. Nov. 13, 1893; daughter of Nathaniel
French and Elizabeth Libby Quimby.

(7) Prof. Dwinal French Thompson, b. Bangor, Me., Jan.
1, 1846; resides at 861 Second Avenue, Troy, N. Y.;
graduated at Dartmouth College, 1869; taught in
Dartmouth College three years;since then he has
held the chair of descriptive geometry, drawing,
etc., at Rensselaer Polytechnic Institute, Troy,
N. Y.; he gathered many Thompson records and
kindly aided in the making of this book; m.,
Jan. 1, 1880, at Troy, N. Y., Mary Lena Burt,
daughter of Solomon Burt and Mary Thompson
Sexton.

(8) Alice Quimby Thompson, b. Troy, N. Y., Dec. 17,
1880.

(8) Gordon Saxton Thompson, b. Lansingburg, N. Y.,
Aug., 1883; m., 1906, Ethel Williams of Troy,
N. Y.

(8) Nathaniel French Thompson, b. Lansingburg, N.
Y., Oct. 16, 1884.

(8) Dwinal Burt Thompson, b. Lansingburg, N. Y.,
Dec. 14, 1886.

(7) Alice Thompson, b. June 1, 1851; d. April 17, 1855.

Children of Joel Thompson and Rachel Wilson:

(6) Rev. Thomas Wilson Thompson, b. Nov. 12, 1814; d.,
Sumner, Me.; a prominent Free Baptist minister;
m. Hannah Harmon.

(6) Jedediah Herrick Thompson, born Jan. 11, 1817; d.,
East Livermore, Me., Jan., 1848.

(6) William Wilson Thompson, b. April 12, 1819; m. Abbie
Clark and resided in Jay, Me.

(6) James Smullen Thompson, b. April 9, 1822; lived in
Rangeley, Me.; m. (first), Lydia Rounds; m. (second), Margaret Alley.

(6) George Owen Thompson, b. March 11, 1826; resides in
Phillips, Me.; m. (first), Marietta Moulton; m. (second), Melisa Tyler.

(6) Actor Patten Thompson, b. April 26, 1828; d. Gardiner,
Me., May 7, 1904, aged 76 years; m. (first), Martha
R. Marston; m. (second), Rose Alley.

(7) Fen B. Thompson, resides in Hallowell, Me.; major
of the Second Regiment of National Guards. "A
fine looking man and a fine officer."

(6) Josiah Sanford Thompson, b. Dec. 4, 1832; resides in

Woonsocket, R. I.; m. (first), Rose Hayford; m. (second), Lena Edson.

(6) Rachel Wilson Thompson, b. March 21, 1835; d. Bangor, Me., April 21, 1889; m. Maj. Warren L. Whitney.

(5) Phineas Thompson, b. May 23, 1786; d. young.

(5) Sarah Thompson, b. March 2, 1789; d. Lewiston, Me., June 12, 1825 (38y.); m., April 22, 1810, William Randall of Lewiston, Me., b. Feb. 19, 1787; d. Feb. 20, 1867; son of Ezra Randall.

(6) Martha Randall, m. Cushman Lee.

(6) Mary Randall, d. young.

(5) Cornelius Thompson, b. April 18, 1791; d. Lisbon, Me., Nov. 15, 1857; educated in the public schools of Lewiston, Me., and when a young man he taught several terms in Lewiston and the adjoining towns. He first settled in Lewiston; then moved to Litchfield, Me., and finally moved to Lisbon, Me., and settled on the farm where he spent the remainder of his days. He was a very successful farmer. In 1835 he built on his farm a sawmill, which, with the aid of his sons, he ran for many years. He came to Lisbon about 1825. He served for a short time in the 1812 War, being stationed at Bath, Me., in the garrison. His company helped fortify Bath against the expected attack of the British; for his services he received a grant of land and his widow received a pension . He was buried in the town of Bowdoin, Me., adjoining his place of residence, in the cemetery of the brick meeting-house at West Bowdoin; m. (first), Nov. 6, 1817, Sarah Cotton of Lewiston, Me., b. July, 1796; d. Dec. 8, 1830; daughter of Isaac Cotton and Elizabeth Slyvester; her father lived in Bowdoin, Me., the last of his life; m. (second), at Freeport, Me., March 14, 1832, Abigail Sylvester[5], b. Freeport, Me., March 14, 1832, Abigail Sylvester (5), b. Freeport, Me., May 4, 1795, d. April 11, 1885; daughter of Boynton Sylvester[4] and Rosanna Jordan; granddaughter of William Sylvester[3] and Mary ———.

Children of first marriage:

(6) Infant son.

(6) Caroline Mehetable Thompson, b., Lewiston, Me., July 2, 1818; d. Lisbon, Me., Oct. 3, 1840.

(6) Henry Herrick Thompson, b. Nov. 1, 1821; d. Feb. 20, 1874.

(6) Elizabeth Sylvester Thompson, b. Nov. 8, 1824; d. Sept. 17, 1826.

(6) Daughters, b. and d. Oct. 7, 1827.

(6) Sarah Thompson, b. Sept. 3, 1829; d. May 11, 1830.

Children of second marriage:

(6) Harriette Thompson, b. Dec. 18, 1832; d. Fall River, Mass., July 14, 1899; m., April 26, 1863, Joseph Healey of Fall River, Mass., b. Jan. 27, 1828; d. Jan. 21, 1901; resided in Fall River, Mass.; cotton mill agent, etc.; son of David Healey and Meribah Hathaway; no children.

(6) Martha Thompson, b. July 3, 1835; has always lived in Lisbon, Me., on the farm where she was born; address, West Bowdoin, Me.; m., Jan. 25, 1863, Cyrus Bede Cox, b. Brunswick, Me., May 17, 1815; d. Lisbon, Me., April 22, 1876; educated at the town schools; farmer; son of Isaac Cox and Desire Estes.

(7) Clara Cotton Cox, b. Aug. 28, 1866; address, Lisbon, or Sabattus, Me.; m., Aug. 4, 1895, Elston A. Jones, b. Worcester, Mass., Oct. 14, 1860; farmer; son of George H. Jones and Sarah Golden.

(8) Blanche Eloise Jones, b. Worcester, Mass., Jan. 25, 1900.

(8) Cyrus Carlton Jones, b. Lisbon, Me., Oct. 22, 1902.

(7) Joseph Henry Cox, b. July 26, 1869; works on the farm and in the sawmill on the old homestead; unm.

(7) Reuben Varney Cox, b. March 3, 1874; graduated from Fall River (Mass.) High School, 1895; resides Cambridge, Mass.; unm.

(6) Sarah Thompson, b. June 26, 1837; resides at 198 Summer St., Auburn, Me.; educated at the Lisbon High School and Litchfield Academy; m., Oct. 23, 1862, Capt. Abram Healey, b. Fall River, Mass., Oct. 3, 1836; d. Fall River, June 18, 1889; son of Abraham Hatheway Healey and Nancy Coombs; his parents moved to Lisbon, Me., when he was a boy; educated in town schools and Litchfield Academy; before he was twenty-one he began going to sea and made that his life work, retiring from it only a few years before his death; his voyages took him to Europe, Asia and Australia; his keen observation added much to his knowledge, and his mingling with men added much to his culture; he was a well-read man and a very successful sea saptain.

(7) Caroline Thompson Healey, b. Lisbon, Me., July 17,

1863; graduated from Fall River (Mass.) High
School, 1884; from Fall River Normal Training
School; resides at 198 Summer St., Auburn, Me.;
m., June 15, 1898, Virgil Theron Healey of Lisbon,
Me., b. Feb. 13; 1872; educated at town schools and
Shaw's Business College, Portland, Me., 1893-'94;
engineer and electrician; son of Theron Adams
Healey and Frances Ellen Nason.

(8) Harold Eugene Healey, b. Jan. 16, 1899.

(8) Ruth Mildred Healey, b. Sept. 29, 1900.

(8) Paul Mariner Healey, b. June 4, 1902.

(7) Carl Ernest Healey, b. April 25, 1871; resides at 41
Lisbon St., Lewiston, Me.; graduated from Fall
River (Mass.) High School in 1889; Brown Uni-
versity, 1894; m., in Lorin, Cal., Feb. 18, 1896,
Elizabeth Augusta Smith, b. Fall River, Mass.,
May 16, 1872.

(8) Alan Thompson Healey, b. Novato, Cal., May 7,
1897.

(8) Carl Smith Healey, b. June 4, 1901.

(8) Donald Royal Healey, b. April 5, 1904.

(7) Hattie Alice Healey, b. July 20, 1873; d. Nagasaki,
Japan, Dec. 26, 1878.

(5) Martha Cotton Thompson, b. April 17, 1793; d. Oct. 13,
1880; m. (first), Jan. 1, 1812, Henry Herrick, b. April
11, 1789; d. July 23, 1816; resided in Greene, Me.; son
of Joseph Herick and Mary Preston. "As he was the
youngest of the family, it was expected that he would
remain on the paternal estate and conduct the various
kinds of business there, and take care of his parents
in their declining years. But he died of consumption
at the age of 27." M. (second), Sept. 8, 1819, Capt.
Nathaniel Eames of Lisbon (now Webster), Me.; b Wilmington, Mass., Jan. 6, 1775; d. April 3, 1827; he m.
(first), 1795, Lucy Curtis of Harpswell, Me., daughter
of James Curtis; he was the son of Joshua Eames.
M. (third), Feb. 23, 1843, Gen. Jedediah Herick of
Hampden, Me., who had first m. her sister, Mehetable
Thompson; no children.

Children of first marriage:

(6) Harriet Jewett Herrick, b. Nov. 28, 1812; d. May, 1838;
m. (as his second wife), Sept. 9, 1835, Horace Corbett, Esq., b. Guilford, Mass., April 13, 1797; d. April
5, 1875; a woollen manufacturer at Lisbon, Me., for

some time; moved to Freeport, Me., 1874, where he d. (By his first marriage he had a daughter and two or three sons.)

(7) Harriet Herrick Corbett, b. Sept. 1, 1836; d. July 13, 1904; m., Sept. 15, 1866, Isaac Cotton Merrill, b. Freeport, Me., June 23, 1838; merchant; d. California, Feb. 12, 1904; son of John Merrill and Lois Cotton of Lewiston, Me.

(8) Horace Edward Corbett Merrill, b. Sept. 5, 1871; d. Aug. 23, 1897; m., Jan. 1, 1894, Georgia S. Dakin of Lewiston, Me., but b. in Scotland May 7, 1872; d. March 8, 1895.

(7) Infant son, unnamed.

(7) Evaline Corbett, b. Sept. 9, 1847; d. April 21, 1875.

(6) Evaline Thompson Herrick, b. Jan. 22, 1814; d. May 8, 1838; m., July 1, 1836, Daniel Weymouth of Topsham, Me. He was a trader at Webster, Me.

(7) Francis Purington Weymouth, b. April 10, 1837; in the Civil War he was lieutenant of a New York Volunteer regiment; resided awhile at Independence, Kan.; 1906, resides in Spokane, Wash.; has been superintendent of the water works in that city.

(8) Eva J. Weymouth, b. Jan. 4, 1866; resides with her father.

Children of second marriage:

(6) Ithamar Bellows Eames, b. June 7, 1822; d. Portland, Me., June 11, 1889. "Think he was a graduate of Bowdoin College. Later he followed the sea and then settled down to a law practice in Shanghai, China. He finally returned to America and spent some of his last days with his half-sister, Mrs. Harriet Corbett." M., Dec. 14, 1862, Emma Hayden of Bath, Me.; daughter of John Hayden; granddaughter of Capt. William Hayden; great-granddaughter of George Hayden and Elizabeth Potter.

(7) Horace Hayden Eames, b. Shanghai, China, Dec. 19, 1863; m., June 18, 1890, Miss Hamilton of Hagerstown, N. J.

(7) Emma Eames, b. Shanghai, China, Aug. 13, 1867. Johnson's Cyclopedia says of her: "Opera singer, born in China, where her parents, who were natives of Boston, were temporarily residing. She studied in Boston under local teachers. In 1883

5

she went to Paris and studied under Mme. Marchesi, and made her début there at the Opera, early in 1889, in Gounod's opera, Romeo & Juliette. In 1891 she appeared in N. Y. as one of Abbey's Company at the Metropolitan Opera House and made a brilliant success during the season, especially in Faust. These operas were taught her by Gounod himself. On July 29, 1891, she married Julian W. Story, the artist, who was b. at Walton-on-Thames, England, Sept. 8, 1856. He graduated at Eton (Brasenose College), Oxford. The son of Wm. W. Story, the famous sculptor." In the winter of 1906 she sang in "Aida" in New York City to a fine audience. When she is not in America her address is No. 7 Place des Etats Unis, Paris, France, and at Tore di Campaignilioni, Vallombrosa, Italy; in America, care of Metropolitan Opera House. Mr. Charles E. Hamlin, of Bangor, Me., who was a dramatic and musical critic in New York City when she made her début, says: "Emma Eames is easily the most notable figure among the women we have on the operatic stage, although Mme. Nordica is entitled to high rank. Mme. Eames has great temperament and passion, although she does not sink herself as completely out of her rôles as Nordica and other artists do. She builds big. She makes a quiet beginning, but after she fairly gets into the work she vitalizes the performance. Her voice is brilliant, strong and sufficiently tinged with sweetness. It has fine dramatic timbre. She completely fills the eye, and sometimes displays great dramatic power in her acting. But her fault is that she is too much herself—and yet she is a regal figure. Her performances are always interesting and moving, if not histrionically convincing." Mr. C. E. Hamlin also furnishes this sketch: "The father of Emma Eames was a lawyer, of Bath; Me., and Miss Eames spent a large part of her childhood in Bath and Boston. Her father practiced his profession in the international courts of Shanghai. Miss Eames gave early evidence of having a rare voice, and she began the study of music in Boston. Prof. John K. Paine, then the leading American composer and professor of music at

Harvard University, was among the first to recognize her great ability, and he encourgaged her to study for grand opera. She removed to Paris, where she resumed her studies, spending two years under Mme. Picciotto and others, learning stage deportment, studying the *mis-en-scene* of various operas, besides perfecting herself in the French language. She made her début at the Paris Grand Opera House March 13, 1889, before one of the most critical audiences in the world, in Gounod's opera, Romeo and Juliet. The de Reszke brothers were in the caste. She was just twenty-one and her success was a happy omen for her future. The directors of the Paris Opera House confirmed her engagement for the next two years. At the end of that time Miss Eames signed a contract to sing at Covent Garden, London, which was a promotion. The result was that Abbey, Achoeffel and Grau engaged her to sing an opera at the Metropolitan Opera House in New York City, where she made her début in 1891, appearing in Romeo and Juliet, the de Reszke brothers in the caste. Her success made her the leading American prima donna. She was regarded as the most beautiful Juliet the American stage ever produced. She revealed great vocal ability and exceptional dramatic temperament and histrionic ability of decided promise. Her greatest success was attained as Margarite in Faust, which was presented that and other seasons with probably the greatest caste with which the opera has ever been performed. She also appeared with success as Elsa in Lohengrin, as Eva in Die Meistersinger, as the Countess in the Marriage of Figaro, and in other rôles which evidenced her versatility. She has been connected with the Metropolitan Opera House for many seasons since her début and has always been a great favorite with the audiences. She is also a great favorite in London and other European cities. One instance of peculiar interest was her first appearance in Maine, October, 1905, which was a veritable triumphal tour."

(6) Lucy Curtis Eames, b. July 8, 1824; d. Oct. 28, 1829.

(5) Ruth Thompson, b. Feb. 9, 1796; d. Jan. 13, 1849; **m.**
Daniel Grant of Hampden, Me.,

   (6) Sabia Grant, m., Feb., 1843, Israel Johnson of Carmel,
Me.

   (6) Joel Thompson Grant.

   (6) Hannah Smith Grant, m. Mr. Johnson.

(5) Hannah Thompson, b. Dec. 3, 1798; d. Aug., 1837; m.
William Davis of Lewiston, Me.

   (6) William Davis.

   (6) Charlotte Davis.

   (6) Nathaniel Eames Davis.

   (6) Martha Cotton Davis.

   (6) Joel Thompson Davis, who d. Jan., 1899.

   (6) Harriet Augusta Davis.

(5) Isaac Cotton Thompson, b. May 22, 1801; d. ———; m.
Mercy Carvill of Lewiston, Me.

   (6) Alfred Herrick Thompson, b. Dec. 7, 1826.

   (6) Theophilus Thompson b. Feb. 15, 1830.

   (6) Harriet Augusta Thompson, b. Dec. 1, 1833.

   (6) Isaac Woodman Thompson b. April 15, 1837.

(5) Theophilus Boynton Thompson, b. June 6, 1803; m.,
Nov. 1, 1841, Charlotte Corbett of Worcester, Mass.,
daughter of Otis Corbett.

   (6) Son, b. Aug. 28, 1842; d. in infancy.

   (6) Charlotte Thompson, b. May 2, 1844; m. Dr. C. H. Hill.

      (7) Florence Hill, b. 1876; m., April 7, 1890, Arthur Pet-
ingill.

      (7) Ethel Hill, b. Aug., 1878.

(5) Horatio Nelson Thompson, b. Dec. 10, 1805; d. 1852;
unm.

    *   *   *   *   *

(4) Richard Thompson, b. Sept. 15, 1755; d. about 1851; a
Revolutionary soldier; lived in Wales, Me.; private in
Capt. James Curtis' company, July 17, 1775; m. Eliza-
beth Ricker.

   (5) Samuel Thompson, m. Mehetable Allen, daughter of
Joseph Allen and Esther Thompson.

   (5) Thomas Thompson, m. Ann Stafford.

   (5) Robert Thompson, m. a widow; went to sea.

   (5) Rhoda Thompson.

   (5) Abigail Thompson, m. Mr. Smith.

   (5) Phœbe Thompson, m. ——— Miller.

   (5) Penelope Thompson, m. ———Jewell.

    *   *   *   *   *

(4) Robert Thompson, b. Sept. 11, 1757; d. 1808 (51y.);

lived on the old Cornelius Thompson homestead at New Meadows; m., May 23, 1783, his cousin, Ruth Thompson[4], b. New Meadows, Me., Dec. 29, 1763; d. Feb. 17, 1838, at Miles Purington's; funeral sermon by Rev. Mr. Conn; Rev. 21 : 4. She was the daughter of Capt. James Thompson[3] and Mrs. Lydia (Brown) Harris.

(5) Mary Hazen Thompson—called Mollie in the old records b. New Meadows, Me., Sept. 14, 1783; d. Peabody, Mass., May 8, 1870; m. Alonzo Cushing of Durham, Me., daughter of John Cushing.

(5) Lydia Brown Thompson, b. Nov. 20, 1875; d. at Lynn, Mass., in her 83d year; unm.

(5) Hannah Smith Thompson, b. June 1, 1788; d. June 19, 1866 (77y., 7m.); m., June 14, 1812, by Rev. Benjamin Titcomb, Daniel Welch, b. Topsham, Me., Feb. 1, 1785; d. Gardiner, Me., May 7, 1868; son of Samuel Welch; resided in Brunswick and Gardiner, Me. "He died in a patient and beautiful old age at the home of his adopted daughter, Mrs. Maria Holbrook Clark."

(6) Samuel Welch, b. Feb. 10, 1819; d. April 8, 1823.

(6) Mary Thompson Welch, b. Brunswick, Me., March 10, 1813; d. at Hallowell, Me., Aug. 3, 1852; m. at Hallowell, Me., by Rev. N. D. Sheldon, July 23, 1843, Joseph Frost Nason, b. Sanford, Me., June 29, 1813; d. at Hallowell, Me., Oct. 27, 1877. He was a dealer in boots and shoes.

The Nason line: (1) Richard Nason; (2) Benjamin Nason; (3) William Nason; (4) Maj. Samuel Nason, b. Portsmouth, N. H., Feb. 1, 1744; served in the Revolutionary War; resided at York and Sanford, Me.; m. Mary Shores, b. Portsmouth, N. H., March 14, 1744; daughter of Peter Shores and Susanna Ball; (5) William Nason, b. York, Me., Aug. 15, 1767, and m. Jane Emery Frost, b. Kittery, Me., June 11, 1778. (See Doctor Stackpole's "Old Kittery, Me.")

(7) Charles Henry Nason, b. Hallowell Me., Nov. 28, 1845; m., at Hallowell, Me., May 23, 1870, Emma Caroline Huntington, b. Aug. 6, 1845; daughter of Samuel W. Huntington and his second wife, Ann Mayo.

(8) Prof. Arthur Huntington Nason, b. Augusta, Me., Feb. 3, 1877; resides University Heights, New York City; graduated from Cony High School, Augusta, Me., 1895; from Bowdoin College, A.

B., 1899; A. M., 1903; teacher of English, Kent's
Hill Seminary, Me., 1899–1902, and at Penn
Charter School, Philadelphia, Pa., 1902; gradu-
ate student and assistant in English at Bowdoin
College, 1902; graduate student in English, Co-
lumbia University, New York City, 1903–'05;
University Fellow in English, 1904–'05; instruc-
tor in English, New York University, since
Sept., 1905.

(7) Aroline Nason, b. Feb. 26, 1850; d. Sept. 27, 1851.

(7) Edwin Francis Nason, b. Oct. 28, 1851; resides at
Augusta, Me.; unm.

(5) Rachel Thompson, b. Sept. 8, 1790; d. Brunswick, Me.,
1856; unm.

(5) Cornelius Thompson, b. Dec. 8, 1791; d. Brunswick, Me.,
June 12, 1850; (58 y.); m. (first), Ann McIntosh of
St. Andrews, N. B., b. Dec. 16, 1799; d. March 28, 1836;
daughter of Capt. John McIntosh; m. (second), Sarah
Branch.

(6) Catherine McIntosh Thompson, b. St. Andrews, N. B.,
August 21, 1821; she now resides at Bath, Me.; m.
Sept. 12, 1844, James Ham[6], Jr., b. April 10, 1819;
d. Bath, Me., Oct. 9, 1883.

His Ham line: (1) John Ham of Portsmouth, N. H.;
(2) Samuel Ham; (3) Joseph Ham; (4) James Ham,
b. Jan. 25, 1776; d. Feb. 13, 1866; he was a farmer at
Brunswick, Me.; m., June 12, 1803, Mary Ham, b. Jan.
7, 1779; d. Feb. 25, 1863; daughter of John Ham and
granddaughter of Tobias Ham.

(7) Hiram Henry Ham, b. Danvers, Mass., 1844; d.
1873; m. Ann Hayward of Washington, D. C.

(7) Charles Albert Ham, b. Danvers, Mass., 1846. He
resides at Bath, Me.; he nearly always lived in
Bath, Me.; graduated at Bath Grammar School,
1861; iron moulder; he has been a rheumatic invalid for over twenty years; m. (first), Jessie
Allen, who d. 1873; m. (second), 1877, Susan Mc-
Kenney.

Child of first wife:

(8) Daniel Herbert Ham, b. Portland, Me., 1869; re-
sides at Islesboro, Me.; graduated from Bath
(Me.) grammar school; steamboat engineer; m.
Laura Stanley.

Children of second wife:

      (8) Lucy Gertrude Ham, b. Bath, July 6, 1883; graduated at Bath High School.

      (8) Walter Chase Ham, b. June, 1886; graduated at Bath Grammar School.

      (8) May Luella Ham, b. Feb. 11, 1889.

    (7) Cornelius F. Ham, b. East Boston, Mass., 1847; m. Ella Given of Bath, Me.

      (8) Winfield L. Ham, b. 1875.

      (8) Harold L. Ham, b. 1883.

      (8) Raymond Ham, b. 1892.

    (7) Ruth Ann Ham, b. Brunswick, 1849.

    (7) Abner Lewis Ham, b. 1851; resides in California; m. Nellie Howard of Lewiston, Me.

      (8) Henry Ham, b. 1875.

    (7) Frank Ezekiel Ham, b. 1853; m., 1873, Eva Graham of Bath, Me.

      (8) William Ham, b. 1874; m., June 28, 1893, Jennie Bimson.

        (9) Ellen C. Ham, b. Bath, 1894.

        (9) Francis W. Ham, b. 1895.

        (9) Edith M. Ham, b. 1896.

        (9) Theodore R. Ham, b. 1900.

      (8) Charles A. Ham, b. 1876.

      (8) Mabel Ham, b. 1879.

      (8) Arthur E. Ham, b. 1882.

      (8) Ethel M. Ham b. 1886.

      (8) Rufus Ham, b. 1890.

      (8) Katherine Ham, b. 1895.

    (7) Eva Jane Ham, b. Bath, Me., 1857; d. 1888.

    (7) Lena Blondell Ham, b. 1860; m. James Chatman of Bath, Me.

      (8) Inez Chatman, b. 1901.

      (8) Mildred Chatman, b. 1902.

  (6) Ruth Thompson, b. June 12, 1822; d. Aug. 18, 1848; m. (first), Stephen Farnham of Canterbury, Conn.; m. (second), Zillah Clark and resides at Westerly, R. I.

Child of first husband:

    (7) Stephen B. Farnham, b. Providence, R. I., May 6, 1848; resides at Westerly, R. I.

  (6) Ann Maria Thompson, b. April 1, 1825; resides at Westerly, R. I.; unm.

  (6) Mary Thompson, b. June 6, 1827; d. West Bath, Me.,

July 20, 1886; m. Charles Donnell of Bath, Me.; no
children.

(6) Isabella Ann K. Thompson, b. Brunswick, Me.; d.
young.

(6) Arabella Thompson, b. Feb. 4, 1833; m. David Davis
of Peabody, Mass.

(5) Ruth Thompson, b. Brunswick, Me., Aug. 3, 1794; d.
Wakefield, Mass., Feb. 9, 1880; m. (first), Jan. 4, 1822,
at New Meadows, Me., by Elder Lamb, Capt. John
Holbrook, b. Bath, Me., Nov. 30, 1789; d. at sea, July
30, 1825; son of John Holbrook and Sarah Higgins;
resided at Topsham, Me. His granddaughter, Mrs.
Medora Small of Oakland, Me., writes: "I have some
letters written by my Grandfather Holbrook before and
after his marriage. In one of these he speaks of being mate with Captain Blakmar, and that the captain
was very abusive to him and the crew. This letter
was written from New Orleans, but the name of the
vessel was not given. Another letter, dated Jan. 21,
1823, states that he is just starting on a voyage with
Captain Farmley in the schooner *Favorite* of Bath,
bound to Demarara and from thence to Coracoa and
then home. The last letter was written from Acquiri,
St. Domingo, July, 1825, and in this he says that he
hopes to see his home in six weeks. He speaks of his
'venture' as if he were captain of the ship. I have the
impression that he died at sea while making this
voyage which he mentions. In a letter dated Jan.,
1823, he states that his brother Wm. was to come the
next week with cotton and other things, and it also
makes mention of his brother Ezekiel. In a letter of
his dated Bath, Me., June 23, 1823, he says that he will
sail on the morrow wih Capt. Riley for some of the
Virgin Islands, and that he will return in Sept." M.
(second), Edward Cunningham of Athens, Me., but
there were no children of this second marriage.

Children of first husband:

(6) John Quincy Adams Holbrook, b. Topsham, Me., May
20, 1823; d. July 3, 1893, in South Boston, Mass.
He was a prominent man; he first kept a restaurant
and later took fine care of a Masonic building in
South Boston, Mass., and also looked very kindly
after the sick brother Masons. M. (first), June 6,
1859, Mrs. Eliza Jane Gibson of Boston; m. (sec-

ond), at New Bedford, Mass., Feb. 15, 1888, Mrs. Lucy Percival; no children.

(6) Maria Ann G. Holbrook, b. Topsham, Me., Jan. 11, 1825; she resides at Lynn, Mass.; she was adopted by her aunt, Mrs. Hannah Smith (Thompson) Welch; m. at Hallowell, Me., Aug. 21, 1848, by Rev. Samuel Field, Nathaniel Clark, Jr., b. Limington, Me., June 10, 1821. He and his wife were members of the Baptist Church at Gardiner, Me., until they moved to Wakefield, Mass.; he was a most efficient deacon in the church; he has always been in the boot and shoe business, having had a store in Gardiner, Me., for some twenty years; he was first in the firm of Cox & Clark, and then in business for himself; the firm name was then changed to Sprague & Clark; was in business in Wakefield, Mass., about 1871; since he gave up work he has resided with his daughter, Harriet, at Lynn, Mass.; son of Nathaniel Clark of Limington, Me., who m. Martha Small, who was b. Jan. 15, 1788, and d. Jan. 20, 1826, and was the daughter of William Small and of his first wife, Mary March, whom he m. Jan. 7, 1782.

(7) Medora Frances Clark, b. Gardiner, Me., Feb. 13, 1850; resides Oakland, Me.; m., at Cliftondale, Mass., Oct. 24, 1888, Maj. A. H. Small of Oakland, Me.

(8) Ralph Hugo Small, b. Oakland, Me., Dec. 27, 1889.

(8) Harold Adams Small, b. Oakland, Me., April 19, 1893.

(7) Howard Ripley Clark, b. Gardiner, Me., Sept. 29, 1862; has resided at Gardiner, Me., Wakefield, Mass., Boston, Mass., Philadelphia, Pa., New York City, Chicago, Ill., etc.; employed by the ·Methodist Book Concern, New York City, for seven years; with A. J. Holman & Co., Philadelphia, Pa.; has been member of the firm of Merrill & Baker, New York City, and of Ridpath History Company, Chicago, Ill.; m., Sept. 24, 1889, Louisa Cecilia Magee, b. Manayunk, Pa., Feb. 25, 1870; daughter of Richard Magee and Louisa Bischoff.

(8) Marie Hildegarde Clark, b. Mt. Airy, Philadelphia, Pa., Aug. 15, 1891; resides at Philadelphia, Pa.

(7) Harriet Ethel Clark, b. Gardiner, Me., July 13, 1869; resides at Lynn, Mass.

(5) Eunice Harding Thompson, b. Sept. 27, 1796; d. Oct. 29, 1879; m., autumn of 1831, as his third wife, Daniel Cole of Cambridge, Me., b. July 30, 1800; d. April 19, 1875; farmer; son of William Cole, b. Greene, Me.; d. Parkman, Me., 1828 (58y.); resided at first at Parkman, Me., then moved to Cambridge, Me.; William Cole was a Baptist minister and m. Rhoda Barker of Lewiston, Me.

(6) Hiram Thompson Cole, b. Jan. 15, 1833; d. Aug. 19, 1899; m. Miranda Watson.

(7) Daughter; m. S. C. Austin.

(8) Sons, Everett and Elwin Austin, live on the old Cole farm at Cambridge, Me.

(5) Robert Thompson, b. Dec. 1, 1798; d. West Bath, Me., Sept. 5, 1882; buried in Brunswick; resided most of his life on the old Cornelius Thompson homestead at New Meadows, until shortly before his death; farmer; m., Nov. 14, 1833, Sylvia Walker of Bath, Me., b. June 12, 1795; d. April 26, 1877; daughter of Abraham Walker.

(6) John Holman Thompson, b. Lisbon, Me., Sept. 19, 1834; d. June 29, 1906; resided at Freeport, Me.; lived at Lisbon, Brunswick, West Bath, Topsham, Pownal and Freeport; farmer; m., June 23, 1869, Margaret Oaks Grows, b. Yarmouth, Me., March 27, 1847; studied in Brunswick (Me.) schools; daughter of Joseph Ross Grows and Caroline Coffin.

(7) Clara Sylvia Thompson, b. Brunswick, Me., May 6, 1870; resides at Freeport, Me.; studied in schools of West Bath and Brunswick, Me., and at Providence, R. I.; m., May, 1894, Jerome F. Thomas, b. Portland, Me., July 5, 1857; studied in Freeport (Me.) schools; druggist; son of John H. Thomas and Eliza A.

(7) Walter Arnold Thompson, b. Brunswick, Me., March 1, 1872; studied at Brunswick (Me.) schools; Tarbox Express Company, Portland, Me., express driver; m., Dec. 26, 1905, Annie Burrows of Green Oaks, N. S.

(7) Charles Holman Thompson, b. Bunganuc, Me., Sept. 25, 1876; studied in Brunswick (Me.) schools; resides at Freeport, Me.; shoe worker; m., May 16, 1903, Birdie Lucinda Cummings, b. Stony Brook,

Me., Nov. 26, 1881; graduated from Freeport (Me.) High School, 1899.

(7) Frederic Eugene Thompson, b. Brunswick, Me., Dec. 30, 1879; studied in schools of Brunswick and Freeport, Me., and in Freeport Grammar School; resides in Freeport, Me; shoe worker; unm.

(7) Chester Ezekiel Thompson, b. Nov. 27, 1885; studied in Freeport (Me.) schools; graduated from Freeport (Me.) High School, 1905; resides Freeport, Me.

(6) Nancy Allen Thompson, b. Brunswick, Me., Feb. 15, 1835/'36; d. July 24, 1892; m., March, 1863, as his second wife, Simeon Purington, b. West Bath, Me., April 23, 1816; d. May 13, 1875 (59y.); farmer; son of Humphrey Purington and Sally Higgins.

(7) Mary Etta Purington, b. May 27, 1864; resides 103 Hamilton Avenue, Lynn, Mass.

(7) Sarah Abbie Purington, b. April 22, 1866; same address as sister in Lynn, Mass.

(7) Miles Stanley Purington, b. Dec. 28, 1868; resides West Bath, Me., near the old Thompson homestead; farmer and mechanic; m., Dec. 19, 1892, Addie Frances Chase, b. West Bath, Me., Dec. 31, 1868; daughter of George E. Chase.

   (8) Two children.

(7) Howard Leslie Purington, b. May 2, 1871; resides at Lynn, Mass.; machinist; m., April 26, 1897; Gertrude Rogers Brown of Lynn, Mass., b. at Frederickton, N. B., July 24, 1877; daughter of Moses Brown and Kate Neals.

(6) Rachel Mary Thompson, b. Oct. 21, 1837; d. Sept. 1, 1906; resided 17 Pine Street, Bradford Division, Haverhill, Mass.; m., in Lynn, Mass., May 11, 1866, John Wesley Dunnells of Buxton, Me., b. Feb. 28, 1840; son of John Sawyer Dunnells and Jane Leavitt of Chatham, Mass.

(7) Idella Maud Dunnells, b. April 4, 1867; d. Plaistow, N. H., 1897; m., Dec. 25, 1893, Willie Brown of Riverside, Mass., suburb of Haverhill, Mass.; he resides in Haverhill and is married a second time.

   (8) Henry Wesley Brown, d. in infancy.

   (8) Babe, stillborn.

(7) Winnifred May Dunnells, b. Stoughton, Mass.—now

Avon—Jan. 1, 1870; m., Oct. 24, 1888, George Albert Gorman, at Haverhill, Mass., b. Newburyport, Mass., Oct. 5, 1867; stationary engineer.

(8) Sylvia May Gorman, b. Haverhill, Mass., Feb. 12, 1889.

(8) Ina Maude Gorman, b. Haverhill, March 16, 1891.

(8) Walter Albert Gorman, b. Plaistow, N. H., June 12, 1892.

(8) George Frederick Gorman, b. Haverhill, Mass., Feb. 20, 1894.

(8) Paul Gorman, b. Haverhill, Mass., Nov. 19, 1897.

(8) Clifton Francis Gorman, b. Haverhill, Mass., March 19, 1900. The children have studied in Bradford and Haverhill, Mass.

(7) Irving Clarence Dunnells, b. Lynn, Mass., Dec. 20, 1872; shoe cutter; m., July 18, 1900, Althea A. Moores of Haverhill, Mass., b. Champlain, N. Y., March 26, 1876.

(8) Ethel Dorris Dunnells, b. July 4, 1901.

(7) Herbert Ernest Dunnells, b. Lynn, Mass., Dec. 16, 1873; resides 392 Washington Street, Haverhill, Mass; graduated from Currier's Grammar School, Haverhill, Mass, 1889; shoe cutter; has resided in Lynn, Mass., Bradford Haverhill, Calais, Me., Plaistow and Pittsfield, N. H.; m., June 15, 1898, Frances Adaline Wilson, b. Haverhill, Mass., April 9, 1879; graduated from Currier's Grammar School, 1895; one year in Wheeler's Academy; daughter of Horace G. Wilson and Edna T. Patten.

(7) Harold Alfred Dunnells, b. Middleton, Mass., Feb. 24, 1875; resides 6 Jackson Street, Haverhill, Mass.; shoe cutter; soldier in Spanish-American War; enlisted at Haverhill, Mass., Jan. 29, 1898, mustered out at Boston, Mass., April 28, 1899; Company F, Eighth Massachusetts Infantry, Capt. William C. Dow; Second Brigade, Second Division, First Army Corps, Capt. William A. Pew, Jr.; m., Sept. 3, 1905, Emma Ellen Carlton, b. Haverhill, Mass., Nov. 16, 1878; studied in Haverhill (Mass.) schools; daughter of Charles Carlton and Margaret Ellen ———.

(7) Fred Thompson Dunnells, b. Bradford, Mass., March 28, 1880; resides at 59 Pleasant Street, Bradford District, Haverhill, Mass.; works for Switchboard

Construction Company, New England Telegraph & Telephone Company, Boston, Mass.; m., at Haverhill, Mass., Sept. 20, 1905, Clara Olive Allen, b. Aug. 15, 1881; daughter of Herbert Melville Allen and Augusta Jane Varney.

(5) Maria Ann Goss Thompson, b. July 27, 1803; d. Oct. 18, 1885; resided at West Bath, Me.,

(5) Ezekiel Thompson, b. Dec. 22, 1805; d. May 30, 1869; one of the chief founders of the Free Baptist Church at Brunswick, Me.

(5) Susannah Thompson, b. May 8, 1810; d. at Brunswick, Me.; unm.

*　*　*　*　*

(4) Phineas Thompson, b. July 21, 1760. "He went to sea with Captain Tracey in 1780." "He was in a United States sloop of war and the vessel was never heard from and was probably captured by an English man-of-war."

CHAPTER IV.

AMOS THOMPSON OF BOWDOIN, ME., AND HIS DESCENDANTS.

His line: (1) William Thompson; (2) James Thompson of Kittery, Me.; (3) Capt. James Thompson of New Meadows, Me.

(4) Amos Thompson, b. Brunswick Me., Sept. 3, 1749; d. Bowdoin, Me., Jan. 6, 1835 (86y.).

His grandson, Amos Thompson of Belleville, Ill., writes of him:

"He lived the greater part of his life on a farm about two and one half miles from Bowdoinham Village. He told me that when he settled there the country was covered with a heavy forest of timber. He said that the bears were so plenty that they would destroy the green corn when it was in the roasting ear, and would also kill the calves, sheep and pigs. He made a snare by bending down a birch sapling, and baiting it with a part of a sheep or calf that the bear had caught the night before. When he went to the snare in the morning he found that he had caught the bear by the hind legs, and the sapling was strong enough to lift him from the ground. The bear was standing on his fore feet with his hind parts in the air. He took his axe and killed him.

"He was eighty years old when I went to visit him, but he was still as straight as a man of thirty years, but he was very bald. He had his coffin made and placed up stairs in the brick house, so it would be all ready when it was wanted. But he did not need it for six years after he made it. I was much interested in looking over the house where this grandfather was born. It had a large chimney in the middle, so that there should be no loss of the heat from the fire. My grandfather told me that he was of English descent. In the fall of 1774 or 1775 he went with General Arnold from Maine to Quebec, for the purpose of capturing Quebec. But the plan was a failure. The army lay on the river below Quebec all that winter and came home in the spring without accomplishing anything.

"My grandmother, whose maiden name was Hannah Wooster, was quite a stout, large woman at that time and appeared to enjoy good health. She said that she was some mixed with French blood."

The following letter from Amos Thompson clearly shows his style of writing, as well as many other interesting things in regard to him. It was called out by matters pertaining to the family of his son, Abel Thompson, who had moved to Illinois some time before:

"Bowdoin (Maine) Monday, May 31st, 1819.
"Kind Respectable Sir:

"I have received your letter of the 2nd of April—last part—and am gratified to hear from you at such an early date, and shall endeavor to forward an answer according to your request. In the first place, sir, you inform me how and by what means I may become Administrator and Guardian of the children, which looks to me most reasonable, but, sir, as you inform me that my son Abel had the desire that the children should enjoy the benefit of his new settlement in that country, I should recoil from interfering in that business, but shall confide in your wisdom respecting my son's children and property to be managed for them according to your discretion Sir, my age and many infirmities of body render me incapable of coming to see you, and the man that I have appointed to go on, namely Mr. Allen, has gone a great distance to the Eastward, so that matter is at an end. But if he had now been at home, under the consideration that my son's children were still to remain there, I should have been very far from recalling them if Mr. Allen had gone to see them. Sir, you inform me that my son died seized of about $16.00, which was all you found, which surprised me much, as he must have had when he went away from us more than $2,000.00, and what should become of it is a great mystery to me, without he meted help to those who moved at about the same time with him. Sir, I have heard that he requested to appoint Mr. Barker (his Christian name I cannot at present recollect), but Mr. Barker may likely inform you, Sir, if you have not come to the knowledge of it, and I hope, Sir, you will be very solicitous to see to the children that they have faithful guardians and places to live at where they may have the instruction that will be necessary for them, and, Sir, my desire for them is fervent, and may the God of the fatherless reward you, Sir, with the blessings of this life and that which is to come. Sir, there are some debts that are due to the Estate of my son from peo-

ple that are living in our vicinity, and some of it may be
collected. Sir, if you think convenient, you may consti-
tute Ezekiel Allen, if you can do it legally, which would
save you considerable pains and trouble, but as I am not at
present able to say how that may be, I shall leave that
matter entirely with you. Sir, you mention one note
given by John Temple of $15.00. I suppose that he is liv-
ing in Cincinnati. Sir, you must act your discretion and
I shall remain satisfied.

"Dear sir, I have written you such things as at present
flow in my mind, but I am loth to trouble you with such
a long harangue, feeling, Sir, a great reliance on your wisdom and candor and shall leave the whole to you, and
subscribe myself,

"Yours, with most profound respect,

"Amos Thompson.

"To Mr. Hugh McClintock, Belleville, St. Clair Co. Illinois Territory.

"P. S. Pray, sir, remember us to our dear grandchildren for whom we feel indissoluble ties of tenderness
and respect. Say to them, as they are able to bear it, that
they are dutiful and kind to those who have care of
them, and to all around them, and to remember their Cre-
ator in the days of their youth. And say to Mehetable, as
the first of age, that she remind her Uncle Barker's children that we remember them with the same tenderness
and respect, and that grandfather and grandmother are
now desirous to hear from you all as often as you can find
an opportunity. And say to Mr. Barker and wife that we
remember them with respect, and that we are enjoying the
blessings of health as our age will permit. Hoping that
these lines may find each of our dear relatives enjoying
the same blessings. Betsy and Hannah and their families
are in good health.

"Amos Thompson."

Hon. Horace Purington of Waterville, Me., a great-
grandson of Amos Thompson, says of him: "He was a
man of great energy and strong will. Nothing was too
hard for him to undertake or overcome. He was a man
of a mechanical turn and somewhat inventive. He built
a saw and gristmill, and operated it for many years, thus
accommodating the country for miles around. Many times
have I heard the old men of the town tell of their going to

this mill with their grists of corn, wheat and rye, which at first they carried on their backs for miles. Later on, horses could be used on the rough roads. Amos Thompson was high sheriff of his town for many years. Many rough men were in the country in those days, but no man too ugly for him to arrest ever crossed the borders of Bowdoin.

"He was a man of keen wit, and many are the stories which are told of the jokes which he played on others when he was sure they would do no personal harm, but fix some needed lesson in the minds of his neighbors. One year the town of Bowdoin offered five dollars per head for every wolf which was caught in the town. At the same time the neighboring town of Topsham offered the same sum for every wolf that was killed in the town. In a few days after this, Amos Thompson caught three wolves in Bowdoin, and promptly received the bounty which was offered for them. He then took the wolves to Topsham and killed them, and got the bounty there. His townsmen tried to get even with him by calling him 'Wolf Thompson,' but each time the nickname was used more and more people laughed at his keen wit. Both towns made their laws in regard to bounties for wolves to harmonize, for they well knew at what points the shafts of wit had been aimed. 'Days of argument would not have accomplished what a few jokes of his did,' was the ready verdict of all who knew Amos Thompson well."

Amos Thompson m. Oct. 15, 1774, Hannah Wooster, b. in 'Falmouth, or Gorham, Me.; d. Bowdoin, Me., Jan. 25, 1835 (84 y.). The marriage intention states that he was then living "without the bounds of the town of Bowdoin." Amos Thompson and his wife lived together 60 years, and her death occurred only four weeks after that of her husband. The records of the children were found in the ancient Bowdoin records. To this Weston Thompson, Esq., of Brunswick, Me., added Betsy, who died at the age of 12 years, and a child which died in infancy.

* * * * *

(5) Abel Thompson, b. Lincoln County, District of Maine, Aug. 15, 1775; d. Randolph, St. Clair County, Ill., Sept. 17, 1818. He is said to have been the second child born in Lincoln County, Me. One writer says he moved to Bowdoin, Me., in 1804. His intention of marriage is dated April 7, 1797, to Mary Haynes[6], b. Oct. 10, 1770; d.

6

St. Clair County, Ill., Sept. 15, 1818; daughter of David Haynes, who was b. at Sudbury, Mass., 1740, and spent most of his life in Bowdoinham, Me.; her mother was Sarah Howland. The Haynes line is: (1) Walter Haynes, b. England, 1583; (2) John Haynes, b. 1621; (3) Peter Haynes; (4) David Haynes; (5) David Haynes, father of Mary. Abel Thompson and wife are buried seven miles southwest of Belleville, Ill. Abel Thompson, with his wife and five children, left Maine for Illinois in Oct., 1816. They arrived in Illinois March 15, 1818, and the following September both the parents died within two days of each other. His son, Amos Thompson, wrote of him: "He joined the Methodist Church when he was a young man. He was a steadfast Christian all his life. How he kept up his church relationship during many years when he had few church privileges was but little short of heroic. Father never accumulated much property. When he died he owned a farm of 140 acres in St. Clair County, Ill."

(6) Betsy Thompson, b. Bowdoin, Me., July 23, 1797 (July 25, 1796); d. Oct., 1834; buried in the Phillips Cemetery near Belleville, Ill.; m., Dec. 8, 1814, Ezekiel Allen, b. Dec. 4, 1792; d. 1819. "A widow with four children, she went to Illinois in 1820 with her uncle, Amos Thompson, who visited Maine that year. Only three of her children went with her, as Margery Allen, the second child, preferred to stay with her father's people in Maine."

(7) Mary Ann Allen, b. June 2, 1815; d. 1840; m. George Stuntz, who was b. Belleville, Ill., March 26, 1810, and d. Sept. 21, 1845; farmer; son of Capt. John Stuntz, who lived near Belleville, Ill.; buried in Stuntz Cemetery, South Newton, St. Clair County, Ill.

(8) Conrad Stuntz, b. July 22, 1835; d. Sept. 6, 1891; he lived in St. Clair County, Ill., save a year or so, about 1864, when he visited in Oregon; he was a school teacher in his younger days.

(8) Child, d. in infancy.

(8) Lucius Dow Stuntz, b. at the house of his grandfather, Capt. John Stuntz, near Belleville, Ill., Jan. 7, 1837; resides Freeburg, Ill.; farmer; m. (first), Feb. 19, 1861, Mary Ann Holcomb, b. near Hecker, Ill., Feb. 19, 1844; d. Oct. 18, 1866; buried

in Richland Cemetery, nine miles south of Belleville, Ill; daughter of John Holcomb and Lavina Potter; m. (second), Sept. 10, 1868, Mary J. Varner, b. Aug. 23, 1841; daughter of Abraham Varner and Edna E. Williams; parents of Virginia.

Child of first wife:

(9) George Osmund Stuntz, b. St. Clair County, Ill., Dec. 15, 1862; resides 453 North Sixteenth Street, East St. Louis, Ill.; began teaching in 1893 and continued until the fall of 1896; was then elected register of deeds for St. Clair County, Ill., and held the position for four years; then entered an abstract title office; is now deputy assessor in East St. Louis, Ill.; m., Aug. 11, 1886, Mary Katherine Spitz, b. Randolph County, Ill., Feb. 21, 1866; daughter of Conrad Spitz and Katharine.

(10) Jessie May Stuntz, b. Sept. 11, 1887.

(10) Harrison Goldwin Stuntz, b. Jan. 16, 1889.

(10) George Washington Stuntz, b. Feb. 22, 1891.

(10) John Arlington Stuntz, b. Nov. 12, 1894.

(10) Clara Matilda Stuntz, b. Jan. 24, 1898.

(10) Helen Edna Stuntz, b. Dec. 3, 1900.

Child of second wife:

(9) Lucius D. Stuntz, Jr., b. April 10, 1874; resides Coulterville, Randolph County, Ill.; in the fruit canning business; m., Oct. 30, 1895, Mary Jeannette Dixon, b. Nov. 26, 1873.

(10) Edna Stuntz, b. Nov. 13, 1896.

(7) Margery Allen, b. Bowdoin, Me., June 4, 1817; "m. Holbrook." "A number of years ago she was a widow with three children."

(7) Hannah Allen, b. Bowdoin, Me., April 17, 1821; d. April 8, 1846; she went to Illinois in 1830 with her uncle, Amos Thompson; m., April 6, 1838, Edward D. Terrell, b. Millersburg, Ky., March 29, 1815; d. May 10, 1904; son of Jeremiah Terrell and Mary Christy of Millersburg, Ky. In May, 1829, Edward D. Terrell went to Belleville, Ill., and in 1860 moved to Holden, Mo.; farmer and merchant; in his old age he spent his very happy days in his pleasant home.

(8) Mary Elizabeth Terrell, b. Belleville, Ill., May 27, 1839; studied in Belleville schools and in Winona

College at Jacksonville, Ill.; for five years she was
a very successful school teacher.

(8) Martha Jane Terrell, b. Aug. 20, 1841; studied in
Belleville schools and in St. Joseph Academy at
St. Louis, Mo.; m. at Holden, Mo., Dec. 1, 1851,
Daniel K. Carmichael, b. near Holden, Mo., July
20, 1837; farmer in Holden, Johnson County, Mo.;
son of Isaac Carmichael and Pamelia Lowrey.

(9) May Bessie Carmichael, b. Holden, Mo., May 27,
1868; d. Nov. 30, 1898; m., July 22, 1887, Benner
F. Shrinkel, b. Thorneville, O., Oct. 26, 1861;
farmer near Holden, Mo.

(10) Mary Elsie Shrinkel, b. Oct 20, 1888.

(10) Carrie Blanche Shrinkel, b. Dec. 20, 1890.

(10) Martha Mabelle Shrinkel, b. July 20, 1893.

(10) Arthur Edward Shrinkel, b. Feb. 29, 1896; d.
June 28, 1896.

(10) Bessie Mildred Shrinkel, b. Oct. 2, 1898.

(9) James Edward Carmichael, b. Holden, Mo., Sept.
17, 1871; farmer at Holden, Mo.; m., May 27,
1894, Katherine Buss, b. Windsor, Mo., Sept. 14,
1870.

(8) James Jeremiah Terrell, b. Belleville, Ill., July 6,
1844; farmer at Holden, Mo.; studied in the Christian Brothers' School at St. Louis, Mo.; soldier in
the Civil War, enlisted Aug. 6, 1862, discharged
Aug. 12, 1865, in the Thirty-third Missouri Infantry; m., at Jacksonville, Ill., Oct. 29, 1873,
Elizabeth Ennis, b. March 6, 1848; daughter of
Henry Ennis and Rebecca Adams.

(9) William Ennis Terrell, b. Holden, Mo., April 4,
1875; merchant at Sedalia, Mo.; m., Nov. 8,
1899, Elizabeth Courtney, b. Dresden, Mo., Dec.
18, 1872; daughter of Peter Courtney and Elizabeth Bract.

(9) Arthur David Terrell, b. Holden, Mo., June 18,
1877; resides at Iola, Kan.; civil and mining engineer; m., July 22, 1903, Nellie Bannon; daughter of John T. Bannon and Elizabeth Foot.

(10) Edward Arthur Terrell, b. Iola, Kan., Jan. 18,
1905.

(9) James Earle Terrell, b. June 5, 1879; farmer at
Holden, Mo.

(8) Hannah Allen Terrell, b. Belleville, Ill., March 25,
1846; d. May 7, 1846.

(7) Betsy Allen, b. Bowdoin, Me., Feb. 25, 1823; d. 1840.

(6) Hannah Thompson, b. Bowdoin, Me., March 20, 1799; d.
July 21, 1886; always resided in Bowdoin, Me., much
of the time with her son, Ezekiel Grover. Her father,
Abel Thompson, cleared a farm in the Bowdoin forests when she was but five years old; when she was
but nine years old she carried corn to the mill, five
miles distant, near the Estey mill, Little River, that
it might be ground into meal. The corn was lashed to
the horse's back, she riding in front of it; there were
then no roads or ways of guidance save the spotted or
blazed trees; the country was full of Indians and wild
beasts; at that time there were no houses or roads at
Lisbon Falls, Me.; m., Sept. 18, 1815, James Grover, b.
Jan. 26, 1790; d. March 26, 1849; he was the son of Andrew Grover, who was twice married. This family resided about two miles from the old Thompson homestead and about four miles from West Bowdoin, Me.

(7) Eliza Jane Grover, b. Bowdoin, Me., March 12, 1816; d.
Taylorsville, Ill. April 7, 1899; m. (first), Mr. Jackson; m. (second), Mr. Goud of Taylorsville, Ill.

(7) Mary E. Grover, b. Bowdoin, Me., July 7, 1818; d.
March 26, 1844; unm.

(7) Abel Thompson Grover, b. Bowdoin, Me., May 27,
1820; d. Bowdoin, Me., June 11, 1901; he moved to
West Bowdoin, Me., March 27, 1858. "He was one of
Bowdoin's oldest and most respected citizens and was
born and brought up on the old place now owned by
Ezekiel Grover, near Cæsar's Pond; he was the only
surviving member of a family of eight boys and four
girls; this farm was taken up by his father, James
Grover, from wild lands, in 1815; he d. on the old
Abel Thompson farm." M., in Webster, Me., Sarah
Hannah Roberts, b. Jan. 15, 1824; d. Dec. 4, 1901.

(8) James A. Grover, b. May 18, 1847; resides Lisbon
Falls, Me.; m., Dec. 29, 1878, Mary A. Grover of
Litchfield, Me., b. March 6, 1860; d. July 4, 1901;
daughter of George Nelson Grover and Emma J.
Buker; farmer.

(9) Gilbert N. Grover, b. Oct. 13, 1880.

(9) Walter L. Grover, b. Sept. 13, 1882.

(9) Mabel Grover, b. Jan. 25, 1886.

(8) Sarah Hannah Grover, b. April 7, 1848; d. Sept. 7, 1850.

(8) Mary Elizabeth Grover, b. March 1, 1850; studied in Bowdoin (Me.) schools; address, Lisbon Falls, Me., R. F. D. No. 1; m. (first), April 18, 1878, Lewis Marcellus Haines, who d. Dec. 8, 1903; carpenter; son of Lyman Haines, formerly of Campton Village, N. H., but now residing at Rangeley, Me., and Sally C. Jones of Campton Bridge, N. H.; she m. (second), April 25, 1906, John Franklin Grover, b. Nov. 26, 1857.

(8) Eldora Grover, b. Jan. 30, 1862; m., Oct., 1885, Granville M. Small of Lisbon, Me.; resides at Lisbon.

(8) George Wilbert Grover, b. May 23, 1865; d. March, 1886; resided in Bowdoin, Me.; farmer; m., in Bowdoin, Feb. 20, 1878, Sylva J. Wheeler, b. Bowdoin, Me.

(8) Abel Thompson Grover, b. July 7, 1867; resides on the old Abel Thompson farm at West Bowdoin, Me.; farmer; m., Dec., 1904, Tinnie Newell of Webster, Me.

(8) King Tallman Grover, dead.

(8) Frederick Grover, dead.

(8) Angelia Grover, b. Dec. 26, 1861; m., at the Grover homestead, Dec. 25, 1881, Hosea Bickford of Bowdoin, Me.; resides at Lisbon Falls, Me.

(8) Sidney Grover.

(8) Eugene Grover.

(8) Persia Grover; d. Jan., 1906.

(7) Clara Grover, b. May 21, 1822; d. April 12, 1882; m., at the Grover homestead, James Barnes of Deering, N. H.; resided at Hillsborough Bridge, N. H.

(7) Ezekiel Grover, b. Aug. 31, 1826; m., Sept. 27, 1866, Maria Ellen Cox, b. April 20, 1828; daughter of Isaac Cox and Desire Estes; no children.

(7) Andrew Grover, b. Aug. 31, 1826; d. at sea, Feb. 8, 1845; unm.

(7) Orrin Grover, b. July 15, 1828; d. Bowdoin, Me., Dec. 1, 1858.

(7) James Grover, b. July 5, 1830; d. Dec. 11, 1852.

(7) George Nelson Grover, b. Bowdoin, Me., July 18, 1832; d. Litchfield, Me., March 7, 1858; farmer; m. (first), in Bowdoin, Oct. 10, 1853, Martha C. Smith of Lisbon, Me., b. July 18, 1838; d. July 26, 1855; m. (second), June 6, 1857, Emma Jane Buker, b. Bowdoin, Oct.

28, 1829; daughter of Timothy Buker and Betsy
Purington.

Child of first wife:

(8) Winfred N. Grover, b. Bowdoin, Feb. 2, 1855; d.
Bowdoin, March 10, 1870.

Children of second wife:

(8) George N. Grover, b. April 8, 1858; mechanic; unm.;
resides at Litchfield, Me.

(8) Mary Grover, b. March 6, 1860; d. July 4, 1901;
lived at Lisbon Falls, Me.; m., Dec. 29, 1878,
James Grover, b. May 18, 1847; farmer; son of
Albert Thompson Grover and Sarah Hannah
Roberts. (See records.)

(8) Emma J. Grover, b. Bowdoin, Me., Feb. 7, 1864; resides at Litchfield, Me.; address, Richmond Corner, Me.; m., Nov. 8, 1882, Horatio C. Allard, b.
April 9, 1854; son of William H. Allard and Elizabeth La Plain.

(9) E. Ethel Allard, b. March 7, 1884.

(9) M. Gertrude Allard, b. July 16, 1886.

(9) Harrie G. Allard, b. June 17, 1889.

(8) Eliza J. Grover, b. Nov. 14, 1866; resides in Bow-
doinham, Me.; m., April 2, 1895, Edward Buker, b.
June, 1868; son of William Greenwood Buker and
Olive Tongue.

(9) William G. Buker, b. Sept. 28, 1896.

(7) King Tallman Grover, b. Jan. 1, 1835; d. March 10,
1875; m., in Bowdoin, Me., Esther Maloon.

(7) Amanda Grover, b. Bowdoin, Me., Jan. 18, 1837; d. New
Haven, Ind., Jan. 9, 1864; moved to Allen County,
Ind., April 10, 1863; m., Oct. 9, 1853, Benjamin Gro-
ver, b. Bowdoin, Me., April 29, 1825; d. in Indiana
Nov. 15, 1906. Benjamin Grover m. (second), Ma-
randa Small of New Haven, Ind.

Children of first marriage:

(8) Sidney Grover, b. Aug. 25, 1854.

(8) Martha Ellen Grover, b. Nov. 25, 1855; d. Dec. 8,
1887.

(8) John Franklin Grover, b. Nov. 26, 1857; resides Lisbon Falls, Me.; m., April 25, 1906, Mrs. Mary E.
(Grover) Haines.

(8) Clara Elizabeth Grover, b. May 11, 1861; d. June 28,
1864.

(8) Amanda Eleanor Grover, b. Allen County, Ind., Oct.
1, 1863.

Children of second marriage:

    (8) Albert and Etta Jane Grover (twins).

    (8) Israel Luther Grover.

    (8) Alice Grover.

    (8) Benjamin W. Grover.

    (8) Nelson P. Grover.

  (7) Fairfield Grover, b. July 26, 1839; d. April 23, 1842.

(6) Boy and girl; d. in infancy.

(6) Mehetable Thompson, b. Bowdoin, Me., May 3, 1806; d. March, 1849; buried in Phillips Cemetery, Belleville, Ill.; m., in Bowdoin, Me., Sept. 9, 1821, Samuel Phillips, b. Oct., 1797; d. Jacksonville, Ill., Oct., 1865; farmer in St. Clair and Jackson counties, Ill.; son of David Phillips of Turkey Hill, Belleville, Ill.

  (7) Daniel Thompson Phillips, b. Belleville, Ill., Jan 27, 1823; d. June 14, 1906; moved to Oregon in 1857; resided at Cornelius, Ore.; brick maker; m., April 17, 1845, Martha Tate, b. Pennsylvania, Dec. 27, 1828; daughter of D. M. Tate and Elizabeth Clamfant.

    (8) Melissa J. Phillips, b. March 17, 1847; m., May 22, 1863, C. W. Purdin and resides at Hillsboro, Ore.

      (9) Mary Ann Purdin, b. 1875; m., March 11, 1888, C. A. Taylor, farmer at Greenville, Ore.

        (10) Two daughters and a son.

      (9) Walter H. Purdin; farmer at Greenville, Ore.; m. in 1893.

        (10) Two children.

      (9) Huston W. Purdin; farmer at Greenville, Ore.; m., 1896; no children.

    (8) Miles C. Phillips; telegraph operator, Forest Grove, Ore.

    (8) Edward M. Phillips; m., 1894.

    (8) Stella Phillips; m., 1893, Greenville, Ore.

    (8) Charles Phillips; clerk at Hillsboro, Ore.

    (8) David H. Phillips; resides at Hillsboro, Ore.

    (8) Otis H. Phillips; resides at Hillsboro, Ore.

    (8) Alonzo Adolphus Phillips, b. St. Clair County, Ill., March 31, 1849; studied in Hillsboro (Ore.) schools; has lived in Cornelius, Ore., since 1865; brick mason, school clerk, notary public, etc.; m., Oct. 15, 1871, Martha Jane Stanley, b. Missouri, 1852.

      (9) Mary Frances Phillips, b. Tangent, Linn County, Ore., Aug. 14, 1872; resides at Monument, Ore.;

studied at Oak Plain School, near Halsey, Ore.;
m., Jan. 1, 1894, George Washington Saunders, b.
Hillsboro, Ore., July 20, 1861; merchant.

(10) Alice Clare Saunders, b. Oct. 14, 1894.

(9) Daniel Webster Phillips, b. Corvallis, Ore., Oct. 15,
1880; resides Baker City, Ore.; m. Alice Endicott.

(9) Hattie May Phillips, b. Corvallis, Ore., Dec. 22,
1882; d. Sept. 4, 1896.

(9) Nellie Phillips, b. Corvallis, Ore., Feb. 17, 1884;
studied in Corvallis schools; lived at Corvallis
until 1904; resides 1543 Valley Avenue, Baker
City, Ore., m., July 9, 1904, George W. Eckerman, b. Albany, Ore., Oct. 19, 1879; merchant;
son of Hiram Eckerman and Minerva J. Harris.

(10) Helen Jeannette Eckerman, b. Nov. 9, 1905.

(9) Lester Phillips, b. May 31, 1894.

(8) Christian N. Phillips, b. Feb. 5, 1851; d. Sept. 16,
1852.

(8) Ellen Phillips, b. Feb. 8, 1853; resides Cornelius,
Ore.; m. (first), Feb. 18, 1869, Mark Hoffman, b.
Illinois; d. 1884; farmer; m. (second), Sept. 15,
1878, Grafton Baker Vickers, b. Sept. 12, 1846;
farmer.

Children of first husband:

(9) Daniel Lee Hoffman, b. Cornelius, Ore., June 30,
1871; studied in Hillsboro (Ore.) High School;
farmer, two miles from Courtney, N. D.; m.,
Dec., 1901, Lulu Wright of Courtney, N. D.

(9) Irving Hill Hoffman, b. May 21, 1874; resides at
Portland, Ore.; graduated from Cornelius (Ore.)
High School; m., 1898, Anna Neep.

Children of second husband:

(9) Rhoda Ann Vickers, b. June 23, 1879; graduated
from Cornelius (Ore.) High School.

(9) Pratt Grafton Vickers, b. Jan. 21, 1881; telegraph
operator at St. Joseph, Ore.; graduated from
Pacific University, Forest Grove, Ore.; m., June
20, 1906, Clara Lund.

(9) William Baker Vickers, b. Oct. 10, 1883; graduated
from Pacific University, Forest Grove, Ore.; con-
fectionery store, Cornelius, Ore.; m., Feb. 5,
1905, Jeannette Ross of Portland, Ore.

(9) Franklin Arthur Vickers, b. June 2, 1885; d. Jan.
23, 1889.

(8) Sarah E. Phillips, b. Jan. 5, 1855; resides at Gaston, Ore.; m. (first), Dec. 26, 1874, Martin Parsons; m. (second), Jan. 5, 1880, Darling Smith.

Children of first husband:

(9) Martha J. Parsons; m. Eben Hall, a farmer, and resides at Dilley, Ore.

(10) Willis Hall, b. 1896.

(9) Rosa May Parsons, b. Jan. 7, 1878; m., Nov. 26, 1894, Robert Hougherty, and resides at Lafayette, Ore.

(10) Fanny Hougherty.

(10) Harold Hougherty.

(10) Earle Hougherty.

Children of second husband:

(9) Lulu Smith; m., Sept. 1, 1898, George Stuart, and resides at Dilley, Ore.

(10) Lilly Stuart.

(10) Tracey Stuart.

(9) Herbert Smith; resides at Westfall, Ore.; farmer.

(9) Nettie Smith; resides at Dilley, Ore.

(9) Vivian Smith, b. 1887.

(9) Roy Smith.

(8) Milly Phillips, b. Dec. 24, 1857; resides at Mist, Ore. m., June 8, 1877, Walter S. Shearer; farmer.

(8) George W. Philips, b. Oct. 6, 1859; resides at Portland, Ore.

(8) Mary F. Phillips, b. Jan. 8, 1862; d. July 2, 1864.

(8) Alice E. Phillips, b. March 14, 1864; resides at Hillsboro, Ore.; m., Sept. 28, 1882, J. E. Found.

(9) Bodie Found, b. Jan. 29, 1883.

(9) Ernest Found, b. Jan. 7, 1885.

(9) Orra Found, b. Jan. 1, 1886.

(9) Albert G. Found, b. May 13, 1888.

(8) Charles W. Phillips, b. March 1, 1867; m., Jan. 11, 1889, Zillah Howard, who d. March 1, 1900.

(8) Albert T. Phillips, b. Nov. 8, 1869; d. April 22, 1900; m., 1894, Sarah S. Huston.

(7) Amos Phillips, b. Jan. 12, 1826; d. Smithton, Ill., June 5, 1905; carpenter and farmer; m., Jan. 5, 1859, Mary Higgins, b. near Smithton, Ill., April 29, 1830; d. April 10, 1904; daughter of Robert Higgins and Sarah Clair.

(8) Sarah A. Phillips, b. July 1, 1852; m., Jan. 30, 1872, at Prairie de Long, Isaac Rettinghouse, b. Hecker,

Monroe County, Ill., Feb. 9, 1848; d. May 31, 1896; farmer.

(9) Charles Alwin Rettinghouse, b. near Hecker, Ill., Sept. 22, 1872; studied in country schools; employed in a creamery; m., Jan. 16, 1895, Susan Coulter, b. near Hecker, Ill., Jan. 19, 1876; studied in country schools; daughter of Al. Coulter and Christiana Woods; resides Hecker, Ill.

(9) Willie Rettinghouse, b. Nov. 26, 1876.

(9) Caleb Rettinghouse, b. July 12, 1880.

(8) Mary Jane Phillips, b. June 5, 1858; resides near Smithton, Ill.; unm.

(8) Deborah Phillips; d. in infancy.

(8) Jerome Phillips, b. on the farm near Smithton, Ill., May 18, 1861; resides at Sherwin Junction, Kan.; m., July 19, 1893, Miranda Jane Miller, b in Illinois, Nov. 15, 1865; daughter of Alexander Miller; moved to Kansas in 1885.

(9) Ethel May Phillips, b. June 19, 1884.

(9) Marilla Caroline Phillips, b. Aug. 20, 1886; d. Nov. 16, 1888.

(9) Amos Alexander Phillips, b. June 29, 1889.

(9) Grace Oliver Phillips, b. Nov. 19, 1891.

(9) Georgianna Phillips, b. Nov. 1, 1893.

(9) Ruth Rowan Phillips, b. July 30, 1896.

(8) Benjamin A. Phillips, b. July 19, 1864; resides at Smithton, St. Clair County, Ill.; studied in schools of Smithton township; farmer; m., Sept. 16, 1905, Kate Frisell, b. Smithton, Ill., June 1, 1872; no children.

(7) Joseph Duncan Phillips, b. Washington County, Ore., May 16, 1829; farmer; m., 1852, Julia Duncan, b. St. Clair, Ill., 1834; d. April 16, 1872.

(8) William R. Phillips, b. Washington County, Ore., Oct. 16, 1857; farmer; lived South from Aug., 1869, to March 11, 1894; resided in Florence, Col., 1896; at Los Angeles, Cal., to Sept., 1900; moved to Washington in 1901; m., Jan. 1, 1882, Alice May Wingate, b. Montgomery County, Ill., Sept. 21, 1862; daughter of Stanley J. Wingate and Anna E. Berry.

(9) Arthur E. Phillips, b. March 6, 1884.

(9) Charley S. Phillips, b. Dec. 23, 1885.

(9) Anna Wingate Phillips, b. Dec. 23, 1885.

(8) Edward Phillips.

(7) Francis Marion Phillips; d. St. Clair County, Ill., Jan. 20, 1849.

(7) Elizabeth Phillips; d. Marion County, Ill., 1877; m. Green Hill.

(7) Wylie Harris Phillips, b. Belleville, Ill., Jan. 1, 1833; resides Shawnee, Okla.; has lived at Georgetown, Ill., Cornelius, Ore., Holden, Mo.; Denison, Tex.; Wichita Falls, Tex.; nurseryman; m., in Davis County, Ky., Sept. 28, 1872, Lydia Elizabeth Bise, b. Deer Valley, O., Nov. 23, 1854; daughter of Henry Lewis Bise and Ellen Sonnels.

(8) Mary Elizabeth Phillips, b. Holden, Mo., Oct. 15, 1878; resides at Turkey, Tex; graduated from St. Louis (Mo.) Kindergarten Normal school; taught two years in El Meta Bond College; has lived at Shawnee, Okla., and Roswell, N. M.; m., Nov. 27, 1901, Garfield Taylor Black, b. Des Moines, Ia., May 17, 1878; graduated Drake University and Columbia School of Oratory; teacher of oratory; on account of ill health became a ranchman; son of Gilson T. Black, b. Louisville, Ky., 1842.

(8) Matibel Phillips, b. Sept. 16, 1880; resides Shawnee, Okla.; graduated Wichita Falls (Tex.) High School; studied five years in music and piano; m., May 26, 1902, Alexander Buford Jones, b. Lexington, Ky., Aug. 25, 1869; farmer and real estate ᴜealer.

(9) Mildred Jones, b. Feb. 9, 1903.

(8) Harris Willey Phillips, b. Holden, Mo., April 29, 1882; address, 108–110 South 8th Street, St. Louis, Mo.; pharmacist; city salesman for Parker, Davis & Co.; studied in schools of Denison, Tex., and at St. Louis (Mo.) College of Pharmacy, June, 1903.

(8) Nellie Pearl Phillips, b. March 23, 1884; resides at Sulpher, I. T.; graduated at Shawnee (Okla.) High School, 1900; studied painting with Mrs. Dodge, at Shawnee, Okla., and is a fine artist.

(8) Guy Francis Phillips, b. Dec. 27, 1886; resides at St. Louis, Mo.; graduated from Shawnee (Okla.) High School, 1902; in University of Oklahoma, Sept. 1903, to March, 1904; Wright's Business College, St. Louis, Mo.; stenographer.

(7) Clarence Phillips.

(7) Hannah Phillips, b. Belleville, Ill., Sept. 30, 1844; resides Kell, Marion County, Ill.; studied in the country schools; after the death of her mother she lived in Jefferson County, Ill.; m., March 20, 1862, Hiram Howard, b. June 13, 1842; son of M. M. Howard and Jane Carpenter.

(8) Marcellus Moss Howard, b. Nov. 14, 1863; farmer, near Divide, Jefferson County, Ill.; m., Sept., 1882, E. Lizzie Howard, b. Wayne County, Ill., Jan. 18, 1867; daughter of Boone Howard and Mary Dols.

(9) Evelyn Howard, b. April 24, 1885.

(9) Orra Belle Howard, b. March 12, 1887.

(9) Clara A. Howard, b. July 14, 1890.

(9) Charles M. Howard, b. Nov. 9, 1893.

(9) William Howard, b. Dec. 15, 1896.

(9) Tinnie Howard, b. Aug., 1899.

(9) Thomas F. Howard, b. March 20, 1901.

(9) Rob Roy Howard, b. Feb. 10, 1903.

(8) Addie Howard, b. Oct. 18, 1869; resides at Centralia, Ill.; dressmaker; m., Dec. 23, 1888, Littleton Davidson Harmon, b. in Tennessee; machinist.

(9) Pansy May Harmon, b. Dec. 15, 1894.

(8) Thomas F. Howard, b. Nov. 8, 1871; resides on the farm with his parents; unm.

(8) Alonzo Howard, b. Dec. 9, 1873; resides near Kell, Ill.; farmer; m., Nov. 17, 1901, Emeline Hawkins, Sept. 14, 1881; daughter of Alonzo Hawkins and Adaline Donaho.

(9) Reuben Howard, b. Aug. 2, 1902.

(9) Clarence Howard, b. Feb. 26, 1904.

(8) Louis Howard, b. Dec. 5, 1875; resides at Kell, Ill.; blacksmith; m., Oct. 4, 1898, Katie Roach; daughter of Woodson Roach and Susan.

(9) Henry Howard, b. Dec., 1889.

(9) Robert Lee Howard, b. Oct., 1902.

(9) Susan Howard, b. Aug. 20, 1904.

(8) Josephine Howard, b. June 10, 1877; resides near Divide. Jefferson County, Ill.; m., Nov. 1, 1899, Albert Brookman; farmer.

(9) Charles Brookman, b. May 10, 1900.

(9) Flossie Brookman, b. Sept. 12, 1903.

(8) Rosa Lee Howard, b. Jan. 6, 1881; resides near Salem, Jefferson County, Ill.; m., Dec. 25, 1900, Etty Early, b. April 8, 1880; farmer.

(9) Addie Josephine Early, b. Jan. 30, 1905.

(7) Mary Ann Phillips; d. in California, 1896.

(7) Thomas Phillips; resides at Pomona, Jackson County, Ill.

(7) Margaret Phillips; d. St. Clair County, Ill., at two years of age.

(6) Amos Thompson, b. Bowdoin, Me., April 26, 1807; d. at the home of his son, Charles H. Thompson at Portland, Ore., Saturday evening, April 13, 1901 (93y., 11 mo., 17d.). His remains were taken back to the old Illinois home, where he had spent nearly all his life, and buried in the beautiful Green Mount Cemetery. Very impressive services were conducted by the pastors of the Baptist and Methodist churches, the large audience room being entirely filled with the old neighbors and friends. The choir tenderly rendered the most comforting hymns, and the organ selections by Miss Zoe Harrison were especially chosen for the occasion. Then the very large funeral cortége wended its way to the cemetery. Standing beside the open grave, the Hon. L. D. Turner delivered the following address:

"Uncle Amos Thompson was my friend, and I approach the story of his life conscious of one's weakness when he speaks of a friend. I loved him, as all did who knew him well, for to know him well was to love him more. My own gentle mother taught me to love him, for she knew him well. And his illustrations of the lessons taught me intensified my love. He and she were sheltered under the same roof, warmed at the same hearthstone, fed the same food, clothed by the same hands, educated in the same log schoolhouse and studied at home by the light of the same tallow candle. Their notions of the present life, and their hopes of the future life, were the same, and their strength of body the same, as they succumbed to death at the same time.

"Amos Thompson was born April 26, 1807, and died April 13, 1901. His parents came to St. Clair County in 1816. His mother protested against the journey, and remarked, 'I am going to my grave,' and her prophecy was fulfilled, as she and her husband died within two days of each other, in less than three months after their arrival in Illinois. After the death of his parents

he lived with a neighbor one year, and when he was
ten years old, he made his home until he reached his
majority, with John Stuntz of Turkey Hill. On May
15, 1831, he married Irene Moore Charles of Twelve-
Mile Prairie and went to farming in High Prairie. The
wife died in 1852. His living children are Charles H.
of Portland, Ore., Alonzo of Fullerton, Neb., Mrs. Theophilus Harrison of Colorado Springs, Col., and Cyrus
of Belleville. He was three times elected to the Illinois
Legislature, the first time in 1842, and succeeded himself in 1844 and was elected again in 1866. In search
of a better climate, he moved to Oregon some five years
ago, but hé always called Illinois his home.

'He still had hopes, his long vexations past,
Here to return and die at home at last.'

"After a very long life of spotless conduct, that comes
only from a heart by nature born of purest impulses,
of perfect integrity, commanding and maintaining con-
tinuously a unanimity of respect from all classes and
kinds of men with whom he came in contact and association, either in a private business way or in a public
way calculated to promote the public weal, or stay the
public woe, our loved friend, our long-time neighbor,
our former citizen, our good, kind, dear old father, has
reached the limits of life's boundary line and has closed
his eyes in the everlasting sleep, and 'joined the innu-
merable caravan that moves to the pale realms of
shade, where each shall take his chamber in the silent
halls of death.' The grave is open and ready to receive
and hide forever from our view that frank, placid countenance; that bent and bowed, yet strong and stalwart,
form. But the memory of his many manly virtues, of
his good deeds done, of his fatherly devotion, 'fadeth
not away.' And if every one upon whom he hath be-
stowed a favor could place but a single petal of a rose
upon his grave, it would be changed from a little
mound of cold clay to a mighty mountain of sweet
flowers. When the electric current flashed over the
Rocky Mountain tops the information of his death, the
tenderest chord is touched and the heart bleeds, and
as the story is repeated on the street a sympathetic
chord is touched in every heart, and in silent cadence
the words are spoken—Amos Thompson is dead.

"In the death of the oldest and charter member of the

Octogenarian Club, the venerable and esteemed Amos Thompson, we mourn the loss of one whose memory we will cherish as long as friendship, founded on virtue and worth, is a cardinal principle of the human heart. His rectitude through a long life elicits our highest admiration. His sound judgment in all temporal affairs, his unswerving integrity in all his dealings with his fellow-men, and his broad charity, have stamped their impress on the community in which he has lived an honored and worthy member. Never a seeker of office, his eminent qualifications commanded the confidence of the discerning public and offices of trust and responsibility were conferred upon him, and in the faithful service rendered he merited their highest respect. Wealth that he accumulated through industry, frugal habits and fair dealing, stimulated no false pride in either feeling or action, but was employed by him in various channels for the benefit of others, and the needy were often and kindly remembered. His influence was always cast on the side of right, and his moral character was above reproach. His gentle manners endeared him to all, and to be numbered among his friends was an honor to be coveted. His kind remembrance of absent members gave evidence of his interest in their welfare and love for the brotherhood. His fair name, and noble example, are an imperishable heritage to his children, and the monument he has built in this community is more lasting than bronze or marble.

"Of this Octogenarian Club, whose memorial I have read, he was a charter member, and lived longer than any other member save one—Col. John Thomas, who lived a little less than one year longer than Amos Thompson. He was a man without enemies. He was loved and admired by everybody. He was the soul of honor and trusted all with whom he dealt. He was not a member of any church, but believed in the immortality of the soul. He was liberal in his views towards all denominations, and his motto was:

'Teach me to feel another's woe,
    To hide the fault I see,
That mercy I to others show,
    That mercy show to me.'

"He verified the old adage, which to him was a very familiar one, 'A punctual man holds his neighbors' purse strings.' At the early age of ten years we find him an orphan boy in a new country, among strangers, homeless, friendless and penniless. Twenty years thereafter we find him in possession of a home and a family, friends in numbers, and pennies in goodly quantity. And yet another twenty years and we find him comfortably located and pleasantly situated, but 'still achieving, still pursuing,' his name extending, his influence widening, his friends increasing, public confidence placed in him, and his voice is heard advocating the cause of the people in the legislative halls in this great and growing state.

"And in yet another twenty years we find him deprived of his wife, but he is not homeless now, for to him sons and daughters were born, and the unspeakable love with which he loved his wife was not buried in the cold earth with her lifeless body, but it lived on, and passed over into and strengthened his lasting, living love for his children and, though there was one vacant chair, the home circle was not broken, and he was not homeless, for his erstwhile home was their home, and their future homes were his home.

"And in this same twenty years not a friend that he had made was lost, not a friendship was broken,—but each one became a better friend,—and to this circle numberless others were added.

"And in this same twenty years not a penny earned in youth was lost in wild speculation or gambling adventures, but the penny once earned was judiciously invested and its increments added thereto. And yet, with all these things accomplished, he is not fifty years old and he lives yet nigh another fifty years before he passes into another life: and he goes on making new friends, and never losing an old one, does public service in many official ways, helps the needy. From his lofty mountain height of success he could take a retrospective view of his past, and could readily see and learn whom to help, when to give, and where to give. His charity was great, and it was not heralded in the public press. Of the poor of our city he was ever mindful, and was always willing to give liberally. With the Woman's Relief Corps he was prodigal. To them he would give fifty dollars, then the same sum, then double that gift. Surely these will feel the breaking of his purse strings.

In stature, Amos Thompson was short and stoutly built, with firm, erect walk, and his countenance was always peaceful. He had done no wrong and there was no heartache to rack his brain and distress his look. He was regular and temperate in his habits and exceedingly industrious. Labor was a pleasure. His education was limited to that of the earlier common school. Then things were rude, indeed, in our new state. But he was a great reader of history and a lover of the poets, and possessed a most wonderful memory. He had the genealogy of the kings and the battles of the nations, at his command, and the songs of the poets were on his tongue. Given the wonderful advantage of the present school, college and university, and the query is, 'What would he not have accomplished?' He was a good, successful and exemplary citizen. And the reason for all this can be expressed in three words, 'He did right.' The world loves and properly appreciates a right thinking man. Success obtained by any other than fair means is a bubble in the air.

"Old classmate of my mother, old friend of my father, I must bid thee farewell. Thou didst awake in the early gray dawn of the most wonderful century of all the ages; thou wert born on the northeastern coast of the most wonderful republic of all the nations, and at thy birth the restless, rolling waves of the Atlantic sang in their foaming spray thy lullaby. And as the bells in the steeples rang out the old century of thy birth, wherein thou hadst witnessed the most wonderful, marvellous discoveries and improvements, on the western coast of the wonderful republic, grown to be the greatest nation among all the nations, there thou didst fall to sleep, and at thy death the smooth, sinking waves of the Pacific sea, washing the most western shores of thy native land, sang thy requiem. And, as thou didst request it to be done, thy body is brought here to the cemetery of thy choice, in 'Sweet Green Mount,' there to be laid in the lap of mother earth. The light of thy star of life is not gone out, but only gone to shine as a brighter life in that world which has no ending. And as on earth thou didst see the worldly cities beside the shore-bound seas where the light of man shone on the streets, so now in Heaven,

'Thou dost see the Holy City,
Beside the tideless sea,
The light of God is on its streets,
The gates are open wide,
And all who will may enter,
And no one is denied.'

"May others like unto thee arise to teach the people and lead our people, glorify our republic and exalt our race, is my prayer at thy grave. For the love I bore him living, for the fragrant memory I cherish of him dead, I come to render this poor tribute of my affection and respect today: This, and more, he would have done for me."

The pall bearers at the funeral of Amos Thompson were Messrs. Hugh W. Harrison, Lee Harrison, Charles W. Harrison, John Heinzelman, William Heinzelman and L. D. Turner.

The Belleville (Ill.) *Weekly Advocate* adds a few facts which are not recorded in the above oration: "On the death of his parents, Amos Thompson found a home with a neighbor named Fowler. He then became an apprentice to John Stuntz, tanner and furrier, who sent him to school, and with whom he remained until he was twenty-one years old. He then learned the carpenter's trade with Mr. Fowler, and worked at it for about twenty years. In 1829 he assisted Mr. Fowler in building the Belleville Court House. In the early '30s he began purchasing real estate, and soon became the owner of large landed interests in St. Clair County, Ill., and in Missouri. After his marriage he was a farmer until 1852. In 1863 he sold his farm and retired from active labors, making his home with his children. He was one of nature's noblemen, gracious and generous to all, and possessed of a high and noble character. He was a Democrat at first, but became a Republican when that party came into power."

From the *Oregonian* of Portland, Ore.: "Probably no voter who cast his ballot for McKinley and Roosevelt in Oregon, Nov. 6, 1900, has a longer and more interesting record than Amos Thompson of Mt. Tabor, who will be 94 years old the 26th of next April. He went to the polls with his sons, Charles and Cyrus, of Belleville, Ill. Thus assisted, he was able to walk most

of the way. Amos Thompson first voted for Jackson
in 1828, and has thus cast nineteen ballots for presidents. He was well acquainted with Stephen A. Douglas and Lincoln."

From the St. Louis *Post-Dispatch* of April 15, 1901:
"Amos Thompson made it a point to distribute his
wealth as he went through this world. He did not
like death-bed bequests or *post mortem* settlements of
estates. Forty years ago he adopted this plan of giving his wealth as he accumulated it. It was a pleasure
to distribute it among his children and see them enjoy
the benefits of his labor and good management. In a
certain way he made them stockholders in all his enterprises. When he amassed any considerable amount
of money he would divide it among his sons and daughter, only reserving enough for his own needs. Before
leaving Belleville, Ill., for Oregon, in 1896, he made a
division of his wealth. It is said that each of his children received $10,000. Up to that time he had attended
to all of his affairs."

The following letter from Amos Thompson, while he
was in the Illinois Legislature, gives a good picture of
his earnest work:

"Springfield, Ills., Feb. 3, 1843.

"Friend Davis:

"Permit me to drop you a few lines. I am enjoying good health, and have done so ever since I have
been here, and hope that you and your family have
been enjoying the same blessing. We have been in
session now two months and we have done little, apparently, although it appears that the members have
been industrious and have lost but little time, and
these members are noted by those who have been acquainted with the Legislatures heretofore, for sobriety. You see no drinking going on here. Sixty-four
members have joined the Washingtonians and there
seems to be a great reformation here in regard to
drinking. At one meeting one hundred and twenty
men and women joined.

"We are trying to District the State. It is more of
a job than I expected. We have too many men who
want Districts to suit themselves. The bill is to the
third reading in the House. I cannot give you the situation of all the Districts. Our District commences at

the mouth of the Ohio, thence north up to Madison County, and the Third Principal Meridian is the East line. You have seen a description of it in the Belleville *Advocate*. But there are many alterations in the plan there proposed. The Democratic Party is very much divided respecting the Districting of the State. On other matters they have acted together as much as could have been expected.

"The last conversation which I had with you you wished me to try to do something in regard to the property that was exempt from execution. You concluded that it had a bad effect on the community. I was of your opinion, but the House of Representatives have gone and passed through their House the Bill exempting in addition to what is already exempt, one stove, two head of sheep, for each member of the family, and a spinning wheel, fuel,—for how long I cannot tell—and feed for a sheep, cow and calf, and several other articles. There is a wonderful spirit of relief here. I did what I could against the Bill, but it went through the House. It has not yet come up in the Senate. Whether they will concur with the house or not is uncertain. It is my opinion it will injure the honest part of the community, and we should not favor the rogues. An honest poor man wants the credit of all the property which he has in his possession. A bill has passed the Senate regulating the interest on money. The school money, according to this Bill, shall hereafter be loaned for 8 per cent lawful interest. In other cases it is to be 6 per cent. How it will go in the House I cannot tell, as it has not yet come up. If it can be defeated, the members from your County will all try to do it. Catlin in the Senate voted for the Bill. I consider that I have no more right to tell you what you shall loan your money for, than to tell you what you shall card your wool for, or the farmer, what he shall sell his wheat for. Demand and supply will always regulate the interest on money, and laws of that kind only tend to cause mankind to avoid the law in place of maintaining it. This afternoon we were at work on the Shawnee Bank and had some fine speeches. What will be the result is uncertain. Some of the members, I think, are a little squeamish. Time, as Burns the poet says, will determine. The Canal Bill has occupied some time and has not yet passed the House. Whether to vote for it or not I do not know. You have seen the plans from the Committee on Canals, I expect. I am afraid of it. I do not wish to sanction any measure that will involve the State in more debt, and the measure, from that Committee, I am fearful will result in nothing more. I am very tired of this place, but will be here till the last of the month.

"If you should see Samuel Stookey please to inform him if he wants his pro rata share of the bank notes that he sent up here by me that I expect the Bank will pay out the silver before I return and I can bring it to him. If he wishes he can write and I will bring either silver or paper.　　　　　Your friend,

　　　　　　　　　　"Amos Thompson.

"To William Davis, Belleville, Ills."

The following reminiscences of Amos Thompson were written by him in 1898, at his home in Mt. Tabor, Ore. A severe illness hindered him from completing them:

"Scenes in strong remembrance set,
　　Scenes never, never to return;
Scenes if in stupor I forget,
　　Again I feel, again they burn."

　　　　　　　　　　—*Burns*.

"Feeling that some recollections of my early days, and how the families of Abel Thompson and Caleb Barker moved to this western country from what then was called the District of Maine, will be helpful and fully believing that such information would be appreciated and valued by those who follow us on the never-ending stream of life, I jot down the following:

"In the spring of 1815 my father was well situated in Maine, with no debts against him, and in possession of a well-stocked farm and a water saw-mill, and apparently lacking nothing but a contented mind, but that is everything in life. He had been reading of the state of Ohio, and some of his neighbors had moved there, and to satisfy himself he made the trip there. He started early in the spring of 1815, having previously placed his farm and mill in the hands of his son-in-law, James Grover. He went with a horse and carriage, and in passing through the Allegheny Mountains, the Indians stole his horse, which he never re-covered from them, and from the place where the horse was stolen he made the balance of the distance to Ohio afoot. He returned from Ohio in the fall of 1815 well pleased with the country, and immediately set to work preparing to move.

"A few weeks after father left home, the saw-mill was burned up with considerable lumber adjoining the mill, which was a great loss to him. He never again re-built the mill, but rapidly went to work selling his stock and farm and preparing to move. Mother was very much opposed to leaving her friends and home in Maine, and often have I heard her expressions that she was going to her grave. But father was deter-mined, as he said, to bring his children into a country where they would not have to labor as hard as he had worked for a living. Could he have pushed the veil aside which hid the transactions of the next thirty months from him, with what horror would he have abandoned his contemplated trip. ('Blindness,' says the poet, 'to the future kindly given, that each may fill the circle marked by Heaven.') For in less than thirty months from the time that they left Maine, father and mother were both dead, and their children orphans among strangers.

"By the middle of October, 1816, he was ready to start on his journey to his future home. Caleb Bar-ker, a brother-in-law to father, and family agreed to go out with him. Barker's family consisted of him-self, wife and five children; namely, Sally, Amos, Sybil, Adeline and Nelson. Father's family consisted of five children, Mehetable, Amos, Eleanor, Haines and Abel,—all healthy children, and I never knew father to be sick until his death sickness in Illinois. James Grover, wife and one child agreed to come out West with father. All three families, Barker's, Grover's and father's, prepared themselves with good comfortable wagons and teams, suitable to make the trip in the winter to Olean Point, at the head of the Allegheny River, where they expected to take water and go down to Cincinnati. Father disliked so much the hogs in the state of Ohio, that he procured three beautiful white guinea pigs to take along with him;—two female and one male. In traveling through the state of New

York, the male pig was stolen and lost. The other two we carried with us to Illinois and they were sold at father's sale;—quite fine, large hogs. Mr. James Grover was living with my father when they were preparing to move, and his parents were very much opposed to leaving them. Father and mother wished their daughter, his wife, to accompany them to the new country. Grover had prepared himself with a good team and wagon suitable for the journey and the day was fixed for starting, and as Grover lived with father, the two wagons and teams started off at the same time together. Grover's team got the advantage of him and ran his wagon up against a log lying near the road, and it is said that one of the axletrees of his wagon was broken. At any rate, the accident so discouraged Grover that he gave up the journey, and bought him a farm nearby and settled on it and raised a large family. He and wife and several of his family are buried there, his wife living to be some eighty-eight years of age. After the accident to Grover, Barker and father proceeded alone on their journey. The first night after we left home, we stayed at Brunswick. From there the most direct road to Olean Point was taken, but winter overtook us long before we reached Olean, and when we arrived there we found many families waiting to go down the river when the spring would open. Father and Barker immediately proceeded to build a flat-boat sufficiently large to transport the two families to Cincinnati. Father being a ship carpenter was of great advantage in building the boat. By the time the river opened in the spring, their boat was ready and was the first boat to leave Olean for Pittsburg. On the boat from Olean to Pittsburg, father and Barker were the only men and we had quite a pleasant voyage to Pittsburg, though nothing of importance transpired during our voyage.

"We found Pittsburg, then the spring of 1817, quite a flourishing little city with foundries for the casting of large cannon, and factories for the cutting of nails,— the first that we had ever seen; also glass works and many other improvements, all of which were very interesting to me, a boy then of ten years of age, and father took great pains to let me see all the factories and novelties of the city. Our stay there was for but a few days as we wished to get to Cincinnati as soon as possible. The Ohio River, which was formed by the junction of the two rivers, Allegheny and Monongahela, was very high, and to my young eyes very beautiful, and many immigrants, like ourselves, were there to descend the river in search of homes in the South and West. I do not recall the exact date that we left the city, but our stay there was quite short. Our boat, containing but the two families, had not descended the river far, before we fell in company with a large flatboat filled with immigrants bound for Louisiana or Mississippi States. They kindly invited us to lash our boats up to theirs, which we did, and in that condition we floated the entire way to the city of Cincinnati. The joining of the boats was a great pleasure to me, and in fact to us all, for I could run about at all times on both boats, and as there were boys on the large boat about my size, the passage down to Cincinnati was very pleasant to us all, old and young. Often have I looked back and recalled the passage down the Ohio River in company with that boat with much pleasure. On our arrival at the city, we looked around the city, which then, in the spring of 1817, was quite large and flourishing to my youthful eyes, with the first steam grist mill that any of us had ever seen, built partly in the river so that boats could load and unload right from the water, the mill being four stories in height, and turning out the flour rapidly. My father was much interested and showed me all about the mill he could. After looking the city over for a few days, father went some eighteen or twenty miles up what was then called Mill Creek, and rented a small home and five acres of ground. He rented the place of a man by the name of Fagan. There were several Fagan brothers and all owning mill property on that stream, called then Mill Creek, all of them being much respected and called Quakers. After father had plowed up the five acres of land and planted it in corn, he left it for me to cultivate and started for the territory of Illinois, as he called it,—Illinois at that time not having become a state. He said he wished to find a country where he would not have to labor so hard to clear out the land.

"Whilst he was gone, he visited Belleville and for

some six weeks he worked for Jas. Tannehill of Belleville at wagon making, and while there he selected the place for his future home in Illinois. His object in the selection of a place was to find one where he could build a water saw-mill, as he was deeply impressed with the importance of having a good saw-mill, and several times before his death in the spring of 1818, pointed out the very spot where he intended to build the mill. His object was more for a mill than for farming purposes, I think, in his selection, although the land was rich and fairly clear and beautiful for cultivation.

"Soon after we arrived in Cincinnati, Uncle Barker and family crossed the river into the state of Kentucky and there he found employment until the return of father from Illinois. On the return of my father, which I think was the latter part of August, 1817, he disposed of the corn that was raised on the five acres of rented ground and then prepared to move to Illinois. At that time there was a man at Cincinnati by the name of Capt. Potter (I call him by that name as he went by no other). He lived in Maine on a farm adjoining that of my grandfather, Amos Thompson, and had left Maine some little time before we left. He and father and a man by the name of Capt. Sparks in company (whether Sparks helped in the purchase or not I do not know positively) bought a large keel boat, sufficiently large to carry six families, and as soon as they could get ready, all left for St. Louis,—Thompson with his family of seven, Barker's family of seven and Potter's family of six. (I think this man Potter was the father of our old neighbor Matthew Potter of High Prairie, for he and his wife died near where Matthew Potter lived.) There was also on the boat a family by the name of Poor, also from Maine, but of his family I knew but little. I think the family was small, probably not more than four or five. In the boat there were also some young men in addition to the families. There was a cousin of Potter's by the name of Reed Potter and another man by the name of Wolcott, and likely more, but the above I well recollect. It was about the middle of October, 1817, that we left Cincinnati for St. Louis. When a short distance from Cincinnati, we had an accident to our boat which caused a great fright among the people on the boat and

delayed us on our journey for about thirty hours. We
had been in the habit of running only in the day time
and tying up the boat at night. The weather was
clear and beautiful and the moon rose about eight
o'clock and they concluded that as soon as the moon
rose they would start out down the river, the boat
having been tied up on the Kentucky shore to wait
until the moon rose. As soon as it was up sufficiently
bright, they pulled out into the stream, or intended to,
but in drifting out we went sideways down stream, and
before we got far from shore the boat struck a snag
and stove a hole in the side and the water rushed in,
alarming the people dreadfully. The point where the
snag struck the boat was under the berth of Capt. Potter and he immediately seized a pillow and kept out as
much of the water as he could. Being near to the
shore the boat was run back and a plank was hastily
put out so that the people could get off, for all thought
the boat would surely sink, and you can imagine what
a scramble there was with all trying to get ashore.
One grown man by the name of Wolcott in walking out
on the plank, fainted and fell into the water and they
thought would have drowned had he not been helped
out of the river. One young man by the name of Poor,
got his little brother on his back, and had to use quite
strong and unbecoming language and not suitable for
a Sunday-school before he could reach the plank, but
both he and his brother got to the shore safely. The
people on the boat, excepting those who were to run the
boat during the night, had gone to bed, and hastily in
their night clothing, men, women and children, old and
young, assembled on the bank, making a laughable appearance. I had got into my bunk and was awakened by
feeling the boat strike the snag, which seemed to keel
the boat over, but I had no trouble in getting ashore.
Neither father nor mother left the boat, father going
into the part of the boat to assist Mr. Potter in keeping
out the water. Father had at that time a flat-boat
lashed to the keel of the large boat, in which he had
some food for his hogs, and by means of a large and
long rope attached to the top of the mast of the keel
boat, and fastened to the flat-boat, they rigged a purchase on that and keeled the boat over so far that the
hole in the boat was above water, and in that condition

we lay until morning, when father, who understood
such work, soon had all things in good condition with
but little damage done by the water that had run into
the boat. We then proceeded on our journey and with
a large sail made fair progress, though I hardly think
we ran much of nights after that, though I do not dis-
tinctly remember. One day as our boat was passing
along the Indiana shore, a man was seen making efforts to attract our attention. It was at a little town
called the Rising Sun, and when we slowed up he
asked us where we were going, and when we told him
to St. Louis he said that was where he wished to go,
and asked if we could take him and a small family
aboard as passengers. We answered in the affirmative
and immediately landed the boat. His name was William Fowler and he had with him his wife and one
young child and an apprentice by the name of John
Dunlap. They were from the northern part of the
state of New York and were on their way to St. Louis.
He had but little freight, a long chest of carpenter
tools and two or three boxes filled with small and good
chopping axes, which found a ready sale in Illinois,
and some household goods such as bedding and clothing. They were taken on board and occupied the part
of the bow of the boat where Barker and father were.
We then had six families. The next town of importance after that was Louisville, at the falls of the
Ohio River on the Kentucky side. At that time, the
fall of 1817, there had been no work done by the government on the falls to improve the river, and to us
the falls presented quite a formidable obstruction to
navigation on the river. About two miles above the
falls the boat was landed and a pilot proceeded to
pilot us over the falls. Privilege was given to all who
wished to leave the boat and walk around the falls,
some two miles, and many who were on the boat got off
and walked around the falls, and amongst them was
William Fowler, but his wife and John Dunlap went
over the falls in the boat. The families of father and
Barker stayed on the boat. The pilot that we had was
an old pilot and considered one of the best. His
charge for taking the boat over was two dollars. At
that time there were three chutes, as they called
them, namely, the Indian or Middle Chute, and one on

the Kentucky side and one on the Indiana side. Our
boat took the Indian Chute. The pilot stood on the
deck of the boat, and his object was to get as much
headway on the boat as possible and to that end had as
many men with oars rowing as there was room for
them to row. As the boat was approaching the falls
the noise of the falls was something appalling and
father ordered me to go below, fearing that I might
be knocked overboard. I stationed myself in the middle of the boat where two men were rowing and anx-
iously awaited the result. And in passing along down
so near did the boat run to a large rock that I could
easily have jumped from the boat to the rock. Yet we
came through all right and without any injury whatever. There was no perpendicular fall of water in the
chute that the boat took, yet in many places the water
fell as much as ten or twelve feet, and the falls at that
time made a loud, roaring noise, and the river at that
place appeared very wide. We proceeded from there
down the river to Cairo, at the mouth of the Ohio,
without any further trouble. Cairo at that time, the
fall of 1817, was a poor place, and what few buildings
there were appeared to be built on stilts, or wooden
posts some fifteen to twenty feet high, so as to keep
dry from the high water. There we met the Mississippi and experienced a great deal of trouble in ascend-
ing that river. When the wind was fair we could use
the sail and do quite well, but the crookedness of the
river and the uncertainty of the wind rendered the
sails of but very little service and we had to depend on
poling or cordeling the boat along, which was slow
and hard work. The cold weather coming on, our
boat was frozen up solid and fast opposite the town of
Kaskaskia, and there the boat lay until spring. My
father and Barker and many others left the boat and
went up where they intended to enter their land.
Deacon Samuel Smith and father were well acquainted
in Maine, and his two sons, Benjamin and James
Smith, must have been on our boat and have come up
with us, and I did not know it, for the two boys, acting for their father, and my father that winter entered
320 acres of land together. Father was to take the
prairie, 160 acres, and the Smith boys were to take the
timber, 160 acres, and then they were to divide the

land East and West and each would have one half of
the timber and one half of the prairie. During the
summer of 1818 the Smith boys got out the timber for
the house that they built for their father; and in the
summer of 1818 my father framed the house for them,
I working with him when he did the work. The Smith
boys went on and finished the house and the old Deacon Smith lived and died in that house. The old Deacon Smith with his family came to Illinois in the
spring of 1819. Timothy Higgins, the father of Robert
Higgins, came to Illinois in the fall of 1818, arriving
shortly after the death of father and mother. There
was another Smith by the name of John Smith,
brother of Samuel Smith, who came with his brother
Samuel in the spring of 1819. This John Smith was
the father of Nathaniel, Benjamin and Valentine
Smith. There were also several other children in the
family. He settled west of where the father of Robert
Higgins settled, but died not many years after coming
to the state, and left a widow, who survived him many
years. Robert Higgins' mother was Samuel Smith's
sister. There were other families who came from
Maine, the Temples,—Richard and John. They also
settled in that section of the country, and it was known
as the Yankee settlement. They were honest, hard-
working men, and men well calculated to improve the
country. All of the old set have died and but few left
of the second generation.

"While our boat was frozen up opposite Kaskaskia,
the men portion of the boat left and came up and built
houses suitable to live in during the summer, and until
better ones could be built. Wm. Fowler and John Dunlap also came, and Fowler entered land adjoining
father's on the North, and his summer house and
father's were not over two hundred yards apart.
Father and Barker worked from the time they left the
boat at Kaskaskia until the boat was ready to move up
to St. Louis, father having employed Barker to work
for him to improve his place. As near as I can recollect the boat with all on board arrived in St. Louis
about the 12th of March, 1818. We stayed in St.
Louis but a few days, and Daniel Moore, a brother of
Smith Moore, moved us from St. Louis to our home on
Richland Creek. The exact time that we arrived there

was between the 15th and 18th of March, 1818. Father, with the help of Barker, immediately went to work making rails and fencing land to put in corn, and father planted that spring about fourteen acres of corn, some eight or ten acres of which yielded at least forty bushels per acre, good sound corn. The year of 1818 was a rather wet year, and father worked very hard in hopes of having a comfortable house for the winter. He repaired the old water-mill owned by James Davidson on the Prairie Du Long Creek, an unhealthy locality for a person not acclimated to the country, and after it was repaired, sawed lumber for his house. He had his house framed and ready to raise, and well dug, before he and mother took sick. As near as I can recollect, father and mother were taken sick about the last week of August in 1818, both being taken down at the same time. Aunt Esther, Uncle Barker's wife, was taken sick at about tne same time, they living some two miles from where father lived. My mother died on the 15th day of September, 1818, and father died on the 17th day of the same month, and Aunt Barker died on the 27th of September. All three were buried within twenty-five yards of where father and mother died. I was the only person in the house excepting father when mother died, and was sitting on the foot of the bed when she breathed her last. She had been unconscious and knew but little for several days before her death. The balance of the children had gone to Mr. Fowler's for their breakfast. Father at that time was so sick that we did not know that he could speak, yet when Mr. Fowler, who accompanied the children home from his house, reached father and shook him and exclaimed to him, "Mr. Thompson, your wife is dead," father raised up and exclaimed, "My poor children, Mr. Fowler, make her a decent coffin," and but very few words he ever spoke to any one after that. He lived only two days longer. The family of five children, the oldest thirteen and the youngest four, surely felt lonesome. There were neighbors and good ones. Mehetable could readily have found a home if she would not take the young child with her, but she would not give him up and consequently she could not get a home. She stayed a few months with Thos. Talbot, but they refused to keep her and the

child both. One of our nearest neighbors, Abner Carr,
who married a sister of Samuel Phillips, agreed to
keep the child through the winter, if Mehetable would
go and live with Mrs. Henry Stout, who was a sister
of Mrs. Carr and had no children. So Mehetable found
a good home and remained there until she was married. Mrs. Stout proved a true mother and Mehetable
found a good home. Nellie (Eleanor) immediately
found a good home with Mrs. George Wilderman and
lived there until she married. Haines found a good
home with Capt. John Stuntz and was bound to him to
learn the tanning business. He lived with him until
he was twenty-one years old. As for myself, I went to
our nearest neighbor's, Wm. Fowler, and asked if I
could stay at his house. He and John Dunlap were
hewing and scoring logs to build a house to live in.
They, up to that time, like my father, had only lived
in a summer house. Says Fowler to me in answer to
my question, "What can you do to pay for keeping
you? Can you score and hew?" I told him that I had
never tried to hew any, but I could use an axe quite
well for a boy. He handed me an axe and told me to
get on a log and let him see what I could do. He was
so well pleased with my work that he let me stay and I
lived about one year with Fowler. I had been with
Fowler only about one month when I was taken very
sick, and was sick most of the winter of 1818. In the
spring of 1819 Mr. Fowler contracted to build a large
house for Samuel Mitchell on Silver Creek, where
Mitchell at that time had a saw-mill. I had regained
my health and Fowler had me to act as cook for his
men while working at the mill. I had from three to
seven or eight hands to cook for, but usually about
three, and got along quite well, but was so much in the
water that at about the time the mill house was finished we all took sick with the fever and ague. In fact
every one of us was down with the ague,—Fowler,
Dunlap, Mrs. Fowler and their only child and myself.
That was about the first of September, 1819. A Mrs.
Hill, mother of David Hill, living not far away, came
to Fowler and persuaded him to let me go and stay at
her house as she said she could soon cure me. I think
it was Sunday that I went with her to her house and
stayed with her for one week, having the chills every

day. She did all that she could for me and the next
Sunday after I got there she had her son, Jonathan
Hill, take me behind him on his horse and carry me to
Capt. John Stuntz's, where brother Haines had been
since father's death. I arrived at Stuntz's about the
15th or 20th of September, 1819, and lived with them
until the 26th of April, 1828, when my apprenticeship
with him expired, I having been bound as was my
brother to learn the tanning trade. At the home of
Mr. Stuntz and his noble wife I must truthfully say the
kindest treatment and best examples were set before
my brother and myself, and sorry was I when the 28th
of April, 1828, arrived when I bade the family adieu.
Abel, if my memory serves me rightly, was taken from
Mr. Carr's and Samuel Smith kept him until Mr. Henry
Null took him the spring or fall of 1820, and he and
his wife treated him as a father and mother would
have done."

(6) Amos Thompson m., May, 1831, Irene Moore Charles,
b. North Carolina, Sept. 14, 1809; d. Jan. 15, 1852. She
was a woman of superior qualities; daughter of Levin
Charles, b. near Cambridge, Md., Feb. 6, 1771; d. Belleville, Ill.; resided for some time at Guilford, N. C.;
moved to Belleville, Ill., soon after his marriage; m.,
about 1801, Eleanor Wright, b. Guilford County, N. C.,
Dec. 13, 1779; d. Aug. 17, 1863. Levin Charles was the
son of Elijah Charles, b. Dec. 17, 1751; d. in Illinois in
1831; m., 1777, Isabella Moore, who lived to be about
ninety years old; she was the daughter of Jonathan
Moore, of a very strong old family, b. in Georgia, Nov.
20, 1799; d. April 19, 1880. Soon after his marriage
Elijah Charles moved to North Carolina and enlisted
in the Revolutionary Army; he rendered important
service as a guide to General Greene's army and was
one of the sturdiest patriots of his day; he moved to
Illinois about 1818; his family was a large and influential one.

(7) Alonzo Thompson, b. Belleville, Ill., Feb. 22, 1832;
office No. 831 Majestic building, Denver, Col.; he
has lived at Maynel, Mo., and St. Louis; he was
Illinois state auditor from Jan. 1, 1865, to Jan.
1, 1869; he is now a dealer in lands; in his early
years he held several offices of honor and trust in
Missouri; he was elected on the Republican ticket,

along with Thomas O. Fletcher, governor, to fill the office of state auditor during the Civil War, 1864, and held the office for four years; he took an active part in the Civil War, helping raise a regiment in northwest Missouri, and served as a scout in various parts of the state; he also represented Nodaway County in the state Legislature for a term of two years; he finished his education in McKendric College, Illinois, graduating in 1853; he was one of the founders of the Platonian Society in that college; m. (first), near Maynell, Mo., Dec. 6, 1857, by Elder B. F. Baxter of the Methodist Episcopal Church, South, Mary Vinsonhaler, b. Maynell, Mo., Sept. 21, 1836; d. March 1, 1877; daughter of Jacob Vinsonhaler and Mary McDonald; m. (second), at Stillman Valley, Ill., April 12, 1880, Mary F. Adams, b. Racine, Wis., Feb. 26, 1847; d. April 13, 1831; no children; m. (third), Oct. 30, 1881, Mrs. Annie Elizabeth (Heard) Jones, b. in Mississippi, Jan. 13, 1851; studied in Crawford Female Institute and Chester Female Institute; daughter of Christopher Columbus Heard and granddaughter of Samuel Smith Heard.

Children of first wife:

(8) Hattie Irene Thompson, b. Nov. 5, 1858; resides at Nevada, Vernon County, Mo.; m., Oct. 27, 1881, at Maynell, Mo., Edward P. Lindley, b. Monticello, Mo., April 25, 1851; he is a very successful lawyer; he studied in several schools and colleges, and graduated at the St. Louis Law School in 1877; he has resided in Washington D. C., Davenport, Ia., Chicago, Ill., St. Louis, etc. His wife was a fine student in several schools, the last one being Brooker Hall, Media, Pa.

(9) Mabel Lindley, b. Aug. 15, 1882; she studied in St. Louis College.

(9) James Johnson Lindley, b. June 18, 1885; studied three years in the Military Academy, Culver, Ind.; in 1906 is in the State University, Columbia, Mo.; is second lieutenant in the Second Regiment Infantry, Missouri National Guard.

(9) Eleanor Lindley, b. Feb. 25, 1888.

(9) Mary Catherine Lindley, b. Aug. 30, 1896.

(8) Fannie Thompson, b. Aug. 31, 1860; d. Dec. 10, 1860.

(8) Elmer Ellsworth Thompson, b. Dec. 6, 1861; d. Aug. 10, 1887; real estate dealer; studied at Phillips Academy, Andover, Mass., and in Yale College; lived in St. Louis, Mo.; m., June 4, 1887, Adele Picot of St. Louis, who is married a second time and resides in Missouri; no children.

Child of third wife:

(8) Alonzo Heard Thompson, b. Jan. 6, 1883; graduated Northwestern Military Academy, Illinois; unm.; resides in Denver, Col.

(7) Mary Eleanor Thompson, b. Belleville, Ill., Oct. 17, 1835; studied in Monticello Seminary, near Alton, Ill., and in Jacksonville (Ill.) Female College; resides in Colorado Springs, Col.; m., Jan. 13, 1856, Theophilus Harrison, b. Belleville, Ill., Sept. 14, 1841; attended McKendric College, Lebanon, Ill., in 1850 and 1853; son of James Harvey Harrison and Lucinda Gooding; the father was b. Feb. 25, 1805, and moved to Illinois in 1807. The grandfather of Theophilus Harrison was Thomas Harrison of Virginia, who was b. Dec. 13, 1779, and was a faithful local minister in the Methodist Episcopal Church. Thomas Harrison had five sons, one of whom died in youth; the other four sons were flour millers in Illinois, and were the first to introduce steam flour mills into Illinois; they built four steam flour mills at Belleville, Ill., and had fine success in business. Mr. Theophilus Harrison is a large manufacturer of agricultural machinery at Belleville, Ill.; these Harrison machine works were established in 1848 and incorporated in 1878.

(8) Lucinda Irene Harrison, b. Belleville, Ill., May 11, 1857; d. May 1, 1861.

(8) Eugene Amos Harrison, b. Nov. 18, 1859; d. Jan. 4, 1861.

(8) Mary Josephine Harrison, b. Dec. 9, 1862; resides at Colorado Springs, Col.; attended Monticello Seminary, Illinois; m., Oct. 17, 1882, at Belleville, Ill., Frank Halliday, b. Oct. 17, 1862; son of Frank Halliday and Ellen Moody of Cincinnati, O.

(8) Annie May Harrison, b. Belleville, Ill., July 12, 1868; resides 1839 Gramercy Place, Los Angeles, Cal.; attended Mary Institute, St. Louis, Mo., and Southern Home School, Baltimore, Md.; graduated from

Miss Brown's School, New York City, 1892; m., at Colorado Springs, Col., June 29, 1892, Frederick Warren Johnson, b. Red Wing, Minn., Jan. 29, 1868; graduated from Harvard College in 1892; real estate dealer; son of Joseph Warren Johnson and Melinda Elizabeth Harrison; has lived in Minneapolis, Minn., and in Iowa City, Ia.

(9) Sydney Warren Johnson, b. June 12, 1893.

(9) Eleanor Irene Johnson, b. May 14, 1897.

(7) Josephine Bonaparte Thompson, b. Belleville, Ill., Aug. 22, 1838; d. April 6, 1882; she resided at Greencastle, Ind.; buried in Green Mount Cemetery, Belleville, Ill.; m., Feb. 14, 1860, John Douglas Truett, b. near Chillicothe, O., Oct. 12, 1835; d. at Atlanta, Ga., Dec. 7, 1897; son of Samuel Truett and Mary Ann Montgomery; he was a dealer in agricultural implements.

(8) Nellie Olive Truett, b. Foot City, Mo., Jan. 3, 1862; resides 1449 Alabama Street, Indianapolis, Ind.; m., Dec. 10, 1884, Andrew Lincoln Lockridge, b. near Greencastle, Ind., March 5, 1862; he is president of the Putnam Creamery Company, Indianapolis, Ind.; son of Robert Z. Lockridge and Melissa Collins.

(9) Robert Truett Lockridge, b. July 19, 1893.

(8) Jennie Douglas Truett, b. Sept. 16, 1866; d. Indianapolis, Ind., April 24, 1887.

(7) Cyrus Thompson, b. on the old Belleville, Ill., homestead, seven miles southeast of the city, Aug. 15, 1845; treasurer of the Harrison Machine Works, Belleville, Ill.; studied in Belleville (Ill.) High School, 1863-'64; Hudson River Institute, 1863-'64; was a clerk and accountant; in 1864-'65 employed by the Harrison Machine Company; from 1865-'75, accounting and warrant clerk in the state auditor's office, Jefferson County, Mo.; in June, 1875, he returned to Belleville, where he purchased a quarter interest in the Harrison Machine Works, and has been treasurer and one of the directors since then; he is a member of no church, but liberal in his views and attends the Baptist Church, of which his wife is a member; he is a sturdy Republican; he and his family spent a year in foreign travel, 1895-'96; m. (first), June 17, 1869, Anna Sophronia Dolph,

b. Corning, N. J., June 13, 1848; d. in Jefferson County, Ill., March 28, 1872 (24y., 2m., 18d.); she and her infant son are buried in Green Mount Cemetery, Belleville, Ill; daughter of John Dolph, b. about 1820; d. March 4, 1856, and of Frances Ann Patrick, b. Wilkesbarre, Pa., April 7, 1821; d. Jan. 7, 1899; the parents d. at Binghampton, N. J., and are buried in the Spring Forest Cemetery at that place; m. (second), Oct. 23, 1874, Louisa Cornelia Boone, b. Fayette, Mo., April 26, 1849; daughter of William C. Boone, who was a nephew of the celebrated pioneer, Daniel Boone.

(8) William Amos Thompson, b. March 6, 1875; resides Belleville, Ill.; secretary of the Harrison Machine Works; attended Colorado College, 1891-'93; m., Jan. 24, 1894, Ondenletta Heinzleman of Belleville, Ill., b. Jan. 25, 1875; studied in Boston (Mass.) Conservatory of Music, 1895-'96; daughter of John Heinzelman and Emoline Middlecoff.

(9) John Cyrus Thompson, b. Jan. 20, 1902.

(9) Ruth Thompson, b. Nov. 9, 1905.

(8) Twin brother; d. at birth.

(8) Theophilus Charles Thompson, b. Oct. 18, 1876; d. Feb. 15, 1903; employed at the Harrison Machine Works, Belleville, Ill.; his boat capsized while he was hunting in the Okaw River, near Posey, Ill.; he died soon after swimming to the land from the cold and his struggles in the swift current; he was one of the most popular young men in Belleville, Ill.; he was a graduate of Colorado College; he was an athlete of local prominence and had a fine reputation as a hunter and fisnerman; attended Phillips Andover (Mass.) Academy, 1896-'98.

(8) Lucy Alice Thompson, b. Feb. 15, 1883; studied in Christian College, Boone County, Mo.

(7) Eugene Thompson, b. Oct. 2, 1848; d. July 30, 1851 (2y., 9mo., 28d.).

(7) Charles Haynes Thompson, b. near Belleville, Ill., Nov. 27, 1850; address, 128 Third Street, Portland, Ore.; real estate, loan, investment and ticket broker, Portland and Spokane; his mother died when he was two years old, and he was kindly cared for by his maternal grandmother, Eleanor Wright Charles; he

attended the district schools and worked on the farm until 1863, when he moved to Belleville, Ill., with his father, where they made their home with his sister, Mrs. Theophilus Harrison; here he attended the public schools; in 1870–'71, he completed his education at Oxford, O.; in the fall of 1871 he went to Lawrence, Kan., where he accepted a position in a large clothing house, where he became very proficient in that line of business; in 1875 he removed to Atchison, Kan., and engaged in merchandising there; in 1894 he went to Fullerton, Neb., and engaged in the real estate business and stock raising; in 1889 he went to Portland, Ore., in business under the name of Thompson & Hathaway, money brokers; he has also been identified with several mining companies and other varied interests, and is looked upon as one of the substantial and reliable business men of Oregon; in 1892 he spent a year in travel, making a tour of the world; through industry and frugality he has accumulated a fine property; he is a sturdy Republican; though not a member of any church, he is always ready to give money for charitable and religious purposes; m., at Atchison, Kan., in 1878, Anna B. Holbert, b. in Atchison, March 17, 1856; graduated from the Atchison High School in 1877; daughter of Charles Holbert and Ann Eleanor; no children.

(6) Eleanor Thompson, b. Oct. 30, 1809; d. July 12, 1854; m., at Nashville, Washington County, Ill., John Alexander, who was b. near Harrisburg, Pa., Feb. 16, 1809; farmer; lived in Nashville, Ill., ten years after his marriage, then in Belleville, Ill., five years, then went to Leeburg, St. Clair County, Ill., where his wife died.

(7) Caroline Alexander, b. March 3, 1830; d. Nov. 22, 1853; m., June 20, 1852, W. R. Podfield, b. Union Grove and lived there after his marriage; no children.

(7) Julie Alexander, b. June 15, 1832; d. Nov. 14, 1845.

(7) Margaret Alexander, b. Aug. 15, 1837; d. Nov. 21, 1884.

(7) Hannah Alexander, b. July 24, 1840; resides Marshall, Saline County, Ill.; m. at Lamar, Mo., Dec. 12, 1872, Cyrus Alexander, b. Lebanon, Ill., July 3, 1837;

farmer; son of Aesophus Alexander and Harriet, who lived on a farm near Philo, Ill., at the time of their death in 1853; no children.

(7) Harris Alexander, b. March 24, 1842; d. near Lamar, Ill., Nov. 12, 1876; farmer; m., Sept. 10, 1871, Martha Corning, b. in Memphis, Tenn., Oct., 1835; she now resides in Fulton, Miss.; no children.

(6) David Haynes Thompson, b. March 27, 1811; d. in Belleville., Ill., Sept. 5, 1834; unm.; called Haynes in the records.

(6) Abel Thompson, b. Bowdoin, Me., April 20, 1814; d. near Belleville, Ill., Sept. 15, 1882; lived in St. Clair County, Ill., all his life; farmer and carpenter; he moved to Illinois in 1818 and his parents died soon after that; he was kindly taken care of and raised up by the good Germans, Henry and Sally Null; he settled twenty miles southeast of St. Louis, in what is now St. Clair County, Ill.; he lived there and in the adjoining town of Monroe, all his life; m., 1839, Delilah Alexandria America Charles, b. Oct. 6, 1820; d. Sept. 14, 1860; b. Alexandria, Ill., near where Cairo now is, and is said to have been the first white child born there, hence the name given her; daughter of Levin Charles and Eleanor Wright.

(7) Alpheus Thompson, b. Dec. 18, 1841; d. at five years of age.

(7) Augustine Thompson, b. Jan. 15, 1845; d. Nov., 1888 (43y.); farmer; lived for some years near Centralia, Ill.; m. (first), Penicy Preston, who d. in 1880; m. (second), and the wife d. in a short time; m. (third), Emma Cunningham of Centralia, Ill., Aug., 1883; she died the following spring:

Children of first wife:

(8) Eva Laura Thompson, b. Nov. 16, 1872; resides in Buxton, Chester County, Ill.; educated in Carlyle schools; lived in Centralia a few years and then in Carlisle; since marriage has lived in Buxton; m., Aug. 25, 1892, William Andrew Sharp, b. Buxton, Ill., June 23, 1866; educated in Carlyle schools; farmer and carpenter; son of Jonathan Sharp and Mary McNeill.

(9) Jonathan Sharp, b. March 21, 1893.

(9) Euterpe Sharp, b. May 23, 1897.

(9) William Ray Sharp, b. Oct. 8, 1902.

(8) Charles Wesley Thompson, b. Jan. 14, 1876; lives five miles south of Salem, Ill.; farmer; educated in the schools of Centralia, Ill.; m., April 10, 1904, Bertha Kell, b. June 15, 1883; daughter of Alexander Porter Kell and Sarah A. Gory.

 (9) Ralph Porter Thompson, b. March 8, 1895.

(7) Melissa Thompson, b. St. Clair County, Ill., April 8, 1845; m., May 1, 1873, Albert E. Wildman, b. on the old homestead where he now lives, five miles southeast of Belleville, Ill.; farmer; son of George Wildman and Nancy Hill.

(8) Luella Caroline Wildman, b. July 1, 1874.

(8) Rosetta A. Wildman, b. Feb. 6, 1876; m., June 18, 1896, Dr. Daniel Le Grand of St. Louis, Mo.

(8) Calvin Abel Wildman, b. Jan. 9, 1878.

(8) Carrie Isabel Wildman, b. July 24, 1880.

(8) Leroy Alfred Wildman, b. Dec. 27, 1882.

(7) Charles Thompson, b. Sept. 4, 1847; d. 1874; unm. He was traveling through Arkansas and was killed by the accidental shot of a revolver at Valley Rock.

(7) Albert Thompson, b. July 5, 1848; d. July 22, 1848 (17d.).

(7) Caroline Thompson, b. St. Clair County, Ill., Dec. 19, 1849; resides at Benton, Ill.; m., Sept. 5, 1871, John Henry Hill, b. Monroe County, Ill., April 27, 1849; farmer; lived in Monroe County, Ill.; moved to Franklin County, near Benton, 1876; son of Henry Bruce and Sarah Ann Sackett.

(8) Cyrus Elmer Hill, b. July 17, 1874; d. Sept. 17, 1905 (31y., 2m.); mail carrier on the Benton, Ill., route nearly four years; m., April 8, 1894, Effie Elenora Doty, b. Franklin County, Ill., March 26, 1876; daughter of John F. Doty and Emily E. McKennie.

 (9) Raymond Floyd Hill, b. March 11, 1895.

 (9) Clifton Hill, b. April 5, 1897.

 (9) Thomas Gordon Hill, b. March 27, 1899.

 (9) Cyrus Elmer Hill, b. Nov. 9, 1905.

(8) Roland Alva Hill, b. Feb. 17, 1877; d. April 12, 1877.

(8) Henry Monroe Hill, b. May 24, 1878; teacher; graduated from a dental school, St. Louis, Mo., May, 1906.

(8) Florence Melissa Hill, b. Jan. 2, 1881; m., Jan. 23,
    1901, James Andrew Hamilton, b. Ewing, Ill.,
    Sept. 14, 1869; farmer and stock raiser; son of
    David S. Hamilton and Susan E. Kidwell.

  (9) Mary Aleen Hamilton, b. Dec. 30, 1901.

(7) Edgar Thompson, b. March 22, 1852; resides at Belle-
    rive, Jefferson County, Ill.; farmer; m., April 14,
    1875, Emma Phillips, b. Aug. 27, 1857; attended
    district schools; daughter of William B. Phillips
    and Rebecca Bevis.

  (8) Fred Thompson, b. Dec. 18, 1876; resides at Belle
    rive, Ill.; farmer and school teacher; attended
    district schools and State Normal School; m.,
    Feb. 18, 1903, Cora L. Smith, b. Jefferson County,
    Ill., Aug. 17, 1880.

  (8) Flora Thompson, b. Sept. 4, 1878; resides at Poplar
    Bluffs, Ill.; m., May 22, 1896, in Jefferson County,
    Ill., James Thomas Byran.

  (8) Stella Thompson, b. July 26, 1881; resides Greene
    County, Ill.; m., Nov. 17, 1899, Charles McKenzie,
    farmer and carpenter.

  (8) Maud Thompson, b. June 25, 1891.

  (8) Son and daughter; d. in infancy.

(7) Dr. Jerome Thompson, b. Feb. 15, 1856, in St. Clair
    County, Ill.; resides Morrisonville, Ill.; has lived
    in Evansville, Ill., Cerro Gordo, Ill., etc.; graduated
    at Miami Medical College, March 7, 1878; m., April
    21, 1880, Sarah G. Booth, b. Newton County, Mo..
    Aug. 13, 1855; daughter of David Booth and Cynthia.

  (8) Anita Mabel Thompson, b. March 7, 1881; graduated
    at Morrisonville (Ill.) High School, 1901.

(7) Dr. William Thompson, b. Feb. 23, 1858; 396 Ridge
    Building, Kansas City, Mo.; resides 623 Walnut
    Street; graduated from Missouri Medical College,
    1881; m., Oct. 1, 1885, Luella Hathorne, b. New
    castle, Pa., May 27, 1856; daughter of Alexander S.
    Hathorne and Salina Boise.

  (8) Fae Thompson, b. Oct. 23, 1887.

  (8) Carylin Thompson, b. June 25, 1893; d. Sept. 24,
    1897.

(7) Albert Thompson, b. St. Clair County, Ill., Oct. 9,
    1860, fifteen miles south of Belleville, Ill.; resides
    at Fullerton, Neb.; attorney-at-law; lived on the
    farm until sixteen years of age, then lived for four

years near Benton, Ill., with his sister, Caroline;
in 1886 he moved to Fullerton, Neb.; taught school
a number of years; attended Ewing College, 1878-
'79; in 1880 went back to St. Clair County, Ill., and
taught three years in Freeburg public schools; law
course in St. Louis Law School; graduated with
LL. B. in the spring of 1885; in the spring of 1888
went West, and has been there ever since; from
1888 to 1893 was in partnership with Hon. George
D. Miklejohn, who was assistant secretary of war up
to Jan. 1, 1891; since 1893 has been in practice
alone; the summer of 1900 was spent with his wife
in Vermont, camping at Thompson's Point, Lake
Champlain, etc.; m., in the Beream Baptist Church,
Burlington, Vt., June 6, 1893, Kate Mary Taggart, b.
East Charlotte, Vt., April 1, 1871; daughter of Benjamin D. Taggart and Emma D. Narramore.

(7) Dr. Eugene Thompson, b. St. Clair County, Ill., Nov.
16, 1864; resides 203 Collinsville Avenue, East St.
Louis, Mo.; graduated from Miami Medical College
March 4, 1890; m., June 14, 1894, Althea L. Gooding,
b. Clinton County, Ill., Feb. 19, 1867; daughter of
Abraham Gooding and Malinda; no children.

*   *   *   *   *

(5) The second child of Amos Thompson and Hannah Wooster, Annah Thompson, b. March 14, 1777; d. Bowdoin, Me.,
Jan. 20, 1860 (82y., 10m.); the "h" is omitted at the end
of her name in most of the old records, but is carefully
added by most of her descendants; m., March 2, 1798,
David Haynes, b. Sudbury, Mass., Dec. 25, 1777; d. Bowdoin, Me., Feb. 15, 1862; he was a brother of Mary
Haynes, who m. Abel Thompson[5]; he came to Bath, Me.,
when he was three or four years old; went to Bowdoin,
Me., when a young man, and remained in that town until his death. He and his wife are buried in the Bowdoinham Village Cemetery.

(6) Sally Haynes, b. Aug. 21, 1798; d. March 5, 1826; m.
Stephen Curtis.

(6) Content Haynes, b. Aug. 8, 1800; d. Nov. 18, 1875; m.
(first), Elisha Doyle; m. (second), Joseph Green; six
children of first marriage.

(6) Capt. Stephen Stockbridge Haynes, b. Sept. 10, 1802; d.
June 11, 1878; m. Mehitable Mosely; a large and fine
number of descendants.

(6) Sophronia Haynes, b. Sept. 7, 1804; d. Jan. 1, 1884.

(6) Saviah Haynes, b. April 22, 1806; d. April 11, 1895; m. Joseph Trufant.

(6) Dwinal Haynes, b. Dec. 2, 1808; d. Sept. 11, 1884; m. Alma Small; six children.

(6) Ayres Haynes, b. Aug. 14, 1811; d. Dec. 16, 1887; m. Matilda Williams; nine children.

(6) James Haynes, b. Feb. 9, 1815; d. Nov. 8, 1902; a noble man; long in the hardware business at Richmond, Me.; m. (first), Nov. 4, 1845, Julia A. Curtis, b. Feb. 1, 1821; d. June 4, 1853; one child; m. (second), Sept. 29, 1853, Elizabeth Lewis Brooks, who d. Aug. 19, 1880; four children; m. (third), Nov. 15, 1882, Melinda Jane Brooks, b. Oct. 23, 1835; d. April 17, 1892.

(6) Francis M. Haynes, b. Feb., 1827, d. at New Orleans, La., Jan. 5, 1860.

*   *   *   *   *

(5) The third child of Amos Thompson and Hannah Wooster, Eunice Thompson, b. Bowdoin, Me., Jan. 10, 1780 (one gives the date 1778); d. March 26, 1842 (60y.); m., 1797, Abizer Purington, b. Sept. 10, 1779; d. June 8, 1858 (78y.); son of Rev. Humphrey Purington[6] and Thankful Snow[5]; Humphrey Purington[6] and Thankful Woodbury; Humphrey Purington[4] and Thankful Harding; Hezekiah Purington[3] and Mary ———; Lieut. James Purington[2] and Mary Scammon; of Ancestor George Purington[1].

One of the descendants has well said: "Grandmother Eunice (Thompson) Purington was very faithful to her thirteen children. She required them to keep the Sabbath according to the Puritan rules, allowing no play and only necessary work to be done. All were expected to attend church services, which were then held in houses and barns. Some must, however, stay at home each Sabbath and take care of the cattle and keep away the wild beasts, which were then so abundant. When two of the sons, Abel and Elisha, were about ten and twelve years of age, they persuaded their father to let them stay at home with their mother, to do the chores on the Sabbath; but it proved that they had most in mind the small brook near what was known as the boiling spring. There they soon cautiously went to play, making water wheels, etc. To correct this matter, the mother told them that if they persisted in such sport the old Scratcher would come after them; but they continued to transgress. One Sabbath morning, while they were busily playing by the brook, the mother dressed herself us as she imagined the Devil or Old Scratcher, as ne was commonly called, looked. She went around through the woods and came up to a fence near the boys and began to lustily scratch upon it. The lads were greatly frightened and ran to the barn as fast as they could. The mother took another path to the house, and got there before the boys, and had the Old Scratcher's clothes tucked away out of sight before the boys came to the log house. They were so frightened and ashamed of their wickedness that they never mentioned the circumstance to any member of the family. It was long afterwards that they knew that the creature that they saw at the fence was their mother. It is needless to say that for a time the two boys sturdily kept the Sabbath.

"A year before his marriage to Eunice Thompson, Abizer Purington went into the wilderness, three miles beyond the other settlers in Bowdoin, Me., keeping his way by spotted trees, and clearing up land and building the log house of one room to which he brought his happy bride. He was a shoemaker and a man of good education. He was industrious to the last, and faithful in all his duties. For many years he was a sturdy, faithful deacon in the Free Baptist Church, of which he and his wife were members. His home was truly one lighted by purest faith and Christian love."

(6) Abner Purington, b. Nov. 20, 1798; d. at sea when a young man.

(6) Esther Purington, b. July 25, 1800; d. May 8, 1884; m. Frederick Buker, and had nine children and thirteen grandchildren.

(6) Fanny D. Purington, b. April 14, 1802; d. Nov. 2, 1884; m. Zaccheus Buker.

(6) Humphrey Purington, b. Feb. 26, 1804; farmer and justice of the peace; m. Harriet Brown; eight children. Rev. Harry M. Purington of the Baptist Church, Mt. Vernon, Me., is a grandson.

(6) Abel Purington, b. March 21, 1806; d. Jan. 22, 1891; m. Mary Raymond; seven children. Rev. Cyrus Purington of the Methodist Episcopal Church, Mt. Vernon, Me., is a grandson.

(6) Abizer Purington, b. March 20, 1808; d. July, 1827.

(6) Betsy Purington, b. Dec. 4, 1809; d. Feb. 28, 1890; m. Timothy Buker. The daughter, Emma Jane, m. Nelson Grover.

(6) Rev. Elisha Purington, b. Nov. 1, 1811; d. Dec. 15, 1880; a very successful Free Baptist minister; m. Deborah E. Brown; six children.

(6) Amos Purington, b. Aug. 17, 1813; d. 1897; m. Margaret Jane Patterson; eight children; one of these, Hon. Horace Purington, is mayor of Waterville, Me; a grandson, Herbert E., is professor at Lewiston, Me.

(6) Cornelius Purington, b. Oct. 17, 1815; m. Hannah Tukey; four children.

(6) Daniel T. Purington, b. Dec. 8, 1817; d. Feb. 12, 1889; m. Pauline S. Mariner; three children.

(6) Eunice Purington, b. Feb. 12, 1820; d. 1895; m. Henry Ridley.

(6) Josiah Purington, b. Oct. 19, 1822; d. Jan. 29, 1890; m. Abbie Ridley; one son. (Full records in "Purington Genealogy," by Rev. Charles N. Sinnett.)

*   *   *   *   *

(5) Tne fourth child of Amos Thompson and Hannah Wooster, Phineas Thompson, b. Bowdoin, Me., Sept. 17, 1782; d. Nov. 22, 1860 (80y.); buried with his wife, near the Gowell farm, Bowdoin, Me.; he spent most of his life in Bowdoin; after his marriage he lived in Lisbon, Me., for awhile, this being the home town of his wife; in 1885 he went to live at Brunswick, Me., with his son, John; he was a faithful farmer and highly respected man; he was a Universalist.

Amos Thompson of Belleville, Ill., writes: "I visited Phineas Thompson in 1829, and found him a stout, hardy man, in the prime of life. I used to go out to the woods with him, across the intervale to his timber, to get firewood. He said that he should soon have to build a new house. He was then living with my grandfather in the brick house. He had taken the farm and was to maintain grandfather and grandmother the rest of their lives. That winter I was several days at his place, and Uncle Abijah Thompson's, as they lived near each other. He was then living with his third wife, and the girls of his second marriage were living with him; tne daughter Elizabeth married a Hinkley shortly after that. When my father, Abel Thompson, left Maine in

December, 1816, Phineas Thompson was living about two miles from my father's place. I think it was called West Bowdoin. I have often been at that place, and his children would come over to our place. In my father's barn I have often played with Wooster and Ray Thompson.

"In Aug., 1884, I visited Phineas Thompson's old place. The lay of the land looked quite natural to me, but the old brick house and the orchard were gone. The new house which Phineas Thompson built on the hill was still there. I was saddened to think of the changes in fifty-five years."

(5) Phineas Thompson m. (first) (publishment dated July 9, 1803), Mehetable Preble[7], b. Wolwich, Me.; d. 1804; daughter of Ebenezer Preble[6] and Martha Smith; Ebenezer Preble[5] and Mary Harnden of Arrowsic, Me.; of Jonathan Preble[4] and Rebecca Harvey, who moved from York, Me., to Arrowsic, Me.; Capt. Abraham Preble[3]; Andrew Preble[2]; Robert Preble[1]. M. (second) (publishment dated Jan. 25, 1806), Mary Metcalf of Lisbon, Me., who d. Dec. 10, 1819 (33y., 7m.); buried on the Gowell farm. M. (third), Nov. 30, 1820, Jemima Blake, b. Harpswell, Me.; d. early in June, 1823, when her only child, John A. Thompson, was but five weeks old; daughter of John Blake and Jennie Webber. M. (fourth) (publication dated Oct. 22, 1823), Sarah Goodwin of Litchfield, Me., who d. about 1853; no children of this fourth marriage.

Child of first wife.

(6) Wooster Thompson, b. Bowdoin, Me., Aug. 13, 1804; d. Nov. 12, 1892 (88y.); lived in Topsham, Me., a number of years and then moved to Brunswick, Me., where he remained until his death; m., in the fall of 1824, Catherine Blake, b. Whaleboat Island, Harpswell, Me., May 7, 1804; d. April 2, 1894; only child of Simeon Blake and Mary. Wooster Thompson and his wife are buried in the Haley Cemetery at Topsham, Me.

(7) Rachel Thompson; d. in one year.

(7) Mary Jane Thompson, b. Brunswick, Me., 1828; d. Brunswick, Me., fall of 1868; buried in Haley Cemetery, Topsham, Me., a mile and a half from Topsham, on the River Road; m. George Lewis Coombs, b. Bowdoin, Me., 1821; farmer and shoemaker.

(8) Ten children.

(7) Elizabeth H. Thompson, b. Topsham, Me., Jan. 14, 1831; d. June 29, 1899; buried in Pine Grove Cemetery, Brunswick, Me.; m., fall of 1857, William B. Speare of Wayne, Me.

(7) Simeon Blake Thompson, b. Topsham, Me., 1833; d. in the Union army in the spring of 1863; buried at New Orleans, La.; enlisted in the winter of 1862 in the Fifteenth Maine Regiment; resided at Brunswick, Me.; m., 1861, Mary Ann Darling, daughter of Andrew Darling of Rhode Island, and wife, Adeline ———.

(8) Simeon Blake Thompson, b. Brunswick, Me., June 7, 1862; resides 59 Water Street, Brunswick, Me.; m., March 18, 1882, Mary Lavina Collins, b. Bath, Me., July 12, 1861; daughter of James Warren Collins and Evelyn Wyman.

(9) Cora Mabel Thompson, b. Brunswick, Me., Aug. 9, 1884.

(9) Alice Mildred Thompson, b. Oct. 2, 1886; d. Jan. 1, 1888.

(9) Forest Blake Thompson, b. Oct. 14, 1893; d. May 21, 1896.

(9) Clarence Fairfield Thompson, b. Sept. 18, 1899.

(7) Martha A. Thompson, b. Topsham, Me., Dec. 2, 1837; d. Brunswick, Me., March 2, 1880; buried in Haley Cemetery, Topsham, Me.; unm.

(7) Caroline M. Thompson, b. Topsham, Me., Nov. 23, 1843; resides 5 Stetson Street, Brunswick, Me., m., in Brunswick, Me., Aug. 23, 1862, John F. Thorn, b. Paris, Me.; only son of John Thorn.

(7) Harriet M. Thompson, b. Topsham, Me., March 15, 1846; m., 1864, James Potter, b. Bowdoin, Me.; d. May 27, 1901; buried Varney Cemetery, Brunswick, Me.; entered the Civil War, 1861; discharged, 1864; Ninth Maine Regiment, Company B.; wounded at Drury's Bluff; son of Jesse Potter and Fannie Kidder of Dixfield, Me.

(8) George E. Potter, b. 1864; m. Laura E. Deming.

(9) Elmer Potter, b. Topsham, Me., July 6, 1895.

(8) Lizzie C. Potter, b. 1871; m. John E. Whitney.

(8) Hattie E. Potter, b. 1876; m. William S. Durrell.

(9) Guy Lester Durrell, b. 1898.

(8) Herbert Potter, b. Feb. 2, 1878; box maker.

(8) Carrie M. Potter, b. Jan. 13, 1881; bookkeeper.

Children of second wife:

(6) Ray Thompson, b. Lisbon, Me., Sept. 19, 1808; d. March 10, 1849; resided at Lisbon, Bowdoin, Gardiner, Me.; owned and operated a sawmill; m., Oct. 3, 1833, Tamsin Bowman, b. Litchfield, Me., Feb. 5, 1808; d. June 26, 1887; daughter of James Bowman and Mary Jewell.

(7) Henry Franklin Thompson, b. Sept. 21, 1836; d. Oct. 3, 1837.

(7) Mary Ellen Thompson, b. Gardiner, Me., Sept 21, 1838; resides Richmond, Me.; m. (first), Nov. 3, 1859, Dr. DeWitt Clinton Chamberlain, b. March 12, 1829; d. Oct. 30, 1870; son of Andrastus Chamberlain and Lucy White; m. (second), Aug. 19, 1873, Alphonso Washington Smith, b. Richmond, Me., April 3, 1842; son of G. W. Smith and Lucretia Catlin; dry and fancy goods dealer.

Children of first husband:

(8) Dr. George Clinton Chamberlain, b. Richmond, Me., Aug. 16, 1860; lived Friendship, Stoughton, Camden, Me.; educated in business college at Poughkeepsie, N. Y.; graduated from Bowdoin Medical College in 1887; m., May 30, 1890, Emogene N. Fisher.

(8) Mary DeWitt Chamberlain, b. Richmond, Me., July 26, 1870; d. Feb. 14, 1873.

Children of second husband:

(8) Alice Gertrude Smith, b. Jan. 18, 1875; resides Holyoke, Mass.; m., June 15, 1896, Charles Warren Lemont, b. July 14, 1874; manager of Western Union Telegraph Company's office.

(8) George Franklin Smith, b. Jan. 5, 1881; d. Nov. 28, 1881.

(8) Ray Smith, b. Nov. 6, 1874; founded the Richmond *Bee;* editor of the Westbrook (Me.) *Gazette* in 1901.

(6) Mehetable Thompson, b. Lisbon, Me.; d. March 19, 1856 (49y.); m., Dec. 31, 1827, Patten Tate, b. April 13, 1801; d. Feb. 26, 1886; educated in common schools; farmer.

(7) Actor Patten Tate, b. Nov. 19, 1828; d. Freeport, Me., July 19, 1888; m., Oct. 8, 1881, Martha Elizabeth Whitmore, b. Bowdoinham, Me., Nov. 28, 1838; she resides in Brunswick, Me.; daughter of Francis Whitmore and Martha Lewis; no children.

(7) William Ray Tate, b. Jan. 26, 1834; d. May 23, 1900;
always resided in Topsham, Me.; farmer; m., June
8, 1858, Mary L. Bradley; daughter of Foster Bradley and Mary Mallett.

  (8) Abbie M. Tate, b. May 18, 1859; bookkeeper at Topsham, Me.; m., at Norway, Me., March 11, 1893,
Ashley Cromwell, who d. March 11, 1893.

    (9) Bernard Cromwell, b. May 26, 1890; lives with his
grandmother Tate.

  (8) Actor Patten Tate, b. Nov. 18, 1861; house carpenter; resides at Portland, Me.

  (8) William Foster Tate, b. April 5, 1863; on the home
farm.

  (8) Alice Lewis Tate, b. May 23, 1869; resides Veazie,
Me.; m., Sept. 7, 1898, Frederick G. Hathorn.

    (9) Daughter, b. winter of 1901.

  (8) Nellie Edith Tate, b. Oct. 6, 1875; resides at home.

(7) Weston Chapin Tate; d. in childhood.

(7) Annie M. Tate, b. about 1848; teacher in Brunswick,
Me.

(7) Tamsin Tate, b. and d. at Topsham, Me.

(6) Sabrina Thompson, b. Lisbon, Me., 1811; d. East Boston,
Mass., Jan. 4, 1894 (82y., 10m., 13d.); m., Oct. 2, 1831,
George Lewis[2], b. Bowdoin, Me., April 26, 1801; d. California, Dec. 9, 1855 (51y.); he was m. in Topsham,
Me., and lived there for some time; he was much interested in military matters; colonel in a Maine regiment; lumbering and milling; son of George Lewis[1]
and Martha Hunt, b. 1765; d. Bowdoin, Me., Nov. 15,
1857 (92y.). George Lewis, Sr., d. at Bowdoin, Me.,
Jan. 23, 1848 (82y.); he came from England with his
widowed mother when a lad; he was a noble man,
and his family a fine one. This family resided in
Brunswick, Me., until the husband went to California,
where he d. in one week after reaching that coast,
from fever contracted on the Isthmus of Darien. The
widow then moved to Boston, Mass., with her children
and remained there until her death.

(7) Mehetable Tate Lewis, b. Brunswick, Me., May 25,
1834; resides 22 Marion Street, East Boston, Mass.;
m., Nov. 20, 1859, James Burdakin.

  (8) Walter Burdakin; resides New York City; m. Jennie Kelsey.

    (9) Margaret Burdakin.

9

(7) Twin, Mary Lewis, b. Brunswick, Me., May 25, 1834; resides 135 Trenton Street, East Boston, Mass.; m., Jan. 10, 1860, Charles Darwin Tisdale.

(8) Frank Lewis Tisdale.

(7) Martha Lewis, b. Brunswick, Me., Aug. 2, 1836; resides 6 Stratford Street, Dorchester Mass., Jewell Park; m., Dec. 15, 1858, Warren Fletcher, b. Arlington, Mass., Oct. 10, 1830; conducts a bakery; son of Walter Fletcher and Matilda Rust.

(8) Grace Lucia Fletcher, b. April 16, 1861; d. Nov. 18, 1872.

(8) Walter Fletcher, d. Dec. 29, 1869 (3d.).

(8) Maud Fletcher, b. East Boston, Mass., Dec. 25, 1870; graduated at Emerson School, June, 1889; resides Brooks Hill Road, Milton, Mass.; m., Oct. 2, 1895, Charles Strout Long, b. Cambridge, Mass., Feb. 2, 1861; graduated from the grammar school, Portland, Me.; traveling salesman; son of Zadoc Long and Ruth A. B. Strout; nephew of Secretary of State John D. Long.

(9) Dorothy Fletcher Long, b. May 15, 1896.

(9) Ruth P. Long, b. May 16, 1896; d. Aug. 13, 1896.

(9) Fletcher Burbank Long, b. Sept. 18, 1898.

(8) Walter Varnum Fletcher, b. East Boston, Mass., Jan. 23, 1873; resides 6 Stratford Street, Dorchester, Mass.; member of the Sons of the American Revolution and of the Sons of Colonial Wars. Capt. Peletiah Fletcher was the Revolutionary ancestor and Gershom Cutter for the Colonial Wars. The Fletcher records reach back to 1630. Wholesale fruit dealer, receiving California, Mediterranean and Spanish fruits that come to Boston; entered this business immediately after completing his education; graduated at the Emerson Grammar School, 1888; at the English High School, 1891; has resided in East Boston and Dorchester, Mass.; m., April 8, 1902, Ella Lowd Vinal, b. Boston, Mass., May 27, 1881; graduated from the Christopher Gibson School, 1896; from Roxbury High School, 1899; daughter of Harry Abbott Vinal and Frances Burnside.

(7) Ray Thompson Lewis, b. Brunswick, Me., June 28, 1838; resides Duluth, Minn. "Resided on the farm at Mere Point, Brunswick, Me., until he was 10 years of

age; then the parents moved to Brunswick village, where he remained until he was 14 years old; attended the public schools; then the mother, who had been a widow for three years, moved to Boston, Mass.; he was employed in a dry goods store on Harrison Street until 18 years of age; then he followed the sea for 22 years, becoming captain at 26 years; he commanded some fine ships for about 15 years, sailing usually out of New York and Boston, the voyages taking him to all parts of the world; doubled the Cape of Good Hope seven times; at the age of 22 years he was first officer on a French transport in the war which England and France had with China; after quitting the sea, in 1879, he went to Leadville, Col., he was in Denver three years, in the real estate and mining business; then he went to Fargo, N. D., for three years; he was then in the real estate business and at one time had a large wheat farm; after that he bought a general store at Red Wing, Minn., and remained there two years; in 1886 he went to Duluth, Minn., and has remained there; he has taken an active part in city affairs; was mayor, 1894–'96; elected by the largest majority ever recorded by any candidate, 3,025 majority—or over 6,000 votes; his opponent, Foster, who was a Populist, Democrat and lawyer, got 3,000 votes; he has been president of the chamber of commerce several years; m., in Portland, Me., Sept. 3, 1864, Mary Anderson, b. Trenton, Me.

(8) Fred A. Lewis; employed in his father's office.

(7) Susan Maria Lewis, b. Feb. 27, 1841, at Brunswick, Me.; resides 35 Falcon Street, East Boston, Mass.; studied in the Chapman School, Boston, Mass.; m. Dec. 25, 1864, Joshua Lazelle Cousens, b. Cohasset, Mass., Jan. 17, 1836; studied in Cohasset schools; in the wholesale flour business; son of George Cousens and Joanna Nichols.

(8) Hobart Everett Cousens, b. East Boston, Mass., April 17, 1867; resides 255 Broadway, Arlington, Mass.; graduated at the Emerson School, East Boston, Mass., June, 1884; bookkeeper; m., June 26, 1888, Carrie Lewis Townsend, b. East Boston, Mass., Nov. 14, 1867; graduated at the Emerson School, East Boston, Mass., June, 1884; daughter of James Townsend and Louisa S. Witham.

(9) Lewis Hobart Cousens, b. East Boston, April 6, 1894.

(9) Harold Franklin Cousens, b. East Boston, May 20, 1899.

(8) Franklin Lewis Cousens, b. May 28, 1872; graduated at the Chapman School and at Bryant & Stratton's Business College; bookkeeper at State National Bank, Boston, Mass.; m., April 1, 1901, Charlotte Ernestine Schwaar, b. Boston, Mass., May 4, 1875; daughter of Charles Theodore Schwaar and Caroline Ogeth Hosfelat; resides 35 Falcon Street, East Boston, Mass.

(7 George Franklin Lewis; lost at sea about 1873; unm.

(6) Elizabeth Thompson, b. Lisbon, Me., Aug. 12, 1812; d. Sept. 18, 1893; went to California in 1864; resided at Fort Jones, Siskyou County, Cal.; m., 1827, Atkins Lombard Hinkley, b. Lisbon, Me., April 26, 1803; d. Fort Jones, Cal., June 14, 1877; he went to California in 1853 and was engaged in milling, mining and farming; son of Samuel Hinkley and Rebecca Lombard.

(7) Mary Ellen Hinkley, b. Bowdoin, Me., Sept. 11, 1831; d. April 2, 1832.

(7) Harden Lombard Hinkley, b. Bowdoin, Me., Jan. 17, 1833; d. Jan. 29, 1875; m., 1860, Abbie Goud, b. Dresden, Me.

(8) Anna Frances Hinkley, b. Brunswick, Me., Sept. 9, 1861; m., at Etna, Cal., Henry Basham of Arkansas.

(7) John Andrew Hinkley, b. Bowdoin, Me., Jan. 26, 1835; d. Feb. 1, 1835.

(7) Priscilla Hinkley, b. Bowdoin, Me., March 21, 1837; d. Aug. 13, 1842.

(7) Mary Ellen Hinkley, b. Bowdoin, Me., April 16, 1840; d. April 28, 1903; m., April 3, 1873, Josh Hanson Rand, b. Albany, Me., and d. in San Francisco, Cal., Aug. 11, 1887; lawyer; resided at Etna Mills, Cal.

(8) John Hanson Rand, b. June 7, 1878; d. June 17, 1878.

(7) Hannah Maria Hinkley, b. Aug. 10, 1843; resides Etna Mills, Cal.; m., at Yuba, Cal., Dec. 15, 1866, Samuel Alden Diggles, b. Taunton, Mass., March 23, 1834; son of James K. Diggles, b. 1808, in London, Eng., and Marietta Alden of Connecticut; she was of the John Alden line.

(7) Elizabeth Ray Hinkley, b. Lisbon, Me., April 6, 1847; resides 24 No. Twelfth Street, Minneapolis, Minn.; educated in Brunswick (Me.) High School; m. (first), June 22, 1867, John Channey Carroll of California, b. in Virginia; lawyer; m. (second), Jan. 22, 1874, at Lewiston, Me., Henry Ellis Wood, b. Litchfield, Me., Feb. 10, 1846; graduated from Maine State Seminary, Lewiston, Me.; lumberman; son of James Smith Wood and Elizabeth Blackwell.

Child of first husband:

(8) Bernard Chancy Carroll, b. Fort Jones, Cal., May 30, 1868; lawyer in San Francisco, Cal.

Children of second husband:

(8) Edith Hinkley Wood, b. Oct. 19, 1874; d. Sept. 22, 1890.

(8) Percy Henry Wood, b. Jan. 18, 1876; railroad man in Minneapolis, Minn.

(8) Fannie Louise Wood, b. Aug. 8, 1885.

(7) Frances Imogene Hinkley, b. Lisbon, Me., Nov. 18, 1858; m., April 3, 1870, Walter E. Tichnor, b. Ravena, O.; d. at Fort Jones, Cal., Sept 15, 1893.

(8) Walter Charter Ticknor, b. Dec. 20, 1871.

(8) Grace Lucia Ticknor, b. Dec. 6, 1873; d. Chico, Cal., March 20, 1888.

(8) Percy Ray Ticknor, b. Aug. 28, 1883.

(8) Beverly Lloyd Ticknor, b. Sept. 3, 1888.

(6) Hannah Thompson, b. April 12, 1815; d. Saco, Me., July 8, 1891; lived Lewiston, Me.; m., as his first wife, Jacob Skolfield, b. April 30, 1810; d. April 14, 1845; went to sea in his early life.

(7) William S. Skolfield, b. Brunswick, Me., March 14, 1840; resides Lewiston, Me.; m. Alice J. Tewksbury.

(6) Franklin Thompson, b. 1818; m. (first), Cornelia Tapley of Gardiner, Me., who d. Bowdoin, Me.; m. (second), in Michigan, Lydia Van Amburgh.

(7) Frank Thompson; resides Claremont, S. D.

Children of third wife:

(6) John A. Thompson, b. Bowdoin, Me., April 29, 1823; d. Brunswick, Me., Feb. 16, 1905 (81y., 9m., 17d.). In early life he conducted the farm that had been owned by his father and grandfather; later on he moved to a a farm in Bowdoinham, Me.; he then went into the clothing business in Fairfield, Me., under the firm name of Thompson & Mariner; about 1880 he moved

to Brunswick, Me., and had a clothing store on the
first floor of the Tontine Hotel Building; he was selectman in Bowdoinham, Me., 1861, 1862 and 1863; he
was known far and wide as an upright and honorable
business man; m., in Bowdoinham, Me., Oct. 21, 1849,
Sarah Dow Stinson, b. at what is now Concord, Somerset County, Me., Feb. 17, 1815; d. Brunswick, Me.,
Jan. 12, 1898; daughter of David Stinson and Mehetable Reirdan.

(7) Hon. Weston Thompson, b. Bowdoin, Me., Aug. 12,
1850; d. Brunswick, Me., Jan. 6, 1907; he grew up on
the farm at Bowdoinham, Me.; studied law with
Hon. S. S. Brown at Fairfield, Me.; admitted to the
bar of the Supreme Judicial Court of Maine at Norridgewock, Me., Sept. 19, 1871, and to the bar of the
Circuit Court of the United States from the First
Circuit of Portland, Me., Sept. 23, 1882; bar of Supreme Court of United States at Washington, D. C.,
Feb. 15, 1880; represented Brunswick, Me., in the
Maine Legislature of 1881 and 1883; was one of the
commissioners appointed by the Maine Legislature
of 1883 to revise and publish the public laws of
Maine. Bowdoin College gave him an honorary degree of A. M. in 1880. He moved to Brunswick, Me.,
in Nov., 1871, and has ever since been one of the
most worthy and helpful of its citizens. He had
been attorney for the towns of Brunswick, Topsham
and Harpswell, and practically for all the large cor-
porations in that vicinity. He organized the Lisbon Falls Fibre Co. and the Pejepscot Paper Co. The
Richmond (Me.) National Bank and the First National Bank of Brunswick, Me.; the Lewiston, Bath
& Brunswick St. Railway Co., and the Portland &
Brunswick St. Railway Co. were among his clients.
The list of law students who read law with him is
a remarkably fine one. In all his extensive law
practice, and in dealing with a great many clients,
it was always a source of satisfaction to him to be of
service and to do the wise and useful thing. He
never advised litigation where he could make a satisfactory settlement for his client. Mr. Thompson's
work was that of a strong man. He was far-sighted
in business and very competent in the organization
of large enterprises. His work in connection with

the organization of the Brunswick & Topsham (Me.)
Water District and the purchase of the plant of the
Maine Water Co. was very thorough and compre-
hensive. Too much could not be written of this
quiet, talented man of such sturdy and sterling qualities.

(7) Eliza Loring Thompson, b. Bowdoin, Me., Dec. 13,
1852; unm.

(7) Harry Floyd Thompson, b. Bowdoinham, Me., July 21,
1857; resides Brunswick, Me.; unm.

(7) Caroline Stinson Thompson, b. Bowdoinham, Me.,
Sept. 28, 1861; d. Oct. 3, 1863.

* * * * *

* * * * *

(5) The fifth child of Amos Thompson and Hannah Wooster,
Esther (called Easter in the old records), b. Bowdoin,
Me., April 19, 1784; d. Illinois, Sept. 27, 1818; m., in
Bowdoin, Me., by Elder Humphrey Purinton, Caleb Barker; he d. in Illinois April 8, 1807, about seventy-seven
years of age; he was a farmer, and went to Illinois with
Abel Thompson in 1816. "On the death of his wife he
was left with five children, the oldest about ten years of
age, and the youngest about three years; he was in a
strange country and with but limited means, so that he
was under the necessity of looking about for some
woman to share with him the cares and sorrows of life,
and assist in raising his children; so in about a year he
married Polly Rittenhouse; she was a woman somewhat advanced in years, with a boy about ten years old
and a girl about seven; she was a good stepmother, and
Mr. Barker was equally kind to her children; that was
a marriage where both parties were benefitted by the
match. After renting land for several years, Mr. Barker
located in Belleville, Ill., and he lived there until his
property became quite valuable, when he sold to good
advantage and moved down to the junction of Forbes'
Fork and the Richland Creek, and there entered or
bought him a piece of land and lived in a very comfortable home. His wife survived him for many years.
There were no children of this second marriage."

(6) Sally Barker; m. Isaac Rittenhouse and soon d.; no
children. The Rittenhouse ancestor settled near
Belleville, Ill., in 1806; the descendants have always
been very enterprising farmers.

(6) Amos Thompson Barker, b. Bowdoin, Me., Sept. 11, 1813; d. April 15, 1892 (78y., 7m., 4d.). He came from Maine to Illinois with his parents when he was about seven years old. He was one of the old settlers at what is now North Belleville, Ill. After his marriage he moved to a farm about seven miles south of Belleville and remained there until about 1856; he then purchased a farm about five miles northwest of Centralia, Ill. He was a successful farmer and a very good man. He was truly a self-made man and was well educated for one who had so few school advantages. Highly esteemed by all his neighbors." M., about 1835, Zadie Rittenhouse, b. 1812; d. Dec. 30, 1890 (78y.).

(7) Louis C. Barker, b. Aug. 21, 1836; d. Feb. 24, 1863; he built a good house on the farm at Centralia, Ill., and always lived there; he had a fine common school education; m., Sept. 3, 1856, Mary Carr, b. St. Clair County, Ill.; daughter of James Carr and Elsa Rettinghouse; she is now Mrs. James Saunders of Centralia, Ill.

(8) Luella Barker, b. July 26, 1860; d. March 4, 1883.

(8) Luna Barker, b. April 12, 1862; d. March 24, 1880.

(7) Sarah Adeline Barker, b. seven miles from Belleville, Ill., June 15, 1839; resides 322 South Sycamore Street, Centralia, Ill.; has also resided at Shattuck, Ill.; m., Dec. 2, 1858, John H. A. Hood, b. Clinton County, Ill., Oct. 11, 1836; d. Dec. 5, 1899; studied in the schools of Clinton County, Ill.; farmer; son of Elisha Hood and Patty Drake.

(8) Florence Vinidia Hood, b. Jan. 18, 1860; d. Jan. 21, 1892; m., Aug. 10, 1882, George H. Gullick, b. April 5, 1860; d. Jan. 21, 1889; son of James Gullick and Martha Jewett.

(9) Minnie Ella Gullick, b. Aug. 26, 1883.

(9) Louis C. Gullick, b. July 18, 1885.

(9) Roy Gullick, b. May 28, 1887.

(9) Daphne Gullick, b. Dec. 10, 1889.

(8) Louis C. Hood, b. Jan. 14, 1866; d. in infancy.

(8) Amos Thompson Hood, b. Jan. 25, 1870; farmer; resides five miles north of Centralia, Ill.; m., Jan. 19, 1890, Marguerite Richard.

(9) Florence V. Hood.

(9) Ira Hood.

(9) Irene M. Hood.

(9) Elmer B. Hood.

(9) Erwin W. Hood

(8) Minnie Hood, b. March 6, 1868; has lived at Centralia, Ill., and Spokane, Wash.; m., Sept. 12, 1894, Alexander Carson.

(9) Alice Carson.

(9) Edward W. Carson.

(9) Dewey V. Carson.

(7) Orzella Barker, b. Jan. 15, 1848; d. Dec. 30, 1895; unm.

(7) Luella Barker, b. 1850; d. 1852 (18m.).

(6) Sybil Barker; b. Dec. 13, 1811; d. May 6, 1897; m., Dec. 18, 1830, John Rittenhouse, who d. Feb. 3, 1901 (90y., 1m.).

(7) Benjamin C. Rittenhouse, b. Oct. 10, 1831; d. Jan. 5, 1895; farmer; buried at Turkey Hill, two miles south of Belleville, Ill.; m., Jan. 19, 1875, Susan Quick, b. St. Clair County, Ill., on a farm ten miles south of Belleville, Ill., June, 11, 1852; resides at Centralia, Ill.

(8) Clifton Rittenhouse, b. Oct. 18, 1878; d. July 21, 1879.

(8) Minnie Rittenhouse, b. Jan. 20, 1883; d. March 15, 1898.

(7) Alonzo P. Rittenhouse, b. Dec. 18, 1833; resides at Hecker, Ill.

(7) Cordelia Rittenhouse, b. Jan. 3, 1836; d. Aug. 18, 1839.

(7) Nelson Rittenhouse, b. Feb. 3, 1838.

(8) Edward Rittenhouse; in California.

(7) Melissa J. Rittenhouse, b. July 11, 1840; resides at Decatur, Mercer County, Ill.

(7) Caleb Rittenhouse, b. Dec. 6, 1842; d. Feb. 3, 1879.

(7) Sarah Rittenhouse, b. April 2, 1845.

(7) Isaac J. Rittenhouse, b. Dec. 9, 1848; d. May 31, 1897.

(7) Olive Franklin Rittenhouse, b. Jan. 20, 1853; resides at Columbus, Kan.

(6) Adaline Barker, unm.

(6) Nelson Barker; m. Polly Carr.

(7) James Barker; resides Walnut Hills, Ill.

(6) Caroline Barker; d. young.

*   *   *   *   *

(5) The sixth child of Amos Thompson and Hannah Wooster, Abijah Thompson, b. Bowdoin, Me., March 23, 1786; d.

Bowdoin, Me., July 23, 1863; farmer, and always resided in Bowdoin, Me.; buried near the old South Church, Bowdoin, Me.; m. (publishment dated Dec. 31, 1808), March 2, 1809, Rachel Woodward, b. Brunswick, Me., June 28, 1782; d. March 13, 1853 (70y., 8m.); daughter of Rev. Samuel Woodward and Mary Coombs.

(6) Mary Ann Thompson, b. Bowdoin, Me., Feb. 2, 1810; d. Feb. 4, 1810.

(6) Julia Ann Thompson, b. Bowdoin, Me., Jan. 24, 1811; d. April 7, 1879 (68y.); m., June 13, 1833, as his second wife, John Carr, b. Bowdoin, Me., Feb. 14, 1796; d. Feb. 6, 1872 (76y., 11m., 23d.); farmer in Bowdoin, Me.; son of Joseph Carr and Molly Eastman.

(7) Rachel Carr, b. April 3, 1834; d. Sept. 23, 1837.

(7) Hannah Carr, b. Oct. 12, 1835; d. Dec. 2, 1841 (6y., 2m.).

(7) Harriet Carr, b. Nov. 12, 1837; d. Sept., 1865; m. Alden Jaques.

(7) Artemas Smith Carr, b. Dec. 21, 1839; resides at Lynn, Mass.; shoemaker; m., Sept. 19, 1863, Sarah E. Gardiner.

(8) Ernest Raymond Carr, b. Nov. 22, 1882.

(7) Hannah Carr, b. Feb. 18, 1841; resides 32 Hamilton Street, Lynn, Mass.; m., Sept. 19, 1863, Josiah H. Preble, b. Nov. 22, 1840; son of Humphrey P. Preble and Sophia W. Mitchell.

(8) George Kimball Preble, b. Feb. 5, 1866; shoe manufacturer at Lynn, Mass.; m., June 20, 1894, Alice Gilman Drew.

(8) Mabel Estelle Preble, b. July 23, 1877; d. April 11, 1879.

(8) Herbert Harmon Preble, b. May 17, 1880; d. Sept. 6, 1900.

(6) Woodward Thompson, b. Bowdoin, Me., June 1, 1812; d. Aug. 15, 1876; he resided in Gardiner, Me., about forty years; shipbuilder and farmer; m. Susan Woodbury, b. May 16, 1818; d. Jan. 24, 1891; daughter of True Woodbury and Sally Jordan.

(7) Annetta Jane Thompson, b. Gardiner, Me., Jan. 3, 1850; studied in Gardiner (Me.) schools; has resided in Gardiner, Monmouth and Norridgewock, Me.; m., Oct. 10, 1871, George Emerson Porter, b. Brunswick, Me., Aug. 18, 1849; studied in Brunswick schools; tailor; son of Nathaniel C. Porter and Hannah Gould.

(8) Cora Edna Porter, b. Jan. 21, 1873; d. April 17, 1873.

(6) Capt. Nathaniel Purington Thompson, b. Bowdoin, Me., Dec. 11, 1813; d. June 21, 1857 (43y., 6m.); he was lost on the ship *William Rogers* on the passage from Liverpool, Eng., to New York; m. Minerva Alezander of Bowdoin; b. 1821; d. March 10, 1847 (26y.); no children.

(6) William Lee Thompson, b. Bowdoin, Me., July 9, 1815; d. Brunswick, Me., May 7, 1900; educated in common schools; farmer; m., June 5, 1841, Elizabeth Mariner, b. Brunswick, Me., Dec. 2, 1816; d. June 15, 1891; buried in Maquoit Cemetery, Brunswick, Me.; daughter of John Mariner and Rhoda Thompson.

(7) Lavina Rhoda Thompson, b. Brunswick, Me., Jan. 7, 1845; d. Poston Mass., April 12, 1872; educated in common schools.

(7) Nathan Thomas Cleveland Thompson, b. Brunswick, Me., May 7, 1843; resides Brunswick, Me.; engineer and carpenter, 26 Mere Point Road; m. (first), Nov. 1866, Rebecca Archibald, b. Maitland, N. S., 1839; d. Aug. 5, 1873 (33y., 10m.); daughter of John Archibald; m. (second), Feb. 22, 1875, Abbie M. Freeman, b. Freeport, Me., March 26, 1850; daughter of Colby Welch and Clarissa Holbrook. Mr. Thompson has lived in Boston, Mass., in Yarmouth and Brunswick, Me.

Children of second wife:

(8) Percy Cleveland Thompson, b. Boston, Mass., Sept. 10, 1877; d. Oct. 20, 1878; buried in Maquoit Cemetery, Brunswick, Me.

(8) Ethel Blanchard Thompson, b. Boston, Mass., April 19, 1881; milliner at Brunswick, Me.

(7) Mary Elizabeth Thompson, b. Brunswick, Me., Sept. 10, 1847; resides 18 Webster Street, East Somerville, Mass.; she and her husband and family are members of the Tremont Temple Church, Boston, Mass.; m., Sept. 12, 1877, Barnard Boynton, b. Washington, Me., Aug. 8, 1848; painter; son of Henry Boynton and ———— Hutchins.

(8) Edith Emma Boynton, b. Oct. 28, 1880; graduated from Edgerly Grammar School, East Somerville, Mass., June, 1895; from English High School, 1899.

(8) John B. Boynton, b. Jan. 12, 1882; d. Jan. 16, 1882.

(8) Edward L. Domineo Hall Boynton, b. Oct. .25, 1883; graduated from Edgerly Grammar School, 1898; painting with his father.

(7) Rachel Anne Thompson, b. Brunswick, Me., May 29, 1856; resides 7 Mabel Street, Woodfords, Me.; m. as his second wife, Dec. 23, 1893, Abizer Curtis Wilson, b. Brunswick, Me., Feb. 19, 1854; mason; son of John Wilson and Susan Ellen Gummer.

(7) Joseph Henry Thompson, b. Brunswick, Me., May 29, 1856; farmer at Brunswick, Me.

(7) James Franklin Thompson, b. Brunswick, Me., Nov. 12, 1860; d. July 5, 1881.

(6) Roxana Thompson, b. Bowdoin, Me., Dec. 16, 1816; d. March 20, 1896; buried in the New Meadows Cemetery; m. her cousin, Gilbert Woodward, b. Brunswick, 1809; d. March 20, 1889; son of Eben Woodward.

(7) Mary Woodward, b. 1840; d. 1854.

(7) Melissa Woodward, b. Brunswick, Me., Nov. 11, 1847; resides 30 Winthrop Street, Augusta, Me.; has resided at Brunswick, Me., Amherst, Mass., St. Louis, Mo., Huntsville, Mo., and Augusta, Me.; m., Aug 26, 1873, Melville Smith, b. Augusta, Me., May 11, 1842; piano and organ dealer; son of Winthrop H. Smith and Mary J. Crockett.

(8) Emma Belle Smith, b. Nov. 25, 1875; m., Oct. 4, 1899, Herbert Parker Doane.

(9) Smith Eaton Doane, b. Nov. 1, 1901.

(8) Ralph Woodward Smith, b. Dec. 23, 1883.

(7) Osborne Thompson Woodward, b. Brunswick, Me., Aug. 2, 1849; resides Brunswick, Me.; m., Jan., 1879, Hattie Alexander.

(8) Lulu M. Woodward.

(8) Samuel Woodward.

(8) Gilbert P. Woodward; d. (4y.).

(6) Abel H. Thompson, b. Bowdoin, Me., Sept. 11, 1818; d. March 13, 1888; buried Riverside Cemetery, Auburn, Me.; lived Gardiner, Brunswick, Harpswell, Island Falls, Bowdoin, Lisbon, Lewiston, Fairfield, all in Maine; blacksmith and farmer; m., 1843, Julia Wakefield, b. Gardiner, Me., Feb. 27, 1820; d. June 19, 1899; educated in Gardiner (Me.) schools; daughter of Jeremiah Wakefield and Elizabeth McKinney.

(7) Julia Ann Thompson, b. Mere Point, Brunswick, Me.,
　　Sept. 16, 1850; resides Fort Fairfield, Me.; has
　　lived in several Maine towns and at Lowell, Mass.,
　　San Francisco, Cal., and at Asheville, N. C.; m., Oct.
　　13, 1884, Levi William Stevens, b. Fort Fairfield, Me.,
　　Dec. 10, 1850; educated in Fort Fairfield schools;
　　lumber manufacturer; son of Hiram Stevens, b. San-
　　gerville, Me., and who went to Aroostook County as
　　a soldier; son of Levi Stevens of Strong, Me., and
　　Dorcas B. Whitney, b. Norridgewock, Me.; d. 1867.

　(8) Anna Lovinia Stevens, b. Dec. 3, 1884; resides at
　　　Osterville, Mass.; m., June 3, 1902, Dr. William B.
　　　Kinney.

　(9) Ortenville Max Kinney.

(7) John Franklin Thompson, b. Mere Point, Brunswick,
　　Me., June 21, 1852; d. 1876.

(7) Lizzie Jane Thompson, b. Mere Point, Brunswick, Me.,
　　Feb. 24, 1854; resides Louisville, Ky.; m., in Lewis-
　　ton, Me., May, 1874, William B. Marinor, manager of
　　cotton mills; lived Bondville, Mass., Fall River,
　　Mass., Cornwall, Ont., Wilmington, Del.

　(8) Gustavus Marinor.

(7) Chapin Edward Thompson, b. Harpswell, Me., Jan. 8,
　　1858; resides Yonkers, N. Y.; has lived at Island
　　Falls, Me., Lisbon, Lewiston, Fort Fairfield, Auburn,
　　and in Lowell, Mass., and Yonkers, N. Y.; studied
　　in the Lewiston (Me.) Grammar School and in a
　　commercial college at Lowell, Mass.; carpenter; m.,
　　Oct. 9, 1886, Nancy Maria Way, b. N. H., May
　　25, 1863; educated in country schools; daughter of
　　Benjamin F. Way and Elizabeth Sweet.

　(8) Unia Ellis Thompson, b. July 20, 1887; graduated
　　　from Erickemeyer School, Yonkers, N. Y., June
　　　25, 1903.

　(8) Norman Abel Thompson, b. Feb. 21, 1891; studied
　　　in Erickemeyer School.

(7) Gilbert Woodward Thompson, b. Island Falls, Me.,
　　May 8, 1858; resides Louisville, Ky.

(7) William Henry Thompson, b. Bowdoin, Me.; d. Oct. 6,
　　1863 (19y.); served in the Civil War in the First
　　Maine Cavalry one and a half years.

(7) George Abijah Thompson, b. Bowdoin, Me.; d. Feb. 14,
　　1864 (20y.).

(6) Samuel Totman Thompson, b. Bowdoin, Me., Sept. 1, 1820; d. Feb. 10, 1897; farmer; m. Lidia Coombs, b. March 19, 1822; d. March 6, 1893.

(7) Viola Vincett Thompson, b. Oct. 4, 1852; resides 193 College Street, Lewiston, Me.; m., Sept. 21, 1877, Orlando Phineas Mosely, b. Oct. 14, 1851; carpenter; son of Phineas Thompson Mosely and Charity Connor.

(8) Ruby Estelle Mosely, b. Dec. 21, 1889; graduated from Lewiston (Me.) Grammar School, 1903.

(6) Abijah Harvey Thompson, b. Dec 21, 1821; d. Feb., 1881; lived in Lewiston and Brunswick, Me., and in Malden, Mass.; m., Nov., 1850, Marcia Ann Beals, b. Leeds, Me., Dec., 1824; daughter of Benjamin Beals and Caroline Leonard.

(7) Harry Leland Thompson, b. Brunswick, Me., Dec. 31, 1851; resides 374 Main Street, Malden, Mass.; educated in Brunswick schools and Portland Commercial College; grocer; m., Jan. 14, 1887, Carrie Lovinia Brooks, b. Boston, Mass., July, 1863; graduated from schools of Malden, Mass.; daughter of Nelson Brooks and Sarah E. Merrill.

(8) Mary Louise Thompson, b. Jan., 1888.

(8) Harry Lewis Brooks Thompson, b. April, 1892.

(8) Lester Beals Thompson, b. May, 1897.

(7) Luella May Thompson, b. Canton, Me., Nov., 1852.

(7) George Knox Thompson, b. Brunswick, Me., July 27, 1864; m., at Malden, Mass., June 21, 1888, Clara E. Keith.

(8) Gladys Josephine Thompson, b. April 22, 1887.

(8) George Kenneth Thompson, b. March 1, 1894.

(8) Arnold Keith Thompson, b. April 15, 1896.

* 　 * 　 * 　 * 　 *

(5) The seventh child of Amos Thompson and Hannah Wooster, Beulah Thompson, b. Bowdoin, Me., March 20, 1789; d. Bowdoin, Me., Jan. 15, 1872 (83y., 10m.); buried at Old South Cemetery, Bowdoin, Me.; m., Feb. 2, 1805, William Moseley, b. Brunswick, Me., 1774; d. Bowdoin, Me., July 11, 1866 (92y.); shoemaker and farmer; lived at Brunswick and Bowdoin, Me.

(6) Mehetable Moseley, b. Jan. 20, 1806; d. Bangor, Me., Feb. 1, 1852; m., Sept. 21, 1825, Capt. Stephen S. Haynes, b. Oct. 19, 1802; d. June 11, 1878; followed the sea for many years and then settled in Bangor, Me.

(7) Mehetable Mary Haynes, b. Aug. 28, 1826; resides 45
    Bedford Street, Bath, Me.; m., in Bangor, Me., Oct.
    15, 1848, William Hogan, b. Bowdoinham, Me., 1824;
    d. Bath, Me., Aug. 1, 1871; resided Bangor and Bath,
    Me.; stonecutter; son of William Hogan and Eliza-
    beth.

 (8) William E. Hogan, b. Aug. 1, 1849; resides 45 Bed-
    ford Street, Bath, Me.; lawyer; graduated at Bath
    (Me.) High School, 1867; at Phillips Andover
    (Mass.) Academy, 1869; Dartmouth College, 1872;
    m., 1889, Estelle Kellett, b. Bath, Me., Nov. 26,
    1852; d. July 7, 1899 (47y., 5m.); daughter of Will-
    iam Kellett and Rachel; no children.

 (8) Clarence Hogan, b. Jan. 10, 1851; d. June 3, 1865
    (14y.).

 (8) Viola G. Hogan, b. Dec. 10, 1853; teacher at Bath,
    Me.; graduated from Bath (Me.) High School,
    1871; taught in the Bath schools for twenty-nine
    years and then in the High School.

 (8) Lilla May Hogan, b. Oct. 24, 1855; d. Nov. 23, 1877
    (24y.); m., Dec. 25, 1875, William Bradford of
    Portland, Me., b. Oct. 27, 1855; spar maker; no
    children.

 (8) Edwin Charles Hogan, b. Nov. 29, 1857; resides at
    Travers City, Mich.; went West in 1877; carpen-
    ter; m., 1882, Helen Elizabeth Wilcox, b. Leslie,
    Mich., April 15, 1862; daughter of John Willard
    Wilcox and Sarah Shane.

  (9) Geraldine Mehetable Hogan, b. March 26, 1900.

  (9) Margaret Sarah Hogan, b. March 26, 1900.

  (9) Alice May Hogan, b. Sept. 23, 1903.

 (8) Dr. Freemont Lincoln Hogan, b. Aug. 25, 1861; re-

 (8) Emma E. Hogan, b. June 17, 1859; d. Aug. 11, 1880
    (21y., 2m.).

 (8) Dr. Fremont Lincoln Hogan, b. Aug. 25, 1861; re-
    sides Lisbon, Me.; graduated from Bath (Me.)
    High School, 1881; at Bowdoin Medical College,
    1894.

 (8) Alice May Hogan, b. March 14, 1863; d. March 22,
    1893.

(7) Deacon Stephen Stockbridge Haynes, b. Bowdoin,
    Me., July 2, 1830; resides Oldtown, Me.; lived some
    time in Bangor, Me.; house joiner and pattern
    maker; m., in Bangor, Me., Nov. 9, 1857, by Rev. C.

F. Porter, Anna Electa Hurd, b. Orrington, Me., July
22, 1837; daughter of Robert Hurd and Orenda
Brown.

(8) Evangeline Mabel Haynes, b. Bangor, Me., Oct. 18,
1858; school teacher; resides Oldtown, Me.

(8) Harold Woodward Haynes, b. March 28, 1874; educated in Bowdoin College.

(7) Rev. Charles Dwinal Haynes, b. Bowdoin, Me., May 15,
1834; resides Traverse City, Mich.; is a preacher and
works on a fruit farm. "When my ninth birthday arrived my mother and her children reached Bangor,
Me., where we resided about 11 years. Then I went
to Bath, Me., and learned the stone cutter's trade,
remaining three years; then went to Columbia, S. C.,
where I worked on the State House two and a half
years. In Feb., before the Rebellion broke out, I
entered the Theological Seminary at Lawrence University, Canton, N. Y., and spent three years there.
I then took a pastorate of three years at Newport
and Middleville, N. Y. I was in Henderson, N. Y.,
one and a half years. In June, 1869, I came to
Traverse City, Mich., and have preached more or
less ever since, and done considerable work on a
small fruit farm." M., July 6, 1863, Adelaide Erexa
Morrill, b. Huntington, Vt., July 16, 1834; d. Oct. 27,
1899; daughter of James Morrill and Eunice Fitch.

(8) Son, b. April 9, 1871.

(7) Susan Moseley Haynes, b. July 8, 1836; m. William
Hall; resides Granger, Idaho.

(7) Phineas Moseley Haynes, b. Bowdoin, Me., Feb. 11,
1843; d. March 11, 1853.

(6) Lovinia Moseley, b. Feb. 29, 1808; d. June 1, 1866; lived
in Litchfield, Me.; m., Dec. 28, 1837, Wyman Gowell, b.
Bowdoin, Me.; he moved from Bowdoin to Litchfield,
Me., in May, 1852; children all born in Bowdoin, Me.

(7) Cora Gowell, b. Oct. 2, 1838; at home.

(7) Johnson Gowell, b. Nov. 23, 1839; d. Bowdoin, Nov.,
1841 (2y., 19d.).

(7) Marilla Gowell, b. April 5, 1842; d. Litchfield, Me.,
Oct. 15, 1868.

(7) Augustus Gowell, b. Feb. 19, 1844. "A very thrifty
farmer on a nicely-located place."

(7) Sawtelle Gowell, b. Oct. 20, 1845; d. Oct. 2, 1849 (4y.,
28d.).

(7) Wyman Woodbury Gowell, b. Dec. 23, 1847; d. Sept.
    24, 1849 (2y., 9m., 28d.).

(6) Elizabeth Moseley, b. July 10, 1810; d. Aug. 31, 1855
    (45y.); buried in Old South Cemetery, Bowdoin, Me.;
    m., Sept. 8, 1853, James Alexander, b. Bowdoin; d.
    April 7, 1882 (81y.); farmer; son of William Alex-
    ander; no children.

(6) Mary Moseley, b. July 23, 1812; m., Oct. 10, 1844, Jona-
    than E. Tedford of Topsham, Me.

(6) Phineas Thompson Moseley, b. Brunswick, Me., Feb. 12,
    1815; d. Lewiston, Me., Jan. 26, 1891 (75y., 11m., 14d.);
    lived in Brunswick, Bowdoin, Litchfield, Me.; car-
    penter; m., Dec. 25, 1839, Charity Connor, b. Bow-
    doin, Me., Oct., 1817; d. Lewiston, Me., Feb. 3, 1881
    (64y., 3m., 10d.); daughter of Simeon Connor and
    Martha Moulton.

    (7) Mary Elizabeth Moseley, b. Feb. 28, 1841; d. Jan. 23,
        1890; unm.

    (7) Alice Moseley, b. May 10, 1843; d. April 4, 1856.

    (7) Alvah Graves Moseley, b. Aug. 1, 1845; d. Aug. 4,
        1882; carpenter; m., Nov., 1877, Ella True, b. Litch-
        field, Me.; resided at Lewiston, Auburn, Portland,
        Me.; no children.

    (7) Orlando Moseley; d. Sept., 1851 (4y., 6m.).

    (7) Charles Connor Moseley, b. Sept. 12, 1849; R. F. D.
        No. 3, Freeport, Me.; educated in Bowdoin (Me.)
        schools and Litchfield Academy; lived Lisbon Falls,
        Portland, Brunswick, Freeport, Me.; carpenter; m.,
        Oct. 9, 1875; Catherine Abbie Cornish, b. June 22,
        1853; studied in Bowdoin schools; daughter of El-
        bridge G. Cornish and Abby G. Small.

        (8) Mabel Florence Moseley, b. June 30, 1877; gradu-
            ated from Portland (Me.) High School, 1895;
            Gorham (Me.) Normal School, 1898; m., July 11,
            1905, Frank Stephens Kendrick, b. Lewiston, Me.,
            Feb. 13, 1875; attended the schools of Bowdoin,
            Me., and Lowell, Mass.; shoe cutter; son of Frank
            William Kendrick and Ada Small.

        (8) Fred Simon Connor Moseley, b. April 10, 1887; at-
            tended Brunswick (Me.) schools; resides Free-
            port, Me.

    (7) Orlando Phineas Moseley, b. Oct. 14, 1851; m. Viola
        Vincett Thompson. (See page 142.)

(7) Clara Emily Moseley, b. Sept. 18, 1853; d. July 5, 1877.

(7) Mary Ellen Moseley, b. Aug. 29, 1855; music teacher; resides 130 College Street, Lewiston, Me.

(7) Simon Connor Moseley, b. Jan. 6, 1858; d. Nov. 29, 1882; graduated from Nichols Latin School, 1873; Bates College, 1877; lawyer; lived in Bowdoin and Lewiston, Me.; unm.; admitted to the Androscoggin bar, Oct., 1881.

(6) Sarah Ann Moseley; b. April 10, 1817; d. Oct. 3, 1883; m., as his second wife, Arthur Edgecombe, b. Oct. 16, 1904; d. Feb., 1880; fifth child of Aaron Edgecombe and Elizabeth Hewey.

(6) William Moseley, Jr., b. July 13, 1819; d. Bowdoinham, Me., Aug. 12, 1865; lived Brunswick, Bowdoin, Portland, Bowdoinham, all in Maine; carpenter and joiner.

(6) Margaret Moseley, b. Dec. 19, 1821; m. Lewis P. Alexander in Topsham, Me., May 13, 1847; he d. Feb. 27, 1895 (75y., 1m.); buried in Old South Cemetery, Bowdoin, Me.

(6) Susannah Moseley, b. Jan. 11, 1825; d. June 27, 1854 (20y.); unm.

(6) Amos Thompson Moseley, b. Sept. 27, 1827; d. Feb. 15, 1850 (23y., 5m.); unm.; buried in Old South Cemetery, Bowdoin, Me.

(6) Caroline Adelaide Moseley, b. Jan. 24, 1829; d. Dec. 18, 1870 (41y., 10m.); unm.

*   *   *   *   *

(5) The eighth child of Amos Thompson and Hannah Wooster, Rhoda Thompson, b. Bowdoin, Me., Feb. 19, 1790; d. April 15, 1866 (76y.); publishment of marriage dated Oct. 30, 1813, to John Mariner, who d. April 15, 1830 (43y.); buried in Maquoit Cemetery, Brunswick, Me.

(6) Jedediah Mariner.

(6) Elizabeth Mariner, b. Dec. 2, 1816; d. June 15, 1891; m., June 5, 1841, William Lee Thompson[6], b. Bowdoin, Me., July 9, 1815; d. May 7, 1900. (See records, page 139.)

(6) Melvin Mariner.

(6) Joseph Mariner.

*   *   *   *   *

(5) The ninth child of Amos Thompson and Hannah Wooster, Lois Thompson, b. Bowdoin, Me., March 4, 1792; m.,

May 10, 1815, by Elder Humphrey Purington, Levi H.
Pratt of North Yarmouth, Me. "Some of the descendants live in Maine and Fall River, Mass."

* * * * *

(5) The tenth child of Amos Thompson and Hannah Wooster,
Sybil (Sebbel in some old records) Thompson, b. Feb.
3, 1794; d. Nov. 5, 1846 (52y.); m., April 22, 1819,
Unight (also spelled Unite) Mariner, b. Brunswick, Me.,
April 20, 1788; d. Sept. 26, 1841; farmer, blacksmith and
bricklayer in Brunswick, Me.; son of William M. Mariner and Elizabeth Moseley.

(6) Paulina Sybil Mariner, b. Nov. 21, 1821; m., April 21,
1846, Daniel T. Purinton, b. Dec. 28, 1817; d. Brunswick, Me., Feb. 12, 1889.

(7) Josiah Purinton, b. April 20, 1847; resides at Betnel,
Me.

(7) Flora E. Purington, b. Oct. 31, 1851; unm.

(7) Daniel Gorham Purinton, b. Dec. 7, 1852; resides at
Brunswick, Me.; m., June 23, 1885, Mary Jane Fer-
rin, b. Brunswick, Me., Feb. 4, 1862; daughter of
David Ferrin, b. Nov. 16, 1827, and Agnes Given
Mariner, b. Sept. 10, 1830.

(8) Grace Agnes Purinton, b. March 20, 1889.

(8) Charles Irwin Purinton, b. Jan. 27, 1892.

(7) Ada P. Purinton, b. Dec. 15, 1854; m., Dec. 21, 1885,
Sumner S. Holbrook, b. Sept. 8, 1839; resides New
Meadows, Me., son of Samuel S. Holbrook[4] and his
cousin, Mercy W. Holbrook.

(8) Allen Jordan Holbrook, b. Oct. 3, 1886.

(8) Irving Whitmore Holbrook, b. July 8, 1888.

(8) Sargent Prentis Holbrook, b. Feb. 27, 1890.

(8) Mercy P. Holbrook, b. Nov. 2, 1891.

(8) Samuel Snow Holbrook, b. April 16, 1894.

(8) Roxana Sybil Holbrook, b. Sept. 16, 1895.

(8) Calista Caroline Holbrook, b. Dec. 14, 1897.

(6) Lettice Mariner, b. July 21, 1824; m., Dec. 27, 1859,
Samuel Woodward; farmer, who has always resided
in Brunswick, Me.; son of Ebenezer Woodward and
Mary Jordan.

(7) Mary Jordan Woodward, b. Nov. 4, 1860; d. May 7,
1888.

(6) Hannah W. Mariner, b. June 17, 1827; d. Feb. 19, 1900;
resided in Brunswick, Me.; m., Dec. 18, 1853, Albert J.

Linscott, b. April 25, 1830; farmer and ship carpenter; son of Abijah Linscott and Betsy Snow.

(7) Georgietta Linscott, b. May 19, 1856; m., Sept. 30, 1877, Robert Jordan.

(8) Mabel E. Jordan, b. March 7, 1878.

(8) Florence R. Jordan, b. Nov. 18, 1886.

(7) Lettice Alice Linscott, b. Feb. 3, 1859; resides Orono, Me.; m., Oct. 17, 1884, Alfred Clifford; carpenter for Maine Central Railroad.

(6) Lois P. Mariner, b. March 31, 1830; always resided in Brunswick, Me.; unm.

(6) Mary E. Mariner, b. Aug. 20, 1832; resides at Bath, Me.; m. (first), Jan. 6, 1852, Henry Scott, b. Freeport, Me., Jan. 10, 1835; ship carpenter; m. (second), William B. Scott.

Child of first husband.

(7) Fred B. Scott, b. Jan. 6, 1854; resides North Bath, Me.; ship joiner; m. (first), Sept. 10, 1878, Lucretia J. Oliver, who d. June 8, 1888; m. (second), June 26, 1889, Anna E. Marr.

Child of first wife:

(8) Ned Scott, b. June 1, 1881.

Child of second wife:

(8) Abbie May Scott, b. Jan. 18, 1891.

Children of second husband:

(7) Lon H. Scott, b. April 4, 1865; resides East Boston, Mass.; dealer in ship chandlery goods; m., March 29, 1889, Eugenie I. Pepper.

(8) Leon B. Scott, b. Jan. 9, 1890; d. Jan. 11, 1894.

(8) Henry M. Scott, b. April 8, 1892.

(8) Ralph B. Scott, b. Feb. 2, 1894.

(7) Susan M. Scott, b. March 25, 1873; resides in Boston, Mass.; unm.

CHAPTER V.

BENJAMIN THOMPSON OF NEW MEADOWS, BRUNSWICK, ME.,
AND HIS DESCENDANTS.

His line: (1) William Thompson of Dover, N. H.; (2)
James Thompson of Kittery, Me.

(3) Benjamin Thompson, b. Kittery, Me., Sept. 9, 1717. Of the
date of his death Ezekiel Thompson, his nephew, says in
his Day Book: "He died 50 years before 1831." One
says: "Benjamin Thompson of Georgetown, Me., purchased of Rebecca Moseley of Dorchester, Mass., the
daughter of Thomas Stevens, seventy-two and one-half
acres of land, stretching across the peninsular from, on the
one side, the waters of Stevens' or New Meadows River,
and on the other side bounded by the waters of Merrymeeting Bay, the latter being where the waters of the Androscoggin River meet, kiss, and mingle with the waters of the
Atlantic, the same as the young and gallant tars did with
the blooming maidens on the return voyage from the high
seas, and thus the place was called Merrymeeting Bay."
This was lot No. 50. "Benjamin Thompson lived at Brunswick and Bath, Me.," "near head of New Meadows River,
where Thomas and Adam Lemont now live." Constable
at Topsham, Me., Nov. 17, 1796, to Nov., 1798. Ezekiel
Thompson, m., Oct. 17, 1744, Abigail Philbrook of Bath,
Me., b. April 9, 1725; baptized at Bath, 1725. She was in
the fifth generation of the Philbrook line. Her father,
Jonathan Philbrook, was a prominent shipmaster. Mr.
Edwin Stockin of Watertown, Mass., gives her Philbrook
line: (1) Thomas Philbrook of Watertown, Mass., who
m. Elizabeth ———; (2) Thomas Philbrook, b. 1624; d.
Nov. 24, 1700; m., July 22, 1669, Hannah (White) French,
daughter of Edward French of Salisbury, Mass., who d.
1624; (3) William Philbrook, b. April 27, 1670; m., Oct.
10, 1869, Mercy Neal, daughter of Walter Neal of Green-
land, N. H.; (4) Jonathan Philbrook, b. 1694, of Green-
land, N. H.; m. Elizabeth, some give the wife's name as
Mann, or Marr; others say Springer.

Ezekiel Thompson in his Day Book, thus speaks of the family of Benjamin Thompson: "Jan. 24, 1831, I hear that Widow Sarah Bates died lately. She was the oldest daughter of my Uncle Benjamin Thompson. Her mother was Abigail Philbrook. After his decease she married old Mr. Tobias Ham, who is since dead (died Oct. 30, 1791) and was called 'Long Tom.' My Uncle Benjamin died about 50 years since. Benjamin Thompson had three sons—Jonathan, David and Alexander. The daughters were Sarah Bates, above mentioned, Abigail, who married Eben Coombs and 2nd Samuel Tebbetts, Esq., and moved to Ohio; Huldah married James Crawford and moved to Pa. Priscilla married Hugh Mulloy, and moved to Ohio; she was tne mother of Ebenezer Herrick's wife. Hannah married a Herrick and lived in Greene. One, whose name I have forgotten, married a Blossom and lived in Monmouth, Me. All these were worthy women and bore a good name."

Two lists of the children of Benjamin Thompson and Abigail Philbrook were furnished. One was from Miss Sarah A. Thompson of Topsham, Me., and the other from E. A. Parker, Esq., of Indianapolis, Ind., who secured them from the town clerk of North Georgetown, Me. Both lists harmonize perfectly.

*　　　*　　　*　　　*　　　*

(4) Sarah Thompson, b. Georgetown, Me., Aug. 21, 1746, and recorded Sept. 13, 1746; d. Jan., 1831; m. Hosea Bates.

*　　　*　　　*　　　*　　　*

(4) Jonathan Thompson, b. Georgetown, Me., July 1, 1748; recorded by Samuel Denny, town clerk, July 16, 1748; lived in Monmouth or Wales, Me.; m., Nov. 23, 1773, Martha Thompson[4], b. Aug. 16, 1751; d. 1849; daughter of Cornelius Thompson[3] and Hannah Smith.

　(5) Jonathan Thompson; m. Miss Jewell.

　(5) Benjamin Thompson; m. Annie Jewell.

　　(6) Jane Thompson.

　　(6) Abigail Thompson.

　　(6) Elbridge Thompson.

　　(6) Phineas Thompson.

　　(6) Corydon Thompson, b. Monmouth, Me., 1806; d. Cundy's Harbor, Me., March 6, 1887 (81y.); ship carpenter; m. Priscilla Curtis, b. Harpswell, Me., Jan. 3, 1809; d. Jan. 3, 1887 (78y.); daughter of James Curtis and Chiloa Raymond.

(7) William Curtis Thompson, b. June 1, 1832; d. June 12, 1901; resided Cundy's Harbor, Me.; joiner and fisherman; m., Nov. 15, 1869, Lydia Florence Watson, b. Gloucester, Mass., Sept. 13, 1840; resides Cundy's Harbor; daughter of Robert Watson and Betsy Younger.

  (8) Charles Wellington Thompson, b. June 15, 1870; unm.

  (8) Sanford Oscar Thompson, b. Nov. 12, 1871; d. April 26, 1889 (17y., 5d.).

  (8) Sidney Watson Thompson, b. Sept. 13, 1873; resides Cundy's Harbor, Me.; fisherman; m., Jan. 1, 1901, Harriet A. Barter, b. Portland, Me., Sept. 29, 1881; daughter of Henry Barter and Mary McKinnon.

    (9) Florence May Thompson, b. Dec. 1, 1900.

    (9) Madaline Thompson, b. Aug. 15, 1902.

    (9) Agnes Ellen Thompson, b. Oct. 6, 1904.

  (8) Albert Trufant Thompson, b. Sept. 9, 1875; unm.

  (8) Harmon Coombs Thompson, b. June 25, 1881; motorman.

(7) Elbridge Thompson, b. Sept. 21, 1834; m. (first), March 19, 1862, Mary Trufant, b. March 16, 1836; d. Sept. 5, 1864 (28y., 6m.); daughter of William Trufant and Lucy Rich; m. (second), Jan. 1, 1866, Alice L. Paul, b. Phippsburg, Me., Aug. 31, 1845; daughter of Moses Paul, b. June 24, 1803, and Lydia Jewell, b. March 11, 1806; d. Jan. 11, 1899.

Child of first wife:

  (8) Edith Thompson; d. Aug. 16, 1864 (2y., 2m.).

Children of second wife:

  (8) Ada E. Thompson, b. East Harpswell, Me., Oct. 15, 1867; resides Cundy's Harbor, Me.; m., Feb. 21, 1887, William Benson, b. Dec. 17, 1856; fisherman; son of Amasa Benson and Deborah Snow.

    (9) Charles L. Benson, b. April 16, 1888.

    (9) George H. Benson, b. Aug. 14, 1890.

    (9) Warren P. Benson, b. March 11, 1892.

    (9) Elbridge A. Benson, b. Jan. 28, 1894.

  (8) Frank L. Thompson, b. Feb. 26, 1869; clerk; resides Sebasco, Me.; m., Oct., 1894, Kate Percy, b. Phippsburg, Me., Sept. 12, 1868; daughter of James Percy and Charlotte Wonson.

(9) Harold P. Thompson, b. July, 1896.

(9) Percy F. Thompson, b. Jan., 1899.

(8) Julia Hatch Thompson, b. Sept. 26, 1871; resides
Cundy's Harbor, Me.; m., Dec. 5, 1895, Wilbur
Augustus Eastman, b. May 8, 1871; son of Levi
Eastman and Betsy Watson.

(9) Alice Bessie Eastman, b. April, 1898.

(9) John D. Eastman, b. July 21, 1901.

(7) Chiloa Ann Thompson, b. Aug. 7, 1836; d. Nov. 1,
1883 (46y., 6m.); m. Capt. Isaac N. Ridley, b.
July 31, 1832; d. Dec. 13, 1901.

(8) Frank Walter Ridley, b. April, 1861; resides
Phippsburg, Me.; merchant; m., Nov. 15, 1883,
Addie Gertrude Trufant, b. Nov. 2, 1865;
daughter of Albert T. Trufant and Sarah B.
Watson.

(9) Sadie Ethel Ridley, b. Nov. 2, 1885.

(9) Leida Dodge Ridley, b. June 2, 1886.

(9) Emma Frances Ridley, b. Aug. 1, 1888.

(9) Walter Everett Ridley, b. June 17, 1890.

(9) Bertie Gordon Ridley, b. Jan. 13, 1896.

(8) Will Harmon Ridley, b. Nov. 13, 1856; clerk in a
grocery store at Cundy's Harbor, Me.; m., Oct.
29, 1898, Isabella A. Holbrook, b. Cundy's Harbor, Sept. 29, 1879; daughter of Samuel H. Holbrook and Adaline Dresser.

(9) Jesse Holbrook Ridley, b. Nov. 25, 1905.

(8) Emma Jane Ridley, b. Cundy's Harbor, Me., June
12, 1858; m., July 14, 1879, Harmon Coombs, b.
Feb. 25, 1853; son of Samuel Coombs and Priscilla Rich.

(7) Joanna Thompson, b. Jan. 25, 1839; resides Bailey's
Island, Me.; m., Jan. 9, 1857, William Henry Sinnett, b. Bailey's Island, Jan. 28, 1836; followed
the sea; then a dealer in cottage lots; son of
Hugh Sinnett and Susannah Orr.

(8) Mary Jane Sinnett, b. May 1, 1860; d. Feb. 23,
1876; m., Dec. 23, 1875, George Albion Johnson,
b. March 10, 1852; son of Elisha Allen Johnson
and Almira Sprague.

(8) Everett Irving Sinnett, b. Sept. 6, 1863; resides
Bailey's Island, Me.; storekeeper; has held sev-
eral town offices; m., Oct. 10, 1885, Fannie M.
Bibber, b. Jan. 24, 1866; daughter of Andrew
Jackson Bibber and Lydia Maria Alexander.

(9) Nina B. Sinnett, b. April 18, 1887.

(9) Irving C. Sinnett, b. March 25, 1892.

(9) Henry Jackson Sinnett, b. Oct. 17, 1895.

(8) Olevia Sinnett, b. Feb., 1867; d. March 20, 1867.

(8) Laura Etta Sinnett, b. Sept. 19, 1873; resides Bailey's Island, Me.; m., May 2, 1888, Capt. George Bernard Johnson, b. Dec. 29, 1869; son of John Merrill Johnson and Almira Susan Johnson.

(9) Freddie Fairfield Johnson, b. Nov. 20, 1889.

(9) Leone Frye Johnson, b. June 30, 1891.

(9) Harry Elroy Johnson, b. March 16, 1894.

(9) Jesse Merrill Johnson, b. Feb. 22, 1904.

(7) Hannah Curtis Thompson, b. Dec. 3, 1841; resides Cundy's Harbor, Me.; m., July 1, 1865, George Washington Sinnett, b. Bailey's Island, Me., Oct. 14, 1839; son of James Sinnett and Hannah Sinnett.

(8) Sanford O. Sinnett, b. July 11, 1867; d. Sept. 16, 1887.

(8) Georgia Anna Sinnett, b. July 23, 1868; resides Cundy's Harbor, Me.; m., March 4, 1889, Capt. Bertrand Boarden Brigham, b. May 16, 1864.

(9) Nellie Hopkins Brigham, b. Oct. 23, 1891.

(9) Harvey Sinnett Brigham, b. Aug. 28, 1893.

(9) Asenath Mary Brigham, b. July 22, 1896.

(9) Edna Curtis Brigham, b. Aug. 8, 1899.

(9) Glendee Emerson Brigham.

(5) Phineas Thompson, m. ——— Allen.

(5) Aaron Thompson.

(5) Judith Thompson.

(5) Abigail Thompson.

(5) Priscilla Thompson; m. (first), Mr. Jewell; m. (second), Nathaniel Donnell of Lisbon, Me.

* * * * *

(4) Abigail Thompson, b. Georgetown, Me., Nov. 22, 1750; recorded by town clerk, 1750; d. Lindale, O., Aug. 13, 1839; m. (first), by Rev. Francis Winter of Bath, Me., Aug. 26, 1773, Ebenezer Coombs, b. Newburyport, Mass., Jan. 31, 1747; d. Oct. 5, 1783; m. (second), Dec. 22, 1788, Samuel Tebbetts, Esq., of Lisbon, Me., who d. in Lindale, O., May 2, 1824 (84y., 6m.); justice of the peace in Lisbon, Me., for many years; moved to Ohio in 1811.

Children of first husband:

154   THOMPSON GENEALOGY.

(5) Andrew Coombs, b. Sept. 2, 1775; d. Lindale, O., Oct.,
     1847; farmer and machinist; m. (first), Dec. 21, 1800,
     Susanah Jackson, b. Jan. 8, 1778; d. March 28, 1816;
     m. (second), Margaret Temple, who d. July 24, 1817;
     m. (third), March 16, 1819, Elizabeth Mitchell.
Children of first wife:
   (6) Abigail Coombs, b. in Maine, Oct. 4, 1801; d. Cincin-
        nati, O., Oct. 3, 1890; m. Amos Conklin, who d. May
        6, 1866; chairmaker and commission merchant.
     (7) Ten children. The son, Oliver Perry Conklin, had a
          fine family.
   (6) Elizabeth Mugridge Coombs, b. Maine, Aug. 12, 1803;
        d. Keokuk, Ia., April 14, 1879; m., May 6, 1827,
        Thomas Jefferson Hilton, b. New Hampshire, May 7,
        1804; d. 1887.
     (7) Child; d. in infancy.
     (7) George Oliver Hilton, b. Clermont County, O., May
          14, 1828; resides San Diego, Cal.; nurseryman and
          fruit grower; m., Jan. 18, 1855, May Elizabeth
          Luce, b. Lancaster, N. Y., Nov. 11, 1832.
       (8) George Frederick Hilton, b. May 2, 1857; d. July
            9, 1900; admitted to the bar; then a very suc-
            cessful Baptist minister in Duluth, Minn., Illi-
            nois, etc.
       (8) Frank Edwin Hilton, b. March 15, 1858; lumber
            merchant at Campbell, Mo.; m., June 17, 1886,
            in Cincinnati, O., Georgie Elstner.
         (9) Elstner Hilton, b. April 9, 1887.
         (9) Franklin Howard Hilton, b. April 26, 1889.
         (9) Harold Henry Hilton, b. April 9, 1892.
         (9) Miriam Hilton, b. Oct. 5, 1899.
       (8) Elizabeth Hilton, b. April 19, 1861.
       (8) Robert Anderson Hilton, b. April 19, 1861; a suc-
            cessful doctor in Chicago, Ill.; m., Jan. 31, 1899,
            Mrs. Etta (Smith) Reed; no children.
       (8) May S. Hilton, b. Dec. 15, 1866.
       (8) Four other children; d. in infancy.
   (6) Andrew Coombs, Jr., b. Dec. 24, 1805; d. May 26,
        1864; farmer and merchant, Lindale, O.; m., March
        29, 1832, Kitty Ann Shannon.
     (7) Maria S. Coombs, b. Sept. 21, 1833; d. Oct. 30, 1880;
          m. Dr. Joseph S. Galloway.
       (8) Edna Maria Galloway; m. E. T. Buffum.
         (9) Howard Buffum.

(9) Stanley Buffum.

(9) Roger Buffum.

(8) James Coombs Galloway; resides Port Allegheny, Pa.

(7) Albert B. Coombs, b. July 23, 1836; killed at the second battle of Bull Run.

(7) Joseph P. Coombs, b. Oct. 12, 1837; d. May 8, 1863; teacher, and brave soldier in the Civil War.

(7) William Cary Coombs, b. Aug. 26, 1840; resides Lindale, O.; farmer; served in the Civil War; m. (first), Mary M. McDonald; m. (second), Sarah A. Cobley.

Children of first wife:

(8) Bertha Coombs; m. George M. Burns.

(9) Fred D. Burns, b. Sept. 6, 1889.

(8) Oliver Andrew Coombs, b. Jan. 21, 1870; d. 1870.

Children of second wife:

(8) Albert Newton Coombs.

(8) Verner Leslie Coombs.

(7) Oliver Coombs, b. Nov. 28, 1843; d. July 26, 1867; a brave soldier in the Civil War.

(6) Joseph Jackson Coombs, b. Oct. 27, 1810.

(7) Mrs. Abbie (Coombs) Getchell, Dorchester, Mass.

(6) Martha Robinson Coombs; m. Rufus Hubbard; a merchant.

(7) Rev. Andrew Coombs Hubbard, b. Lindale, O., Jan. 23, 1839; a successful Baptist minister; m., Jan. 1, 1861, Abby Maria Melliken.

(8) Martha Clement Hubbard, b. Feb. 16, 1862; m. J. A. Skinner of Holyoke, Mass.

(8) Harry Gregory Hubbard, b. April 24, 1864.

(8) Francis Wayland Hubbard, b. Dec. 6, 1866; resides St. Louis, Mo.; m., 1897, May E. Flather.

(9) Sophia Hubbard.

Children of third wife:

(6) Susanna Jackson Coombs, b. May 6, 1820; d. July 14, 1849; m. Rev. William Cox.

(7) Harvey Coombs Cox; drowned while in United States naval service.

(6) Thomas Mitchell Coombs, b. Jan. 18, 1823; d. in California in 1856.

(5) Cynthia Coombs, b. May 26, 1778; m. Silas Dalie.

(5) Ebenezer Coombs, Jr., b. June 30, 1782; d. Feb. 6, 1792.

*   *   *   *   *

(4) Huldah Thompson, b. Georgetown, Me., Aug. 24, 1752; birth recorded by Georgetown town clerk, Sept. 5, 1752; m. James Crawford and moved to Pennsylvania.

*   *   *   *   *

(4) Priscilla Thompson, b. Georgetown, Me., May 13, 1754; birth recorded by the town clerk, Sept. 10, 1754; she d. New Richmond, O., April 4, 1819; marriage intention recorded at Georgetown, Me., May 13, 1776; date of marriage June 25, 1776, to Hugh Mulloy, b. Albany N. Y., Dec. 4, 1751; d. New Richmond, O., July 11, 1845 (94th y.). (The full records of the children and descendants are given in Chapter VI.)

*   *   *   *   *

(4) David Thompson, b. Georgetown, Me., March 26, 1756; recorded by Samuel Denny, town clerk, April 7, 1756; resided in Topsham, Me. "He was killed at the battle of Monmouth in the Revolutionary War."

*   *   *   *   *

(4) Alexander Thompson, b. Georgetown, Me., May 7, 1758; recorded July 7, 1758; d. at Amelia, O., Oct., 1830. About 1815 he moved to Amelia, O., arriving there in the fall; he always made his home in that town, and is buried in the family cemetery near there.

"He made his way in a rough cart over the mountain roads to Pittsburg, Pa. He and his family went down the Ohio River on a raft of logs which they made. In 1827, when he was nearly 70 years old, he built a church. It was dedicated to God alone; to the free worship of every people who there wished to learn of God. It did not belong to any denomination; it was not built for any sect; it was not erected to further his opinions, or any man's opinions about God and religion. No intermediary of saint or book, or tradition, was to come between the devout soul and the God of its worship. It was not even called a church of the Christian religion, but free for every people to worship God in. Climbing upon the frame of this new meeting house as it neared completion, Alexander Thompson dedicated it with these words: "Here stands a fine frame, and it should have a good name. It shall be called Republican—free for all denominations to worship God in.' And nearly every denomination in that part of Ohio at some time worshipped in the Republican Meeting House, including

Jews and Mormons. Among the denominations which used the church with some regularity in those early days were Christians, Universalists, Protestant Methodists and Presbyterians. In it was held a memorable debate, said to have been of several weeks' duration, between Hon David Fisher, a neighbor of Mr. Thompson, and a Universalist missionary."

M. (first), about 1778, Hannah Baker, b. Falmoutn, Me., Feb. 3, 1754; d. about May, 1821; daughter of Capt. Elisha Baker and Sarah Wilson of Monmouth, Me. Some report that her father served in King Philip's War; others say such service was rendered by her grandfather, Captain Wilson; m. (second), Widow Cushman, who m. as her third husband, Mr. Thomas and moved to Brown County, O; no children.

Children of first wife:

(5) Olive Thompson; d. Porter's Landing, Freeport, Me., Sept. 15, 1871 (93y.); m., Feb. 7, 1801, Jeremiah Coffin of North Yarmouth, Me.; farmer; always lived at Porter's Landing, Freeport, Me.

(6) Olive Coffin, b. Dec. 30, 1801; d. 1889; m. Capt. George B. Randall, b. Freeport, Me., 1800; d. 1883.

(7) Gen. George W. Randall, b. Freeport, Me., Aug. 13, 1827; d. May 20, 1897; m. Martha L. Armstrong.

(8) Blanche Randall, b. June 3, 1859.

(8) Martha Lee Randall, b. June 2, 1862.

(7) Archella Randall, b. March 24, 1829; d. Sept. 30, 1831.

(7) Electrus Gancello Randall, b. 1832. "When a young man he went to California and remained there; m. there, and his wife now resides in Mass."

(8) Minnie Randall.

(8) Katie Randall.

(8) Platt Randall.

(7) Archella Helen Randall, b. Freeport, Me., March 28, 1833; m., 1851, Andrew Litchfield.

(8) Leonora Litchfield, b. Sept., 1852.

(8) Eugenia A. Litchfield, b. 1857.

(8) Lemont Litchfield.

(7) Charlotte Randall, b. Freeport, Me., March 6, 1835; m., June 1, 1856, William Anderson, b. Freeport, Me., Jan. 22, 1834; d. Oct. 17, 1892 (62y.); studied in Webster (Me.) common schools; master painter.

(8) William Norwood Anderson, b. Dec. 9, 1857; re-

sides Freeport, Me.; studied in schools of Auburn and Freeport, Me.; farmer and master painter; m., Nov. 16, 1887, Maggie Lydia Parker, b. Phillips, Me., Sept. 6, 1851; studied in Farmington (Me.) schools; daughter of Joseph W. Parker and Harriet Toothaker.

  (9) Oscar Norwood Anderson, b. Nov. 8, 1888; educated in North Yarmouth (Me.) Academy.

  (9) Leslie Garland Anderson, b. Nov. 16, 1889.

(8) H. Delmont Anderson, b. Feb. 26, 1859; resides Freeport, Me.; m., April 26, 1885, Hattie L. Randall.

  (9) Lousia Georgianna Anderson, b. Sept. 1; m., June 26, 1901, Charles Beck Mallett.

(7) Rosilla Randall, b. March 2, 1837; d. Aug. 24, 1838.

(7) Ansil N. Coffin Randall, b. Aug. 31, 1841; d. Sept. 17, 1843.

(7) Roselia Coffin Randall, b. Nov. 7, 1839; m., 1874, Emore Townsend; d. 1894.

  (8) Archelina E. Townsend, b. Litchfield, Me., July 16, 1875.

(6) Franklin Coffin, b. Sept. 5; d. Oct. 17, 1804 (1y).

(6) Roxilania Coffin, b. May 28, 1805; d. Oct. 14, 1806 (14m.).

(6) Louisa Coffin, b. July 20, 1807; d. Oct. 1, 1893; resided Freeport, Me.; m. Thomas Chase, b. Dec. 23, 1801; d. Jan. 27, 1883.

  (7) Thomas Franklin Chase, b. Oct. 20, 1826; d. Freeport, Me., Jan. 13, 1895.

  (7) Quincy Acastus Chase, b. Nov. 20, 1830; resides 2065 Webster Street, Oakland, Cal.

  (7) William Ira Chase, b. Jan. 25, 1832; resides Freeport, Me.

  (7) Jere Ansyl Chase, b. April 14, 1835; resides Freeport, Me.

  (7) Edward Joseph Chase, b. Oct. 9, 1838; resides Freeport, Me.

  (7) Charles Marshall Staples Chase, b. Feb. 19, 1843; resides Freeport, Me.

  (7) Andrew Kohler Chase, b. Dec. 18, 1850; d. March 5, 1885.

(6) Jeremiah Thomas Coffin, b. Aug. 28, 1809; d. June 28, 1842 (33y.); resided Pownal, Me.; m., Dec. 30, 1830, Mary Lunt; daughter of Judah Lunt and Elizabeth Brewer.

(7) Ira Stanciles Coffin, b. Freeport, Me., March 25,
    1832; d. Jan. 19, 1900; lived at Little River, Me.,
    for a few years; carpenter; also a photographer
    for some time; m., May 9, 1871, Helen Tracey
    Cornish, b. Dec. 7, 1849; educated in Little River
    (Me.) schools; daughter of John Cornish and
    Hannah Tracey.

   (8) Willis Coffin, b. Dec. 26, 1873; m., Sept. 5, 1900,
       Anna Louisa Brewer.

   (8) George Everett Coffin, b. Feb. 28, 1877; m., Sept.
       10, 1902, Lucretia West.

      (9) Elizabeth Cornish Coffin, b. July 2, 1903.

   (8) Andrew Kohler Coffin, b. Dec. 20, 1885.

(7) Olive Elizabeth Coffin; m. ——— Coombs.

(7) Emery Oscar Coffin, b. Freeport, Me., May 1, 1836;
    address, Freeport, Me., R. F. D. No. 4, box 26; has
    lived at Bath, Minot, Winthrop and Freeport, Me.;
    for some twenty years a photographer; now on a
    farm; m., Nov. 19, 1857, Louisa Jane Frazier, b.
    Dartmouth, N. S., June 1, 1840; daughter of Jacob
    Frazier, of a good old Scotch family; she lived
    in Nova Scotia till eight years old, then in East-
    port, Bath, etc.

   (8) Boy; d. at birth.

   (8) Boy; d. at birth.

   (8) Louisa Evira Coffin, b. April 13, 1863; d. Port-
       land, Me., Dec. 28, 1895 (32y., 8m., 14d.); buried
       at Freeport Me.; studied in Winthrop (Me.)
       schools; m., Aug. 10, 1880, Emery S. Adell.

      (9) Viola Leslie Adell, b. Sept. 3, 1889.

      (9) Emerald Evvira Adell, b. May 14, 1890.

   (8) Irving B. Coffin, b. May 27, 1865; d. Philadelphia,
       Pa., May 6, 1884 (18y., 11m., 9d.); graduated at
       Winthrop (Me.) High School; employed in
       stamping oilcloth.

   (8) Iola Eudell Coffin, b. Feb. 10, 1868; studied in Win-
       throp (Me.) High School; resides Freeport, Me.;
       m., April 20, 1889, Linwood E. Varney.

      (9) Linwood Irving Varney, b. Oct. 9, 1889.

      (9) Nellie Hazel Varney, b. March 4, 1891.

      (9) Joseph Emery Varney, b. Sept 11, 1892.

      (9) Cyral Blanchard Varney, b. March 1, 1895.

      (9) Louise Eunice Varney, b. April 14, 1897.

      (9) Gerald Ernest Varney, b. June 20, 1898.

    (9) Iola Christine Varney, b. Dec. 18, 1900.

    (9) Charles Adell Varney, b. May 19, 1902.

    (9) John Frederick Varney, b. May 7, 1904.

    (9) Vivia Varney, b. March 25, 1905; d. April 20, 1905.

    (9) Edna Nathalie Varney, b. March 17, 1906.

  (8) Archie Leland Coffin, b. March 1, 1871; resides Freeport, Me., R. F. D. No. 4; m., Nov. 28, 1901, Mary Graves.

  (8) Violet Alma Coffin, b. Feb. 24, 1873; resides at Harpswell Center, Me.; m., March 18, 1896, Eugene Coffin Bibber[5], b. July 29, 1862.

    (9) Marguerite Avice Bibber, b. Oct. 14, 1896.

    (9) Eugene Coffin Bibber, b. Jan. 5, 1898.

    (9) Emery Oscar Bibber, b. Dec. 11, 1899; d. March 6, 1900 (2m., 23d.).

    (9) Emery Oscar Bibber, b. Nov. 10, 1902.

    (9) Violet Adelaide Bibber, b. May 26, 1905.

  (8) Edwina Elice Coffin, b. May 26, 1878; studied in Freeport and Portland, Me.; resides Freeport, Me., m., May 9, 1900, Daniel P. Allen.

    (9) Elvira Louise Allen, b. Aug. 19, 1901.

    (9) Edwina Viola Allen, b. Oct. 15, 1903.

    (9) Agnes Allen, b. April 17, 1905.

(7) Alice Coffin, b. 1838.

(7) Henry Coffin; d. at 2 years.

(7) Archelia Ann Coffin; d. at one year.

(6) Roxana Coffin, b. Dec. 17, 1811; d. Jan. 2, 1838 (25y.).

(6) Ira Preble Coffin, b. March 8, 1814; d. Dec. 9, 1814 (9m.).

(6) Constant Converse Coffin, b. Nov. 10, 1816; d. Oct. 7, 1881; always lived Porter's Landing, Freeport, Me.; farmer; changed his name to Constant Converse when he was a young man; m., Sept. 6, 1846, Susan Maria Coffin, b. Freeport, Me., 1825; d. Sept. 25, 1900; daughter of David Coffin and Jane Welch.

  (7) Mary Susan Converse, b. June 19, 1847; m. Charles C. Soule; resides Calumet Street, Peabody, Mass.

  (7) David G. Converse, b. April 4, 1849.

  (7) Lorana J. Converse, b. Nov. 15, 1851.

  (7) Eunice Maria Converse, b. Freeport, Me., Oct. 2, 1856; resides Peabody, Mass.; lived Freeport and Portland, Me., and Beverly, Mass.; m., Dec. 25, 1874, David Franklin Randall, b. Freeport, Me., Jan.

4, 1853; educated in Mast Landing and Freeport
schools; barber; son of Daniel Franklin Randall
and Rebecca Sylvester.

(8) Herman Ellsworth Randall, b. Portland, Me.;
barber at Little's Lane, Peabody, Mass.; m.
Miss P. Ferren.

(8) Ethel Belle Randall, b. April 9, 1885; graduated
from Peabody (Mass.) High School.

(8) Pearl Elwin Randall, b. Nov. 13, 1889; studied in
Peabody (Mass.) High School.

(8) Bessie May Randall, b. July 15, 1891.

(8) Ray Franklin Randall, b. Oct. 15, 1895.

(7) John Dennison (adopted son), b. March 15, 1842.

(7) Sarah Emma Converse; d. at one year.

(7) Edith Converse; d. at one year.

(7) Ethel Converse; d. at two weeks.

(7) Albra Converse.

(6) Cordelia Arabine Coffin, b. June 1, 1818; d. Nov. 27,
1894 (76y., 5m., 27d.); m. Andrew Kohler and went
to California.

(7) One daughter, who d. when she was about five years
old.

(6) Ansel Baker Coffin, b. March 17, 1821; d. Jan., 1903
(82y.); m., Oct. 26, 1847, Rhoda Coombs, b. Liverpool, N. S., June 16, 1825; d. Aug. 27, 1857.

(7) Otis Learned Coffin, b. Feb. 4, 1844; m. Hattie
Almira Harrington, b. Cushing's Island, Me , June
28, 1847.

(8) Ernest Linwood Coffin, b. Freeport, Me., Jan. 17,
1866; d. May 26, 1877.

(8) Arthur Bailey Coffin, b. Freeport, Me., May 28,
1867.

(8) Lillian Delnoria Coffin, b. Freeport, Me., Jan. 3,
1871; resides Freeport, Me.; m. James E. Gettings of Massachusetts.

(9) Stella Gettings, b. Oakland, Cal.

(9) Mildred Adelia Gettings, b. Oakland, Cal.

(9) Cordelia Arabine Gettings, b. Oakland, Cal.

(8) Wellington Bennett Coffin, b. Freeport, Me., June
15, 1873; went to California; m. Marcia Davis.

(9) Ernest L. Coffin.

(8) Rose O. Coffin, b. Freeport, Me., May 29, 1874.

(8) Violet Arabine Coffin, b. Freeport, Me., Nov. 25,
1881; m. Lewis Munroe of Illinois.

   (7) Marcellus Kohler, b. Freeport, Me., May 28, 1848; m.
      Sophia Harabush, b. Vienna, Austria, March 21,
      1861; d. March 15, 1899.

   (7) Olive Arobine Coffin, b. Freeport, Me., April 1, 1851;
      m., Portland, Me., by Rev. A. K. P. Small, Aug. 22,
      1869, Andrew Bradley, b. Portland, Me., Aug. 4,
      1845.

     (8) William Ansyl Bradley, b. Portland, Me., Dec. 14,
        1871; m., at South Gardiner, Me., June 19, 1895,
        Frances Collins, b. South Gardiner, Me., 1868.

      (9) Ina Louise Collins, b. South Gardiner, Me., Nov.
         22, 1900.

     (8) Charles Henry Bradley, b. Portland, Me., Jan. 11,
        1874; d. Sept. 22, 1895.

     (8) Leonard Andrew Bradley, b. Freeport, Me., Aug.
        15, 1880.

     (8) Clifford Carrol Bradley, b. Freeport, Me., June
        22, 1882.

     (8) Melvin Albion Bradley, b. Freeport, Me., Jan. 22,
        1883; d. March 16, 1887.

     (8) Bertha Louise Bradley, b. Freeport, Me., Jan. 24,
        1888.

     (8) Kohler Coffin Bradley, b. April 14, 1894.

   (7) Susan Louise Roxiana Coffin.

(5) Rev. David Thompson, b. 1780; d. in Jennings County,
    Ind., 1861; m., in Maine, April 18, 1804, Mary Reed
    of Freeport, Me.

   (6) Rev. David Thompson, b. 1806; d. Van Buren County,
     Ia., 1878; m. Miss Layrock.

    (7) Rev. David Thompson.

    (7) William Thompson; m. ——— Bingaman.

    (7) George Thompson.

    (7) Daughter, m. Mr. Church.

   (6) William Reed Thompson, b. April 30, 1808; m. Ruth
     Paine.

    (7) Origen Thompson.

   (6) Horatio Nelson Thompson, b. Dec. 15, 1810.

   (6) Mary Ann Thompson, b. Feb. 3, 1812; m. Mr. Grisson.

   (6) Hannah Thompson, b. Nov. 22, 1814; m. ——— Strong.

   (6) Jane Thompson, b. Feb. 18, 1817; m. James Donham,
     brother of Mary Ann Donham, who m. Alexander
     Thompson.

   (6) Elbridge Thompson, b. June 14, 1820; d. in Kansas,
     1899.

(6) Lewis Thompson, b. April 21, 1823.

(5) Jeremiah Thompson; d. young.

(5) Charlotte Thompson; m., Oct. 30, 1808, Edward Welch, b. Monmouth, Me., April 24, 1782; he was a farmer at Monmouth, Me.; son of John Welch and Elizabeth Baker. "When Elizabeth (Baker) Welch was 96 years old she had her second sight and second set of teeth."

(6) Franklin Otis Welch, b. April 1, 1810; d. April 20, 1869; he was a druggist at Albany, Ga.; m. (first), Hannah Gookin of Saco, Me., daughter of John Gookin; m. (second), Phœbe Huntington of Pine Plains, N. J.

   (7) One child; d. young.

   (7) Franklin O. Welch.

   (7) Phœbe Welch.

   (7) Fannie Welch; d. at 14 years.

(6) Emery Welch, b. Sept. 22, 1811 (or 1813); d. 1846; m. Lydia Fairbanks of Boston, Mass.

   (7) Henry E. Welch, b. 1841; d. Albany, Ga., 1877; unm.

   (7) Elizabeth Welch, b. 1843; m. Fred Newton.

    (8) Agnes Newton; dead.

    (8) Ernestine Newton; d. in infancy.

(6) John Baker Welch, b. Monmouth, Me., May 2, 1814; d. March 4, 1888; buried at Oak Park, Ill.; m. Mary Davis of Rockport, Mass., b. April 28, 1815; d. Feb. 27, 1881; son of Capt. John Davis (keeper of the Straits Mouth Light many years) and Esther Carter. "John Baker Welch was a cabinet maker. In 1855 he moved to Lake Village, now Lakeport, N. H. In 1856 he moved to Janesville, Wis. In 1872 moved to Vineland, N. J. He was a man of fine character; kind and loving in his ways."

   (7) Mary Eliza Welch, b. Monmouth, Me., June 11, 1840; lived Janesville, Wis.; m., Dec. 1, 1859, Nathaniel Dwight Crosby, b. Fredonia, N. Y., Jan. 18, 1836; address, Oak Park, Ill.; son of Nathaniel Crosby and Sarah Leonard.

    (8) Bessie E. Crosby, b. Wisconsin, Feb. 4, 1855; resides Oak Park, Ill.

    (8) Laura E. Crosby, b. Jan. 23, 1868; d. Janesville, Wis., Aug. 7, 1870.

   (7) Delia Emerson Welch, b. Monmouth, Me., Nov. 14, 1841; d. Albany, Ga., Oct. 4, 1855.

   (7) Laura Esther Welch, b. April 25, 1843; d. Feb. 9,

1881; lived Janesville and Monroe, Wis.; m. Andrew S. Douglas, a prominent lawyer of Monroe,
Wis.; he was mayor of Monroe, where he still resides with his second wife.

(8) Arthur Douglas; m. and lives Milwaukee, Wis.

(8) Malcolm C. Douglas.

(8) Helen Douglas; resides Monroe, Wis.

(7) Edward Franklin Welch, b. Monmouth, Me., July
14, 1845; d. River Forest, Ill., July 10, 1901; he
was a bank clerk at Janesville, Wis.; m., Aug. 25,
1868, Elizabeth Hodge, b. Colchester, Vt., Jan. 3,
1848; she resides at 1410 Gerard Avenue, Washington, D. C.; she was the daughter of Rev. Marvin G. Hodge, a very prominent and much beloved
Baptist minister, and her mother was Harriet Kel-
lam of Irasburg, Vt.; the father was instrumental
in the building of the Hanson Place Baptist
Church at Brooklyn, N. Y. Mrs. Edward Franklin Welch is the seventh generation from John
Hodge, b. 1643, who m. Susanna Denslow. (See
Hodge Genealogy, by Col. O. G. Hodge, 1096 Eu-
clid Avenue, Cleveland, O.)

(8) Raymond Franklin Welch, b. Janesville, Wis.,
Aug. 18, 1869; in 1885 he went to New York
City and has resided there ever since; retail
druggist; care of J. Milhans' Son, druggist,
corner Broadway and Courtland streets; unm.;
May 1, 1898, he enlisted in the Spanish-American War, naval department, with title of junior
medical officer, having charge of the drugs and
physicians' supplies on the steamer; he was stationed on the receiving ship *Vernon* for about a
month and then transferred to the *Hannibal*,
which was a supply boat, and he went with it
to the fleets near Cuba and Porto Rico; he enlisted for a year, but received an honorable discharge Oct. 18, 1898.

(8) Marvin John Welch, b. Janesville, Wis., March 20,
1872; address, 277 Park Avenue, River Forest,
Ill.; in 1891 he went to reside in Milwaukee,
Wis.; during the summer of 1893 he was official
court reporter in Rhinelander, Wis.; went to
Chicago in Jan., 1894, and was private secretary
for three years to F. J. V. Skiff, director of the

Field Columbian Museum; is now assistant purchasing agent with the American Cereal Company, 1341 Monadnock Block, Chicago, and has been there nearly four years; unm.

(8) Harold Cameron Welch, b. Janesville, Wis., Aug. 15, 1875; resided in Kalamazoo, Mich., for a year, and then went to Chicago, in 1896; electrician and machinist, and was connected with the Western Electric Company of Chicago for about three years; in April, 1900, he went to Brooklyn, Wis.

(7) Arthur E. Welch, b. Sept. 28, 1846; resides Marinette, Wis.; unm.; in 1856 he went to Janesville, Wis., with his parents; in New York City he was connected with a large book concern for a number of years; he has lived in Philadelphia, California and Milwaukee.

(7) Reuel Howard Welch, b. May 22, 1849; d. Jan. 19, 1901; enlisted as a drummer boy in the Civil War and served several years; he was quite a prominent citizen of St. Louis, Mo., and was in a book publishing house; m. Mattie Rice; address of the family, 4012 Morgan Street, St. Louis, Mo.

(8) Lollie Welch.

(8) Reuel Welch, Jr.

(7) John Leonard Welch, b. Dec. 13, 1852; d. Oct. 19, 1901; resided at Elgin, Ill., for awhile; m., Nov. 24, 1880, Elizabeth Katherine Case, b. Wood Haven, Long Island, N. Y., July 5, 1855; daughter of Conrad Case and Eva Kinsley; his address, 533 Garden Street, Kenosha, Wis.

(8) Everett G. Welch, b. Vineland, N. J., Oct. 4, 1881.

(8) John Baker Welch, b. Vineland, N. J., Oct. 2, 1884; d. Oct. 31, 1887.

(8) Sarah L. Welch, b. Vineland, N. J., June 22, 1886; d. July 3, 1887.

(8) Mary Eva Welch, b. Elgin, Ill., June 24, 1888.

(8) Howard F. Welch, b. Aug. 15, 1889.

(8) Alvah L. Welch, b. May 23, 1891.

(8) Willard C. Welch, b. Elgin, Ill., March 18, 1899.

(7) James Henry Welch, b. Lake Village, N. H., May 2, 1856; resides 827 Cass Street, Milwaukee, Wis.; court reporter in Milwaukee, Wis., 1877–'82; member of the State Assembly, 1897–'99; 1906, official

court stenographer; educated in the public schools of Vineland, N. J.; lived in Vineland, N. J., Monroe, Wis., Janesville, Wis., Milwaukee; m., April 22, 1879, Kate Sophia Andrews, b. June 12, 1836; educated in Gardiner (Me.) High School; daughter of Greenleaf Andrews and Charlotte Elizabeth Welch.

(8) Carrie Louise Welch, b. Sept. 4, 1880; graduated from Milwaukee (Wis.) schools and from State Normal School; unm.

(8) Bessie Eliza Welch, b. Nov. 14, 1883; educated in Milwaukee schools and State Normal School.

(8) Edith Welch, b. Sept. 27, 1884; d. Sept. 9, 1901.

(8) Arthur Welch, b. May 27, 1887; educated in Milwaukee schools.

(6) Charlotte Elizabeth Welch, b. Monmouth, Me., May 19, 1818; lived in Monmouth, Me., 26 years, then went to Albany, Ga.; m. there in 1845; then went to New Orleans, La., and returned to Albany, Ga., for three years; then lived seven years in Gardiner, Me.; lived in Vineland, N. J., with her brother, John Welch, for seven years, then went to Milwaukee, Wis.; m., at Albany, Ga., 1845; Capt. Greenleaf Andrews, b. Monmouth, Me., June, 1819; d. Kissimer Valley, Fla., June 27, 1842; steamer captain; son of Arthur Andrews and Olive Welch.

(7) Edward Andrews, b. Dec. 25, 1847; d. March 21, 1848.

(7) Howard Andrews, b. Dec. 13, 1848; d. Oct. 25, 1849.

(7) Walter Andrews, b. Oct. 1, 1850; d. April 18, 1851.

(7) Baxter Andrews, b. Nov. 20, 1854; d. Aug. 25, 1855.

(7) Kate Sophia Andrews, b. June 12, 1856; resides 827 Cass Street, Milwaukee, Wis.; m. Charles Henry Welch. (See records above.)

(6) William Welch, b. April 19, 1820; d. 1854; m. Elizabeth Baker Welch of Monmouth, Me.; lived near Albany, Ga.; only child d. young.

(6) Sophia Welch, b. Monmouth, Me., April 20, 1822; resides San Diego, Cal.; resided Winthrop, Me.; lived San Francisco, Cal., Nov., 1851, to 1857, save a few months spent in Sacramento; to Watsonville for a few months; spent six years in Lower California and Mexico; over 21 years in Spring Valley, four miles from San Diego, Cal.; m. (first), March 21,

1843, Edward Moody, b. Monmouth, Me., July 9, 1820; d. Boston, Mass., Oct., 1851; farmer; m. (second), Dec. 21, 1852, Rufus King Porter, b. Cambridgeport, Mass., Aug. 9, 1820; farmer; engaged in mining and salt works in Lower California and Mexico; one year in a hotel at San Pedro; for many years raising stock and farming at Spring Valley, San Diego, Cal; son of Rufus King and Eunice Twombly.

Child of first husband:

(7) Marietta Moody, b. Monmouth, Me., April 9, 1848; re-rides San Diego, Cal; m., Sept. 29, 1864, Franklin Augustus Gregory.

(8) Marietta Gregory, b. San Diego, Cal., Nov. 15, 1867; m., Nov. 15, 1886, James F. Jones, b. Covington, Ind., 1856; contractor; son of Alfred White Jones and Sybil Asburn.

(9) Helen Jones, b. Sept. 27, 1887.

(9) Clyde Rufus Jones, b. Aug. 15, 1893.

(9) Clifford White Jones, b. Feb. 10, 1895.

(9) Boy and girl; died.

(8) Anginette Gregory, b. May 30, 1870; resides San Diego, Cal.; m., Dec. 14, 1901, Guy Little; son of E. Little and E. T. Miller.

(8) Irena B. Gregory, b. Nov. 2, 1887; resides San Diego, Cal.

Child of first husband:

(7) Rufina Augusta Porter, b. Nov. 23, 1854; resides San Diego, Cal.; m., Oct. 16, 1873, Charles S. Crosby of Billerica, Mass., b. Sept. 6, 1848; real estate dealer; son of John Crosby and Isabella.

(8) Lottie May Crosby, b. June 23, 1874; m. April 4, 1903, Frank D. W. Putnam; resides San Diego, Cal.

(8) Frederic Arthur Crosby, b. June 3, 1875; graduated at Normal School and Leland Stanford University; physical secretary of Y. M. C. A. in Pennsylvania; m., at Harrisburg, Pa., June 26, 1903, Frances S. Taylor; resides 351 So. Thirteenth Street, Harrisburg, Pa.

(8) Ethel Crosby, b. May 4, 1886; graduated from the Normal School; resides San Diego, Cal.

(8) Oliver Crosby, b. Sept. 2, 1893; graduated from the Normal School; resides San Diego, Cal.

(6) Catherine Herrick Welch, b. Monmouth, Me., Dec. 20, 1824; d. July, 1836; m. Hazard Swinney.

(7) Lizzie Swinney, b. 1855; trained musician in New York City.

(6) Leonard Edward Welch, b. Monmouth, Me., Jan. 1, 1829; resides Albany, Ga.; real estate business and insurance, with office in the First National Bank. "I have been a druggist most of my life; I have been superintendent of the schools of this, Dougherty County, most of the time since 1871." He moved to Albany, Ga., March 18, 1847; m., July 14, 1860, Laura Isabel Spencer, b. Sept. 25, 1839; daughter of John Spencer of New York.

(7) Leonard Edward Welch, Jr., b. March 13, 1866; doctor in Albany, Ga.

(7) Agnes T. Welch, b. March 20, 1868; m. Solomon Hoge of Macon, Ga., where she now resides; the husband is a druggist.

(8) Solomon Hoge, Jr., b. April 27, 1890.

(8) Agnes F. Hoge, b. July 6, 1892.

(8) Leonard Welch Hoge, b. Feb. 20, 1896.

(8) Florence Hoge, b. July 30, 1901.

(5) Alexander Philbrook Thompson; lived Amelia and Bethel, O.; m. (first), Betsy Chase; m. (second), Mary Ann Donham.

Children of first wife:

(6) Lorena Thompson; m. Hiram Wheeler.

(7) Elizabeth Wheeler, m. Nelson Lythe.

(8) Edward Lythe.

(8) Albert Lythe.

(8) Clara Lythe.

(8) Orrin Lythe.

(8) Harry Lythe.

(8) Bert Lythe.

(7) John Albert Wheeler.

(7) Jane Wheeler; m. B. Frank Wylie.

(7) Olive Wheeler; m. Ben P. Daily.

(6) Orren Thompson; d. in Illinois.

(7) Only son, David Thompson; m. Molly Lutz.

(6) Roxanna Thompson; m. William Armstrong.

*   *   *   *   *

(5) Rachel Thompson, b. Nov. 3, 1789; d. June 16, 1847; m., Feb. 11, 1813, Otis Andrews of Wales, Me., b. Oct. 17, 1788; d. March 13, 1873; a prosperous farmer and in-

fluential man; son of John Andrews and Olive Baker; lived in Monmouth, Me.

(6) Everett Andrews, b. March 22, 1814; d. July 15, 1817.

(6) Harriet Elizabeth Andrews, b. May 21, 1816; d. Jan. 3, 1887; resided Monmouth, Me.

(6) Sophia Ann Andrews, b. June 26, 1818; d. Dec. 7, 1895; m., Dec. 12, 1841, Walter Olney Hooker, b. Feb. 17, 1818; d. Feb. 7, 1887; son of Reverius Hooker and Huldah Cannon; resided Gardiner, Me.

(7) Otis Everett Hooker, b. Oct. 31, 1842; m., Nov. 23, 1886, Margaret Marson, b. Dec. 13, 1849; daughter of Capt. George Marson and Hannah Yeaton; no children.

(7) Olevia Ann Hooker, b. Nov. 28, 1843; d. Jan. 23, 1906; m., Nov. 21, 1861, Capt. James F. Wright, b. Oct. 2, 1836; son of James P. Wright, b. Lewiston, Me., and Fanny Hewey. They resided at Bath, Me.

(8) Benjamin Franklin Wright, b. Phippsburg, Me., March 20, 1863; m., Nov. 6, 1886, Margaret Archibald Parker of Musquodoboit, N. S., b. Feb. 3, 1864, daughter of Francis Parker and Mary Kent; police inspector.

(9) Eva May Wright, b. Lynn, Mass., July 7, 1888.

(9) Walter Olney Wright, b. June 8, 1890.

(8) Melville Otis Wright, b. Phippsburg, Me., July 24, 1864; m., Oct. 1, 1906, Lillian Maud Coombs of Bath, Me.

(8) Harold Beaufort Wright, b. Aug. 11, 1870; m., May 7, 1893, Winnifred Hunter, b. Bath, Me., Jan. 18, 1873; daughter of Winchell Hunter and Anna Collins.

(9) Olevia Alma Wright, b. May 20, 1894; resides Allston, Mass.

(9) Harold Hunter Wright, b. Feb. 15, 1896.

(9) Riverius Hooker Wright, b. Nov. 4, 1897.

(9) Barbara Archila Wright, b. Oct. 4, 1900.

(9) Frederick Winchell Wright, b. Oct. 17, 1902; d. Nov. 14, 1902.

(8) Ella Annie Wright, b. Bath, Me., June 19, 1873; d. March 1, 1874.

(8) Linwood Palmer Wright, b. Bath, Me., Dec. 4, 1874; m. (first), Feb. 4, 1898, Martha M. Varney, b. Wiscassett, Me., July 17, 1876; d. June 21, 1891; daughter of Joseph M. Varney and Melora

Kasson; resides Readville, Mass.; m. (second), Jan. 31, 1905, Aimee Louise Sparks; daughter of Charles Louis Sparks.

Child of first wife:

(9) Caroline Linwood Wright, b. Feb. 4, 1899.

(7) Harriet Jane Hooker, b. May 7, 1845; d. April 30, 1849.

(7) Ella Rachel Hooker, b. June 22, 1847; d. May 26. 1849.

(7) Walter Olney Hooker, b. April 17, 1849; d. Aug. 14, 1878; he graduated from Bowdoin College in 1872; a very successful teacher; he was master of the ship *Virginia* in 1876; in 1878 he took charge of the ship *Harry Morse*, going to Rio Janiero, where he died; unm.

(7) Millard F. Hooker, b. June 9, 1850; d. Nov. 19, 1851.

(7) Ella Jane Hooker, b. Gardiner, Me., Jan. 14, 1852; resides Augusta, Me.; of grand help in the writing of this book; m., Dec. 16, 1874; George Nickels Lawrence, b. Pittston, Me., Dec. 2, 1846; for years extensively engaged in the ice business on the Kennebec River; later general manager of the Maine America Ice Company, at Augusta, Me.; son of Daniel Lawrence and Sophia Duell.

(8) Bertha Sophia Lawrence, b. June 29, 1877; m., Oct. 26, 1900, Dr. Herbert Allen Black, b. Oct. 10, 1874; graduated at Cony High School, Augusta, Me., 1894; Bowdoin College, 1897; member of the Colorado Medical Society; resides Pueblo, Col.

(9) George Lawrence Black, b. Pueblo, Col., Nov. 22, 1903.

(6) Hannah Olevia Andrews, b. Sept. 3, 1820; d. May 9, 1840.

(6) Charlotte Maria Andrews, b. Oct. 26, 1822; d. June 26, 1863.

(6) Lydia Adelaide Andrews, b. Oct. 30, 1824; resides Monmouth, Me.; m., Jan. 10, 1849, Charles W. Goodwin, b. Monmouth, Me., Oct. 5, 1823; d. Sept. 24, 1873; son of Charles Goodwin and Olive Trufant; no children.

(6) Rachel Jane Andrews, b. March 10, 1827; d. May 18, 1888; studied in Monmouth (Me.) Academy: m.,

Oct. 11, 1862, as his second wife, John C. Ham of Wales, Me.; son of Thomas Ham and Hannah Smith of Wales, Me.; resides Wales, Me.

(7) Charlie Andrews Ham, b. May 22, 1865; resides Wales, Me.; farmer; studied in Monmouth (Me.) Academy and in a business college; m., Sept. 10, 1889, Elsie M. Maxwell of Wales, Me., b. Dec. 17, 1868; daughter of David Maxwell and Mary E. Davis.

(8) Clinton Ham, b. March 26, 1897.

(8) J. Raymond Ham, b. Feb. 20, 1901.

(6) Otis Wilson Andrews, b. July 17, 1829; d. June 27, 1830.

(6) Otis Wilson Andrews, b. Jan. 10, 1832; he resides on the old homestead at Monmouth Ridge, Me.; studied in Monmouth Academy; he taught school for a number of years, and has been prominent in town affairs; has filled the offices of selectman, superintending school committee and representative in the Legislature; m. (first), March 15, 1855, Augusta D. Chick, b. Monmouth, Me., Sept. 30, 1833; d. Oct. 14, 1866; daughter of Levi Chick and Cordelia Allen; m. (second), Orra D. Chick, b. March 12, 1841; d. Dec. 30, 1873; m. (third), Marilla V. Dixon, b. Feb. 1, 1852; daughter of Nathaniel Dixon and Lucy Maxwell of Wales, Me.

Children of first wife:

(7) Ernest C. Andrews, b. Sept. 11, 1857; resides Monmouth, Me.; m., June 5, 1889, Harriet M. Pierce, b. Wantoma, Wis., March 3, 1862; daughter of Capt. Harry O. Pierce and Martha Storm of Monmouth, Me.; resides Monmouth, Me.

(8) Harold Pierce Andrews, b. Monmouth, Me., Sept. 6, 1895.

(8) Helen Elizabeth Andrews, b. Dec. 18, 1897.

(7) Herbert C. Andrews, b. June 21, 1859; resides Kingsley, Ia.; farmer; m., Sept. 26, 1887, Drusilla Dodson, b. May 31, 1863; daughter of George Dodson and Mary Marsh.

(8) Mary A. Andrews, b. Sept. 10, 1892.

(8) Esther A. Andrews, b. Dec. 12, 1897.

(7) Augustus Wilson Andrews, b. Oct. 19, 1865; resides Salem, Mass.

(6) Leonard C. Andrews, b. Feb. 15, 1835; m., Nov. 1, 1865, Lucinda Walker, b. May 4, 1843; d. March 9,

1877; daughter of Rev. Obed Burnham Walker and
Julia Works; farmer at Monmouth, Me.

(7) Olive Thompson Andrews, b. March 16, 1870; m.,
Dec. 2, 1892, Walter Jackson, b. April 26, 1867;
son of John W. Jackson of Woodstock, N. B., and
Anna P. Allen; resides No. Livermore, Me.

(8) Cyril Walker Jackson, b. Aug. 6, 1896; resides
No. Livermore, Me.

(7) Lottie M. Andrews, b. Aug. 13, 1873.

(5) Sophia Thompson, b. Bath, Me., July 6, 1794; d. Amelia,
O., Oct. 18, 1869; m., at Sebec, Me., March 24, 1813,
Josiah Fairfield, b. Kennebunk, Me., March 20, 1785;
d. Amelia, O., July 20, 1874; he followed the sea from
1800 to 1812; lived in Sebec, Me., 1813-'15; lived in
Amelia, O., 1815-'69; he was a farmer while living in
Ohio; son of Samuel Fairfield and Sarah Huff; of
the seventh generation. His Fairfield line: (1)
John Fairfield, was at Charlestown, Mass., in 1638;
moved to Salem, Mass., 1639; m., Elizabeth
————; (2) John Fairfield, b. Salem, Mass., m. Sarah
————; (3) John Fairfield of Boston; m. Mary ————;
(4) Capt. John Fairfield of Boston, Mass.; moved to
Kennebunkport, Me.; m. Mary Emery (or Hills);
(5) John Fairfield, b. Kennebunkport, Me.; m. Mary
Burbank; (6) Samuel Fairfield, b. Nov. 24, 1752; d.
1828; m. Sarah Huff, b. 1756; d. 1817. (George W.
Fairfield, Allston, Mass., has many Fairfield records.)

(6) Hannah Baker Fairfield, b. March 20, 1814; d Feb.
22, 1893; buried, Eureka, Kan.; she lived Amelia, O.,
Merom, Ind., Garden City, Kan., and Edenton, O.;
m., Dec. 12, 1833, Enos Smith, b. near Atlantic City,
N. J.; d. Oct. 22, 1883; carpenter and a Methodist
exhorter; son of John Smith, who came from Holland
or Germany.

(7) Washington Perry Smith, b. Oct. 17, 1834; resides
Merom, Ind.; m. Emma Brown.

(7) Sarah F. Smith, b. May 26, 1837; m. Sydney Turner.

(7) John J. Smith, b. Sept. 30, 1841; m. Lucinda Saunders.

(7) Henry Clay Smith, b. Sept. 30, 1841; d. Oct. 6, 1841.

(7) Rev. Thomas Corwin Smith, b. Nov. 27, 1842; Presbyterian D. D. and A. M.; m. Marie E. McConnell;
resides Springville, Utah.

(7) Sophia Ann Smith, b. Aug. 12, 1845; d. Dec. 12,
1888; m. William M. Weir.

(7) Hannah Maria Smith, b. July 18, 1851; d. Oct. 3, 1851.

(7) Mary Maria Smith, b. July 26, 1852; d. Sept. 2, 1853.

(7) Wilbur E. Smith, b. Feb. 25, 1855; m. Eudora Titus; resides Neosha, Mo.

(6) Sarah Huff Fairfield, b. Dec. 8, 1815; d. Feb. 13, 1837; m., April 13, 1836, Moses Leeds, b. Clermont County, O.; no children.

(6) Cyrus Fairfield, b. Dec. 14, 1817; d. Jan. 21, 1904; studied in Amelia (O.) schools; merchant; m., Dec. 15, 1850, Mary Pease, b. Amelia, O., June 30, 1818; d. April 21, 1891; educated in Amelia (O.) schools; daughter of Capt Martin Pease and Deborah Butler.

(7) Mary Etta Fairfield, b. Amelia, O., July 11, 1858; resides Muncie, Ind.; has lived Amelia, O., Newcastle, Ind., and Belle Fontaine, O.; educated in the schools of Amelia, O., and Newcastle, Ind.; m., at Newcastle, Ind., April 24, 1878, David T. Youngman, b. Logansville, O., May 2, 1849; educated in the schools of De Graffe, O.; merchant; son of Richard T. Youngman and Susan Ambrose.

(8) Clara Youngman, b. De Graffe, O., Feb. 16, 1882; resides Muncie, Ind.; educated in Muncie (Ind.) public schools, Oldenby Academy and Hamilton College, Lexington, Ky.; m., Nov. 26, 1902, David Ferel Case, b. Muncie, Ind., April 20, 1881; educated in Muncie public schools; tailor.

(6) Lorenzo Dow Fairfield, b. Nov. 21, 1819; d. Aug. 3, 1886; a tinner by trade; lived Batavia. O., Oquawka, Ill., Merom, Ind., and Amelia, O.; m., in Batavia, O., April 15, 1845, Tabitha Jeffries, b. Bellemont County, O., Aug. 12, 1823; d. Sept. 30, 1882; daughter of Blair Jeffries.

(7) Olive Fairfield, b. Feb. 22, 1846; d. Nov. 22, 1846.

(7) Barton Warren Stone Fairfield, b. Amelia, O., April 17, 1849; resides Mayfield, Cal.; gradauted at Antioch College, Yellow Springs, O.; lived Merom, Ind., Yellow Springs, O., Cincinnati, O., Fargo, N. D., Chicago, Ill., Evanston, Ill., Dunkirk Ill., Palo Alto, Cal.; groceryman; store destroyed in earthquake, 1906; now in the lumber and planing mill business; has been through a North Dakota cyclone and was burned out in the Fargo, N. D., fire, 1893; still brave and hopeful; m. at New-

castle, Ind., Sept. 5, 1877, Clara Florence Bond, b. Washington, Wayne County, Ind., May 7, 1857; graduated from Newcastle High School; daughter of Calvin Bond and Mary M. Murphy.

(8) Edith May Fairfield, b. Fargo, N. D., Sept. 6, 1883; educated in Fargo and Chicago schools; graduated at Dunkirk (Ind.) High School and Leland Stanford University, Palo Alto, Cal.; m., June 29, 1906, Raymond August Fuller, b. Putnam, Conn., Aug. 7, 1881; graduated Leland Stanford University 1906; mining engineer; son of Lucius Henry Fuller and Abby Clara Cundall of Putnam, Conn.

(8) Earl Bond Fairfield, b. Fargo, N. D., Feb. 14, 1887; d. Fargo, July 30, 1887.

(8) Clarence Herbert Fairfield, b. Fargo, N. D., Sept. 30, 1890; d. Fargo, N. D., Nov. 22, 1891.

(7) Evan Blair Fairfield, b. Amelia, O., May 28, 1851; d. Newcastle, Ind., May 29, 1893; m., at Newcastle, Ind., Dec. 23, 1877, Nora Woodward; Mrs. Nora (Fairfield) Hobam, Chesterton, Ind.

(8) George Albert Fairfield, b. Newcastle, Ind., Oct 11, 1880; m., at Valparaiso, Ind., July 17, 1901, Edith Robinson.

(9) Donald F. Fairfield, b. 1903.

(7) George Washington Fairfield, b. Feb. 22, 1854; d. Dec. 8, 1857.

(7) Charles Howard Fairfield, b. July 20, 1856; d. April 2, 1870; lived on the old farm near Amelia, O.

(7) Otho Pearre Fairfield, b. Amelia, O., Oct. 25, 1863; resides Alfred, N. Y.; graduated from Union Christian College, Merom, Ind.; received A. B. from University of Chicago, 1896; professor in Latin and English at Alfred University, Alfred, N. Y.; lived Amelia, O., 1863–'79; Merom, Ind., 1879, 1882, 1892; Clarinda, Ia., 1892–'95; Chicago, Ill., 1895–'96; Alfred, N. Y., 1896–1906; m., Dec. 24, 1886, Clara Ada Hutson, b. Owensville, Ind., Aug. 8, 1867; graduated from Union Christian College, Merom, Ind., 1885; daughter of Austin Hutson and Louise Warwick Wasson.

(8) Irving Hutson Fairfield, b. Merom, Ind., Sept. 16, 1889.

(8) Mary Fairfield, b. Merom, Ind., April 2, 1892.

(8) Clara Louise Fairfield, b. Alfred, N. Y., Nov. 28, 1897.

(7) Wm. Grant. Fairfield, b. Jan. 1, 1866; resides 615 So. Noble Street, Indianapolis, Ind.; banker; m., Nov. 17, 1883, at Newcastle, Mary E. Modlin, b. Aug. 28, 1866.

(8) Warren Edward Fairfield, b. Feb. 25, 1885; m., in Indianapolis, Ind., Feb. 22, 1906, Nora ———.

(8) Arthur Blair Fairfield, b. Fargo, N. D., Dec. 27, 1886; d. Dec. 29, 1886.

(8) Grace Tabitha Fairfield, b. Chicago, Ill., Jan 6, 1890.

(8) Hazel Delilah Fairfield, b. Chicago, Ill., March 6, 1894.

(6) Albert Alexander Fairfield, b. Feb. 12, 1822, d. June 7, 1898; carpenter; lived Battle Creek, Mich.; m., Aug. 13, 1843, Melissa B. White.

(7) Orilla Fairfield.

(7) Myers Fairfield.

(7) Anna Fairfield.

(7) Goff Fairfield.

(7) William J. Fairfield.

(7) Wheeler Fairfield.

(6) Samuel Rogers Fairfield, b. Amelia, O., Feb. 7, 1824; d. Nov. 4, 1904; resided Amelia, O., 1824–'56; Mt. Pleasant, Ia., 1857–'59; Syracuse, Mo., 1859–'60; Mt. Holly, O., 1861–'65, 1866; Yellow Springs, O., 1886–'91; Merom, Ind., 1891–1904; carpenter from 1857–'70, then a farmer; m., March 23, 1861, Mary Robinson, b. Amelia, O., Sept. 22, 1831; since Nov. 4, 1904, has resided at Sullivan, Ind.; son of Charles Robinson and Sarah Hulick, whose name is some- times written Gullick.

(7) Charles Robinson Fairfield, b. Mt. Holly, O., Jan. 25, 1862; resides Merom, Ind.; merchant, surveyor and farmer; has lived Mt. Holly, O., Batavia, O., Mesilla Park, N. M., San Diego, Cal.; graduated from the Union Christian College at Merom, Ind., 1885; m. (first), Olive McKinney; m. (second), Rilla Buser.

(8) Alveda Clara Fairfield, b. Palestine, Ill., Aug. 7, 1884; resides Shelburne, Ind.; m., Aug. 7, 1902, Bruce C. Haskinson; she graduated at Union Christian College, Merom, Ind.

(7) Rev. Oliver Jay Fairfield, b. Mt. Holly, O., March

15, 1866; resides Ware, Mass.; attended Antioch
College (O.), 1888; Harvard Divinity School,
1892; has lived Bedford, Mass., Spokane, Wash.,
Ware, Mass.; Unitarian minister; m., Nov. 22,
1892, Eulalie Deming Guthrie, b. Yellow Springs,
O., Feb. 25, 1865; graduated at Antioch College
(O.), 1887; daughter of James Guthrie and Jose-
phine B. Deming.

(8) John Guthrie Fairfield, b. Bedford, Mass., Aug. 1,
1893.

(8) Mary Juniata Fairfield, b. Bedford, Nov. 12,
1894.

(8) Priscilla Blanche Fairfield, b. Spokane, Wash.,
April 14, 1896.

(8) Faith Janet Fairfield, b. Spokane, Wash., March
18, 1896.

(7) Sadie Sophia Fairfield, b. Batavia Township, Cler-
mont County, O., June 15, 1870; resides Sullivan,
Ind.; has lived Yellow Springs, O., Merom, Ind.,
Lafayette, Ind., etc.; graduated from Union
Christian College, Merom, Ind., with B. A., 1893,
and M. A., 1896; m., March 3, 1901, Rollin A.
Plunkett[6], b. La Motte, Ill., Jan. 26, 1874; gradu-
ated from Union Christian College with B. A.,
1897; photographic artist; son of Rev. John M.
Plunkett[5], b. Crawfordsville, Ind., 1848; pastor of
the Christian Church, Palestine, Ill.; m. Anna
Shore, b. Sullivan, Ind.; daughter of Isaac M.
Shore and Rebecca Butner. (The Plunkett an-
cestry: [1] Lord Plunkett of Ireland, who settled
in Virginia; [2] Jesse Plunkett, b. Virginia. m.
Miss Mosely; [3] Robert Plunkett, b. Kentucky,
m. Nancy Hartly; [4] Robert Plunkett, b. Shelby
County, Ky.; m. Christina Andrews; daughter of
John Andrews and Nancy McPheely.)

(6) Emeline D. Fairfield, b. Dec. 2, 1825; resides Mt.
Holly, O.; m., Nov. 4, 1849, George Darlington Edwards, b. July 19, 1821; d. July 21, 1876; studied in
Decatur schools; harness maker; son of John Edwards and Miss Jacobs.

(7) Cora Rosella Edwards, b. Dec. 3, 1856; d. July 28,
1879; studied in Amelia (O.) schools.

(7) Cassius M. Edwards; resides Mt. Holly, O.

(7) Julius Fairfield Edwards, b. Amelia, O., June 8,
1858; address, 514 Byrne Building, Los Angeles,

Cal.; J. F. Edwards & Co., general agents of real estate and insurance; attended Batavia (O.) High School; graduated from John Grundy's Commercial College, Cincinnati, O., 1874; m., in Batavia, O., June 29, 1874, Ella Moore, b. Batavia, O., Sept. 5, 1856; daughter of Lester G. Moore and Eliza Rust.

(8) Grace Maud Edwards, b. Batavia, O., Aug. 6, 1875; resides 713 East Twenty-seventh Street, Los Angeles, Cal.; educated in Chicago (Ill.) public schools; m., Dec. 24, 1894, Harry Ellsworth Needham, b. Newcastle, Ind., May 23, 1873; educated in Newcastle schools; real estate dealer.

(9) Earl Harry Needham, b. San Francisco, Cal., June 27, 1898.

(8) Clarence Oscar Edwards, b. Pulaski, Tenn.; educated in Chicago schools; resides Los Angeles, Cal.

(8) Lester George Edwards, b. Chicago, Ill., July 21, 1893; resides Los Angeles, Cal.

(7) Otho Sheridan Edwards, b. Clermont, O., June 25, 1868; address 705 and 706 Atwood Building, Chicago, Ill.; manager of the Atwood Agency of Mutual Life Insurance, etc.; graduated from Jacksonville (Ill.) High School, 1886; has lived in Ohio, Tennessee and Illinois; m., July 3, 1889, Sara Gilhurley, b. Chicago, Oct. 22, 1868; daughter of Jesse G. Gilhurley and Jane Phillips.

(8) Howard Fairfield Edwards, b. April 20, 1891; graduated from Alcott Grammar School, Chicago.

(8) Gail Phillips Edwards, b. Oct. 4, 1895.

(8) Liston Myron Edwards, b. June 10, 1897.

(6) Sophia Olive Fairfield, b. Amelia, O., June 29, 1828; d. Yellow Springs, O., Aug. 12, 1877; lived in Ohio towns, Amelia, Eaton, Lebanon and Yellow Springs, in Covington and Merom, Ind.; studied in Parker's Academy, New Richmond, O.; m., at Fairfield Farm, Clermont County, O., June 13, 1851, Rev. Evan William Humphreys, b. Pentone, Cardiganshire, Wales, Jan. 11, 1816; d. Yellow Springs, O., Jan 8, 1884; studied in the schools at Caermarthen, Wales. and Meadville (N. J.) Theological Seminary; minister

of the Christian Church; son of Evan Thomas Davyth Humphreys and Margaret Williams.

(7) Margaret Humphreys, b. Felicity, O., Aug. 3, 1854; resides 2700 Thirteenth Street, Washington, D. C.; studied at Antioch College, Yellow Springs, O., Granville (O.) Female College and the University of Michigan; m., at Ann Arbor, Mich., July 25, 1885, Elmer Ellsworth Paine, b. Xenia, O.; studied at Antioch College and Ohio State University; journalist; editor of Akron (O.) *Beacon*, 1888–'96; now a member of the Associated Press staff, Washington, D. C.; son of Dr. George Lane Paine, dentist at Xenia, O., and Eliza A. Barkalow.

(8) George Humphrey Paine; d. at birth, Oct. 7, 1886.

(8) Roger Warde Paine, b. Springfield, O., Sept. 7, 1887; graduated from Capital High School, Washington, D. C.; appointed to Annapolis, Md., by President Roosevelt.

(8) Margaret Raymond Paine, b. Akron, O., Aug. 6, 1890; attends Washington schools.

(8) Dorothy Olive Paine, b. Akron, O., Dec. 15, 1891; attends Washington schools.

(8) Janet Eleanor Paine, b. Akron, O., Nov. 1, 1893; attends Washington schools.

(7) Florence N. Humphreys, b. Covington, Ind., May 27, 1856; d. Yellow Springs, O., Jan. 29, 1874.

(7) Alfred Evan Humphreys, b. Eaton, O., Oct. 25, 1860; resides Snyderville, O; studied at Antioch College, Ohio; farmer; m., Dec. 24, 1885, Jessie Elizabeth Minnick, b. Clark County, O., Nov. 13, 1864; studied at Antioch College; daughter of John Minnick and Mary Caroline Layton.

(8) Mary Sophia Humphreys, b. Dec 13, 1886.

(8) Evan Minnick Humphreys, b. Aug. 7, 1888.

(8) Felix Otho Humphreys, b. Jan. 1, 1890.

(8) John Rogers Humphreys, b. Oct. 3, 1891.

(7) Otho Fairfield Humphreys, b. Eaton, O., July 6, 1864; resides Newark, N. J.; has lived at Lebanon and Yellow Springs, O., Springfield, Mass., Milwaukee, Wis., Newark and West Orange, N. J.; graduated, June, 1893, from Episcopal Theological School, Cambridge, Mass.; Episcopal clergyman; m., Jan. 1, 1895, Sarah Luddington Patton, b. Milwaukee, Wis., Sept. 12, 1868; daughter of

James Edward Patton and Sarah Elizabeth Luddington.

(8) James Patton Humphreys.

(8) Otho F. Humphreys, Jr.

(8) Sarah Luddington Humphreys.

(8) Frances Eliza Humphreys.

(8) Margaret Humphreys.

(6) Aseneth Martin Fairfield, b. Sept. 28, 1830; resides
Poplar Valley Farm, Merom, Ind., in Clermont
County until 1864; then settled on a tract of land
two miles north of Merom, Ind., where a beautiful
farm of 300 acres has been cleared and developed;
m., Oct. 28, 1853, Jonathan Bragdon, b. Union Township, near Withamsville, O., Dec. 11, 1827; he and
his wife studied in the common schools; son of
Benjamin Bragdon and Rebecca Wood; grandson of
Jotham Bragdon, who went from Maine to Ohio
with his wife, Sarah Bradley. The following children were given a good education, and are settled
near their parents:

(7) Benjamin Rush Bragdon, b. near Amelia, Clermont
County, O., July 13, 1854; d. near Merom, Ind.,
June 7, 1876.

(7) Emma Bell Bragdon, b. Amelia, O., July 22, 1856;
resides Brazil, Ind.; studied in Union Christian
College, Merom, Ind., m., Sept. 28, 1881, by her
cousin, Rev. J. C. Smith, Dr. George William Finley, b. near Harmony, Ind., April 29, 1855; graduated from Union Christian College and the Medical College of Indiana; at Harmony and Brazil,
Ind., since 1880; son of James M Finley and
Sarah Belk. The Finleys came from Ireland to
Maryland; one, Dr. Samuel Finley, was a president of Princeton College. The Finleys removed
to North Carolina before the Revolutionary War;
from thence to Ohio and Indiana, about 1830.

(8) Dorathea Pearl Finley, b. Harmony, Ind., Dec. 21,
1883; graduated from Brazil (Ind.) High
School, 1904; now studying in Indiana University.

(8) Lois Ruby Finley, b. Harmony, Ind., Feb. 3, 1887;
graduated from Brazil (Ind.) High School,
class of 1906.

(8) Rebe Crystal Finley, b. Harmony, Ind., Oct. 11,
1891; in Brazil High School.

(7) Sophia Rebecca Bragdon, b. July 22, 1858.

(7) Jotham Josiah Bragdon, b. Amelia, O., Oct. 3, 1860;
successful farmer; m., March 23, 1890, Olive Wible,
b. Sullivan, Ind., June 6, 1868; only daughter of
William Wible and Miss Davis.

(8) Charles Rush Bragdon, b. Nov. 17, 1891.

(8) William Franklin Bragdon, b. Sept. 2, 1893.

(8) Bernice Bragdon, b. Jan. 23, 1895.

(8) Ross Jotham Bragdon, b. May 17, 1903.

(7) Voorhees Vallingham Bragdon, b. Amelia, O.,
March 1, 1863; farmer at Merom, Ind.; m., Oct.
19, 1887, Clara Amy Smith, b. New Albany, Ind.,
Sept. 17, 1865; d. Merom, Ind., May 16, 1905;
daughter of Philip Smith and Julia Cline.

(8) Vita Blanch Bragdon, b. Aug. 20, 1888; graduated
Merom (Ind.) schools, and is now a student in
Union Christian College, Merom.

(8) Ralph Emerson Bragdon, b. Jan. 13, 1893.

(8) Benjamin Murray Bragdon, b. Nov. 7, 1898.

(8) Hugh Carlton Bragdon, b. Sept. 1, 1902.

(8) Hervey Smith Bragdon, b. May 1, 1905.

(7) Clara Asenath Bragdon, b. near Merom, Ind., Aug.
21, 1868.

(6) Otho Pearre Fairfield, b. June 25, 1835; d. Nov. 1,
1835.

(6) Melissa Pearre Fairfield, b. March 25, 1836; d. March
26, 1836.

(6) Otho Pearre Fairfield, b. Sept. 18, 1837; d. Nov. 8,
1864; lived Amelia, O., and in Merom, Ind., 1861-
'62; teacher; he was lieutenant in Company B,
Eighty-ninth Ohio Volunteers; was in Libby Prison
from Sept., 1863, to Oct., 1864; taken from Libby
Prison to Columbia, S. C., where he died; he enlisted Aug. 11, 1862, took command as first lieutenant April 10, 1863; captured by the enemy at
Chickamauga, Sept. 20, 1863.

(5) Elisha Baker Thompson, b. April 6, 1797; d. Bethel, O.,
July 26, 1885; In 1815 he moved from Maine to near
Amelia, O., and was there until March, 1827, when he
moved to near Bethel, O.; in 1865 he went to Five
Mile, Brown County, O.; in 1882 he moved back to
Bethel, O.; buried at Bethel, Clermont County, O.;
farmer; m. (first), March, 1816, Mary Douglass, b.
Maine, Oct. 16, 1795; d. Aug. 8, 1864; m. (second), au-

tumn of 1865, Mrs. Mary Ann (Dunham) Thompson, widow of his brother, Alexander Thompson; daughter of Jonathan Dunham and Lucy ———; no children of this second marriage.

Children of first wife:

(6) Charlotte Welch Thompson, b. Sept. 9, 1816; d. Dec. 14, 1873 (57y., 3m., 3d.); m. Jan. 19, 1845, Ezekiel Edwin Turner, b. Dec. 17, 1817; d. June 2, 1889. This family lived on a farm two and one-half miles south of Bethel, O., on the Cincinnati Pike; this was sold to Mr. Poole and a farm purchased on the same road in Brown County, three and one-half miles east of Bethel, O., of 213 acres, to which forty acres of timber land were added. Mr. Turner started in life without means, but by hard work he became well-to-do; he was a good business manager, a good neighbor, and always ready to help the sick and dying all that lay in his power. Of the wife no one could speak too highly in praise; her life was regarded as a well-nigh perfect one; among the sick and dying she was of the strongest help; for seven days and nights she waited on a sick orphan girl, who was an entire stranger to her, with the most loving care; Mrs. Fred Morgan, who had lived beside her for twenty years, declared that she had never seen a woman like her for helpfulness; she was one of the finest spinners, and in the fall before she died she spun twenty-four cuts of long-reeled yarn as a day's work; she was a good weaver.

(7) Mary Adelaide Turner, b July 28, 1846, near Bethel, O.; d. April 6, 1862 (15y., 8m., 8d.).

(7) Melissa Jane Turner, b. on the Bethel, O., farm, Oct. 24, 1848; d. Aug. 29, 1888 (39y., 10m., 4d.); m., Feb. 14, 1872, by Rev. A. J. Lockwood, William C. McMurchy, b. on the homestead one and a half miles from Freeburg, O., Jan. 21, 1846; after his marriage he settled on the farm two and one-half miles west of Homerville, O.; his address is Homerville, O.; son of John McMurchy and Eliza Ann Wells.

(8) Archie Leland McMurchy, b. Feb. 25, 1875; resides Bethel, O.; studied in Spring Grove schools; dairyman and farmer; m., Dec. 31, 1902, Edna Minton.

(8) Anna Elizabeth McMurchy, b. March 25, 1880; studied in the Spring Grove schools.

(8) Florence Isabel McMurchy, b. Nov. 21, 1885; resides Sioux City, Ia.; unm.

(7) Lucy Ann Turner, b. near Bethel, O., July 25, 1850; d. Dec. 8, 1893 (42y., 4m., 13d.); m., Aug. 15, 1869, Alonzo Wood, b. Point Pleasant, O., Oct. 5, 1848; d. May 30, 1893; for two or three years they lived near Bethel, O., and then moved to Edgar County, Ill.; after awhile they lived again on the old Ohio farm for a couple of years; from Sept., 1877, to Oct., 1891, they lived on a farm near Felicity, O., then moved to Science Hill, Pulaski County, Ky., where Mr. Wood d. in May, 1893, and his wife the following December. They are buried in Union Cemetery, three miles east of Science Hill, Ky.

(8) Frank Clarence Wood, b. May 9, 1870; resides Kneeland, Ill.; farmer; studied in common schools; in Sept., 1894, he went to Milwaukee, Wis., to work for the Chicago, Milwaukee & St. Paul Railroad Company; he then stayed on a farm at Kneeland, Wis., for a short time, moving back to Illinois in 1905; m. (first), Jan. 30, 1894, Emma E. Ivens, who d. Jan. 30, 1899, on the hour on which she was married; daughter of John P. Ivens and Caroline; m. (second), April 4, 1900, Barbara A. Harsh, b. Hagerstown, Md., Aug. 4, 1876; daughter of Daniel Harsh and Sarah Hoover.

Children of first wife:

(9) Raymond George Wood, b. Aug. 7, 1895.

(9) Everett Harding Wood, b. Jan. 12, 1899.

Children of second wife:

(9) David Edward Wood, b. April 20, 1901.

(9) Clarence Richard Wood, b. June 17, 1905.

(8) Lottie May Wood, b. Feb. 7, 1872; resides Kenesaw, Neb.; m., Aug. 15, 1894, Francis Brady McGiff; he was located on his father's farm at Science Hill, Ky., until Nov., 1898, when he moved to Kenesaw, Neb..

(9) Nellie McGiff; d. in her first year.

(9) Daughter and son.

(8) Walter George Wood, b. Sept. 20, 1872; resides Science Hill, Ky.

(8) Carl Erwin Wood, b. Dec. 4, 1874; in 1895 went
to Milwaukee, Wis., on a dairy farm and remained there until Sept., 1897; then was a fire-
man on the Chicago, Milwaukee & St. Paul Railroad; sent by the Railroad Company to Sioux
City, Ia., where he now resides; m., June 5,
1900, Addie R. Allen of Shell Rock, Ia.

(9) Son.

(7) Laura Elizabeth Turner, b. near Bethel, O., Dec.
26, 1853; studied in Yankeetown and Spring
Grove schools; joined the Christian Church at
Bethel, O., when 15 years old; resides Homerville, Brown County, O.; m., Feb. 7, 1877, Henry
H. Day, b. Felicity, O., Nov. 18, 1854; son of Jesse
Day and Mary A. Fusler; educated in Benton and
Antioch (O.) schools; an elder in the Christian
Church; soon after marriage he moved to a farm
three miles west of Felicity, O., and remained
about eighteen months; then to a farm two and
one-half miles west of Homerville, O.; farmer
and insurance agent.

(8) Lillie Maud T. Day, b. near Homerville, O.,
April 9, 1880; educated in Homerville High
School; joined the Christian Church at fifteen
years; resides 2002 College Avenue, Indianapolis, Ind.; m., Jan. 7, 1900, Charles C. Jones, b.
near Georgetown, O., March 26, 1877; carpenter;
united with the Christian Church at seventeen
years; son of Christopher Jones and Mary La-
rock.

(9) Edna Elizabeth Jones, b. Oct. 21, 1900.

(9) Carl E. Jones, b. Nov. 12, 1902.

(8) Edna Erett Day, b. Nov. 16, 1883; attended
Homerville (O.) High School; united with the
Christian Church at twelve years.

(8) Loren Wellington Day, b. Jan. 21, 1885; attended
school at Pride Hill, O.; united with the Christian Church at fourteen years.

(6) Adeline Donham Thompson, b. on the farm near
Amelia, O., March 19, 1818; d. March 9, 1896 (78y.);
m., March 13, 1842, Samuel M. Cook, b. Montgomery
County, Md., March 6, 1815; d. June 2, 1891; he
went from Maryland at the age of thirteen years to
near Bethel, O., and remained there all his life;

farmer; son of Amos Cook and Anna ———. Of the wife it is written: "Her parents moved to near Bethel, O., in 1827, and in this locality she spent the balance of her days; she united with the Christian Church at Bethel, O., Sept., 1832, when in her fourteenth year. For a period of sixty-four years she was one of the most faithful members of that church. And her children also became active members of it. For several years she suffered much from sickness, but was always a patient Christian, looking with joyous hope to her meeting with her Savior and the loved ones who had gone before her She showed rare fidelity, patience, godliness, and untiring devotion to all her duties in all her relations of life."

(7) Perry Thomas Cook, b. April 24, 1843; resides Brookville, Ky.; school teacher and then a lawyer; m., April 4, 1867, Elizabeth M. Frank of Brookville, Ky.

(8) Gloie Melinda Cook, b. Oct. 31, 1869; d. Sept. 21, 1905; resided Brookville, Ky,; m., Sept. 2, 1890, George Gibson, b. Brookville, Ky., Sept. 12, 1865. "He raised tobacco for awhile and then became partner in a gristmill; of late he has farmed some."

(9) Georgia Gibson, b. Oct. 26, 1901; d. Oct. 26, 1901.

(9) Carroll Slater Gibson, b. Jan. 2, 1903.

(7) Amos Baker Cook, b. Feb. 25, 1845; d. Aug. 24, 1896; m., March 4, 1873, Malinda Ulrey, who d. April 3, 1894; school teacher and farmer.

(8) Lona Blanche Cook, b. April 19, 1878.

(7) Sarah Jane Cook, b. Feb. 24, 1847; d. Oct. 14, 1898; m., Oct. 13, 1889, William Clark McMurchy, b. near Bethel, O.; wife is a milliner.

(7) Cyrus Fairfield Cook, b. April 2, 1849; farmer near Bethel, O.; m., Feb. 27, 1876, Lucinda Amelia ———.

(8) Inez Bessie Cook, b. Aug. 15, 1878; school teacher.

(8) Edora May Cook, b. March 1, 1883.

(7) Mary Letitia Cook, b. July 29, 1851; resides near Bethel, O.; educated in the public schools; prepared for a teacher.

(7) Anna Elizabeth Cook, b. Oct. 2, 1853; resides Bethel,

O., m., April 16, 1884, Augustus Eugene McGohan, b. near Bethel, O., May 5, 1852; farmer, son of Andrew Jackson McGohan and Lucinda Thompson.

(7) Charles William Cook, b. near Bethel, O., June 2, 1857; resides Bethel, O.; farmer; m., Dec. 16, 1883, Mary Ellen Ulrey, b. near Bethel, O., Sept. 30, 1861; daughter of Samuel Ulrey and Glovina Sentry.

(6) Everett Andrews Thompson.

(7) The daughter, Mrs. Mary J. Marsh, resides at Celina, Mercer County, O.

(6) Benjamin Alexander Thompson, b. Feb. 2, 1827; d. March 3, 1891; resided Bethel, O.; farmer and teacher; unm.

(6) Alvah K. Thompson; resides Sanford, Ind. "The only child now living."

(6) Otho P. Thompson; d. young.

(6) Alonzo A. Thompson; d. young.

(6) Converse Conkling Thompson; b. near Bethel O., Nov. 9, 1816; resides near Bethel, O.; farmer; member of the Christian Church; m., Oct. 11, 1860, Mary Frances Edwards, b. near Bethel, O., Dec. 28, 1840.

(7) George Quincy Thompson; b. near Bethel, O., Sept. 19, 1861; d. July 5, 1894; lived at Bethel, O., until nearly five years old, then went to Windsor, Ill., with his mother; farmer; m., Oct., 1884, Callie Ellen Beck, b. Milroy, Ind., Nov. 9, 1865; daughter of William Nelson Beck and Mary Ellen ———.

(8) William Converse Thompson, b. Oct. 27. 1885.

(8) Thomas Roy Thompson, b. Jan. 4, 1888.

(8) Mary Ruth Thompson, b. July 2, 1894.

(6) Matthew Gardner Thompson, b. Clermont County, O., July 6, 1823; d. Bethel, O., Oct. 9, 1893; went to Bethel, O., 1867; m., in Buckner County, O., April 14, 1846, Sarah E. Day; she resides at Bethel, O.

(7) Percy E. Thompson; d. in infancy.

(7) William R. Thompson, b. Buckner County, Ky., May 15, 1854; address, box 112, Bethel, O.; carpenter and builder; m., Jan. 17, 1875, Olive Ulrey of Bethel, O.

(8) William A. Thompson, b. June 11, 1876; barber.

(8) Charles E. Thompson, b. Sept. 13, 1879; barber.

(8) Lucinda Maud Thompson, b. April 11, 1886.

(7) Baker B. Thompson, b. June 28, 1856; in 1891 went
    to Newport, Ky.; in the railroad business; m.,
    in Brown County, in 1877.

*   ·   *   *   *

(4) Hannah Thompson, b. Georgetown, Me., April 20, 1760;
    recorded by the town clerk May 20, 1760; m. Eli Her-
    rick of Greene, Me.; son of Israel Herrick and Mary
    Bragg; no more in the Herrick genealogy; no children.

*   *   *   *   *

(4) Mercy Thompson, b. Georgetown, Me., Dec. 3, 1762; d.
    Dec. 31, 1826; m. Mathias Blossom[6], b. Sept. 12, 1765; d.
    June 1, 1804. The Blossom line: (1) Ancestor Thomas
    Blossom, b. 1632/'33; started with the Pilgrims on the
    Speedwell in 1620, but finally came to Plymouth, Mass.,
    1629; he was the first deacon of the Plymouth Church; m.
    Anna ——; (2) Peter Blossom m. Sarah Bodfish, daugh-
    ter of Robert Bodfish; resided Barnstable, Mass.; (3) Jo-
    seph Blossom, b. Dec. 10, 1673; resided Barnstable, Mass.;
    m. June 17, 1696, Mary Pincheon, who d. April 6, 1706;
    (4) Joseph Blossom, b. March 14, 1703; resided Barn-
    stable, Mass.; m., March 30, 1727; Temperance Ful-
    ler[5], b. March 7, 1702; daughter of Benjamin Fuller[4] of
    Barnstable, Mass.; he was of the fourth generation and
    the son of Samuel Fuller[3], who was baptized Feb. 11,
    1637/'38; d. before 1691; m., April 8, 1635, Anna Fuller,
    who d. before 1691 (she was a daughter of Matthew Ful-
    ler and supposed to be a granddaughter of the Samuel
    Fuller mentioned above); Samuel Fuller[2] d. Oct. 31,
    1683; resided Barnstable, Mass.; m. Mary Lothrop, b.
    Sept. 14, 1614; daughter of Rev. John Lothrop of Scitu-
    ate, Mass. Edward Fuller[1] of the *Mayflower;* (5) James
    Blossom, b. Feb. 9, 1731; lived Barnstable, Mass., and
    Monmouth, Me.; m. Bethiah Smith. Her ancestry is
    as follows: (1) Thomas Smith; (2) Rev. John Smith;
    (3) Joseph Smith, b. April 29, 1689; m. Anna Fuller;
    (4) Mathias Smith, b. Barnstable, Mass., July 10, 1697;
    m., Sept. 3, 1730, Hannah Fuller; (5) Bethiah Smith
    (above). Records of Hannah Fuller, who m. Mathias
    Smith, named above: She was the daughter of Lieut.
    John Fuller, b. Oct., 1689; d. July 20, 1710, and resided
    at Barnstable, Mass.; Lieut. John Fuller m. Thankful
    Gorham, b. Feb. 15, 1690/'91; she was the daughter of
    Lieut.-Col. John Gorham, b. Feb. 20, 1651/'52; d. Dec. 9,

1716; lived Marshfield, Mass.; m., Feb. 24, 1674/'75, Mary Otis, daughter of John Otis of England, b. 1621, who m. Mary Jubb. The above John Gorham was the son of Capt. John Gorham, baptized 1620 and m., 1643, Desire Howland, daughter of John Howland of the *Mayflower*. The above Lieut. John Fuller was the son of Dr. John Fuller, who. d. 1691, and a grandson of Capt. Matthew Fuller.

(5) James E. Blossom, b. Monmouth, Me., Feb. 15, 1788; d. Jan. 29, 1858; m., April 27, 1824, Anstris Wilcox, b. Feb. 28, 1791; d. Aug. 10, 1883; daughter of Capt. John Wilcox.

  (6) Delia A. Blossom, b. Feb. 27, 1827; resided Monmouth, Me.; unm.

  (6) James G. Blossom, b. Sept. 23, 1828; resides Watertown, Mass.; m. Mary A. Adams; daughter of John W. Adams; no children.

(5) Ira A. Blossom, b. Dec. 24, 1798; d. Oct. 2, 1856; m. Eunice Hubbard of Buffalo, N. Y.

  (6) Lucy Blossom; deceased.

(5) Samuel Franklin Blossom, b. Nov. 25, 1791; d. Dec. 15, 1840, at Amherst, N. Y.; m. (first), March 20, 1820, Julia Morrill of Monmouth, Me., b. Sept. 2, 1796; d. Dec. 20, 1828; daughter of Abraham Morrill; m. (second), June 20, 1829, Jane Hillman, b. Livermore, Me., 1796; d. Buffalo, N. Y., Feb. 6, 1877; daughter of Rev. Samuel Hillman.

Children of first wife:

  (6) Maria G. Blossom, b. Nov. 19, 1820.

  (6) Ira Harrison Blossom, b. March 11, 1822; d. Jan. 11, 1855; m. Laura Church.

  (6) Two children.

  (6) Mary Morrill Blossom, b. Jan. 23, 1824; d. Brunswick, Me., July 18, 1846.

  (6) Sarah Elvira Blossom, b. Aug. 14, 1827; d. Buffalo, N. Y., June 15, 1853.

Children of second wife:

  (6) Samuel Hillman Blossom, b. Sept. 10, 1831; d. Buffalo, N. Y., April 13, 1880; m., Feb. 15, 1865, Ellen Phillips.

    (7) Mary Ellen Blossom, b. March 18, 1866; resides Buffalo, N. Y.

    (7) Samuel F. Blossom, b. May 22, 1867; d. April 12, 1901.

(6) Albert Harrison Blossom, b. Aug. 14, 1833; m., Feb. 12, 1870, Mary E. McLean.

 (7) Charlotte Blossom, b. July 9, 1872; m. (first), June 13, 1891, B. F. Miller; m. (second), Jan. 29, 1899, W. H. Newman.

  (8) Warren Newman.

  (8) Nellie Newman, b. June 6, 1892.

(6) Julia Ellen Blossom, b. June 13, 1875; d. St. Louis, Mo., Dec. 30, 1867; m., April 9, 1867, Hiram P. Thompson.

(5) Harrison A. Blossom, b. Jan. 17, 1794; d. Aug. 23, 1795.

(5) Sally H. Blossom, b. Monmouth, Me., May 8, 1796; d. March 31, 1850; m., April 25, 1826, Ira Towle, b. Sept. 15, 1794; d. May 2, 1881.

(6) Ira Scott Towle, b. April 19, 1827; d. Feb. 18, 1857; unm.

(6) Cyrus Edwin Towle, b. Oct. 15, 1828; m.; Oct. 15, 1853, Jane Webb.

 (7) Ira Edwin Towle, b. July 8, 1854.

 (7) Daniel Webb Towle, b. July 14, 1855; married; no children.

 (7) Eugene Towle; d. young.

 (7) Helen Medora Towle; m. Robert Stark of Waltham, Mass.

  (8) Two children.

 (7) Walter Scott Towle, b. Oct., 1861; m. (first), Mary Owen; m. (second), Edna ———; no children.

 (7) Charlotte Towle; d. young.

(6) Susan Towle, b. March 4, 1830; d. June 4, 1860; m. John M. Bent.

(6) Helen Medora Towle, b. Monmouth, Me., July 6, 1832; resides Watertown, Mass.; m., Aug. 3, 1858, Abner Chase Stockin, b. Aug. 30, 1831; d. Jan. 11, 1901; graduated from Bowdoin College, 1857; teacher 12 years; educational publisher 30 years; son of Thomas Blossom Stockin and Lydia Ann Chase.

 (7) Edwin Stockin, b. Monmouth, Me., Jan. 22, 1862; resides Watertown, Mass.; graduated at Watertown High School, 1880; publisher of the *Youth's Companion* of Boston, Mass.; m., Oct. 7, 1885, Eleanor Stafford Green, b. Boston, Mass., Nov. 19, 1861; graduated from the Watertown High School, 1880; daughter of John Henry Green and Helen M. Stafford.

(8) Albert Edwin Stockin, b. April 16, 1887; graduated from Watertown High School; in Harvard
University in 1906.

(8) Eleanor Charlotte Stockin, b. April 17, 1895.

(7) Arthur Stockin, b. April 19, 1864; d. Jan. 29, 1901;
illustrator; graduated from Watertown (Mass.)
High School, 1882; m., Feb. 28, 1889, Alice L.
Draper, b. 1864; d. Feb. 8, 1901; lived South Berwick, Me., Penacook, N. H., Chelsea, Mass., Watertown, Mass.

(8) Helen Louise Stockin, b. May 31, 1892.

(8) Dorothy Bowditch Stockin, b. Nov. 12, 1894.

(7) Annie Stockin, b. Aug. 25, 1864; resides Watertown,
Mass; graduated from Watertown High School,
1883; unm.

(6) David Quimby Towle, b. Oct. 26, 1833; d. Oct. 5, 1856;
unm.

(6) Charlotte Augusta Towle, b. Nov. 26, 1836; resides
Lewiston, Me.; unm.

(5) Winter Green Blossom, b. Jan. 21, 1799; d. March 10,
1818; unm.

(5) Thomas Blossom, b. March 3, 1801; m. Charlotte Strong;
no children.

(5) Sophia Maria Blossom, b. March 2, 1803; d. Jan. 12,
1804.

CHAPTER VI.

PRISCILLA THOMPSON AND LIEUT. HUGH MULLOY AND THEIR DESCENDANTS.

Priscilla Thompson's line: (1) William Thompson of Dover, N. H.; (2) James Thompson of Kittery, Me.; (3) Benjamin Thompson of New Meadows, Brunswick, Me.

(4) Priscilla Thompson, b. Georgetown, Me., May 13, 1754; d. New Richmond, O., April 4, 1819. "She was a woman of that force of character which was necessary in those early, trying times. Yet she was possessed of a gentle spirit. She was a noble, self-reliant woman who has sent the grand influence of her life down the long line of her descendants. She was a true type of many Thompson daughters in many neighborhoods and states."

M., June 25, 1776, Hugh Mulloy, b. Albany, N. Y., Dec. 4, 1751; d. New Richmond, O., July 11, 1845 (94th y.). This family moved to Ohio in 1817.

The epitaph from the tombstone of Hugh Mulloy: "In memory of Hugh Mulloy, a Lt. in the Revolutionary War; b. Albany, N. Y.; married one of great worth; joined the army at Cambridge, 1775. He was personally acquainted with Washington and Lafayette; was in the retreat from Ticonderoga; in both battles at Saratoga; lay at Valley Forge; was at Monmouth; and was thrice wounded—once at Hubbardstown in 1780. Among the bravest he was brave. He came to Ohio in 1817 and died July 11, 1845 in the 94th year of his age."

He and his wife were buried in the cemetery at Boat Run, O., but as the river was washing away the ground there, Mr. J. G. Mulloy, now of Fremont, Neb., and others, removed the remains to the old cemetery between Mt. Hygiene and New Richmond, O.

O. B. Clason, Esq., of Gardiner, Me.: "Hugh Mulloy was one of the pioneers of Litchfield, Me. His ancestors came from the north of Ireland and were of Scotch-Irish extraction. When a boy he emigrated to the then province of Maine and lived in Brunswick and Georgetown. While

home on a furlough from the Continental Army he married
Priscilla Thompson. When the news of the battle of Bunker Hill was received he, with other patriots from his lo-
·cality, started for Boston. He at once enlisted in the
army at Cambridge as a private. In April following he was
promoted to Corporal; promoted in the June following to
Sergeant, and was commissioned Nov. 6, 1776, as ensign in
the Co. of which George White was Captain. His commission was issued at Boston, by order of Congress, and
signed by John Hancock, President. In May, 1778, he was
promoted again to the rank of First Lieutenant. He was
in the battle of Ticonderoga, in May, 1777; was in the
battle of Hubbardstown; in both battles of Saratoga
(Stillwater); and witnessed the surrender of Burgoyne,
Oct. 17, 1777. He was in several skirmishes, in one of
which he was wounded. At the battle of Monmouth he
was twice wounded severely, and one of these wounds
subsequently proved so troublesome as to incapacitate him
from active duty, and he was honorably discharged from
the service. This discharge was written on the back of
his commission in the handwriting of Gen. Washington.
This paper, which was on file in the pension department
at Washington, was destroyed in 1814 by the British when
they sacked the town.

"Lt. Mulloy had a personal acquaintance with Washington and Lafayette. He was initiated into the mysteries of
Free Masonry in Washington's tent, and was secretary of
the lodge which existed in the army. Immediately after
his discharge from the army, he moved with his family
to Monmouth, Maine, and was among the first settlers
there. He held several positions of trust in the Plantation,
among them Plantation Clerk. It was subsequently found
that the land he had settled upon belonged to Gen. Dearborn; and the Gen. bought out his improvements, giving
him a note of the following tenor:

"'Wales, Me., June 27, 1783.

"'For value received I promise to pay Hugh Mulloy the
sum of fifty Spanish Milled dollars by the 15th day of Oct.,
1784, with interest until paid. (Signed) Henry Dearborn.'

"Upon selling out his interest in Monmouth, Me., Hugh
Mulloy settled in Litchfield, Me., upon land now owned by
Warren R. Buker, by the side of Pleasant Pond, where he
made his home for more than thirty years. He was frequently moderator of the town meetings, and also a mem-

ber of the school board, and took a lively interest in education. In 1817 Mr. Mulloy moved to near Williamsburg,
Clermont Co., Ohio, where he ever after made his home.
At the time of his death he was the last commissioned officer of the regular Continental army, and as such his por-
trait was painted by Frankenstein, the celebrated artist.
The Legislature of Ohio made an appropriation for this
painting.

"Old Masons say that it is handed down by tradition that
the Masons in Gardiner, Me., early in the present century,
used to go by boat or canoes, out to Mr. Mulloy's home, by
the side of the beautiful Cobbosseecontee Pond, and meet
in Masonic brotherhood, and that he frequently met them
in Gardiner. They had no lodge there then, or until the
last of Hugh Mulloy's living there, but kept up occasional
meetings for the work of the order."

Mr. A. E. Parker writes: "Hugh Mulloy, the dear old
man, how well I remember him as he came down from
Williamsburgh in his little Dearborn wagon, to see my
mother. His hair was white and his step was feeble. But
he would enthusiastically tell of all the hardships of his
service in the Revolutionary days."

Parker Donaldson: "Hugh Mulloy was a stern-spirited,
brave man."

       *   *   *   *   *

The following list of the children of Priscilla Thompson
and Hugh Mulloy was taken from the Litchfield, Me., town
records and from the old family Bible in the possession of
his grandson, Moreton Mulloy, son of Thomas Mulloy.

       *   *   *   *   *

(5) David Mulloy, b. Litchfield, Me., Oct. 15, 1779; he lived in
    Litchfield until 1817, when he moved to Ohio; shortly
    after this he moved to Oregon, where all trace was lost
    of him; m., March 3, 1803, Mary Stevens, b. March 8,
    1780; d. Gardiner, Me., Nov., 1879, almost one hundred
    years old; she and her daughters remained in Maine
    when the husband went to Ohio. She is said to have m.
    (second), in Litchfield, Me., Dec. 28, 1828, Robert Edge-
    combe; m. by John Smith, justice of the peace.

(6) John Mulloy, b, Litchfield, Me., Dec. 3, 1803; d. March 3,
    1804.

(6) Jonathan T. Mulloy, b. Litchfield, Me., April 15, 1804;
    he went to Ohio with his father.

(6) Mary L. Mulloy, b. Litchfield; d. Caribou, Me., about 1896, aged 86 years; she m. (first), Hiram Anderson; m. (second), Elisha Burgess.

(6) Lucinda Mulloy, b. Litchfield, Me., June 15, 1809; d. July 24, 1857; m. Elijah Closson and lived Richmond, Me. Another account says: "M., Jan. 18, 1831, Hezekiah Richardson. Her daughter, Mrs. Charles Bennet⁷, resided in Augusta, Me."

* * * * *

(5) The second child of Priscilla Thompson and Hugh Mulloy, Abigail Mulloy, b. Litchfield, Me., Friday, July 31, 1781; m. (first), Feb. 3, 1805, David Colson and resided Bath, Me.; m. (second), Jeremiah Norton and lived several years in Wales, Me.

(6) James Colson, b. 1812; he was an old and honored citizen of Gardiner, Me., for many years; he was lieutenant in Company C, Third Maine Regiment, in the Civil War.

(7) James M. Colson; a brave soldier in the Civil War; killed in a railroad accident after the war.

(7) John Colson; crippled by an accident.

(7) Margaret Colson; resided in Massachusetts.

* * * * *

(5) John Mulloy, b. Litchfield, Me., Monday, Aug. 27, 1783; d. June 1, 1802.

* * * * *

(5) Catherine Mulloy, b. Litchfield, Me., Jan. 11, 1786; d. Edina, Mo., when nearly ninety years of age. Hon. Hugh Mulloy Herrick of Patterson, N. J., writes: "She was a woman of strong mentality, and she and hers were well and favorably known in the communities where she lived." Eben A. Parker says, "The last time she came to visit us she was nearly eighty-eight years old, but still wide-awake and active. In 1850, when she was 64 years of age, she taught school with the zeal which had characterized her work along those lines in her younger days." Catherine Mulloy m. (first), Oct., 1807, Samuel Herrick, b. Greene, Me., Dec. 11, 1784; d. July 4, 1822. He d. of yellow fever on a New Orleans steamer bound up the river; this family moved from Maine to Ohio in 1813. M. (second), William O. Bowler; she lived in Indiana for awhile and then settled in Edina, Mo.;

13

there are said to have been eight children of her marriage with Samuel Herrick.

(6) Hannah Thompson Herrick; m., Feb. 18, 1836, William E. Davis of Clarksburg, Ind.; she lived at Edina, Mo., for some time. Her mother wrote in 1850, "She has three little boys." The mother states, "At the time of her death she left three sons: George W., Francis Marion and Andrew Jackson."

(7) Arthur Davis.

(7) Jesse Davis, b. Nov. 14, 1836.

(7) Andrew J. Davis; in the Civil War in the Ninth Iowa Regiment; his wife d. at Christmas, 1870, her babe dying at the same time, and left the husband with a little daughter of four years.

(7) George W. Davis, a faithful soldier in the Civil War; d. in the hospital at Quincy, Ill., 1864.

(7) Francis Marion Davis. "He was wounded by the bursting of a musket in the hands of another soldier; after great suffering for a long time, he regained his health in a measure."

(6) Matilda Herrick.

(6) Catherine Herrick; d. 1834; m., 1832, Stephen Parker of Indiana.

(7) Mary Parker. "She was a lone one. Her mother died before she could well remember, and her father did not long survive. She was mostly raised by her uncle, William Parker. She m. Mr. McCall, and lived at New Hope, Ohio."

(6) Eli Herrick. "Killed in a negro insurrection."

(6) Mary Herrick.

(6) Martha Herrick.

(6) Sophia Herrick.

Children of second husband.

(6) Samuel Bowler; a brave soldier in the Civil War.

(6) Martha E. Bowler; m. Mr. Hoback. "She left three children when she died." In 1850 she was a second time married.

(A long search was made for the full records of the children and descendants of this noble Catherine Mulloy (Herrick) Bowler; but it was nearly in vain; but her niece, Mrs. Abbie C. Hitch of Catawba, Ky., kindly loaned the letters which were written to her and her mother when Catherine Mulloy Bowler was an aged woman; these letters are herewith printed, as giving glimpses of her family, and as showing forth her sturdy strength and trust in the midst of many sorrows and in the stress of the Civil War, in which so many of her loved ones were taking part.)

"Edina, Mo. Mch 18, 1850.
"(To Mrs. Martha [Mulloy] Sherwin, Catawba, Ky:)

"Dear and much loved sister. I owe you an apology for my delay in writing—I know not whence this delay. It is always a source of satisfaction to hear from you by your own hand. In the first place I will say that I am in the possession of a reasonable state of health, and also the rest of our family, except Priscilla. She was taken with a bad cold, or influenza, the first of the winter, and her lungs appear to be much disordered, though she is able to be up and oversee her domestic concerns. I feel concerned for her safety.

"I am now teaching a small school eight miles from my home, among our old neighbors. Four weeks are now expired. If I continue through the quarter I think I shall go home and not be persuaded to leave again. Samuel and Raphael are working in partnership. They have rented Mr. Boone's farm this year—his sons being in California. One will follow the prairie breaking, and the other will tend the crop, as they did last year. They have now paid up for their team. If they are blest with health, I hope they will do tolerably well during the ensuing year.

"I hope that when I hear from you again that your son will have returned to the loving arms of his beloved parents and friends with an ample reward for his toil.

"O, sister, how rejoiced we should be to have a visit from you when he returns. If fortune favors, do try to come. It is not so much to travel, as to contemplate the journey beforehand.

"It is now some time since I commenced this letter. Priscilla is much better than she was. The rest of the family are all well. I have had my health better this winter than I have had for a long time. I have been able to attend to my school every day since I commenced. We have had a very pleasant winter, with very little snow. If it continues as it is now people will be plowing the coming week.

"I know that you will write to me as soon as you receive this. Let me know how you all do. I believe that I wrote to you since I received a letter from Mr. Hoback. If I have, I wrote the particulars. I will state that he is married, and I have not heard from him since. His wife is of a respectable family, but I am not personally acquainted with her. He wrote that the children were all doing well. I think that I shall soon write to him. He stated that he was in better circumstances than he had ever been. He plans to move to the north part of the State the coming fall, where his mother and brothers are gone.

"Wm. L. Davis and family are all well and send their best respects to you and yours. The three little boys are doing well. They have been at school all winter. They are writing very well. They are reading in the Fourth Reader and the U. S. History, and have commenced in arithmetic.

"Priscilla's daughter is now grown. Though small, she is a fine promising girl and a great comfort to her mother, though she is not very healthy.

"I regret not seeing your family when I was in Ohio. And when you write give me the particulars from James and likewise from all the rest. I hear that the men who were in California have gone to Oregon the past winter. I have delayed writing so long that it seems as if I cannot write at all as I wish to, nor half what I could say if I could see you.

"Raphael and Samuel will commence the prairie breaking tomorrow. The health of the country is good, except some cases of whooping cough, and that is more favorable than common.

"Please accept and excuse my poor letter, for on reviewing it I perceive that it is altogether disjointed, and my mind is in accordance with it. Remember me to all our dear relatives and accept my warmest love and best wishes for you and yours.

"C. Bowler.

"P. S. I have never heard from Nancy J. Parker, except what brother wrote. If you have heard anything since then please inform me."

*   *   *   *   *

To her niece, Mrs. Abigail C. Hitch:

"Edina, Mo., May 19, 1862.

"My Dear Friends and Relatives in Ky.:

"I received your letter on March 5th and am glad to hear that you are all well and are measureably secluded from the troubles that we have in this State. Since I wrote to you before another of my grandsons is gone to try the realities of another world. He was accidentally shot at Pittsburgh Landing but a short time before the battle. Samuel W. Joliffe, his father and older brother, were with him. Perhaps he was taken from the evil to come. He was a promising youth, dearly beloved by all his family and by all his acquaintances. I feel the blow repeated. But my trust is in God that ere long I shall meet them all again where troubles never come.

"I received a letter from my son last Saturday. He was well and was still at Hanibal. I don't know how long he will remain there, or when he will be home. I have not seen him since Feb. I am now home again on your own little place in the country with Mr. Foss and Martha Jane. They are still planting here. The weather has been very dry for a long time. May 20. No rain yet.

"Catherine and the children were here yesterday, and all well. She brought a letter she had just received from her father. He and William were in the battle. They lost everything they had and have never drawn a cent of pay since they have been there. They have not a cent to buy anything with. He wrote to her to send some paper and stamps. Their letters have been written with a pencil on the leaf of an old book. The letters are sent by the Adjutant to Cairo. They are mailed there, a soldier's letter, and we pay at Edina post office. Many others come that way. They are in the vicinity of Corinth, Tenn., and every day expecting a battle.

"I have not heard from my grandson Herrick Hoback since he was wounded in the battle. I am looking every day for a letter from his sister, in hope to get news. There are now upwards of 200 militia stationed in Edina. We have no courts here since the War commenced. The soldiers are quartered in the Court House. It is fortified, and a large flag floats from the cupola. The jail is used for the prisoners and is never empty. There are scouts constantly scouring the country and bringing in more or less prisoners. How long this bloody strife will last God only knows. It has been viewed in the distance for nearly fifty years, but I have always hoped that I should never live to see the time when it would occur. Nor do I grieve for my three daughters who died before their sons fell in this dreadful war. If it is my son's lot to end his life there I feel as if I could not long survive him.

"My granddaughters all wish to be kindly remembered to you and all. Tell Susanna that this is for her as well as for you. If she will write to me and her husband we will respond. Tell her that I cannot write to her individually, for I do not know her name. Give my kind respects to your father, sister and family, and accept the same for yourself and husband. Please both write soon. Writing, reading, and receiving letters, helps to buoy me up.

"I remain your Affectionate Aunt,

"C. M. H. Bowler."

*   *   *   *   *

To her niece, Mrs. Abby C. Hitch:

"Flora, Ills., Sept. 30, 1864.

"Dear Niece:

"I received a letter from my granddaughter, Catherine E. Munns, informing me that you had written to her and that she intended answering it the coming day. So I am in hopes that you have heard from her before this time. And now that our correspondence is renewed I hope it will be continued. I hardly know why it was broken off so long. I was exceedingly glad to hear from you again. But she stated no particulars. When you receive this you will respond and let me know about the welfare of yourself and family. I am in the usual health, though old and infirm. I have no right to complain. I am as comfortable as can be expected at my age. I feel thankful that I am able to read and write, so as to correspond with my friends.

"My son, my only living child, has been in the army ever since the commencement of the War. Last Feb. he reënlisted for three years more. He nas lately been home on a furlough. When he returned I came with him to St. Louis where he put me on the cars that I might come to some of our friends in Ills. I plan to stay there until he returns, if it please God that he does return.

"Your cousin Hannah Davis left three sons, George W., Francis M., and Andrew J. They are all in the War from the first. George died in the hospital at Quincy, Ills. Marion was wounded by the bursting of a musket in the hands of another soldier. After extreme suffering for a long time he recovered, but is nearly ruined for life. Andrew is in the Iowa Cavalry, Company M., at McDougall's Bluff, Arkansas. They are in Steele's Division of the Cavalry that my son is in. His address is the 3d Mo. Cavalry, Co. E., Little Rock, Arkansas. These two forts are 60 miles apart.

"I hope before this time you have got Catherine Munn's letter which will inform you all about her mother's family and her own. Your cousin Catherine Parker left one child, Nancy J. Both parents died when she was young. She was left to the care of her Uncle Wm. Parker after her grandpartnes died, where she lived until she was married. Her address is Mrs. Nancy J. McCall, New Hope, Ohio. Please write to her and form an acquaintance with her, for which I know that she would be very grateful. I believe that she has two half brothers in the army, but she is a lone one on her mother's side.

"Martha E. Hoback left three children: Herrick, Catherine D. and Nancy Priscilla. Herrick was killed at Pittsburgh Landing, as you have been informed. Kate was married to Frederic Martin, who is also in the Army. They live in Cassville, Howard Co., Iowa. Nancy is not married. Her father (Mr. Hoback) was a Methodist preacher for several years previous to the War. But his patriotism for his country was so great that he went out Capt. of a Co. in 1861. But his health did not permit him to continue. He resigned after getting his health mended up a little. He commenced preaching again. He writes to me that the state of his health demands him to locate and he thinks of coming to the West to settle.

"Now, dear Abby, please write to me a good long letter. Tell me of all your friends, your dear old father, your sister Susan, your friends in California, and about your husband and children in particular. Give me your sister's address, for you and she were made up in the bundle with the other dear ones that I wish to hear from. Adieu.

"Yours Truly,   Catherine Bowler,"

*   *   *   *   *

To her niece, Mrs. Abby C. Hitch:

"Edina, Mo., Apr. 8, 1870.

"My Dear Niece:

"I take up the pen once more to inform you that I am still living and that I am in as good health as is commonly allotted to old age. I am feeble. My sight and hearing both fail. But still I can walk about the house, and truly thank God that I am no worse. I am subject to spells of sickness. But now is my time of best health. In looking over some old letters that I had preserved, I found your photograph. It brought past recollections, both of you and of your beloved mother, so to my mind that I resolved to write to you. But I can see these lines but very faintly, and perhaps you will not understand what I am trying to write.

"Two years before the War ended I was in Ills. with my step-grandchildren. Samuel came to me there. Then we staid two years longer and came back to Mo. two years ago last month. We came to David Munn's. You know she is your cousin, Catherine Joliffe, that was. This has been my home ever since.

"I am comfortably provided for, but live very retired. They take me twice a year to see Martha. They live ten miles from here. She is Catherine's married sister, and her youngest sister is now eighteen years of age. Jane had two sons and two daughters. Catherine has four children living, two daughters and two sons. She lost two children. Her sister Matilda lives with her and her youngest brother, Thomas Benton, is now 15 years old.

"I have not heard from your Aunt Parker for a long time. But I am looking for a letter from her. Dear Abby, please write to me. I long to hear from you all. Your respected old mother, sisters and brothers. I think Dr. Carr came back from California and settled in Iowa. I am glad to hear that Nancy has come back to the States. I always thought I should be un-happy out where she has been. Tell me all about Susanna and her family. Give my love to her and give me her address.

"Tell about your brothers. Do not fail to write, for I am old and lonely. It comforts me to hear from my dear distant friends. Catherine and Matilda join with me in love to all. Farewell.

"Your Aunt, C. H. Bowler."

* * * * *

To her niece, Mrs. Abby C. Hitch:

"Edina, Mo., Apr. 14, 1871.

"Dear Niece Abby Hitch:

"I have been in poor health for a month past though not confined to my bed. But my great age for-bids my being long on this earth. My earnest prayer is to be ready when God calls for me. I was 84 last January. The family is as well as usual. Martha Jane was here last Saturday and she and her family are well.

"Your cousin, Andy Davis, who lives at Gosport, Ind., lost his wife last Christmas. He thinks of com-ing back to this place in the summer. His brother is in Kansas. They are all that is left of your cousin Hannah's family.

"Mch 12 I got a letter from your Aunt Parker. Her health is reasonable for one of her age. She keeps house, with hired help. She is able to drive out in her little carriage, or walk to the Academy. She said she had her garden ploughed to plant peas and early potatoes. I have no doubt that she will be working in her garden all the spring. Her letters are very satisfactory. Catherine has four children. Her oldest, Ella is in her 14th year. Robert the youngest is 20 months old.

"Martha has four children. Samuel is here with me. His health is not very good. He has been afflicted with neuralgia for several years. He suffers much at times, but is not often laid by altogether, and works very hard. He sends his love to you all, especially to William, if he is with you. You said you expected him but of his return we have never heard. Your Aunt wrote that Nancy was still in Iowa. Your cousin, Nancy Jane McCall, that lives at New Hope,

Ohio, is of my daughter Catherine Parker. She wrote to me a year ago that she was in bad health, and did not expect to be better. Tell Martha to write to Matilda Joliffe. She still lives with Catherine. Sarah lives with Martha J. Fox

"My granddaughters are busy planting the garden.
"Your loving Aunt,   Catherine Bowler."

*   *   *   *   *

(5) James Mulloy, b. Litchfield, Me., Thursday, March 13, 1788, and probably died young, as no further mention is found.

*   *   *   *   *

(5) Hannah Mulloy, b. Litchfield, Me., Saturday, July 3, 1790; d. New York, Nov., 1839; m., intention dated April 22, 1810, to Hon. Ebenezer Herrick, b. Lewiston, Me., Oct. 10, 1785; d. Lewiston, Me., May 7, 1839; he was the son of John Herrick, a leading citizen of Lewiston, Me., and his mother's maiden name was Griffin; he was a brother of Oliver Herrick, who m. Lydia Thompson, daughter of Ezekiel Thompson, and he was a grandson of Maj. Israel Herrick. The Herrick line of Hon. Ebenezer Herrick: (1) Henry Herrick of Leicestershire, England, who came to America, 1653, and settled on a large tract of land at Beverly, Mass., and his descendants settled near him, and from this line came all the Herricks in America; the fifth son of Sir William Herrick was (2) Henry Herrick; (3) Israel Herrick, grandson of this Henry Herrick, entered the British Colonial Army in 1745 as a lieutenant, and commanded a Beverly, Mass., company at the battle of the Plains of Abraham, when General Wolfe fell in victory; he also fought in a campaign against the French and Indians; resigned from the army as major, 1765; his military experience was valuable to him in organizing the colonial troops previous to the battle of Bunker Hill, and he fought in that famous battle; when the army left Cambridge his age and disabilities compelled him to resign; he afterwards moved with his sons to Lewiston, Me., where he settled; his son Eli m. Hannah Thompson, daughter of Benjamin Thompson of Bath, Me., Sept. 5, 1759; d. 1844; no children; Hon. Ebenezer Herrick was a member of Congress from Maine for several terms; he was a lawyer, but he did not follow his profession; for a time he was professor of logic and rhetoric in Bowdoin College, Brunswick, Me.; he

was a member of the convention at Portland, 1819,
which framed the constitution of Maine in 1821; representative to Congress for six years, 1821–'27; state senator, 1828–'29; he was the first principal of the academy
at Monmouth, Me.; he was a resident of Bowdoin, Me.,
when he was married; soon after 1819 he moved to Lewiston, Me., and lived there many years

(6) John Herrick; b. Aug. 5, 1810; d. Dec. 6, 1830; unm.

(6) Hon. Anson Herrick, b. Jan. 12, 1812; d. New York City,
Feb. 6, 1868; he was publisher and editor of the New
York *Atlas;* alderman of the Nineteenth Ward of New
York City, 1853–'57; naval store keeper of Brooklyn
Navy Yard for the Eighth District of New York,
1863–'65; he was one of the few Democrats in the
House of Representatives who voted for the constitu-
tional amendment abolishing slavery, and thus secured
its submission to the Senate. New England Historic
Genealogical Register, July, 1868: "He received a common school education; at the age of 15 years he was
apprenticed to the printer's business; 1836, settled in
New York City; continued in the same employment
until 1838, when he commenced the weekly publication of the journal called the *Atlas,* of which he has
since been the editor and proprietor; in 1862 he was
chosen alderman and served three years; by President
Buchanan he was appointed naval store keeper for
New York, which he held till 1861; in 1862 he was
elected representative from New York to the Thirty-
eighth Congress." M. Mary Wood of Wiscasset, Me.,
who d. at Paterson, N. J., Nov. 28, 1881; Hon. Anson
Herrick had nine children; the records of a few are
given:

(7) Mary Wood Herrick, b. Wiscasset, Me., June 30, 1834;
unm.; resides at Paterson, N. J., with her brother,
Carlton M. Herrick.

*   *   *   *   *

(7) Carlton Moses Herrick, b. New York City, Nov. 4,
1836; graduated from Columbia College, 1854; A. M.,
1857; Columbia Law School, 1861; admitted to the
bar; was editor and one of the proprietors of the
New York *Atlas* after the death of his father;
moved to Paterson, N. J., where in 1881 he was editor and publisher of the daily and weekly *Guardian*

*   *   *   *   *

(7) Anson Herrick, b. Dec. 26, 1838; d. June 15, 1878; one
of the proprietors of the New York *Atlas;* on a paper at Paterson, N. J., with his brother, Carlton; m.
Mary Scheffelin of Catskill, N. Y.

(6) Mary Gove Herrick, b. Jan., 1813; d. at Yellow Springs,
O., May 20, 1870; m., Jan. 13, 1833, John Tyler Blaisdell of Lewiston, Me., b. Feb. 18, 1808; d. Yellow
Springs, O., May 24, 1880; son of Walter Robie Blaisdell and Sarah Tyler; farmer, carpenter, etc.; there
were nine children.

(7) Walter Robie Blaisdell, b Nov. 5, 1833; d. April 15,
1834.

*   *   *   *   *

(7) Hannah Herrick Blaisdell, b. Yellow Springs, O., Oct.,
1834; resides Jefferson, Tex.; m., Oct. 16, 1855, Samuel McCulloch, a carpenter and undertaker.

(8) Samuel Herrick McCulloch, b. Dec. 14, 1856; resides Cañon City, Col.

(8) Mary Agnes McCulloch, b. March 5, 1858; d. March
5, 1863.

(8) Anna Donaldson McCulloch, b. Jan. 21, 1862; d. Oct.
12, 1863.

(8) Archie McCulloch, b. Oct., 1863.

(8) Mary McCulloch, b. Sept. 18, 1868.

*   *   *   *   *

(7) Mary Elizabeth Blaisdell, b. near Lewiston, Me., May
23, 1836; d. Auburndale, Mass., Dec. 25, 1905; she
lived Lewiston, Me., New York City, Brooklyn, N. Y.,
Clermont, O., Yellow Springs, O., and moved to Auburndale, Mass., 1894; she studied in Antioch College; a noble woman; m., Aug. 21, 1862, Archibald
McNair, b. Clermont County, O., Feb., 1830; d. Nashville, Tenn., March 11, 1865; a teacher and farmer;
son of John McNair and Sarah McMurchy.

(8) Anna Donaldson McNair, b. Clermont County, O.,
June 21, 1863; resides 40 Auburn Place, Auburndale, Mass; graduated from Antioch College, Yellow Springs, O., 1886, and in 1890 from Doctor Sargent's School of Physical Training, Cambridge,
Mass.; she was the director of the gymnasium of
Bryn Mawr College, 1890–'94; also in the Friends'
Hospital, Fairford, Pa., 1891–'93; m., June 28,
1894, Amos R. Wells of Glen Falls, N. Y., b. Dec.
23, 1862; he graduated from Antioch College, 1883;

editor of *Christian Endeavor World* and writer of
books and many periodicals; son of Amos P. Wells
and Mary ———.

(9) Mary Elizabeth Wells, b. Auburndale, Mass., Aug.
9, 1895.

(9) Margaret Anna Wells, b. Feb. 8, 1899; d. Aug. 10,
1905.

* * * * *

(7) Minerva Huntington Blaisdell, b. Oct. 3, 1837; resides
Richmond, Ky.; m., April 2, 1861, Rev. Charles K.
Marshall, minister of Disciples Church.

(8) Mary Ella Marshall, b. May 20, 1862; d. Aug. 1,
1863.

(8) Jessie Blaisdell Marshall, b. July 21, 1863; d. Oct.
13, 1864.

(8) Lena Hannah Marshall, b. May 7, 1865.

(8) Kate Frazier Marshall, b. Sept. 14, 1867.

(8) Harmon Marshall, b. Sept. 23, 1870.

(8) John Blaisdell Marshall, b. Sept. 12, 1872.

(8) Sallie Woolfolk Marshall, b. March 18, 1875.

(8) Charles Kingsley Marshall, b. March 14, 1877.

(8) Mary Hattie Marshall, b. April 14, 1881; d. Oct. 29,
1882.

* * * * *

(7) Elvira Priscilla Blaisdell, b. July 3, 1839; d. Feb. 17,
1842.

* * * * *

(7) Walter Scott Blaisdell, b. Sept. 22, 1847; d. Sept. 30,
1878; m., March, 1873, Mary Elizabeth Edwards of
Paris, Bourbon County, Ky.

* * * * *

(7) Elvira Susan Blaisdell, b. July 24, 1850; resides 259
Harrisville Avenue, Ogden, Utah; m., Aug. 6, 1881,
Dr. James M. Harris of Yellow Springs, O.; gradu-
ated A. B. from Antioch College; and from Bellevue
Homeopathic Hospital, New York City, 1868; mem-
ber of medical society of Clark County, O.

(8) Ten children; one of them Walter B. Harris, b. Feb.
23, 1882.

(6) James L. Herrick, b. June 4, 1815; d. 1838.

(6) Elvira Priscilla Herrick, b. Oct. 25, 1816; d. 1850.

(6) Laura Herrick, b. May 1, 1819; d. Feb. 23, 1878; m. George Ogden of Jersey City, N. J.

  (7) Caroline Augusta Ogden, b. Jan. 30, 1842.

*   *   *   *   *

  (7) Lydia Herrick Ogden, b. Oct. 17, 1843; resides Asbury Park, N. J.; m., Oct. 4, 1860, William E. Barnes of Jersey City, N. J.; commission merchant. Ten children, part of whom are as follows:

    (8) William E. Barnes, b. Nov. 11, 1865.

    (8) Laura Louise Barnes, b. June 14, 1867.

    (8) Edward Vanderpool Barnes, b. Dec. 23, 1868; d. July 31, 1869.

    (8) Lydia Herrick Barnes, b. June 7, 1870; d. Aug. 16, 1870.

    (8) Charles Francis Barnes, b. May 7, 1872; d. May 28, 1872.

*   *   *   *   *

  (7) George L. Ogden, b. Aug. 16, 1843.

*   *   *   *   *

  (7) William Sickles Ogden, b. June 17, 1847; resides Jersey City, N. J.; m., Aug. 1, 1867, Minerva A. Rowe.

    (8) William R. Ogden, b. Sept. 17, 1867.

    (8) Minerva A. Ogden, b. Nov. 13, 1869.

    (8) Lillian Ogden, b. Oct. 10, 1871.

    (8) Clara Ogden, b. May 17, 1873.

    (8) Fannie Ogden, b. May 9, 1875.

    (8) Laura Ogden, b. 1877.

*   *   *   *   *

  (7) Laura Ogden.

(6) Hugh Mulloy Herrick, b. at the old Herrick homestead, Lewiston, Me., July 3, 1829; resides 105 Carroll Street, Paterson, N. J.; journalist and editor; in 1842 moved to New York City; clerk of the court of common pleas, New York City, 1850–'61; in 1872 moved to Paterson, N. J.; 1872, on the Paterson *Daily Guardian* as associate editor; received an academic education in Monmouth (Me.) Academy and in Clermont (O.) Academy; in 1850, when 21 years old, established a weekly newspaper at Richmond, O.; in 1852 went to New York City; was attached to the editorial staff of the New York *Atlas*, published by his brother; took an active part in politics; June 1, 1856, was appointed

clerk of the trial department of the New York court
of common pleas; held the place until 1862, then became chief entry clerk of the naval office of the New
York Revenue Department, which he held until the
spring of 1871; in the meantime he kept up his practice of journalism and was a writer for, and a contributor to, several New York daily and weekly jour-
nals; on the Paterson (N. J.) *Daily Guardian* for many
years; in 1888 proprietor of the *Repuolican*, a large
paper at Hackensack, N. J.; in 1901 sold this newspaper establishment and retired from business, making
his home in Paterson, N. J.; a well-known political
leader in New Jersey, and an influential editor; m., at
New Richmond, O., Aug. 9, 1853, Louisa Malvena Tremper, b. March 4, 1834; daughter of Johnson Tremper of
Kingston, N. Y., b. 1809; d. New Richmond, O., and
Laura Jeffers.

*　*　*　*　*

(7) Alma Elmira Herrick, b. July 15, 1854; graduated
from the High School of Jersey City, N. J., 1868; resides Auvergne-by-the-sea, Long Island, N. Y.; m.,
Jan. 14, 1874, Henry E. Knight, b. Brooklyn, N. Y.,
1847; silk commission merchant of New York City;
son of Francis E. Knight.

(8) Edith Herrick Knight, b. Nov. 20, 1875; m., Nov.
28, 1905, Emerson W. Montrose.

(8) Frank Robinson Knight, b. Oct. 13, 1877; address,
592 One Hundred and Fifty-first Street, New York
City; in silk business with his father; resides
Bensonhurst, L. I.; m., April 19, 1899, Mary Byrne
of New York City.

(9) Henry E. Knight, Jr.

(9) Frank Robinson Knight.

(8) Henry Eliott Knight, b. Feb. 7, 1881; unm.; fruit
raiser in Porto Rico.

*　*　*　*

(7) Mary Herrick, b. Sept. 11, 1856; m., Oct., 1883, Edgar
I. Talman, b. Massachusetts, 1858; he is now superintendent of a silk manufactory at Astoria, L. I.

(8) Louise Herrick Talman, b. Sept. 11, 1856; graduated from the New York Training School for
Teachers, Nov., 1884.

(8) Irving C. Talman, b. May, 1886.

(8) Shirley Talman, b. July, 1890.

(8) Malcolm H. Talman, b. Aug., 1896.

     *   *   *   *   *

(7) Richard Cummings Herrick, b. New York City, July 13, 1859; resides Indianapolis, Ind.; assistant to general manager of Indianapolis *News;* printer and ranchman; has lived New York City, Passaic and Jersey City, N. J.; in Colorado towns: Monimet, Rockyford, Pueblo, Denver, and in Pasadena, Cal., Iron Mountain, Mich., and Indianapolis, Ind.; only had primary school education; went into a printing office at 12 years of age; m., Sept. 7, 1882, Martha Ann Kenyon of Kansas, b. Aug. 11, 1861; daughter of John Kenyon and Asenath Wessner.

(8) Frank Kenyon Herrick, b. Indianapolis, Ind., June 21, 1883; d. of pneumonia, March 15, 1904; was in United States Navy with the Asiatic Squadron; was rising rapidly in the navy; graduated from high school, 1901; yeoman of the second class in the navy.

(8) Hugh Mulloy Herrick, b. Rockyford, Col., May 8, 1890; freshman in Indianapolis (Ind.) High School, 1906.

     *   *   *   *   *

(7) Carlton Tremper Herrick, b. July 6, 1867; d. Feb. 14, 1902; unm.; finished his education in the Paterson (N. J.) High School and Paterson Classical Institute; graduated from College of Ophthalmia in Chicago; was the leading optician in Paterson, N. J.; his office was burned in the great fire at Paterson, N. J., and he took cold while searching for a new office and died suddenly of pleuro-pneumonia.

     *   *   *   *   *

(5) Priscilla Mulloy, b. Litchfield, Me., Saturday, May 18, 1793; d. Mount Hygiene, Clermont County, O., Sept. 4, 1874. Of her Mr. Parker Donaldson of Cincinnati, O., gives the following sketch:

"Priscilla Mulloy early manifested superior powers of mind and an unusually resolute, ambitious spirit. We learn from some friends of her youth that she was remarkably handsome and attractive. Mrs. Abigail Conklin says she well remembers being told by her mother, in her childhood, to get her work done and prepare to meet her handsome cousin Priscilla. And when she arrived she remembers looking upon her as a stately, beautiful woman. A much more important fact is, that, while she was quite young, she made a decision to embrace the religion of Jesus. She frequently and affectionately spoke of her first pastor, Elder Stinson, and of his wife. This wife was a remarkable woman for those times. So earnest was she in coöperating in the good work of her husband in urging sinners to repent, that the deacons of the church felt called upon to admonish her that she was transcending the bounds of propriety for a woman by praying and speaking in public. Possessing a spirit meek as well as earnest, she resolved to heed the admonition of the brethren. But when she came again into the meetings she was so filled with the love and spirit of the Master that she could not forbear to speak. This seemingly incoherent item is mentioned because of its effect on the mind of the young Priscilla in that susceptible age. The effect was so great as to become in a measure a life-long inspiration to her, and for years she has been known to obey religious impulses in a similar manner. She said that no sermon ever seemed to move the people as did the words and example of the godly Mrs. Stinson.

"In her early girlhood Priscilla Mulloy was also deeply impressed by an interesting scene which she witnessed. It was the baptism of a little friend, Benjamin Ring. He was so young and small that Elder Stinson took him in his arms, carried him down into the water and baptized him, and bore him to the shore again in his extended arms. Always when she related this incident she would stand with her arms extended in imitation of the elder. No doubt that scene made an impression upon her that was never obliterated. At the age of eighteen Priscilla was baptized and united with the church. The resolution thus to obey her Savior was made at a meeting held by Elder Stinson at a new barn in the neighborhood. Among the obstacles, hindrances and crosses, which usually beset one's pathway in taking such a step, one usually looms up above all others. Her particular cross was the supposed opposition of her father. Although of an age when she could act for herself, yet her sense of obligation to her parents induced her to go to them and make her wishes known. What was her joyful

14

surprise to find entire willingness on their part. Her father said that he never planned to control his children in matters of religion. Thus she began her Christian career.

"Mother Parker, as she was always called in Ohio, did not at any time turn away from or neglect religious duties. But, like many others, for a few years, she seemed to have fallen asleep in reference to them. Not having brought a church letter with her from the East, she did not, for many years, assume any church connection. But in the time of great revival from 1836 to 1840, she was among the number who were awakened to duty, and she united with the Free Baptists at what is now called the Lindale, O., church. From that time, for many years, she was remarkably active and zealous in her religious duties. No ordinary circumstances, not even boisterous winds, nor pelting rains would keep her from the meetings of the church. And yet she was often heard—more of late years—to deplore her delinquencies and lack of faith. She sometimes said, 'I am a natural infidel.' Few, if any, were more faithful to convictions of truth and duty, or stood forth with more moral courage to advocate the great principles of practical Christianity, even though they were unpopular and persecuted. She was impatient of opposition and delay. She was early in the anti-slavery cause and continued a zealous advocate and worker so long as the institution of slavery lasted. She once made a pilgrimage into Kentucky, calling on her old friends and exhorting them concerning their sin. She was no less interested in the temperance cause. Not only did she participate in the Temperance Crusade in a quiet way, but she, in company of Dr. Rogers and Mrs. Mary Applegate, made a similar crusade. They entered every grocery, dramshop and tavern, in New Richmond, O., where drinks were sold, and exhorted the proprietors to desist from their traffic. They, being American gentlemen, heard the appeal, and in course of time, though not immediately, abandoned the business. Succeeding this, there was a time when New Richmond, O., was reported to be the most orderly town and to possess the most temperate, intelligent inhabitants of any in that country. When David Gibson came to reëstablish and extend the whiskey business it was a sorrowful day for lovers of Temperance and Sobriety, and to none was it more so than to Mother Priscilla Mulloy Parker and her good husband. Both of them personally remonstrated with Mr. Gibson, only to be repulsed by him with derision. Mother Parker addressed letters to him on the subject as long as he would take them from the post office and read them. But these pungent truths he could not bear, and he finally told her he would never read another letter of hers.

"Mother Parker was in the habit of examining every new subject which was brought before the public notice, heartily endorsing whatever in her judgment seemed to contain truth. Among them was Spiritualism. This, for a time, drew her away from the ordinary forms of religious service and proved a manifest injury to her spiritual state. But in the course of time, the *Banner of Light*, and such literature, was discontinued. The *Journal and Messenger*, and other religious papers, and the old Family Bible, were substituted. Her old devotional spirits and habits returned. Again she frequented the House of God and participated earnestly in the prayer and social meetings. Often, in the last years of her life, she exhorted the young people to espouse the religion of Christ. Gospel preaching again had its wonted influence over her. As constantly as she was able to do so, she attended the ministrations of Elder Drinkwater and enjoyed them much, being greatly encouraged and benefitted by them. She often said that his Thanksgiving sermons were a comfort to her. In her last sickness she often asked for Scripture reading, singing, or prayer, at her bedside, and sometimes she designated the portion of Scripture which she would like to hear. The songs which she chose were chiefly those used in the Temperance Crusade.

"In whatever good she engaged she came as nearly as anyone to fulfilling the Scriptures, 'She hath done what she could.'

"Her childish friendship with Benjamin Ring, which has already been referred to, ripened in maturer years into the pure esteem and affection which can be experienced but once. She married this life-long lover, and moved to Hallowell, Me., where she spent some of the happiest days of her life. In her own narrative she says, 'In the early part of the autumn of 1810 we were married and I rode home with my young, beautiful husband to Hallowell in a chaise. We did not dream that any one could have a greater share of happiness than had fallen to our lot. The town was beautiful, and the society was delightful to me. Time glided by; all things were dressed in golden hues to my enraptured vision.'

"The husband, Benjamin Ring, was a merchant and took great pleasure in supplying her with all personal household comforts in that cosy, complete, and frugal style which comported with that day in our country's history. But alas, as the poet has said, sadly, and perhaps truly, 'You may suspect some danger nigh when you possess delight.' So in a few months this companionship came to a sad end. In Dec., 1814, Benjamin Ring started for Boston, Mass., to purchase goods for his store. The schooner on which he took passage was capsized in a gale and he, with all the passengers but one, were frozen to death. One says, 'The sorrow which then began in the heart of the widowed wife never ceased, though she bore it all with a wonderful fortitude. I once called on her on a gloomy day, the anniversary of Mr. Ring's death. She said she had lived all her early bereavement over again, as if it had just occurred. But her trust was firmly anchored in her Lord.'

"The only child of her marriage to Mr. Ring was Benjamin[6], b. 1814, and d. of fever in Ohio in the winter of 1815.

"In 1815, as soon as her affairs could be adjusted after the loss of her husband, she started with her infant son in her arms, in company with some friends who were emigrating to Ohio. They came in wagons to the Ohio River, and thence down the River on flat boats and landed on the Frandon Farm below New Richmond, Ohio. Then she was taken to the neighborhood now known as Lindale, O., where she was kindly received into the home of her cousin, Deacon Andrew Coombs. In that vicinity she taught her first school in the West. There, too, she was laid low by the malignant fever which prevailed at the time in that new country. Her babe was also smitten. While she was still prostrate the dead body of her Bennie, beautiful even in death, was brought to her bedside. On her return to health she went to teach in Kentucky, nearly opposite Point Pleasant, Ohio. She boarded in the family of Esquire James Kennedy, a Scotch gentle-

"Mount Hygiene," the home of Rev. Daniel Parker and his wife, Priscilla Mulloy. It faced the Ohio River. The first house was burned and this was built on the same site.

erect as a queen beside her husband when some one whispered, but loud enough for her to hear, "She will not always sit as straight as she does now." She at once, and quietly, resolved that she would sit as then—and maintained her queenly bearing down to her old age.

A short time previous to his marriage Father Parker, as he was always called, was delighted to find that Mr. David Moreton was willing to sell the half of his farm on which he then resided. This became Mount Hygiene, on the Ohio River, near New Richmond, Clermont County. This included the sawmill which the Moretons had built on Boat Run. Daniel Parker at once secured this property, in 1818, and it was their happy home through the long years of their married life. There they lived in comfort, though they toiled hard to get the farm paid for and to procure the means of living.

Mother Parker taught several select schools after her marriage. She also taught all that she could in her home, as the country districts could then afford only a few months of school in the winter, and that not of the best quality. Mr. John Cooper, who became a merchant at Point Pleasant, O., and Mr. David Moreton, were, however, fine teachers, whose good influence was long felt in that community.

As their children grew up, Father and Mother Parker felt a deepening interest in the education of these dear ones. Mother Parker was one day in the company of Mr. Cathcart, who was teacher of a select school in Cincinnati, O. When she heard him remark that he hoped to educate his son and daughter so that they might be able to conduct an academy, she was inspired to resolve that she would adopt the same plan for her oldest children, James and Susanna. As soon, therefore, as they were old enough, they were sent to New Richmond, O., where they could enjoy advantages superior to those at home. Susanna was in the schools of Miss Sarah Ann Molyneaux, afterwards Mrs. John Rogers and Mrs. John W. Weekly. Besides this, Dr. James T. Johnson, a very intelligent, scholarly and public-spirited man of that town, gave free lectures on English grammar and botany. Mother Parker generally attended these lectures with her children, being an enthusiastic lover of these and of other sciences, and thus inspired in her children a deep love of the same things. Doctor Johnson's lectures were well attended. Among the pupils were Capt. John Comers and wife—then young and single; Mrs. Sarah Walker, who became Mrs. Moreton of Marietta, O.; Miss Lydia Applegate; Dr. Knox Rotchford, who settled in Alexandria, Ky., but who was then a student of medicine with Dr. John Rogers; and numerous others whose scholarly ways and fine characters were of great help to the Parkers and their children. A few years later Rev. James Walker, an eminent divine and author, the pastor of the Presbyterian Church in that place, gave a very able and instructive course of lectures in geology. And all this did much to make the "Golden Age" in New Richmond, O.

Finally Mother Parker conceived the idea of erecting a school building on the farm in which the older children might teach and help educate the younger ones. After much deliberation Father Parker acquiesced in the plan. Lack of means was the great obstacle. With a family of ten members to maintain by the proceeds of a small farm, and spending much of his time away preaching for a very meagre remuneration in money, such an undertaking was to him almost impossible. Moreover, the principal of the proposed academy was then a youth entirely unqualified for such a position. He must be educated by means which were wholly unseen. The prospect was by no means flattering, and none but an ambitious and determined spirit would have entertained the thought. But Mother Parker possessed such a spirit, while her husband, while slower of decision, and more timid of venture, when he had once made up his mind to try anything, especially if it involved a duty, or a moral principle, was resolute and persevering to execute. Father Parker secretly resolved on trying to save from his scanty income, by small sums, $200, to begin with. He said to himself that if the Lord would enable him to do this he would take it is an indication of His favor, and venture on. In the course of time he succeeded in saving this sum, and it was very interesting to hear him tell how the Lord had blessed him in his efforts, throwing into his hands here a little and there a little, through unexpected channels, in several cases for ministerial services for which, before that, he had seldom received any compensation.

In 1839 the building of the famous Clermont Academy was finally begun and carried on to completion in the spirit of prayer and consecration. In the meantime the teacher was away at school trying to acquire the necessary qualifications for the responsible position. Mother Parker's heart rejoiced when she beheld the darling object of her desire and long expectation in operation. Never for a moment in its history did her interest in its prosperity abate, nor her watchfulness wane. All the examinations, exhibitions, social meetings, reunions, etc., especially the lyceum meetings, have witnessed the fervor of her zeal and the intense delight which she always took in the culture and development of the youthful mind and heart. No entertainment seemed to give her so much pleasure as the literary and religious exercises in which the students were engaged, and in which she always participated when she was able, either by reading from her prose or poetic writings, or selections, or in the way of debate or criticism.

Father Parker, though equally interested in the history at heart in the establishment and prosperity of Clermont Academy, was nevertheless always ready to recognize his wife as the leading spirit in its incipiency. On one occasion, at the close of one of the annual exhibitions, he was making some remarks, reciting some of the history of the school, and relating some of the labors and anxieties connected with its history, and also speaking his gratitude and gratification in tne good results already realized. Dr. Nathaniel Culver of Cincinnati was present. When Father Parker had done speaking, the doctor said in substance: "That is just such a history as a woman would instigate. Now tell me, was not your wife the prime mover in this enterprise?" Thereupon Father Parker, with his characteristic candor, replied, "Yes, she was;" so cheerfully giving up to her a large meed of praise.

Mother Parker once wrote thus of the school: "It was in the summer of 1816 that my late husband, Rev. Daniel Parker, came riding down the Franklin Road, passing by what has since become the Browning farm. As he approached the descent of the hill, in full view of the Ohio River, and of the hills beyond, clothed in the rich foliage of an unbroken Kentucky forest—the beautiful expanded area before him combined the grand and the picturesque—he contemplated the extended prospect with delight, while a halo seemed to his impressable imagination to

Clermont Academy.

Clermont Academy, and Bock Row, in which roomed students from a distance.

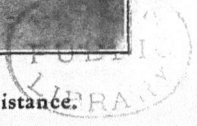

(6) James Kennedy Parker, b. Clermontville, O., Sept. 22,
        1817; d. June 14, 1894. The mother gave him, and her
        other children, careful educational training at home.
        When not six years old he was a pupil of Mr. David
        Moreton. Under John Cooper, later on, he not only
        studied the common school branches, but trigonometry
        and bookkeeping in the log cabin schoolhouses of those
        times. As soon as he and his sister Susanna were old
        enough they were sent to New Richmond, O., where
        they could enjoy superior educational advantages. He
        was under the fine training of Rev. Charles Swain,
        Clement Pierce, Rev. Josiah Denham, Rev. Mr. Blake-
        ley and others ' In the school of Mr. John W. Wheeler,
        on the closing day of school, July 4, 1839, James K.
        Parker made his first public address. He studied in
        South Hanover Presbyterian College, near Madison,
        Ind., entering May, 1835; entered Pleasant Hill Acad-
        emy, near Cincinnati, O., May, 1839; he had some fine
        training in the Lebanon (O.) Normal School; he was
        a scholar of great ability and untiring industry. In
        1839 he became principal of Clermont Academy; he
        continued in that position until 1892, except sixteen
        months which he spent in Wilberforce University,
        Green County, O. He was familiarly known through-
        out a large section of the country as "Teacher Par-
        ker," and his work was of the most careful and endur-
        ing character. M., Dec. 25, 1842, Sarah Preston Ba-
        ker, b. Georgetown, O., Dec. 6, 1823; d. New Richmond,
        O., May 8, 1901; studied at Clermont Academy and Leb-
        anon (O.) Normal School; daughter of James O. Baker,
        b. Maryland and d. Clermontville, O., summer of 1859;
        ne resided in several Ohio towns; millwright and house
        builder; m. Henrietta Hermason, b. West Hartford,
        Conn., and d. New Richmond, O.

              *   *   *   *   *
              *   *   *   *   *

(7) Charlotte Frances Parker, b. Mount Hygiene, O., Dec.
        23, 1844; resides 71 Oxford Avenue, Dayton, O.;
        graduated at Clermont Academy, June, 1863; also
        from Young Ladies' Institute, Granville, O., June,
        1866; school teacher and music teacher; m., in
        Lowell, Mass., Dec. 25, 1867, Rev. Charles Warren
        Currier, b. Lowell, Mass., Dec. 22, 1842; d. Winfield,
        Kan., April 17, 1889; Baptist clergyman; son of Seth

James Kennedy Parker, Principal of Clermont Academy.

(8) Alan Kent Stuckey, b. Mount Hygiene, O., Sept. 11, 1885; resides 301 Delaware Avenue, N. E., Washington, D. C.; civil engineer.

*　　*　　*　　*　　*
*　　*　　*　　*　　*

(7) Eva Parker, b. Mount Hygiene, O., March 29, 1860; resides Martin's Ferry, W. Va.; graduated from Clermont Academy, 1880; m., July 7, 1881, Rev. Edward Andrew Read, b. Norton, Mass., April 27, 1852; Baptist minister; graduated from Colby (Me.) University, 1875; Newton (Mass.) Theological Seminary, 1878; son of Rev. William Read and Susan Austin.

(8) Austin Parker Read, b. Clermontville, O., June 24, 1887.

(8) Mason Kent Read, b. Wauseon, Fulton County, O., March 12, 1891.

*　　*　　*　　*　　*
*　　*　　*　　*　　*

(7) Dr. James Kennedy Parker, b. Wauseon, O., April 6, 1862; d. Denver, Col., Sept. 29, 1889; studied at Clermont Academy and Miami Medical College with Doctor Scudder; m., June 9, 1889, Ella Carey Smith, b. Dec., 1861; no children.

(6) Susanna Everts Parker, b. Mount Hygiene, O., April 28, 1819; d. Penmaen, New Richmond, O., March 5, 1890; she and her brother James were sent to New Richmond, O., to school; she studied in the school of Miss Sarah Ann Molyneaux, who became Mrs. Doctor Rogers; also in the school of Mrs. John J. A. Weakley; she was also under the influence of the lectures of Dr. James T. Johnson, a very intelligent, scholarly and public-spirited man, who gave free lectures on English and botany; m., Aug. 31, 1827, Thomas Donaldson, b. London, Eng., Nov. 27, 1805; d. Penmaen, New Richmond, O., Jan. 27, 1894; soon after his marriage he bought a tract of land, then covered with forest, and made it into a fine farm; his daughter, Mrs. Elvira Barkley, resides on this old homestead; he was a man of many noble qualities.

*　　*　　*　　*　　*
*　　*　　*　　*　　*

(7) Emily Hough Donaldson, b. Mount Hygiene, O., Jan. 7, 1838; d. Penmaen, O., Feb. 19, 1884; m., Oct. 2,

View up the valley of Boat Run Creek, Ohio, from the home of James Kennedy Parker. On the left is a rear view of Clermont Academy.

d. Feb. 16, 1897; Clarence Tell Barkley[3], b. July 30, 1876. James M. Barkley[2], b. Jan. 24, 1831; d. Sept. 4, 1851.)

*   *   *   *   *
*   *   *   *   *

(7) Jessie Donaldson, b. Penmaen, O., Sept. 2, 1851; d. July 14, 1877; studied in Clermont Academy; m., June 18, 1870, Thomas Winfield South; resided Tacony and Philadelphia, Pa.

(8) Mamie Ditson South, b. Dec. 5, 1874; d. Philadelphia, Pa., Oct., 1880.

*   *   *   *   *
*   *   *   *   *

(7) Parker Donaldson, b. Penmaen, O., Feb. 13, 1860; graduated from Clermont Academy; United States Engineer's office, room 405, Cincinnati, O.

(6) Dr. William Tell Parker, b. Mount Hygiene, O., May 18, 1821; d. Tracy City, Tenn., Oct. 12, 1876; m. (first), Oct. 10, 1859, Ann Denman, b. Erie County, O., Aug. 27, 1826; d. Henry County, O., Oct. 10, 1849; studied at Clermont Academy, Carey Academy (afterwards known as College Hill, Cincinnati, O.); studied medicine in the office of Dr. W. P. Kincaid at Neville, O., at the same time teaching in that town; attended the full course of lectures at Eclectic Medical College, Cincinnati, O., graduating in 1847; he began the practice of medicine at Birmingham, O., but left in two months for the California gold fields, where he remained two years, at Marysville, etc.; returned to Birmingham; resided on a farm in Henry County and in 1869 went to Tracy City, Tenn.; m. (second), at Sandusky, O., Dec. 23, 1860, Sarah Maria Aumond, b. Feb. 11, 1839; she resides 522 West Fourth Avenue, Denver, Col.

*   *   *   *   *
*   *   *   *   *

Children of first wife:

(7) Frederick Donaldson Parker, b. Clermont County, O., Sept. 1, 1850; resides 1716 Marion Street, Denver, Col.; graduated from Prof. Job Fish's Select High School, Birmingham, O., and Clermont Academy; has lived in Ohio towns: Birmingham, Norwalk, Akron, and in Tracy City, Tenn., Des Moines, Ia.,

Susanna Everts Parker.

Thomas Donaldson.

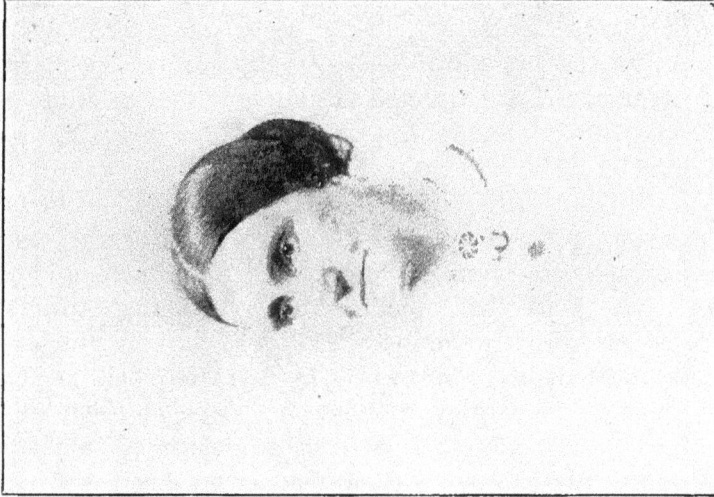

schools of his neighborhood and in Carey's Academy,
near Cincinnati, O.; attended Cincinnati (O.) Medical College and graduated from Starling's Medical College, Columbus, O., 1850; in the latter college he occupied for awhile the chair of demonstration of anatomy; m., Oct. 4, 1853, Sarah Maria Lakin, b. April 8,
1829; d. Fayette, Ia., Dec. 5, 1888; daughter of William
P. Lakin and Sarah ———; she studied in Clermont
Academy. "On account of her gentle Christian ways
she left a precious memory in the community where
she lived."

"In 1855 Dr. Parker, desiring a wider field of labor,
went on horseback from Louisville, Ky., and decided
to build his home at Fayette, Ia. The natural beauty
of the place attracted him, and its being the seat of
Upper Iowa University. This was a struggling school
to be helped. For awhile he lectured there on chem-
istry and anatomy without any hope of pecuniary reward. For 45 years he was a trustee of this school,
aiding its growth with a zeal, enthusiasm and single-
ness of purpose."

The funeral sermon was by Rev. J. L. Paine, and
was published by request and widely and eagerly read.
It was from the verse which he thought most nearly
described the doctor's loving, earnest life. "Ye are
our epistle, written in our hearts, and known and
read of all men." The following are among some of
the glowing tributes:

"Fifty years ago last December I was teaching in the
log school house which stood in the grove hard by the
residence of Brother James Robertson, who was one
of the directors. According to the custom of that day,
the teacher 'boarded round,' and the Robertson home
was my first place of entertainment. Dr. Parker and
his excellent wife had just arrived, and were staying
with Brother Robertson until their own house could be
occupied. Amid the freedom of frontier conditions, a
week under the same roof furnished an excellent opportunity for intimate acquaintance. I recognized at
once the princely character of the man, and his generous nature seemed to reach out and embrace me, and
we were close friends at once and ever after.

"Dr. Parker's devotion to his wife attracted my at-
tioned and won my admiration from the first. Every

degree of tenderness, every measure of affection, was manifest and shown, not by sentimental words, but by kindliest action. He was a lover to the last—dignified, but informal, chivalrous and sincere.

"As children came to bless the home the same traits were prominent. Their physical, moral and intellectual well-being were carefully guarded, and no outside interest, however pressing, was permitted to come between him and his family.

"But his solicitude for his family did not stop with them; it reached out to all his acquaintances, and especially to those to whom he ministered professionally. He did not choose his profession merely as a means of worldly gain and promotion, but as offering him the best field in which to exercise his God-given talents and by that exercise to bless humanity. He felt tnat, having entered this work, responsibility was laid upon him by the Almighty, from which he did not wish nor dare to flinch. Wherever there was a wail of distress, brought to his ear, be it from hovel or palace, with promise of reward or without hope of emolument, by night or by day, in heat or cold, there lay his path of duty and he faltered not.

"I see him now, as memory's picture brings before me those early days, sitting on his little brown mare, plunging into the oncoming darkness, out onto the unfenced and almost trackless prairie. The cry of the afflicted was to him the cry of God. Kindness was in the very warp and woof of his being, and extended to all animals as well as to men.

"Dr. Parker was eminently industrious. He seemed to act upon the conviction that he was debited with sixty minutes of each waking hour, and for each minute thus debited he sought to show a corresponding credit of something worthy accomplished. One day I entered his office and said, 'Dr., if you are not busy, I wish you would look at my arm, though if you are in a hurry I can come in again.' With the trace of a smile coming over his usually grave countenance, he replied, 'I am always busy, but never in a hurry.' It was the key to his busy life and shows how he was able to accomplish so much.

"While carrying a large practice, he found time to study and keep abreast with the very front of his profession, taking part in public enterprises, mingling largely in social life, and cultivating, chiefly with his own hands, vegetable and flower gardens which were the pride and admiration of the city. He once said, 'I never allow a weed to go to seed in my garden.'

"With him a dollar given to better the condition of a fellow being, or a call made to relieve human suffering, though it brought no moneyed return, was not deemed lost. It was so much laid up. He preferred to suffer inconvenience himself rather than to distress another. I remember in a time of great stringency, I was talking with him about his financial affairs. He was in need of money, and I said to him, 'You have a large amount on your books—why not urge collections more vigorously? Your accounts are good, are they not?' And I shall never forget his grave, earnest look; half reproach, half sympathy, as he said, 'Yes, they are nearly all good, sometime, and I am urging those who are in circumstances to pay to do so now. But most of them are very hard pushed just now. I went to them to relieve their suffering, and I cannot bring myself to distress them again unless I am in great personal need.'

"And so when it was said, 'Dr. Parker is dead,' many said with trembling voice and moistened eye, 'Oh, dear old Dr. Parker!' He was thus rich in the truest riches. And the memory of his noble deeds will never fade away."

Many other noble tributes were given by those who had long known Doctor Parker. Dr. J. W. McLean said, "He passed from the ranks of living members of his profession without an enemy, bearing with him the confidence, esteem and love of all who knew him. From an intimate professional association with him of more than twenty years, I can say that I never knew a more noble, pure-minded, unselfish, conscientious physician than he. Anywhere and everywhere among his professional brethren, or at the bedside of the sick, he was always the courteous, sympathetic, Christian gentleman."

     *   *   *   *   *

     *   *   *   *   *

(7) William Lakin Parker, b. Point Pleasant, O., Feb. 5, 1855; d. Sept. 15, 1855.

(7) Rev. Daniel Mason Parker, b. Fayette, Ia., Oct. 29, 1856; resides New Hampton, Ia.; Methodist Episcopal minister; graduated from Upper Iowa University, Fayette, Ia., 1879; preaching points: Lansing, Ia., 1880–'83; New Hampton, Ia., 1884–'87; Grafton, N. D., 1887–'88; Jamestown, N. D., 1888–'89; Hawley Circuit, Ia., 1889–'90; Waucoma, Ia., 1890–'93; Nora Springs, Ia., 1893–'97; Hawkeye, Ia., 1898–'99; Waucoma, Ia., 1899–1900; Postville, Ia., 1900–'02; New Hampton, Ia., 1902–'06; m., Jan. 21, 1887, Sarah Emeline McDonald, b. Dundee, Ill., 1869; daughter of Robert P. McDonald and Kate Sherman.

  (8) Charles Sherman Parker, b. Grafton, N. D., Feb. 17, 1888.

  (8) Sarah Blythe Parker, b. New Hampton, Ia., Nov. 22, 1897.

  (8) Laurice Daniel Parker, b. Postville, Ia., July 16, 1902.

*   *   *   *   *
*   *   *   *   *

(7) Charles Lucius Parker, b. Fayette, Ia., Aug. 1, 1859; address, 209–210 *Globe* Block, Seattle, Wash.; attorney-at-law; graduated from Upper Iowa University, Fayette, Ia., 1881; law department, University of Michigan, 1894; resided as follows: Fayette, Ia., until 1880; West Union, Ia., 1880–'82; Bathgate, N. D., 1882–'89; Ann Arbor, Mich., 1893–'94; moved to Seattle, Wash., 1894; m., at Decorah, Ia., Aug. 20, 1884, Violet Truman, b. July 5, 1857; studied at Upper Iowa University, Fayette, Ia.; daughter of Thomas Truman and Elizabeth Boyles; no children.

*   *   *   *   *
*   *   *   *   *

(7) Sarah Priscilla Parker, b. Fayette, Ia., April 27, 1863; d. Feb. 6, 1870.

*   *   *   *   *

(7) Carrie Ritchy Parker, b. Fayette, Ia., Oct. 29, 1865; d. Aug. 21, 1880.

*   *   *   *   *

(7) Dr. James Donaldson Parker, b. Fayette, Ia., Feb. 11, 1868; doctor and surgeon; resides Fayette, Ia.; graduated Upper Iowa University, Fayette, Ia., 1889; Uni-

versity of Michigan, 1892; m., Aug. 23, 1892, Nellie
R. Klemme, b. Howard County, Ia., March 10, 1871;
graduated from Upper Iowa University, 1890; daughter of William H. Klemme and Mary A. Bolles.

(8) Hugh Klemme Parker, b. April 11, 1894.

(8) Dorothy Lakin Parker, b. March 28, 1896.

(8) Eleanor Bolles Parker, b. Oct. 31, 1905.

(6) Daniel Mulloy Parker; b. Montgomery, O., Nov. 23, 1825;
d. Franklin, O., Aug. 3, 1878; attended Clermont (O.)
Academy; teacher and farmer; m., Dec. 25, 1856,
Harriet Cook, b. Franklin, O., Nov. 16, 1826; resides
Pueblo, Col.; educated in the public schools and Cler-
mont (O.) Academy; daughter of William Cook, b.
Pennsylvania, Aug. 25, 1799; d. April 10, 1877; farmer;
and Sophia Inloes, b. Maryland, April 11, 1807; d. Feb.
16, 1884; daughter of William Inloes and Elizabeth
Petticourt.

     *   *   *   *   *

(7) Josephine Parker, b. Mount Hygiene, O., June 1, 1859;
attended the public schools and took a partial course
at Parker's Academy, Clermont, O.; taught five years
in the public schools of Clermont County, O.; five
years in Manitou Springs, Col., and ten years in Pueblo, Col.; unm.

(6) Mason Doane Parker, b. Clermont County, O., March 17,
1828; d. Cincinnati, O., March 29, 1865; studied in Clermont Academy; resided Cincinnati, O.; teacher and
superintendent of public schools; m., July 24, 1856,
Lucy E. Herron, b. Cincinnati, O., Sept. 24, 1831; d.
Nov. 30, 1898; graduated at Cincinnati (O.) Wesleyan
College, 1848; daughter of Joseph Herron and Elizabeth Rogers.

(7) Lucie Mason Parker, b. Cincinnati, O., July 6, 1857
(resided Washington, D. C.); graduated from
Wesleyan College for Women, Cincinnati, 1875; from
Dayton (O.) Normal School, 1877; taught, Monnett
Hall, Ohio Wesleyan University, fall of 1875–'76; Cincinnati Wesleyan College, 1878–'79; Chickering Institute for Boys, Cincinnati, O., 1879–'80; Nashville College for Young Ladies, 1886–'89; Mount Vernon Seminary, Washington, D. C., 1889–'94; Central High
School, Washington, D. C., 1894–1905; m., Nov. 15,
1905, Earl Cranston, b. Athens, O., June 27, 1840;
groduated from Ohio University, Athens, O., 1861;

elected bishop of Methodist Episcopal Church, 1896;
entered the ministry, 1867; pastor and presiding
elder until 1884; publishing agent, 1884–'96; served
in Civil War as private, orderly sergeant, first lieutenant, adjutant and captain; son of Earl Cranston
and Jane Montgomery; no children.

* * * * *

(7) Lillie Rogers Parker, b. Cincinnati, O., Aug. 22, 1861;
d. April 19, 1862.

(6) Eben Armstrong Parker, b. Mount Hygiene, O., Jan. 27,
1831; d. Indianapolis, Ind., Sept. 12, 1898; attorney-at-
law; m., July 24, 1860, Elizabeth Rebecca Barkley, b.
Laurel, O., Feb. 26, 1837; d. Indianapolis, Ind., Jan.
22, 1898.

* * * * *

(7) Mattie Maria Parker, b. Milford, O., Aug. 8, 1861;
graduated at Indianapolis (Ind.) High School, 1880;
resides Franklin, O.; m., July 18, 1883, Samuel Alva
Wilson, b. Greenwood, Johnson County, Ind., May 28,
1851; real estate and insurance business; son of
William Wilson and Jane ———.

(8) Julia Lyle Wilson, b. Franklin, Ind., Feb. 26, 1884;
in Franklin College in 1906.

(8) Elizabeth Jane Wilson, b. June 16, 1886; in Franklin College in 1906.

(8) Ida Maria Wilson, b. May 31, 1890; in Franklin High
School in 1906.

(8) Parker Jones Wilson, b. Oct. 28, 1894.

* * * * *

(7) Barkley Parker, b. Nov. 5, 1865; resides 114 North
Street, Indianapolis, Ind.; unm.

* * * * *

(7) Sarah Belle Parker, b. Indianapolis, Ind., Dec. 25,
1867; resides with her brother, 114 North Street,
Indianapolis, Ind.; unm.

(6) Mary Priscilla Parker, b. Mount Hygiene, O., March 3,
1837; d. Cincinnati, O., Oct. 16, 1880; m., June 25, 1860,
George B. Nichols, b. Clermont, O., Oct. 7, 1835.

* * * * *

(7) Edwin True Nichols, b. Terrace Park, O., Dec. 18,
1867; m., June 23, 1897, Henrietta R. Danks, b. Cincinnati, O., Feb. 27, 1875.

(8) Ruth Nichols, b. July 7, 1898.

* * * * *

(5) Martha Mulloy, b. Litchfield, Me., Feb. 20, 1796; d. Friday, Jan. 2, 1857; buried in Concord Cemetery.

"Martha Mulloy went to Ohio with her brother Thomas. She was a woman of wonderful fortitude and practicability. She and her brother, Thomas Mulloy, were possessed of strong intellectual faculties and deep religious convictions. They were soon leaders in society and the church."

Mrs. Abby C. Hitch, Catawba, Pendleton County, Ky., says: "She died trusting in her Savior. The night before her spirit left the body she insisted that all of us who were watching by her bed should lie down, for she wanted to be alone with the angels. We did not sleep. For some time we could hear her whispering as if she were in conversation or prayer. Then she took a coughing spell. In the morning she passed away to her Heavenly home."

M., Nov. 28, 1820, William Bacon Sherwin, b. near Waterville, Me., July 13, 1796; d. Thursday, Nov. 30, 1887; he conducted a cooperage business in connection with his farming; he lived near Point Pleasant, O., until long after the birth of Gen. U. S. Grant, with whose parents the Sherwins were intimately connected; before the Civil War the Sherwins moved to Kentucky and located on the banks of the Licking River, about thirty miles from Cincinnati, O.; William Sherwin was the son of Elnathan Sherwin and Abigail Bacon, who lived near Waterville, Me.; the brothers and sisters of W. B. Sherwin were: Josiah Sherwin; Sophia Sherwin, who m. Mr. Belknap and lived near Waterville, Me.; Charlotte Sherwin, who m. Mr. Cathcart and lived in Dayton, O.; Caroline Sherwin, who m. Mr. Reddington; Nancy T. Sherwin, who m. Lee Thompson and lives at Point Pleasant, O.; Elbridge Torry Sherwin, who m. Mary Ann Debrular and lived at Point Pleasant, O.; most of these Sherwins came to Ohio about the time the Mulloys moved there; the parents are buried on the home place; Elnathan Sherwin was in the Revolutionary War, near Canada.

(6) Justice Mulloy Sherwin, b. Nov. 13, 1821; d. Aug. 17, 1843.

(6) James Leander Cathcart Sherwin, b. Sept. 10, 1825; resides Bishop, Cal.; he went to California in March, 1859; he went by ship to the Isthmus of Panama and walked to the Pacific coast and embarked on another

vessel; he made money enough to return home for his wife; they made the journey to California over the plains in wagons, and were six months on the way; they had many hardships and had many dangers from the Indians; but they kept on their way with sturdy zeal. Doctor Carr and his wife, Nancy Sherwin, went with them; Mr. Sherwin was a cooper by trade; in California he was engaged in prospecting and farming; m., Dec. 16, 1858, Nannie E. Colvin, b. four miles from Falmouth, Ky., Sept. 21, 1833; d. May 5, 1905; she taught school for five years and was very successful; daughter of Birkett Colvin and Nancy Minor.

(7) Lilly May Sherwin, b. Ophir, Nev., May 17, 1863; resides 2240 Rose Street, Berkley, Cal.; m. (first), Feb. 18, 1885, Robert Frederic Brooks, b. New York City, May 21, 1836; deceased; studied in high school of Bishop, Cal.; merchant; m. (second), C. C. Radcliffe; deceased.

Children of first husband:

(8) Blanche Edna Brooks, b. July 19, 1884; a teacher for two years at Bishop, Cal.

(8) Frederic Sherwin Brooks, b. Sept. 21, 1885; helps his mother in her store.

(8) Floyd Clenlon Brooks, b. Feb. 21, 1887.

(7) Nannie Minor Sherwin, b. Nevada, July 31, 1865; resides Round Valley, Inyo County, Cal.; studied in Round Valley and Bishop (Cal.) schools; m., Feb. 18, 1885, John Prince Smith, b. June 24, 1861; farmer.

(8) Grace Birdena Smith, b. Oct. 26, 1886; educated in Round Valley and Bishop (Cal.) schools and the Union High School.

(8) Russel Colvin Smith, b. June 28, 1889.

(8) Henry Foster Smith, b. April 8, 1891.

(8) Esther Marion Smith, b. July 29, 1893.

(8) Birkett Smith, b. Feb. 14, 1896.

(8) Blanche Minor Smith, b. Aug. 24, 1899.

(8) Prince Lyle Smith, b. March 13, 1904.

(7) Martha Katherine Sherwin, b. Round Valley, Cal., Feb. 11, 1867; studied in Round Valley and Bishop (Cal.) schools.

(7) Grace Sherwin, b. Round Valley, Cal., Dec. 25, 1869; resides Round Valley, Cal.; studied in Round Valley schools and in Inyo Academy; m., Dec. 29, 1887, Isaac Foster Smith, b. Oct. 26, 1856; farmer.

(8) Ella May Smith, b. Dec. 25, 1888.

(8) Deborah B. Smith, b. Sept. 28, 1890.

(8) Walter Smith, b. Feb. 3, 1892.

(8) Isaac Foster Smith, b. Nov. 26, 1897.

(8) Grace Elizabeth Smith, b. Oct. 11, 1898.

(8) Arthur Smith, b. April 21, 1901.

(8) Laura Smith, b. March 4, 1903.

(7) Birkett Elnathan Sherwin, b. Round Valley, Cal., April 21, 1871; resides 2240 Rose Street, Berkley, Cal.; civil and mining engineer; attended Round Valley schools and graduated from Inyo Academy May 17, 1893; m., Jan. 20, 1900, Christine Gregory, b. Bodie, Cal., Feb. 18, 1880; educated in Bodie schools and Stockton (Cal.) business college; daughter of Nathan Gregory and Katherine Cook.

(8) Marvin Birkett Sherwin, b. Aug. 28, 1901.

(8) Vernon Gregory Sherwin, b. Sept. 21, 1905.

(7) James William Sherwin, b. Sept. 24, 1875; resides Bodie, Cal.; educated in Round Valley schools and Inyo Academy; civil and mining engineer; m. Idella Gregory.

(8) Guinevere Sherwin, b. Sept. 11, 1901.

(8) Dorothy Sherwin, b. June 28, 1906.

* * * * *

(6) Nancy Thompson Sherwin, b. Feb. 29, 1827; d. Peach Grove, Ky., Jan. 11, 1879; lived Kentucky, Iowa and California; m., Oct. 22, 1845, Dr. Lancelot Carr, b. Ohio, Feb. 2, 1819; d. Peach Grove, Ky., April 10, 1887; parents were of Baltimore, Md.

* * * * *
* * * * *

(7) Charley Edwin Carr, b. Oct. 16, 1848; resides Emerson, Iowa; plasterer and brick layer; m. Sadie Sheldon of Emerson, Ia.

(8) Florence Carr, b. Dec. 8, 1874; resides Mitchellville, Ia.; m. Walter Sharp.

(8) Rose Myrtie Carr, b. Aug. 2, 1877; d. Sept. 8, 1878.

(8) Byron Lancelot Carr, b. June 11, 1882.

(8) Hazel Nell Carr, b. Sept. 13, 1891.

* * * * *
* * * * *

(7) Lizzie Carr, b. Dec. 19, 1849; d. Peach Grove, Ky., July 5, 1882; m., in Ames, Ia., Sept. 16, 1869, W. J. Bundy.

(8) Harry E. Bundy, b. Emerson, Ia., Nov. 20, 1870; m. Mabel Naught of Bakersville, Cal.

  (9) J. Harold Bundy, b. Santa Anna, Cal., April 18, 1902.

  (9) Emery Bundy, b. Santa Anna, Cal.

(8) Nellie Bundy, b. Emerson, Ia., Feb. 28, 1872; d. May 29, 1890.

    *   *   *   *   *
    *   *   *   *   *

(7) Nannie Carr, b. Flamertown, Ky., Oct. 21, 1853; resides Quincy, Plumas County, Cal.; educated in the public schools and Girls' Seminary, Ames, Ia.; m., at Ames, Ia., May 17, 1870, Henry White, b. Bridgenorth, Eng., March 8, 1837; educated in the common schools; miner and farmer; son of John B. White.

(8) Nellie Maude White, b. Quincy, Cal., July 21, 1871; resides Quincy, Cal.; m., Dec. 12, 1896, Clarence Gilbert Weldon, b. near Quincy, Cal., June 18, 1869; educated in the country schools; son of Allen John Weldon and Lucina Morey.

  (9) Clarence Sherwin Weldon, b. May 31, 1903.

  (9) William Weldon, b. Aug. 15, 1904.

(8) Harold J. White, b. Quincy, Cal., June 15, 1882; resides Quincy, Cal.; graduated from State Normal School and now a student in University of Nevada; studying to be a sculptor.

    *   *   *   *   *
    *   *   *   *   *

(7) James William Carr, b. Nelson Point, Cal., Dec. 27, 1860; d. Aug. 7, 1863.

    *   *   *   *   *
    *   *   *   *   *

(7) Martha Ellen Carr, b. Nelson Point, Cal., Oct. 20, 1865; resides Elsinore, Cal.; graduated from Clermont (O.) Academy, June 23, 1883; has lived Emerson, Ia., Ames, Ia., Tustin, Cal., Corona, Cal., Elsinore, Cal.; m., at Tustin, Cal., July 31, 1895, Ralph Lewis Eddy, b. Bay City, Mich., April 5, 1867; educated in Tustin (Cal.) public schools; blacksmith; son of Samuel Eddy and Sarah A. Hutchinson.

(8) Harry Sherwin Eddy, b. Tustin, Cal., April 5, 1897.

(8) Sara Eddy, b. Tustin, Cal., Oct. 7, 1898.

    *   *   *   *   *

(6) William Thomas Sherwin, b. Aug. 12, 1830; went to California in 1859; unm.

*   *   *   *   *

(6) Abigail Charlotte Sherwin, b. April 26, 1832; resides Catawba, Pendleton County, Ky.; went to Kentucky in 1844; educated in Point Pleasant (O.) schools and Clermont Academy; m., July 2, 1849, Robert Hamilton Hitch, b. Poplar Grove, Ky., Feb. 26, 1815; d. Aug. 23, 1877; studied in Ash Run schoolhouse, made of logs and with split logs for benches; farmer; in the Civil War he was a faithful Union man; he was of a very honest, industrious family; his father, Joseph Hitch, d. Sept. 26, 1847; m. Sarah Muir, b. April 22, 1782; d. June 17, 1852; he moved from Maryland to Kentucky in 1808; he settled at Poplar Grove, about five miles from Falmouth, Ky.; Robert Hamilton Hitch was the youngest son and so inherited the old farm.

*   *   *   *   *

(7) William Shakespeare Hitch, b. Sept. 9, 1850; resides Catawba, Ky.; studied in Ash Run schoolhouse; farmer; m., March 6, 1872, Catherine Brown Crosier, b. Nicholsville, Jessamine County, Ky., Feb. 18, 1845; studied in Danville, Ky.; son of David Crosier and Margaret Crisman.

(8) Agnes Hitch, b. Feb. 20, 1875; d. Jan. 6, 1896.

(8) Walter Clark Hitch, b. May 1, 1877; d. Dec., 1895.

(8) Mabel Abigail Hitch, b. Feb. 8, 1880.

*   *   *   *   *

(7) Martha Muir Hitch, b. March 2, 1853; studied in Ash Run schoolhouse; resides Falmouth, Ky., R. F. D. No. 1; m., March 10, 1870, Henry Sanford Marshall, b. Pendleton County, Ky., Jan. 10, 1840; educated in Ash Run schools; merchant.

(8) Edward Lee Marshall, b. Catawba, Ky., Dec. 6, 1870; d. Berry, Harrison County, Ky., Oct. 20, 1890.

(8) Charlie Randolph Marshall, b. Aug. 26, 1874; unm.

(8) Charlotte O'Neal Marshall, b. Sept. 27, 1877; unm.

*   *   *   *   *

(7) James Henry Hitch, b. Hitch homestead, Sept. 7, 1855; studied in Ash Run schoolhouse; address, 12 West Third Street, Covington, Ky.; foreman in steel construction works; m., Sept. 4, 1877, Malvina Fitslan Sullivan, b. Rock Springs, Ky., Nov. 6, 1851; edu-

cated in Midway (Ky.) school; daughter of Austin Wells Sullivan and Perlina Norris.

(8) Helen Hitch, b. Dec. 31, 1879; unm.

(8) Louise Hitch, b. Dec. 24, 1883; educated in Falmouth (Ky.) schools; unm.

(8) Susannah Hitch, b. Feb. 21, 1893; educated in Covington schools.

*   *   *   *   *

(7) Chilcarra Stewart Hitch, b. Poplar Grove, Ky., April 13, 1858; studied in Concord (Lewis County, Ky.) schools; address, Falmouth, Ky., R. F. D. No. 1; m., Dec. 22, 1880, Harden Ellis, b. Pendleton County, Ky., Oct. 23, 1856; studied in Lovejoy (Ky.) schools; farmer; son of James Ellis and Sarah Isabelle Beckett.

(8) Sarah Abbelyn Ellis, b. Oct. 6, 1881; educated in Pleasant Hill school; m., Oct. 19, 1904, Albert Perley Owen; son of Robert Walter Owen and Theresa Mains.

(8) Edith Marie Ellis, b. July 30, 1883; educated in Pleasant Hill school.

(8) Robert James Ellis, b. Aug. 19, 1884; educated in Pleasant Hill school.

(8) Faye Josephine Ellis; b. Nov. 11, 1891; educated in Pleasant Hill school.

(8) Hilton Hayden Ellis, b. July 26, 1895.

*   *   *   *   *

(7) Susanna Jane Hitch, b. Poplar Grove, Ky., Jan. 23, 1861; d. Aug. 5, 1897; educated in Ash Run school; m., Feb. 25, 1880, Richard Stewart; taught school in Florida; no children.

*   *   *   *   *

(7) Thomas T. Hitch, b. Poplar Grove, Ky., Aug. 11, 1863; educated in Concord (Ky.) schools; farmer; address, Catawba, Ky.; m., April 4, 1903, Nora Del Redmon, b. Mount Auburn, Ky., Sept. 7, 1881; educated in Irving schoolhouse; daughter of Nathan Redmon and Lucinda B. Baxter.

(8) Georgia Lallas Hitch; d. at two years of age.

(8) Alice May Hitch, b. June 24, 1906; d. Nov., 1906.

*   *   *   *   *

(7) Mary Ruby Hitch, b. Feb. 1, 1866; studied in schools of Concord and Butler County Academy; address,

Falmouth, Ky.; m., Oct. 29, 1890, George Lawrence Myers, b. near Felicity, O., 1854; educated in the stone schoolhouse, Clermont County, O.; machinist, carpenter and millwright; son of David Myers and Belinda Howell.

(8) Harry Sherwin Myers, b. March 20, 1892.

* * * * *

(7) Nalbro O'Neal Hitch, b. Pendleton County, Ky., April 24, 1869; educated in Concord district schools; resides 1811 Eastern Avenue, Cincinnati, O.; pipe fitter; a member of the official board of McKendree Methodist Episcopal Church, Cincinnati, O.; m. (first), July 3, 1892, Tillie Florence Hart, b. Pendleton, Ky., Sept. 7, 1864; d. Jan. 14, 1898; educated in Lovejoy district school; daughter of John M. Hart and Marenda Hendricks; m. (second), Sept. 12, 1901, May Hanson Simmons, b. Newport, Ky., May 5, 1873; educated in the Fourth District School of Cincinnati, O.; daughter of Benjamin H. Simmons and Cordelia Kelsey.

Child of first wife:

(8) Ethel Marenda Hitch, b. June 29, 1893.

Child of second wife:

(8) Mildred Kelsey Hitch, b. Jan. 18, 1903.

* * * * *

(7) Annie Sherwin Hitch, b. Jan. 5, 1871; d. Sept. 11, 1896; educated in Concord (Ky.) schools; m., Oct. 5, 1892, James Fields, b. Concord, Ky., March 23, 1868; educated in Concord schools; farmer; son of Newton Fields and Emily Hitch; resides Falmouth, Ky., R. F. D. No. 1.

(8) Bernard Hitch Fields, b. Sept. 20, 1894.

(8) Charlotte Emily Fields, b. July 7, 1896; d. Sept. 21, 1896.

* * * * *

(7) Robert Hugh Hitch, b. Poplar Grove, Ky., March 14, 1873; educated in Concord (Ky.) schools; farmer; resides Catawba, Pendleton County, Ky.; unm.

* * * * *

(7) Arthur Eugene Hitch, b. Poplar Grove, Ky., Feb. 25, 1876; studied in Concord schools; resides 2212 Eastern Avenue, Cincinnati, O.; steel worker; m., June 18, 1903, Fannie M. Oatley, b. Batavia, O., July 8, 1875;

daughter of Luther Oatley and Sarah B. Perkins; no children.

(6) Susanna Priscilla Sherwin, b. near Point Pleasant, O., Sept. 16, 1834; d. March 9, 1886; in 1844, with her parents she moved to near Boston Station, Pendleton County, Ky.; studied at Parker's Academy, Clermont County, O.; m., May 10, 1855, Thomas Cass Houston, b. March 23, 1829; farmer; son of James Houston and Amanda Cawden.

(7) James William Houston, b. April 24, 1856; d. April 6, 1863.

(7) Walter Augustus Houston, b. Jan. 23, 1858; address, Boston Station, Ky.; farmer; m., Nov. 16, 1880, Margaret Elizabeth Rush, b. March 20, 1859; daughter of Daniel Rush and Martha McKee.

(8) Anna Grace Houston, b. Feb. 21, 1882; m., April 8, 1903, Cassie Elbert Barnhill; d. April 11, 1905.

(9) Willard Roy Barnhill, b. Sept. 26, 1904; d. Nov. 25, 1905.

(8) Lizzie Louise Houston, b. Jan. 2, 1890.

(7) Charles Mulloy Houston, b. June 3, 1860; graduated from College of the Bible of Kentucky University, June, 1892; he is a Christian minister at Rosehill, Madison County, Ky.; m., April 19, 1900, Rebecca Frances Troynham, b. Jan. 4, 1875; daughter of Thomas B. T. and Sallie Frances Lawson; these parents were of Halifax County, Va.

(8) Charles Walker Houston, b. Madison County, Va., March 15, 1901.

(8) Lucy Lawson Houston, b. Madison County, Va., March 16, 1904.

(7) Nancy Ann Houston, b. Oct. 19, 1862; m., Nov., 1884, Alva Milton Mulloy, b. Clermont County, O., Aug. 1, 1859; lived as a farmer in Pendleton County, Ky.; son of Isaac Mulloy and Elizabeth Aultman; resides Butler, Ky., R. F. D.

(8) Haseltine Lee Mulloy, b. July 10, 1886.

(8) Hugh Houston Mulloy, b. June 23, 1890.

(8) Mary Susanna Mulloy, b. Nov. 7, 1895.

(7) Robert Marion Houston, b. Oct. 31, 1864; in 1900 he moved from Kentucky to Oklahoma and took his family there in 1901; farmer in Grear County; m., Dec. 28, 1892, Minnie Alice Northcutt; daughter of Uriah Milton Northcutt and Elizabeth A. Kendive.

(8) Shirley Thomas Houston, b. Nov. 11, 1893.

(8) Osla Northcutt Houston, b. Dec. 3, 1894.

(8) Susanna Elizabeth Houston, b. Dec. 7, 1898.

(8) Daniel Robert Houston, b. Oct. 8, 1905.

(7) Martha Pepper Houston, b. Jan. 4, 1867; m., Jan. 23, 1887, William Grant Frazer, b. Aug. 12, 1863; son of Alfred Frazer and Melissa Hitch; he and his family were born and raised in Pendleton County, Ky.; located in Falmouth, where he is an undertaker and sells furniture; after awhile he sold monuments, tombstones and musical instruments; address, Falmouth, Ky.

(8) Charles Roy Frazer, b. April 11, 1888.

(8) Cecil Priscilla Frazer, b. March 26, 1891.

(8) Mildred Virgiline Frazer, b. July 19, 1899.

(8) Alma Louise Frazer, b. Nov. 16, 1900.

(7) Leona Priscilla Houston, b. Feb. 2, 1869; d. Oct. 24, 1900; m., Oct. 19, 1892, George Herman Schubert, b. March 24, 1865; son of Fridellen S. and Susannah Lancha; parents of Germany; after his wife's death Mr. Schubert went from Pendleton County, Ky., to Oklahoma, where he m. again; lives near Hammon, Custer County; is farming and carpentering; took his children there in 1904.

(8) Frederic Sherwin Schubert, b. Aug. 30, 1892.

(8) Carra Christianna Schubert, b. Dec. 20, 1895.

(8) Walter Alton Schubert, b. Jan. 6, 1898.

(8) Charlottie Gertrude Schubert, b. Nov. 27, 1899.

(7) Nellie M. Houston, b. Aug. 20, 1871; m., Dec. 23, 1891, George Pribble, b. Feb. 5, 1868; son of John M. Pribble and Martha Lancaster; address, Boston Station, Ky.

(8) Charles Francis Pribble, b. Feb. 15, 1893.

(8) Lulu Florence Pribble, b. Aug. 8, 1895.

(8) Burkett Lee Pribble, b. Aug. 19, 1900.

(8) Hallie Maude Pribble, b. April 18, 1905.

(7) Joseph Carr Houston, b. Aug. 23, 1873; d. Dec. 21, 1874.

(7) Mary Abigail Houston, b. Jan. 1, 1876; d. Jan. 6, 1876.

(7) Thomas Allen Houston, b. Nov. 29, 1878; teacher in Dayton, O.

(6) Hugh Elnathan Sherwin, b. Dec. 3, 1836; d. March 22, 1857. "He went to California with his brothers and died among strangers."

*   *   *   *   *

(5) Thomas Mulloy, b. Litchfield, Me., Monday, May 14, 1798;
d. Moscow, Clermont County, O., May 3, 1863. He came
to Ohio and became one of the leading farmers in the
section of Ohio where he lived; resided a short time at
Boat Run, O.; also a short time at Cincinnati, O.; then
in Nicholsville, Clermont County, O., until 1859; then
moved to near Moscow, Clermont County, O.; besides
farming he operated a sawmill and chair factory for
six or seven years at Nicholsville, O., a quarter of a
mile from town; m. (first), July 29, 1824, Susannah
Moreton, b. March 12, 1805; d. May 9, 1840; studied
in Pennsylvania schools; daughter of Isaac Moreton
and Jane McCully; m. (second), March 28, 1841, Susannah Rogers, b. Stepstone, Montgomery County, Ky.,
March 17, 1812; d. Aug. 12, 1901; buried in the Ridge
Cemetery, Fremont, Neb.; daughter of John Rogers, who
lived on a farm about ten miles from Laurel, O.; he was
a prominent citizen, justice of the peace, auctioneer, officer in the militia, etc.; he m. Elizabeth Gustin, descended
from an old English family, and reared in Lexington,
Ky.; d. April 6, 1866; they, like many others, bought
land and paid for it; then a claimant appeared; some
thus abandoned their land, but the Rogers family paid
for their land a second time; this trouble was caused by
the different surveys overlapping.

*　　*　　*　　*　　*

Children of first wife:
(6) David Mulloy, b. Clermontville, O., June 21, 1825; d.
Aviston, Clinton County, Ill., Aug. 20, 1854; studied at
Parker's Academy, Clermont County, O., and at Eclec-
tic Medical College, Cincinnati, O. "He became an
eminent physician; he first settled in Milwaukee, Wis.,
and then went to northern Illinois, where he died."
M., April 11, 1849, at Milwaukee, Wis., Elizabeth Agnes
Cecilia Burke, b. Dublin, Ireland, Jan. 25, 1823; d.
Sept. 11, 1895; daughter of William Burke and Mary
Ann Eagan.

*　　*　　*　　*　　*

(7) Susanna Theresa Mulloy, b. Milwaukee, Wis., Jan. 29,
1850; m., at Richmond, Ind., Dec. 24, 1873, William
H. Middleton.
(8) Walter Guy Middleton, b. 1874; graduated from
Earlham College, Richmond, Ind.; studied at Ar-
mour Institute, Chicago, Ill.; head of the engi-

neering department of Twin City Telephone Company, Minneapolis, Minn.

(8) Joseph Burke Middleton, b. 1880; in telephone work in Seattle, Wash.

(8) Elizabeth Alice Middleton, b. 1883; at present taking a master's degree in University of Minnesota.

(8) Donald Rich Middleton, b. 1885; in telephone work in Seattle, Wash.

(6) Hugh Mulloy, b. Dec. 19, 1827; d. Milwaukee, Wis., Sept. 25, 1850; studied in Parker's Academy, Clermontville, O., and at Eclectic Medical College, Cincinnati, O.; physician; resided Milwaukee, Wis.; unm.

(6) Isaac Mulloy, b. Cincinnati, O., June 26, 1830; resides Butler, Ky., R. F. D.; farmer; studied in district schools; m. Jennie Aultman, who d. July 8, 1863; daughter of Daniel Aultman and Ann Boggers.

* * * * *

(7) Alva Milton Mulloy, b near Bethel, O., Aug. 1, 1860; farmer in Pendleton County, Ky.; m., Nov., 1884, Nancy Ann Houston, b. Oct. 19, 1862. (See records of family, page 237.)

* * * * *

(7) Wilbur Mulloy; killed by lightning.

* * * * *

(7) Frank Mulloy, resides Boston Station, Ky.
(8) Two children.

(6) Moreton Mulloy, b. Clermontville, O., July 29, 1832; d. June 29, 1904; studied in Parker's Academy; lived in Ohio at Clermontville, Nicholsville and Madisonville; teacher and farmer; m., April 20, 1854, Hannah Fitzpatrick, b. Madisonville, O., Oct. 23, 1833; d. July 27, 1898.

* * * * *

(7) Dr. Thomas Benton Mulloy, b. July 20, 1855; resides Newtown, O.

* * * * *

(7) Charles Moreton Mulloy, b. Nov. 1, 1856; d. Feb. 27, 1860.

* * * * *

(7) Laura May Mulloy, b. Jan. 13, 1860; resides Madisonville, O.; m., Dec. 28, 1892, Chas. Atchley.

* * * * *

(7) Son, b. Aug. 30, 1861; d. Sept. 18, 1861.

*   *   *   *   *

(7) William T. Mulloy, b. Aug. 12, 1863; carpenter at Madisonville, O.; m., Feb. 18, 1887, Permelia Heltman.

(7) Lettie Kate Mulloy, b. Jan. 12, 1865; resides Cincinnati, O.; m., Dec. 28, 1888, Chas. Heltman.

*   *   *   *   *

(7) Minnie Sue Mulloy, b. Nov. 7, 1866; d. Sept. 15, 1868.

*   *   *   *   *

(7) Lida Luella Mulloy, b. Sept. 6, 1869.

*   *   *   *   *

(6) William Mulloy, b. Boat Run, O., Nov. 8, 1835; resides Bethel, O.; studied in Moore's district school, Monroe Township, O., and at Clermont Academy; farmer; m., June 23, 1857, Phœbe Ann Hardy Crane, b. June 30, 1836; daughter of Oliver Crane and Eliza West.

(7) Alfred J. Mulloy, b. May 4, 1858.

(7) Thomas Oliver Mulloy, b. Nov. 23, 1860.

(7) Eva May Mulloy, b. July 23, 1865.

(7) Mina Moreton Mulloy, b. Nov. 1, 1868.

(7) Jimmie Claud Mulloy, b. May 23, 1874.

(7) Maggie Luella Mulloy, b. April 30, 1878.

(6) Susannah Mulloy, b. Boat Run, now Clermontville, O., Dec. 1, 1838; resides Madisonville, O.; educated in common schools and Parker's Academy; m., Feb. 22, 1859, William Boggers Aultman, b. Bethel, O., Sept. 20, 1828; d. July 9, 1898; studied in country schools; carpenter; son of Daniel Aultman and Ann Boggers.

*   *   *   *   *

(7) Ida May Aultman, b. Nov. 22, 1859; d. Dec. 10, 1862, at Nicholsville, O.

*   *   *   *   *

(7) Cassius Mulloy Aultman, b. Jan. 20, 1861; resides Madisonville, O.; cabinet maker; m., Oct. 8, 1885, Ella A. Griffin of Rushville, Ind., b. Columbus, Ind., July 6, 1862; educated in the Rushville (Ind.) schools; daughter of Jesse R. Griffin and Mary E. Johnson; their three children were educated in the schools of Rushville, Ind., and Madisonville, O.

(8) Roy C. Aultman, b. July 26, 1886.

(8) Hazel Lynn Aultman, b. June 24, 1892.

(8) Helen Aultman, b. April 25, 1894.

*   *   *   *   *

(7) Eben Lee Aultman, b. Nicholsville, O., Jan. 22, 1864; resides Cincinnati, O.; educated in country schools and Normal University at Lebanon, O.; employed in railroad freight department; m., Feb. 21, 1903, Cora Settles Ward, b. Madisonville, O., Oct. 25, 1872; a high school graduate; daughter of Luke M. Ward and Caroline Settles.

*   *   *   *   *

(7) Bernice Aultman, b. Nicholsville, O., Dec. 18, 1879; clerk in Madisonville, O.

*   *   *   *   *

Children of second wife:

(6) John Rogers Mulloy, b. near Nicholsville, Clermont County, O., April 22, 1842; d. Fremont, Neb., Oct. 28, 1877; in the spring of 1863 he moved to Colorado; in 1865 went to Nebraska; in 1868 he moved to Dodge County, Neb.; taught school in Ohio and Nebraska; he was candidate for county superintendent of public instruction in the fall of 1877; studied in Clermont (O.) Academy; farmer for some years; m., at Jamestown, Neb., Sept. 22, 1875, Ann Catherine Watt, b. Rebe, Denmark, Aug. 10, 1857; she came to America with her parents when she was about two years old; she moved to Fremont, Neb., with her parents in 1865; graduated from the high and normal schools; studied and taught music; has played the church organ with great skill for over thirty years; she is now organist of All Saints Church, Seattle, Wash.; resides 4335 Eastern Avenue, Seattle, Wash.; daughter of Soren Mason Watt and Anna Marie Shon; the wife d. at 28 years of age, leaving three children, and after three years Mr. Watt married a second time.

(The widow of John Rogers Mulloy m. [second], at Fremont, Neb., in St. James Episcopal Church, June 28, 1893, Edward J. Seykora of North Bend, Neb., b. Iowa City, Ia., Dec. 25, 1863; at the age of 14 years he was apprenticed to a druggist and has been in that line of work ever since; in South Omaha, Neb., under the firm name of E. J. Seykora & Co.; was in North Bend, Neb., 1899, and in Seattle, Wash., 1904; his family moved there April 8, 1905. Children of this second marriage: Anna Marie Seykora, b. South Omaha, Neb., April 9, 1891; Ethel Elizabeth Seykora, b. South Omaha, Neb., May 31, 1892; John Edward Seykora, b. South Omaha, Neb., Feb. 8, 1894; Frederic Watt Seykora, b. South Omaha, Neb., March 26, 1897.)

*   *   *   *   *

*   *   *   *   *

(7) Edwin Mason Mulloy, b. Jamestown, Neb., Jan. 12, 1877; resides Chicago, Ill.; stenographer and bookkeeper. As his father died when he was nine months old he was brought up among his mother's people; graduated from the country district school, 1892; commercial department of the Fremont (Neb.) Normal School, 1894; lived on a farm near Fremont, Neb., until 1899; in Chicago until March, 1902; in New York City until Aug., 1902; in Chicago since then; now a traveling salesman and general office man, with Hine-Watt Manufacturing Company; m., June 27, 1906, Carrie Mattie Anderson, b. Jamestown, Neb., Nov. 10, 1878; graduated from country school, 1894, and from Fremont (Neb.) Normal School, teachers' course, 1898; scientific course, 1903; pedagogy course, 1903; daughter of Nels S. Anderson and Laura Miller.

*   *   *   *   *

(6) James Guston Mulloy, b. near Nicholsville, Clermont County, O., Jan. 28, 1845; resides Fremont, Neb.; educated in the district schools of Clermont County, O.; lived at Batavia, O., from March, 1862, to May, 1863, then near Moscow, O.; in March, 1870, moved to Ames, Dodge County, Neb., and has lived there ever since; farmer; m., in Omaha, Neb., March 16, 1871, Mary Eliza Norris, b. Laurel, Clermont County, O., Sept. 12, 1844; educated in the public schools; daughter of John Norris and Harriet Uling.

*   *   *   *   *

*   *   *   *   *

(7) Nannie Mulloy, b. Ames, Neb., Dec. 16, 1871; resides Somers Avenue and Thirteenth Street., Fremont, Neb.; educated in the common schools and at Fremont Normal College; was a most successful teacher for eight years; m., May 20, 1896, Milton Asbury Mark, b. Marion County, Ia., May 10, 1860; educated

in country schools and Fremont (Neb.) Business College; carpenter; son of John A. Mark and Mary
West.

(8) Marie Alta Mark, b. Fremont, Neb., June 22, 1903.

     *   *   *   *   *
     *   *   *   *   *

(7) Charles William Mulloy, b. Ames, Neb., Feb. 24, 1874;
educated in country schools of Ames and Riverside,
Neb., Fremont Business College and State University at Lincoln, Neb.; resides Somers Avenue
and Twelfth Street, Fremont, Neb.; letter carrier;
m., June 26, 1900, Harriet May Horton, b. Centerville,
Neb., Sept. 8, 1872; educated in the schools of
Ridgely, North Bend, Neb., and Central and high
schools of Fremont, Neb; daughter of George Horton,
who resides in Oregon, and Jerusha King, who d.
Dec., 1877.

(8) Caroline Marie Mulloy, b. March 13, 1901.

(8) Hugh William Mulloy, b. Feb. 20, 1904.

     *   *   *   *   *
     *   *   *   *   *

(7) Hugh Clarence Mulloy, b. Ames, Neb., May 12, 1877;
accidentally killed by the discharge of a gun July 1,
1899; educated in Fremont schools and Fremont Normal College.

     *   *   *   *   *
     *   *   *   *   *

(7) Susanna Elizabeth Mulloy, b. Ames, Neb., Dec. 18,1880;
studied in Riverside District School No. 53, Dodge
County, Neb., and in Fremont (Neb.) High School;
resides 3224 Orchard Street, Lincoln, Neb.; m., Sept.
27, 1905, Percel Lyman Baldwin, b. David City, Neb.,
Aug. 7, 1876; educated in David City schools and
Fremont (Neb.) Normal College; employed in the
dairy department of the state farm; son of Charles
Biles Baldwin and Sarah Whitmore Lyman.

     *   *   *   *   *
     *   *   *   *   *

(7) John Rogers Mulloy, b. Ames, Neb., March 4, 1882; resides Fremont, Neb.; educated in Fremont Normal
Business College and Nebraska State Agricultural
School; he has taken charge of his father's home
farm, about four miles west of Fremont, Neb.; m., in

Omaha, Neb., April 30, 1906, Lucile Vavra, b. Schuyler, Neb., Oct., 1883; graduated from Fremont, (Neb.) Normal Business College; daughter of Adolph Vavra, who d. March 16, 1902, and of Marie Peshek, who resides Schuyler, Neb.

*   *   *   *   *

(6) Elizabeth Priscilla Mulloy, b. Nicholsville, O., March 28, 1847; resides South Omaha, Neb.; lived Nicholsville and Moscow, O., Fremont, North Bend and South Omaha, Neb., Champaign, Ill.; educated in the schools of Nicholsville, O., and Clermont Academy; m., near Moscow, O., Nov. 19, 1867, Albert Dawson of Moscow, O., b. near New Richmond, O., Dec. 18, 1844; d. Sept. 14, 1896 (51y., 8m., 26d.); educated in Franklin and Moscow (O.) schools and Clermont Academy; farmer; son of Joseph Dawson and Sarah Boss Gates.

*   *   *   *   *
*   *   *   *   *

(7) Owen Everett Dawson, b. Dec. 18, 1868; d. March 5, 1871 (2y., 5m., 15d.).

*   *   *   *   *
*   *   *   *   *

(7) Clarence Lester Dawson, b. March 1, 1870; d. Dec. 14, 1874 (4y., 9m., 13d.).

*   *   *   *   *
*   *   *   *   *

(7) Mattie Elvira Dawson, b. Dec. 20, 1871, near Moscow, O.; educated in the schools of Dodge County, Neb., Champaign, Ill., Kearney, Neb., etc.; resides Ogallala, Neb.; m., in Lincoln, Neb., Nov. 28, 1894, John Levi Wells, b. Clark County, Ill., Aug. 21, 1869; farmer and ranchman; son of J. B. Sidney Wells and Elizabeth Cox.

(8) Elizabeth Wells, b. and d. Sept. 17, 1895.

(8) Ralph Sidney Wells, b. March 23, 1897; educated in the schools of Keith County, Neb.

(8) John Lawrence Wells, b. Dec. 3, 1900.

(8) Albert Beckworth Wells, b. July 19, 1903.

*   *   *   *   *
*   *   *   *   *

(7) Jesse Thomas Dawson, b. Jan. 28, 1874; resides South Omaha, Neb.; laundryman; studied in schools of

Kearney, Neb.; m., Oct. 25, 1902, Ella Belle Billings, b. Ashland, Neb., Oct. 25, 1875; studied in Ashland schools; children of wife's first husband:
James Henry, Hattie Olive, Ethel Eula, Mary Nettie.

*   *   *   *   *
*   *   *   *   *

(7) Joseph Alvah Dawson, b. Jan. 26, 1877; studied in
Champaign (Ill.) schools; resides South Omaha,
Neb.; brick and stone mason; m., July 11, 1900, Leah
Mary Hoenstine, b. May 22, 1881; educated in schools
of Rollersville, O., and Louisville, Neb.; daughter of
Zeigler Hoenstine and Hattie M. Robert.
(8) Vera Allyn Dawson, b. Oct. 4, 1902.
(8) Myrtle Priscilla Dawson, b. June 6, 1905.

*   *   *   *   *
*   *   *   *   *

(7) Asa Dawson, b. Jan. 25, 1880; d. Jan. 30, 1880.
(7) Claude Sylvanus Dawson, b. Dec. 16, 1881; resides
Ogallala, Neb.; studied in schools of Champaign,
Ill., etc.
(7) Osia Myrtle Dawson, b. July 15, 1884; resides South
Omaha, Neb.; studied in schools of Kearney and
Louisville, Neb.
(7) Gracie Dawson, b. March 22, 1889; d. March 24, 1889.
(7) Susannah Mulloy Dawson, b. May 16, 1891; resides
South Omaha, Neb.

*   *   *   *   *

(6) Elvira Herrick Mulloy, b. near Nicholsville, O., March
29, 1849; d. Dodge County, Neb., May 19, 1899; studied
in common schools and Clermont Academy; lived Moscow, O.; moved to Dodge County, Neb., spring of 1870;
thence to Ames and near North Bend, Neb.; m., March
12, 1872, Alonzo Parrish, b. Tuscarawus County, O.;
in Aug., 1844, moved to Iowa with his parents, when
quite a small boy; served three or four years in the
Civil War in an Iowa City regiment; resides Oklahoma.

*   *   *   *   *
*   *   *   *   *

(7) Musetta Iduma Parrish, b. Monday, June 9, 1872, in
the country at Dodge County, Neb.; resides Webster, Neb.; address, R. F. D., Scribner, Neb.; studied
in North Bend (Neb.) schools; m., Wednesday, Feb.
27, 1895, Christopher Andrews, b. Christiania, Nor-

way, Oct. 3, 1869; came to America when 13 years old; blacksmith; children all born in Webster, Dodge County, Neb.

(8) Forrest Leroy Andrews, b. Monday, Feb. 8, 1896.

(8) Raymond Bernard Andrews, b. Saturday, April 27, 1897; d. Aug. 12, 1902.

(8) Oscar Adolph Andrews, b. Saturday, June 11, 1898.

(8) Laura Iduma Andrews, b. Saturday, April 21, 1900.

(8) Harry Christopher Andrews, b. Monday, April 28, 1902.

(8) Frances Christinia Andrews, b. Thursday, May 19, 1904.

(8) Baby, b. April 16, 1906.

*   *   *   *   *
*   *   *   *   *

(7) Maud Leona Parrish, b. Maple Grove Township, Dodge County, Neb., July 4, 1875; resides Sturgeonville, Alberta, Canada; a graduate of Maple Grove School, April 6, 1894; m., in Maple Grove Church, Neb., Feb. 18, 1900, William T. Banghart, b. Ridgeley, Neb., Nov. 4, 1871; studied in Ridgeley schools; on his father's farm for six years after his marriage; in the spring of 1906 moved to Sturgeonville, Alberta, Can.

(8) Van Glidden Banghart, b. Ridgeley, Neb., Dec. 17, 1900.

(8) Zeta Mae Banghart, b. Ridgeley, Neb., Feb. 16, 1904.

*   *   *   *   *
*   *   *   *   *

(7) Raymond Hugh Parrish, b. Maple Grove Township, Neb., Jan. 26, 1879; resides White Earth, N. D.; graduated from Maple Grove Township school, April 6, 1894; student at Fremont (Neb.) Normal College.

*   *   *   *   *
*   *   *   *   *

(7) Alice Eugena Parrish, b. near North Bend, Neb., Aug. 27, 1882; resides Hooper, Neb.; graduated from the common schools of Dodge County, Neb.; m., Nov. 29, 1899, John Henry Hubler, b. Jones County, Ia., April 14, 1877; studied in common schools of Stephen County, Ill.; engineer; son of David Milton Hubler, who resides Scribner, Neb., and Laura Albertina Margity.

(8) Earl William Hubler, b. Nov. 26, 1900.

CHAPTER VII.

ALEXANDER THOMPSON OF TOPSHAM, ME., AND HIS DESCENDANTS.

His line of descent: (1) William Thompson of Dover, N. H.; (2) Alexander Thompson, who m. Anna Curtis; (3) Benjamin Thompson, who m., 1726, Hannah Smith, daughter of Joseph Smith of York, Me.; (4) Benjamin Thompson, b. Sept. 7, 1727, resided Kennebunk, Me.; m. (first) Eunice Lord, daughter of Nathaniel Lord; (second), Mary Foster.

(5) Alexander Thompson, b. Arundel, now Kennebunk, Me., Aug. 27, 1757; d. Topsham, Me., Feb. 23, 1820. "He was four years in the Revolutionary Army." Moved to Topsham, Me., 1785, he and his wife riding thither on horseback; resided sixty years on the fine farm, Topsham, Me.; a man of sterling qualities; m., April 8, 1784, Lydia Wildes, b. Arundel, Me., 1764; d. Topsham, Me., April 17, 1858; buried Brunswick, Me., upper cemetery, on the Lisbon Road.

(6) Jane Thompson, b. Nov. 7, 1785; m., Feb. 17, 1810, Maj. Nathaniel Walker, b. Arundel, Me., Sept. 26, 1781; d. Topsham, Me., Aug. 17, 1851. "When a boy he came with his father to Topsham, Me., and in that town passed the greater part of his life. He was a warm-hearted patriot, and served in the 1812 War. In 1814 he was captain of the Topsham (Me.) Artillery Company when it was called out and ordered to defend the city of Bath, Me. He was afterwards promoted to major. He filled various public offices. He was town clerk for a series of years, postmaster for some length of time and justice of the peace. He was an efficient member of the Citizens' Fire Company, in which he always manifested a great deal of interest. He was much interested in the lumber business, and his chief occupation was surveying lumber. He was an energetic and able business man. He had a strong constitution and was never sick until the time of his death. In 1809 he built the Walker homestead." He was the son of Gideon Walker of Arundel,

Me., and Mary Perkins; grandson of Gideon Walker, and great-grandson of John Walker.

(7) Elinor Walker; d. at 15 years.

(7) Wildes Perkins Walker, b. Topsham, Me., May 8, 1814; d. Topsham, Me., June 20, 1888; went to Boston in 1850, and to New York City in 1860; was a prominent merchant in Boston, then a lawyer in New York City; m. (first), in Boston, Mass., July 5, 1840, Catherine Fulton Patten, b. Bath, Me., July 3, 1821; d. May 5, 1875, on a steamer on the Bay of Naples, Italy; daughter of George Ferguson Patten and Hannah Thomas; granddaughter of Thomas Patten and Katherine Fulton; m. (second), Priscilla I. McManus of Brunswick, Me., daughter of Robert McManus and Priscilla Purington; no children.

Children of first wife:

(8) Catherine Patten Walker, b. Boston, Mass., April, 1841; m., April, 1867, Edward Warden, who d. London, Eng., Jan. 19, 1892.

(9) Francis Warden, b. Paris, France, Dec. 2, 1868.

(9) Clarence Patten Warden, b. Aug. 18, 1870; d. Nice, France, April 23, 1896.

(9) William Warden, b. Aug. 18, 1870; d. Paris, France, 1871.

(9) Reginald Warden, b. Brighton, Eng., April 10, 1872.

(9) Katherine Patten Warden, b. Brighton, Eng., Feb. 2, 1874; m., in England, April, 1904, Sir Peter Leicester.

(9) Edward Warden, b. Brighton, Eng.

(9) Julian Warden, b. Paris, France, 1877.

(9) Vera Lydia Warden, b. 1877.

(8) Georgianna Veazie Walker, b. Bath, Me., July 26, 1842; d. Bonn, Germany, May 11, 1897.

(8) Caroline Sears Walker, b. Bath, Me., Feb. 14, 1844.

(7) Elizabeth J. Walker; d. July 23, 1853 (82y., 8m., 6d.); m. (as his first wife), July 1, 1840, Woodbury Bryant Purinton, b. Topsham, Me., Dec. 24, 1814; d. Sept. 19, 1895; son of Humphrey Purinton and Sarah Emery.

(8) Jennie Walker Purinton, b. 1841; resides Commonwealth Avenue, Boston, Mass.; m., April 25, 1866, D. Webster King of Boston, Mass.

(9) Bessie Woodbury King; m., Sept. 12, 1900, Rev. Edward Henry Newbegin of Bangor, Me., rector of Episcopal Church, Bangor, Me.; he d. April 14, 1906 (38y.).

(10) Henry Webster Newbegin, b. Aug. 3ʊ, 1901.

(10) Edward Newbegin, b. Jan. 11, 1903.

(10) Elizabeth Newbegin, b. Dec. 15, 1904.

(10) Robert Newbegin, b. Feb. 5, 1906.

(9) Tarrant Putnam King; m., Feb. 17, 1898, Marica Appleton, daughter of Gen. Francis Appleton.

(10) Appleton King, b. March 15, 1899.

(10) Dorothy King, b. Oct. 2, 1901.

(10) Putnam King, b. Sept. 4, 1903.

(8) Annie E. Purinton, b. June 9, 1845.

(7) Caroline Walker; m. William Tebbetts.

* * * * *

(6) Eunice Thompson, b. Topsham, Me., March 17, 1788; d. Dec. 20, 1878; m., Dec. 31, 1818, Col. John Wilson, b. April 3, 1770; d. Topsham, Me., Feb. 6, 1832. "He came to Harpswell, Me., on a small schooner, with his parents, James Wilson and Ann Henry of Providence, R. I., which was a forty days' journey, owing to storms, etc."

(7) Ann Wilson, b. Aug. 13, 1821; m., Dec. 7, 1842, Rev. A. B. Pendleton, a Baptist minister.

(8) Charles A. Pendleton, b. Aug. 28, 1844; d. Sept. 11, 1844.

(8) Theodosia Pendleton, b. Aug. 11, 1846.

(7) Theodosia Wilson, b. March 20, 1822; d. Oct. 8, 1875; unm.

* * * * *

(6) Lydia Thompson, b. Topsham, Me., April 17, 1790; d Brunswick, Me., July 2, 1876; m. Elias Pierce of Brunswick, Me.

(7) Elias D. Pierce, b. Jan. 4, 1815; d. Feb. 14, 1872; served in the Civil War; m. (first), by Rev. George E. Adams, April 1, 1837, Mary A. Beard of Brunswick, Mê.; m. (second), Dec. 28, 1861, Mrs. Sarah Thomas.

Child of first wife:

(8) Abigail Isadore Pierce.

* * * * *

(6) Hannah Thompson, b. June 1, 1792; d. Brunswick, Me., Feb. 5, 1857; m., June 7, 1819, Calvin Fairbanks⁷ of Monmouth, Me., b. Winthrop, Me., Aug. 5, 1789; d. Brunswick, Me., Feb. 28, 1856; went to Brunswick, Me., in early manhood; stone mason. The family line of Calvin Fairbanks: (1) Jonathan Fairbanks of Dedham, Mass., who m. Grace Smith; (2) John F. Fairbanks, m. Sarah

Fiske; (3) Joseph Fairbanks, m. Dorcas ———; (4) Joseph Fairbanks, m. Abigail Deane; (5) Joseph Fairbanks of Winthrop, Me., m. Frances Estey of Stoughton, Mass.; (6) Col. Nathaniel Fairbanks of Winthrop, Me., m. Hannah Metcalf of Wrentham, Mass.

(7) Lydia Maria Fairbanks, b. March 20, 1820; d. Taunton, Mass., July 30, 1864; m., 1841, Rufus Frank Huckins, who d. Ossipee, N. H., Dec. 20, 1893 (72y.).

(8) Frank Rufus Huckins, b. May 16, 1848; d. Westboro, Mass, Oct. 20, 1889.

(8) Mary Frances Huckins, b. Sept. 1, 1862; unm.

(7) Alexander Fairbanks, b. Aug. 17, 1821; m. Margaret Hume of New Orleans, La.

(8) Alexander Hume Fairbanks, b. Boston, Mass., April 14, 1850; d. at New London, Conn., May 6, 1894; seafaring man; lived Boston, Portland, Me., Jersey City, N. J., New York City, New London, Conn., etc.; m., May 29, 1869, Harriet Ann Sanders, b. Devonshire, Eng., April 19, 1850; resides New London, Conn.; daughter of William Sanders and Maria Walters of Devonshire, Eng.

(9) Mary Maria Fairbanks, b. Portland, Me., March 6, 1870; d. Jersey City, N. J., Jan., 1875.

(9) Margaret Ann Fairbanks, b. Portland, Me., June 11, 1872; since her marriage has lived in New York City, 430 Sixty-second Street, Brooklyn, N. Y.; studied in New London (Conn.) schools; m., April 23, 1891, William Selden Carroll, b. New London, Conn., May 15, 1870; construction engineer; son of James N. Carroll and Mary Jane Bailey.

(10) Edward Ferdinand Carroll, b. New London, Conn., May 1, 1892.

(10) Lloyd Hume Carroll, b. New York City, Aug. 9, 1895.

(9) Lydia Pierce Fairbanks, b. Jersey City, N. J., June 12, 1874; resides Apponaug, R. I.; has lived England, New York City, New London, Conn., etc.; educated in New London schools; m., Sept. 30, 1896, Frank J. Whitcomb, b. New London, Conn., Sept. 14, 1869; educated in New London schools; son of Henry F. Whitcomb and Sarah Kesterton.

(10) Henry A. Whitcomb, b. Feb. 3, 1898.

(10) Robert W. Whitcomb, b. Jan. 27, 1890.

(10) Frank S. Whitcomb, b. May 3, 1903.

(9) William Henry Fairbanks, b. June 22, 1876; d. April 1, 1903.

(9) Beaxy Hume Fairbanks, b. Devonshire, Eng., March 28, 1878; resides New London, Conn; studied in New London schools.

(9) Alexander Thompson Fairbanks, b. New York City, Aug. 23, 1881; machinist.

(9) Edwin Thompson Fairbanks, b. Mystic, Conn., Dec. 3, 1883.

(7) John Calvin Fairbanks, b. Feb., 1828; d. Santa Barbara, Cal., April 20, 1874; m., Oct. 29, 1859, Abby Eliza Macomber of Quincy, Mass., b. Feb. 15, 1839; daughter of Oliver T. Macomber and Abigail D. H. Shaw.

(7) Eliazbeth Hannah Fairbanks. "She went to sea with her uncle, Capt. Wildes Thompson; died in some foreign port, when about 25 years old, and her body was brought to Brunswick, Me., for burial." B. March, 1825; d. July 21, 1856.

(7) Dixey Alpheus Fairbanks, b. 1830; d. in Boston, Mass., May 1, 1858.

(7) Frances Ellen Thompson Fairbanks, b. Brunswick, Me., May, 1832; d. Aug. 8, 1847.

* * * * *

(6) John Thompson, b. Topsham, Me., Aug. 11, 1794; d. Oct. 13, 1857; he lived on his father's homestead in Topsham, Me., the greater part of his life, and was a very successful farmer and one of the kindest neighbors; he was a man of good intellectual ability, a great lover of books and a well-read man for those days. It was intended that he should enter Bowdoin College, but his health was not considered strong enough for that work; he m., Feb. 11, 1824, Mary Mustard, b. Topsham, Me., Jan. 28, 1799; d. Oakland, Cal., Jan. 15, 1875; daughter of Capt. Charles Mustard and Margaret Fulton.

(7) Dixey Wildes Thompson, b. April 8, 1826; d. Santa Barbara, Cal., April 16, 1903; studied in the schools of Brunswick and Topsham, Me.; he m, Oct, 22, 1872, Nancy Parker Swett, b. Georgetown, Me., June, 1844; daughter of Hon. Woodbury Swett and Lydia Owen; a very kind and helpful woman.

"Among the sons of Maine who have emigrated to the West to grow up with the new country, and have achieved renown and fortune, was Dixey W. Thompson. At twenty years of age he adopted the seafaring life, and rose from the lowest grade to be commander of one of the finest ships that sailed on the Kennebec River of Maine. His first venture was in the ship *Richmond*, with Capt. Mustard of Brunswick, Me., the ship having been built at Richmond, Me., himself becoming shipowner and manager in his eventful career in after life. When the 'California fever' broke out he retired from the sea and became a '49er. He crossed the Isthmus of Panama. Arriving in San Francisco, Dec. 28, 1849, he joined in the following summer a party of Maine men in an unsuccessful mining venture at Marysville. Finding employment in San Francisco not to his taste, he took to the sea again, and in course of time, 1852–'57, commanded several vessels, employed mostly in the cotton trade, a lucrative service in those days. He finally purchased the *Sophia*, in commerce between Santa Barbara Islands and the mainland. Then, with his indomitable enterprise, he turned his attention to the acquisition of real estate in that section of California which comprises the rich counties of Santa Barbara and Ventura. Among his purchases were some 300 acres west of Santa Barbara and adjoining Ventura City, and extending several miles along the coast below that city. Within the borders of these two counties he owned and cultivated the largest bean ranch in the world, covering 2,300 acres of the richest land in California, and for which he once refused the offer of half a million of dollars. The utilizing of his landed possessions required the use of a hundred horses and supported 150 dairy cows.

"Dixey W. Thompson was also the extensive owner of city property in Santa Barbara, upon which notable improvements were constantly in progress. The captain's popular reputation extended all through the state and far beyond its boundaries, not only as a man of affairs, but as a pioneer of California. With a chivalrous trait of character, he was noted for genial and open hospitality, and was almost always foremost in entertaining distinguished guests whose steps led them to the gates of Santa Barbara. A marked trait of his private life was open-hearted generosity, and he never failed in his practical aid to the unfortunate whose wants came to his knowledge. He often gave employment to working men in times of business depression, when the work gave him but the slightest profit. Quietly and heartily he did all such work.

"In Captain Thompson's stable of fine horses was his favorite Tecumseh, on which he rode on his silver saddle. When any civic parade was held in any large California city he and his steed were in earnest request. When he could accept such invitations he formed a notable feature in the processions in the last ten years of his life.

"Although 75 years of age when he passed away in his Santa Barbara home, he had been a vigorous man until a fatal disease seized him. At the time of his death he was the well-known owner of the San Miguel Rancho, of 2,500 acres, which joins Ventura on the east. His Santa Barbara interests included 300 acres of land west of that city, a half block on Chaplin Street, a half block on State Street., opposite the post office.

"While landlord of the Arlington he was very popular. In those early times there were no railways, and the steamships called only on specified days. It was rather hard to provide amusement in a dull, small, and very peculiar town that had hardly learned its place on the map. But Captain Thompson could organize a series of specialties that were so new and interesting to visitors from such cities as New York and Boston, that their fame is not yet dim. He offered his guests free trips to the great ranches, gave them picnics in the wonderfully beautiful cañons, had Spanish dances in the royal parlors and fine feats of horsemanship by Californian riders on the hotel grounds. The drowsy, soft music of the violin and the guitar became the fad, and the daredevil riding of the vaqueros was an eye-opener to the Eastern tourists. Presents of flowers and fruits were unostentatiously but frequently made. Old legends were rehearsed. So, notwithstanding the mails were often delayed two weeks, time flew fast and the days were very pleasant.

"But, in the midst of all his marvellous successes in the far West, his loyalty to his Pine Tree State never waned. Thither he returned to wed his gifted and kind-hearted wife, and in scores of other ways he showed that he still tenderly loved his home town by the Androscoggin. In return, Topsham was full of love and pride for this her noble son."

(7) George Wildes Thompson, b. Feb. 15, 1828; drowned in the Androscoggin River, Aug. 3, 1839.

(7) Charles Alexander Thompson, b. May 9, 1830; d. March 22, 1833.

(7) Margaret Thompson, b. April 6, 1833; d. May 4, 1841.

(7) Francesca Carillo Thompson, b. May 26, 1837; d. June 28, 1866; unm. "She was a remarkably gifted woman."

(7) Georgianna M. Thompson, b. July 14, 1841; resides Santa Barbara, Cal.; a woman of great ability and kindness; graduated from Brunswick (Me.) High School, 1858; m., July 10, 1872, Thomas Jefferson Potter Lacey, b. Penfield, N. Y., Feb. 17, 1832; d. Feb. 10, 1883; graduated at Union College, Schenectady, N. Y.; civil engineer; son of John Lacey and Louise Potter.

(8) Mildred Brayton Lacey, b. Jan. 24, 1874.

(8) Madeline Potter Lacey, b. Oct. 24, 1875.

(8) Georgianna Isabel Lacey, b. May 17, 1877; m., Dec. 6, 1905, James Makee Spaulding, b. Hawaii, Dec. 6, 1876; educated in Paris and Rome; he is an artist of great ability; he is now superintendent of his father's large sugar plantation on the Island of Kauai, Hawaiian Islands. His father was a colonel in the Civil War, and is one of the largest sugar planters on the island.

(8) Lloyd Thompson Lacey, b. Feb. 24, 1879; a real estate dealer in Oakland, Cal.

*   *   *   *   *

(6) Capt. Alpheus B. Thompson, b. Jan. 27, 1797; he was a famous sea captain and visited California in 1822. He lived at Santa Barbara, Cal.; by his marriage he became possessed of a half interest in Santa Rosa Island; m. Francesco Camillo, daughter of General Camillo, who was one of the governors of California.

(7) Isabella Thompson; resided Santa Barbara, Cal.

(7) Caroline Thompson; m. John Dana and resided Nimpo, Cal.

(7) Elena Thompson; m. Mr. Tyng and resides Victoria, Tex. This family is now traveling in Europe.

(8) Charles Tyng.

(8) George Tyng.

(8) Francis Carillo Tyng.

(7) Charles Alexander Thompson, b. Santa Barbara, Cal., May 18, 1845; resides Santa Barbara; studied at Santa Clara College, Cal.; attorney-at-law and searcher of titles; deputy clerk for fourteen years; councilman and deputy sheriff; school trustee; m., April 12, 1874, Maria Eulalia Andonaegui, b. Santa Barbara, Cal., Feb. 12, 1856; studied in Santa Barbara public schools; daughter of Jose Marie Andonaegui and Estefania Echeverria.

(8) Charles Lawrence Thompson, b. Santa Barbara, Cal., March 4, 1875; resides San Francisco, Cal.; graduated from Santa Barbara High School, Leland Stanford University and Hastings Law School; admitted as attorney-at-law in the Supreme Court of California; m., in San Francisco, Sept. 9, 1904, Gertrude Boynton.

(8) Frances E. Thompson, b. Santa Barbara, Cal., Oct. 3, 1876; graduated from Santa Barbara High School and Academy of the Sacred Heart, San Francisco, Cal.; unm.

(8) Lorena Anita Thompson, b. Santa Barbara, Cal., Oct. 11, 1890; student in Santa Barbara High School.

(7) Francis Thompson; lived and died in Los Angeles, Cal.; his widow resides there.

(8) Five children.

(7) Adelbert Thompson; d. Santa Barbara, Cal.; unm.

*   *   *   *   *

(6) Mary Thompson, b. April 9, 1799.

*   *   *   *   *

(6) Capt. Wildes T. Thompson, b. March 20, 1801; d. at Oakland, Cal., 1871. He was a very genial and lovable man; of retiring disposition; very much devoted to his family; highly respected by all who knew him; very successful while he followed the sea. Just before he died he roused himself and cried, "Call the pilot!" M. (first), Sept. 10, 1834, Wealthy Robinson of Bath, Me., who d. Dec. 6, 1843 (27y.); m. (second) at St. Louis, Mo.

Children of first wife:

(7) Frank Wildes Thompson; d. 1905; unm.

(7) Chas. Robinson Thompson; deceased; made a fine record in the Civil War; brevetted brigadier-general; m. Octavia Putnam of Bath, Me.; daughter of Dr. Israel Putnam, mayor of Bath.

(8) William Putnam Thompson; graduate of Bowdoin
College; lawyer in Boston, Mass.

Children of second wife:

(7) Alice Wildes Thompson, d. San Francisco, Cal., 1877;
m. William M. Jordan; attorney-at-law in San Francisco.

(8) Daughter; m. Charles Kierulff; resides Berkeley, Cal.

(9) Son.

(7) Daughter.

(6) Capt. Dixey Wildes Thompson, b. May 2, 1803; d. San
Francisco, Cal., May 2, 1900 (77y.); m., June, 1833, Sarah
E. Purinton, b. Topsham, Me., April 24, 1806; d. Nov. 16,
1844; daughter of Humphrey Purinton and Sarah Emery.

(7) Sarah Purinton Thompson, b. Topsham, Me., July 2,
1837; d. Bangor, Me., July 21, 1905.

"She was educated at Pittsfield, Mass., where she
attended the Maplewood School, conducted by Doctor
Agnew, a noted educator of his day. She left there in
1855 to attend the Hubbard School at Hanover, N. H.,
where she remained until 1856. An intimate friend
of those days wrote of her: 'She was a rarely beautiful girl. Her sweet disposition, gentle ways and pure
character, made her a general favorite. She naturally
drew people to her, and all her schoolmates who knew
her intimately, sought her when in trouble. She
soothed and encouraged them. She was always genuine and sincere, and was governed by a loving heart
such as few possessed. She was naturally retiring in
disposition, but her natural qualities and her firm ad-
herence to principle made her very nearly the central
figure of her school life. The instructors were fond of
her. She was a conscientious pupil. She had good
judgment and good reasoning powers. Her intuitions
were marked. She had very remarkable powers for
the reading of character; but her strongest characteristic was her sweetness of disposition, which made
her loved by all who knew her. The child was the
mother of the woman.'"

She m. Gen. Charles Hamlin of Bangor, Me., whom
she had known as a student in Bowdoin College, where
he graduated in 1857. They met when they were
scarcely more than sixteen years old. They were soon
engaged. Their married life of forty-five years was a
perfect union. In early life she began to lose her hear-

17

ing, and in her last years she was totally deaf. This was the only cloud on her life. But of this no one ever heard her utter a word of murmuring or complaint. She accepted her affliction in a truly Christian spirit. It served to intensify her great devotion to her family. While she was in retirement she had a very large circle of the most devoted friends. She followed the different members of her family with unusual interest and judgment through their various occupations in law, drama, medicine, engineering and business, and she often gave them advice which evidenced rare good sense and taste. She was a very faithful member of the Unitarian Church. M., Nov. 28, 1860, Gen. Charles Hamlin, and settled in Bangor, Me., soon after the Civil War. He was b. at Hampden, Me., Sept. 13, 1837, the second son of Hon. Hannibal Hamlin and Sarah Emery; he resides at Bangor, Me.; he was educated at Hampden, Bridgton and Bethel (Me.) academies, and graduated at Bowdoin College in 1857; he read law with his uncle, Stephen Emery, who was then attorney-general of Maine; he began his law practice at Orland, Me. At the opening of the Civil War he entered the recruiting service and was appointed major of the Eighteenth Maine Infantry, afterwards the First Maine Heavy Artillery. He left the defense of Washington, D. C., to enter active service as assistant adjutant-general, Second Division, Third Army Corps, Army of the Potomac; he took part in the battles of Gettysburg, Kelly's Ford, Locust Grove, Mine Run, etc.; promoted to brevet brigadier-general of volunteers; he was asked to enter the regular army, but he resigned and returned to his law practice in Bangor, Me. He has been city solicitor for Bangor, Me.; United States register of bankruptcy, 1869–'79; speaker of the Maine House, 1885; recorder of decisions of Supreme Court, 1888–'94; United States commissioner; chairman of Executive committee of the Maine Gettysburg commission; commander of the Maine Loyal Legion; president of the Eastern Maine General Hospital; author of several legal works, etc.

(8) Charles Eugene Hamlin, b. Orland, Me., Oct. 11, 1861; educated in Bangor (Me.) public schools; graduated Phillips Exeter (N. H.) Academy, 1880; graduated at Harvard College, 1884; has been connected with the

New York *Tribune*, New York *Morning Advertiser*, *Commercial Advertiser*, and other newspapers, from 1885 to 1895, as general political writer, dramatic and musical editor, managing editor, etc.; he is the author of "The Life and Times of Hon. Hannibal Hamlin," composer of the romantic opera "Nicolette," and co-author of the play, "Geraldine;" a most graceful and faithful writer in all lines; m., April 15, 1886, Louise Sawyer, b. Cambridge, 'Mass., July 2, 1857; daughter of Frederick A. Sawyer, United States senator from South Carolina, and Delia E. Gray; she is the author of many children's books. "The Nan Series," "Nan at Camp Chicopee," "Nan in the City," etc., have made her widely known as a writer.

(9) Myra Louise Hamlin, b. Brooklyn, N. Y., April 26, 1887.

(8) Addison Hamlin, b. Georgetown, D. C., March 30 1863; in the real estate business at Bangor, Me.; educated in Bangor (Me.) public schools; graduated from Phillips Exeter (N. H.) Academy, 1880; Harvard College, 1884; at Fryeburg, Saxony, 1884-'85; employed by the United States mint in Philadelphia, Mexico, etc.

(8) Cyrus Hamlin, b. Bangor, Me., Aug. 18, 1869; educated in Bangor (Me.) public schools; graduated from University of Maine, 1891; from Long Island (N. Y.) Hospital College, 1895; studied in Brooklyn Hospital; visiting surgeon to city institutions; United States pension examiner, etc.; m., Oct. 8, 1901, Hattie Bennion, b. Sanghall, Chester, Eng., June 22, 1874; educated in the schools of Chester, Eng.; daughter of Samuel Bennion and Annie ———.

(9) Sarah Emery Hamlin, b. Brooklyn, N. Y., Nov. 23, 1902.

(9) Hannibal Hamlin, b. Feb. 10, 1903.

(8) Edward Thompson Hamlin, b. Bangor, Me., June 6, 1872; resides 80 Park Street, Lynn, Mass.; graduated at Cornell University, 1895; mechanical engineer.

(7) Willie P. Thompson, b. May 14, 1840; d. Nov. 1, 1840.

(7) Dixey Thompson, b. May 14, 1840; d. Jan. 11, 1859, at Havana, Cuba, of yellow fever. "The embalming of the body was imperfect and he was buried in the sea."

(7) Capt. Edward Humphrey Thompson, b. July 29, 1844; d.
     April 19, 1902 (67y.); resided Brunswick, Me.; m.,
     Sept. 14, 1866, Jane Murray, b. June 11, 1838; daugh-
     ter of Capt. William Murray and Jane Lemont.

(8) Adopted daughter, Emma Sewall, b. Nov. 20, 1880; m.,
     July 18, 1900, Wilbur Fisher Center, b. Greenland,
     N. H., March 22, 1873.

(9) Edwin Murray Center, b. July 8, 1901.

(9) Wilbur Center, b. Sept. 5, 1902.

(6) Capt. Francis Alexander Thompson, b. June 27, 1807; d.
     Sumatra, July 1838; lived Bath, Me.; he was a remark-
     ably handsome man, of fine military carriage; studied
     West Point Military Academy; m., May 5, 1834, Sarah
     Richardson of Bath, Me.; daughter of John Richardson
     and Sarah Tibbetts.

(7) Francis Thompson; unm.

CHAPTER VIII.

LEMUEL THOMPSON OF TOPSHAM, ME.

His line of descent: (1) William Thompson of Dover, N. H.; (2) Alexander Thompson, who m. Anna Curtis; (3) Benjamin Thompson, b. Oct. 14, 1702; m., 1726, Hannah Smith, daughter of Joseph Smith of York, Me.; (4) Benjamin Thompson, b. Sept. 7, 1727; resided Kennebunk, Me.; m. (first) Eunice Lord, daughter of Nathaniel Lord, Jr.; (second). Mary Foster; (5) Lemuel Thompson, son of the first marriage with Eunice Lord.

(5) Lemuel Thompson, b. Kennebunk, Me., April 22, 1764; d. Topsham, Me., April 2, 1861 (97y.). The late Isaac N. Thompson of Brunswick, Me., gave this sketch of him:

"My grandfather, Lemuel Thompson, when a young man, came to Topsham, most of the way by spotted trees, distance of about sixty miles. He passed over this route, barefooted, in one day. His shoes were tied in a bundle with his axe and a few clothes. His cash capital was twenty-five cents. With a brave heart he at once took up some wild land at Topsham, out of which he made a valuable farm. It was four miles from Topsham (Me.) Falls, and there he spent all his days. The house which he built is still standing and is occupied by Mr. Charles Barnes. Lemuel Thompson gathered a good property by his honesty and industry, and owned quite a good deal of shipping, etc. He gave his farm to his son, Lewis, with whom he lived in his last days."

Lemuel Thompson, m., Sept. 27, 1792, Susanna Haley, b. Kittery, Me., Nov. 7, 1761; d. Topsham, Me., June 18, 1831 (67y.); daughter of Peletiah Haley of Kittery, Me., who moved to Topsham, Me., May, 1761. His wife was Elizabeth Lewis. Susanna Haley was the granddaughter of Andrew Haley and Mary Bryar, and great-granddaughter of Andrew Haley and Elizabeth Scammon, daughter of Humphrey Scammon; great-great-granddaughter of Andrew Haley, the ancestor, of the Isles of Shoals, called "King of the Shoals," who bought land at York, Me., 1662, and who m, Deborah Wilson, daughter of Gowen Wilson.

* * * * *

(6) Benjamin Thompson, b. Sept. 6, 1793, d. March 6, 1885 (91y.). A man of his father's sturdy type; he settled on a farm about a mile from his father's homestead; he was also a successful shipowner and civil engineer; m., in Bowdoin, Me., by Justice of the Peace John Potter, Jan. 16, 1825, Hannah Pennell, b. Dec. 11, 1798; d. March 4, 1858; daughter of Stephen Pennell, who moved from Falmouth (now Portland), Me., and settled in Topsham, Me.; he m. Mary Cotton, daughter of Thomas Cotton; granddaughter of Thomas Pennell and Rachel Riggs of Falmouth, Me.

(7) Charles Lewis Thompson, b. Topsham, Me., Nov. 12, 1825; d. Portland, Me., June 23, 1897; busied in Evergreen Cemetery, Portland, Me.; studied in the common schools; ship carpenter and builder; of most upright and industrious life; resided Topsham, Me., 1825–'50, in Brunswick, Me., 1850–'70, in Portland, Me., rest of his life; m., Oct. 13, 1853, Clarissa Dunning[5], b. Brunswick, Me., Nov. 24, 1829; d. March 16, 1888; daughter of James Dunning[4] and Elizabeth T. Elkins; Andrew Dunning[3] and Mrs. Margaret (Miller) Ransom; Lieut. James Dunning[2] and Martha Lithgow; Ancestor Andrew Dunning[1] and Susan Bond.

(8) Sarah Pennell Thompson, b. July 19, 1855; resides Woodfords, Me.; studied in Brunswick (Me.) schools; m., March 11, 1878, Henry Irving Nelson, b. Jay, Me., May 14, 1846; studied in Portland (Me.) schools; commercial traveler; son of Lot Packard Nelson and Caroline Starr.

(9) Philip Henry Nelson, b. Dec. 11, 1879; resides Woodfords, Me.; graduated Westbrook (Me.) Seminary, 1902; Maine Central Railroad employé.

(9) Charles Howard Nelson, b. March 23, 1881; graduated Deering (Me.) High School, 1900.

(9) Ralph Holden Nelson, b. July 29, 1883; graduated Westbrook (Me.) Seminary, 1903; bank clerk.

(8) Benjamin Thompson, b. Brunswick, Me., Oct. 13, 1857; resides Portland, Me.; studied in Portland (Me.) schools; course in Lewiston (Me.) Business College; studied law in Portland, Me., with Hon. Thomas H.

Haskell, late associate justice of the Supreme Judicial Court of Maine; admitted to the bar in Portland, Oct. 19, 1881; a very successful attorney-at-law; a generous helper in many good causes; m., Oct. 19, 1882, Emma Stuart Duffett, b. Montreal, Can., Feb. 9, 1859; graduated from Portland (Me.) High School, 1877; daughter of Walter White Duffett and Mary Stuart.

(9) Marion Stuart Thompson, b. Dec. 30, 1884.

(9) Eleanor Thompson, b. March 13, 1891.

(9) Clara Dunning Thompson, b. April 7, 1894.

(9) Nathan Webb Thompson, b. Sept. 30, 1895.

(9) Helen York Thompson, b. June 3, 1899.

(8) Elizabeth Dunning Thompson, b. July 11, 1864; resides Lynn, Mass.; studied in Portland (Me.) schools; a very successful music teacher; m., Aug. 13, 1903, H. E. Pinkham of Lynn, Mass.

(7) Otis F. Thompson, b. Oct., 1827; d. Oct., 1896; m., 1866, Fidelia Stover, b. Harpswell, Me., Oct. 12, 1825; daughter of John Stover and Deborah Clark.

(7) Minerva E. Thompson, b. July 16, 1836; m., Jan. 9, 1866, Charlie O. Hunt, b. Nov. 19, 1829; d. Jan., 1897.

(7) Lavina Carr Thompson, b. Aug. 18, 1839; d. May 2, 1885 (46y.); m., Nov., 1865, George L. Wilson, b. Jan. 1, 1838; d. March 9, 1877.

(8) Jennie M. Wilson, b. June 7, 1871; m., Sept. 14, 1892, Dwight W. Pierce.

(9) Son, b. Sept. 5, 1894.

(8) Hattie E. Wilson, b. Jan. 1, 1874; d. May 6, 1893; m. Winfield S. White.

(6) Peletiah Thompson, b. Topsham, Me., April 4, 1795; d. May 1, 1871 (76y.). "When a young man he went to West Virginia and married. He then moved to Springfield, O., where he bought land, which he afterwards sold for house lots at a good profit; a successful farmer. He invented a fanning mill for winnowing grain. After an absence of twenty-seven years he visited his parents and friends in Maine." M. (first), Mrs. Wilson; m (second), Unity Bucknam.

(7) Emily Thompson.

(7) Charles Thompson.

(7) Levi Thompson.

(7) Lydia Thompson.

(7) Peletiah Thompson.

*　　*　　*　　*　　*

(6) Capt. Isaac Thompson, b. Topsham, Me., May 10, 1797; d.
July 4, 1848 (51y.). He was commander of the Topsham
military company for several years; when a young man
he was a very successful school teacher. Mr. Jellison,
one of his pupils, said: "Our school had the reputation
of being a hard one; several teachers had to leave on account of the unruly conduct of some of the larger boys.
When Isaac Thompson took charge of the school there
were several scholars much larger than himself. Pretty
soon the boys began to snowball the schoolhouse; the
teacher told them not to do it again, as he would punish
the first one who disobeyed. He went to his boarding
house to dinner; when he came back all the larger boys
and some of the smaller ones, were snowballing the
schoolhouse at a great rate; he called the school to order
and requested some of the smaller scholars to bring in
some stout birch sticks; he then invited two of the
larger boys to stand in the floor; he began with the
largest boy and applied to him the birch rod until he had
handsomely promised to obey all the rules of the school.
He gave the same medicine to all the boys who had been
engaged in the mischief, being most severe with the
larger ones. The whole neighborhood was elated over
this victory. The scholars all soon learned to love as
well as they feared their faithful teacher; they made
rapid progress in their studies, and the school was a
very profitable one. The boys who had been the leaders
in disobedience became lifelong friends of Mr. Thompson,
who taught in that school for several terms. He bought
land next to his brother's and was a very successful
farmer. He and his wife were very faithful members of
the Topsham (Me.) Baptist Church." M., Sept. 17, 1824,
Jane E. Wyer, b. Orr's Island, Me., Nov. 4, 1795; d. Jan.,
1881; daughter of Robert Wyer and Agnes Ewing;
granddaughter of William Wyer of Boston, Mass.

(7) Peletiah Haley Thompson, b. July 16, 1825; d June,
1883; m., Aug. 20, 1850, Jane Parker, who d. July,
1896.

(8) Daniel P. Thompson, b. 1851. "Went to Minnesota,
1868."

(8) Alfaretta Thompson, b. 1853; d. 1864.

(8) Lewis Alfred Thompson, b. Nov. 29, 1854; address,
box 45, Bemis, Tenn.; left Maine in May, 1899;
overseer of weaving mills for over twenty-five years;

now foreman in a cotton mill; m., Dec. 5, 1878, Caro Frances Coffin, b. Thorndike, Me., Oct. 17 1855; graduated from Amity (Me.) High School; daughter of John Coffin and Lavina ————; no children

(8) Emery Austin Thompson, b. March 9, 1857; resides Abbeville, S. C. "On the 9th of March, when I was nine years old, I walked with my father 25 miles over the ice and snow to Mr. Calvin Mowers', in Greene, Me., where for three years I worked on the farm for my food and clothes. I then went home to my father, who had moved to Brunswick, Me. and staid with him until I was 15 years old. I worked some on the farms for our neighbors. I then worked in the cotton mill of the Bates Mfg. Co. at Lewiston, Me., for 17 months. I worked in the Androscoggin Mills at Lewiston until I was 25 years old, with the exception of six months, when I was employed by the Cabot Mfg. Co. at Brunswick, Me. In 1882 I went to Biddeford, Me., and worked for the Pepperell Mfg. Co. Aug. 29, 1888, went to Vacluse, S. C., in the employ of the Graniteville Mfg. Co., makers of cotton goods, and continued there 12 years as boss weaver. March 1, 1898, became Supt. of Abbeville S. C., cotton mill." M., Aug. 19, 1876, Hannah Josephine Fox of Portage Lake, Aroostook County, Me., b. Nov. 13, 1852; daughter of Edward Fox and Clarissa Alice ————.

(9) Alfaretta May Thompson, b. Nov. 7, 1879; d. Dec. 4, 1881.

(9) Ralph Lathrop Thompson, b. Jan. 25, 1882.

(9) Emery Austin Thompson, Jr., b. and d. Sept. 18, 1886.

(9) Gladys Teague Thompson, b. June 2, 1895.

(8) Mary Thompson; d. March, 1864.

(8) Thomas Curtis Thompson, b. Topsham, Me., Oct. 4, 1861; resides South Fayette, Me., P. O. box 38, Wayne, Me. "When I was a very small boy my parents moved to Lewiston, Me. I was in the public schools until I was 18 years old. I had a desire to 'see the world.' I went from Boston to the West Indies, where the Am. Consul secured me a responsible position as engineer with a R. R. Co., with Keith & Wilson, who represented an English Syndicate which was constructing roads in Central America.

Four years in that most interesting country were
passed in novel experiences. I was then a sailor on
the Pacific for several years, touching at South American and foreign ports. At Point Lemon, on the coast
of Central America, I went ashore with the captain
to transact some business. We were attacked by a
band of Indians who were in rebellion at the time.
We fled for our lives. On reaching the shore we
found that our boat and crew had gone. They had
been fired on, but had escaped to the ship, thinking
that we were safe in the town. There are no docks
at this port, and the ships are obliged to anchor far
out from shore, lighters being used in the shallow
water. Just as we reached the water's edge, Capt.
George Lyford was shot by the pursuing Indians,
but we both leaped into the water and attempted to
swim to the ship. We were but a little ways out
when the captain gave a cry, threw up his arms, and
began to sink. I swan to his rescue and secured
a floating plank some distance away, and put him
upon it. We pushed out to sea amid a shower of
bullets, and reached the ship much exhausted.
When we got on board we found that we were
bleeding profusely from our many wounds. I had received two bullets in the upper part of my body, of
which I still bear the ugly scars. We were well
taken care of by our good surgeon, Dr. Bird of Philadelphia. At New Orleans I left the ship and trav-
eled through the length and breadth of the U. S. and
Canada. One day at Tacoma, Wash., I met an old
acquaintance from Maine, and that evening I longed
to see my home again. In due time I' reached Lewiston, Me. I entered the cotton mills and made myself proficient in all the departments where I worked.
I then became Supt. of the bag department of the
Victoria Mills, Newburyport, Mass. After awhile I
returned to Maine, where I have remained ever
since. In all my wanderings I held fast to my boy-
ish love for the girl who is now my wife." Mr.
Thompson is tall and straight, with a very muscular
frame, dislikes a crowd, and takes great pleasure in
the hunting and fishing in which he is always so
successful. M., Dec. 17, 1894, Eleanor Sullivan, b.
Readfield Corner, Me., Aug. 1, 1868; only daughter of

Gen. John O'Sullivan and Margaret ———; no children.

(8) William Henry Thompson, b. Topsham, Me., June 19, 1864; resides 4 Harvard Place, Waltham, Mass.; studied in the schools of Lewiston, Me.; went to Boston, Mass., 1884; worked for the Waltham, Mass., Watch Company for eighteen years; is now chaffeur for the Orient Automobile Company; m., July 6, 1886, Annie Jane Kelley, b. Waltham, Mass., April 1, 1867; studied in Waltham schools; daughter of John Kelley and Mary Jane Killopps.

(9) Annie Albretta Thompson, b. July 26, 1893.

(9) Lewis William Thompson, b. Oct. 31, 1897.

(9) William H. Thompson, Jr., b. Oct. 8, 1899.

(8) Fred S. Thompson; resides 259 Charles Street, Waltham, Mass.

(8) Cynthia Patten Thompson, b. Brunswick, Me., April 20, 1869; resides Lannett, Ga.; m., Oct. 18, 1895, James Edward Coburn, b. Biddeford, Me., Feb. 13, 1869; son of Edward Coburn and Lucy Jane ———; he has been overseer of weaving in cotton mills.

(9) Mandy Lucy Thompson, b. Aug. 18, 1898.

(7) Alfred S. Thompson, b. April 18, 1827; drowned Aug. 10, 1847.

(7) Mary Simpson Thompson, b. Feb. 13, 1829; d. April 24, 1896; resided Upper Main Street, Lewiston, Me.; m., Jan. 20, 1850, at Topsham, Me., John Parker of Greene, Me., b. June 17, 1820; farmer on the old Greene (Me.) homestead; the eighth child of William Parker, b. Freeport, Me., Jan. 1, 1783, and of Hannah Larrabee, b. Greene, Me., Oct. 11, 1785; they were married in Greene, Me., March 13, 1808, and had thirteen children.

(8) Corris Anna Parker, b. Dec. 27, 1850; d. May 29, 1886; m., Dec. 24, 1871, Charles Foss of Turner, Me.; farmer.

(9) Bertha Idella Foss, b. Aug. 8, 1874; resides Lewiston, Me.; m. (first), Dec., 1892, Frank Briggs of Auburn, Me., who d. Oct., 1897; m. (second), Feb. 11, 1899, Ernest W. Furbush of Lewiston, Me.; grocer.

Children of first husband:

(10) Charles Seth Briggs, b. June 18, 1893.

(10) Melvin Leonard Briggs, b. Nov. 12, 1895.

(8) Daughter; d. in infancy, March 9, 1852.

(8) John Stinson Parker, b. May 27, 1853; d. Feb. 22, 1858.

(8) Clinton Thompson Parker, b. Feb. 24, 1856; farmer at West Farmington, Me.; m., Dec. 31, 1887, Cora Libby of Carthage, Me.; no children.

(8) John Herbert Parker, b. June 20, 1858; farmer at Leeds, Me.; m., March 30, 1884, Mary J. House of Leeds, Me.

   (9) John Stinson Parker, b. April 24, 1885.

   (9) Benjamin Forest Parker, b. Oct. 22, 1886; d. Oct. 16, 1897.

   (9) Amos Roland Parker, b. Nov. 24, 1892; d. Oct. 3, 1895.

   (9) Herbert Ozro Parker, b. Nov. 15, 1895.

(8) Jemima A. Parker, b. Dec. 21, 1860; resides Greene, Me.; m. (first), Dec., 1882, George Briggs of Turner, Me.; m. (second), Oct., 1888, Charles Foss, a farmer.

Child of first husband:

   (9) Charles Arthur Briggs, b. June 29,.1883.

Child of second husband:

   (9) Daughter, b. Oct., 1890.

(8) Minnie Rosabelle Parker, b. June 22, 1864; resides Greene, Me.; m., Jan. 1, 1884, Walter E. Rose, b. Auburn, Me., Jan. 1, 1856; farmer; son of Elisha K. Rose and Mary E. Morse.

(8) Isaac Newton Parker, b. Dec. 4, 1866; farmer at Greene, Me.; m., March 25, 1893, Clara G. Moore of Howard Lake, Minn. On April 14, 1893, this family moved to the old Greene (Me.) homestead.

   (9) Marguerithe May Parker, b. Nov. 24, 1895.

   (9) Harlan Newton Parker, b. April 6, 1898.

   (9) Paul Dixon Parker, b. May 19, 1899.

(8) Myrtie May Parker, b. Nov. 18, 1869; resides Greene, Me.; m., Oct. 18, 1888, Herbert A. Stevens.

   (9) Paul Linwood Stevens, b. May 17, 1889.

   (9) Parker Francis Stevens, b. March 26, 1894.

(7) Isaac Newton Thompson, b. Topsham, Me., Sept. 11, 1833; d. Brunswick, Me., July 11, 1904 (70y., 10m.). "In 1854 he was in the milk business in Boston, Mass. About a year later he moved to Bowdoin, Me., where for 19 years he carried on the large farm which he had purchased. In Bowdoin he was ever regarded as one of the prominent citizens. He served on the board of selectmen for several years. He was chairman of that board when he left Bowdoin in 1874. He then lived in Webster and Greene, Me. He moved to Brunswick,

Me., about 1894. Here he did a large business in mowing machines, which he sold for over 35 years. For some time he had charge of a large territory as agent for the McCormick Harvestry Co., of Chicago, Ill. He won one of the four prizes offered to New England agents who sold the largest number of machines in one season. They gave him a free trip to the St Louis Exposition. He was a wonderfully energetic and successful man, and this was in spite of the fact that both his hands were badly crippled when he was an infant, his fingers having been drawn up by some terrible burns. The only two fingers which were saved from this early accident were lost in a machine later on in life. He had the genuine Thompson grit, and this and his shrewdness and ability overcame all obstacles in his way." He helped greatly in the writing of the Thompson history, and all that he sent was neatly and clearly written. M., in Topsham, Me., Oct. 24, 1854, Betsy Jane Jones, who d. Dec. 31, 1905 (74y., 8m., 23d.); daughter of Elijah Jones and Betsy Whitney.

(8) Frank Jones Thompson, b. Bowdoin, Me., Sept. 20, 1855; a prosperous farmer at Webster, Me.; in Bowdoin until 1882; in Monmouth until Feb., 1885; in Lewiston until 1896, then to Webster; m., Aug. 30, 1874, Emma Jane Roberts, b. Bowdoin, Me., Aug. 30, 1855; daughter of Nathaniel Roberts and Eliza Jane Grover.

(9) Isaac Nathaniel Thompson, b. Bowdoin, Me., Jan. 23, 1876; resides on a farm at Wales, Me.; studied in grammar school, Lewiston, Me.; m., Nov. 4, 1903, Cora B. Frost of Wales, Me.

(9) Bertha Marcia Thompson, b. Bowdoin, July 4, 1877; d. Webster, Dec. 11, 1897.

(9) Emma Thompson, b. Bowdoin, March 6, 1881; resides Lisbon Falls, Me.; m. Joel M. Ham of Wales, Me., a painter.

(10) Frank Newton Ham, b. Jan. 16, 1905.

(9) Celestie Mae Thompson, b. Monmouth, Me., Aug. 20, 1883; graduated Sabattus (Me.) Grammar School, 1903.

(9) John Fred Thompson, b. Lewiston, Me., Jan. 16, 1888.

(8) Alfred Moses Thompson, b. Bowdoin, Me., March 24, 1859; a successful farmer at Greene, Me., R. F. D. No. 2; studied in Litchfield (Me.) Academy; m., March 22, 1886, Rhoda Ann Cushman, b. Oakfield,

Me., May 20, 1870; daughter of Sullivan Cushman
and Maria W. Briggs.

(9) William Lester Thompson, b. July 14, 1887.

(9) Winifred Alice Thompson, b. Aug. 2, 1888.

(9) Annie May Thompson, b. June 1, 1893.

(9) Alfred Newton Thompson, b. Feb. 8, 1896.

(9) Ethel Irene Thompson, b. March 28, 1906.

(8) Emma Jane Thompson, b. June 26, 1865; resides Brunswick, Me.: studied in Sabattus (Me.) High School;
m., Nov. 4, 1882, John William Edwards, b. Dexter,
Me., Feb. 12, 1862; farmer; son of Simeon Edwards
and Mary Ann Feltham.

(9) Ethel Maud Edwards, b. Aug. 10, 1883.

*   *   *   *   *

(6) Eunice Thompson, b. Topsham, Me., Aug. 25, 1799; d.
March 4, 1885 (85y.). "Single. Lived on the old Thompson homestead, beloved by all who knew her."

*   *   *   *   *

(6) Moses Thompson, b. Topsham, Me., Aug. 1, 1801; d. May 22,
1878 (76y.); a successful farmer at Topsham, Me.; m.
Eliza Jameson, b. Topsham, 1795; d. 1843.

(7) Frances Ellen Thompson, b. Topsham, Me., Jan. 9, 1837;
d. Bath, Me., May 12, 1887; m., Feb. 24, 1860, Lorenzo
Totman, b. East Harpswell, Me., Oct. 19, 1831; d. Bath,
Me., Dec. 19, 1885; sail maker; son of Elisha Totman
and Lucretia Wyer.

(8) Ida Eliza Jane Totman, b. March 3, 1861; R. F. D. No.
1, Jacksonville, Fla; resided in Topsham four years,
then in Bath, Me., until marriage; since then in
Florida; graduated from Bath (Me.) High School,
June, 1880; m., July 23, 1889, Eugene Buck, b. Credo,
W. Va., Oct. 15, 1860; dentist; son of Lorenzo Buck
and Octavia Gilman.

(7) Oliver Franklin Thompson, b. Topsham, Me., 1840; m.
(first), Sarah Hamilton Small of Lewiston, Me.; m.
(second), Ella Small of Lewiston, Me. *Ella Hamilton Small*

Children of first wife:

(8) Minnie Thompson; d. 1884.

(8) Frank Thompson.

(8) Mrs. Lizzie Chesley. *Gurney Jan. 6, 1857 D. 1945*

Children of second wife:

(8) Leona Thompson. *Jan 12 - 1856*

(8) Maurice Thompson. *Nov 14 - 1858*

*   *   *   *   *

(6) David Thompson, b. Sept. 11, 1803; d. Feb. 14, 1884 (80y.);
farmer at Topsham, Me.; m. (first), Harriet Snow, b.
Brunswick, Me., March 7, 1801; d. Aug. 27, 1846; daughter of Aaron Snow and Hannah Aubens; no children; m.
(second), Dec. 30, 1849, Abigail Hersey Dill, b. Falmouth,
Me., July 2, 1816; d. Dec. 12, 1893; daughter of Enoch
Dill and Draxa Fields.

(7) Emily Amanda Thompson, b. Nov. 24, 1850; m., Nov. 21,
1876, Joseph Whitney, b. Topsham, Me., Oct. 18. 1850;
farmer; son of Jeremiah Fowler Whitney and Charity
Rogers Hunter.

(8) Ella Charity Whitney, b. Nov. 21, 1877.

(8) Horace Jere Whitney, b. July 31, 1879; graduate of
Topsham High School, 1896; farmer.

(8) George David Whitney, b. Nov. 15, 1881; d. June 14,
1899.

(8) Mary Abbie Whitney, b. Sept. 23, 1887.

(7) David Lemuel Thompson, b. Topsham, Jan. 14, 1852; d.
Feb. 22, 1884. "He went to the cemetery to select and
arrange for his father's grave, changing his heavy
footwear for thin; took a violent cold and soon died.
His baby boy, David, died in a few months so that
three David Thompsons died in one house in less than
a year, and left no son in the family to retain the
Thompson name." Farmer; graduated from Farmington (Me.) Normal School; m., June 24, 1875, Huldah
Crawford Hyde, b. Topsham, Me., April 7, 1853; daughter of Jude Hyde and Bethiah Ward.

(8) Edith May Thompson, b. Topsham, Me., March 26,
1878; resides Brunswick, Me.; graduated Topsham
High School, June 22, 1894; m., April 20, 1904, George
Irving Prince, b. Brunswick, Me., Dec. 21, 1873;
farmer; son of A. J. Prince and Corilla Given.

(8) Bessie Garfield Thompson, b. Nov. 7, 1881; resides
Bath, Me.; graduated from Topsham High School;
m., June 23, 1904, Lendall E. Knight.

(8) David Otis Thompson, b. March 1, 1884; d. Aug. 18,
1884.

(7) Abbie Esther Thompson, b. Topsham, Me., Aug. 30, 1857;
resides Hopkinton, Mass.; has lived Belfast, Me., and
in Massachusetts, Worcester, Milford and Hopkinton;
m., July 21, 1880, Hiram Franklin Gowell, b. Bowdoin,
Me., Sept. 12, 1851; farmer; son of Alfred Gowell and
Elizabeth Brown.

*   *   *   *   *

(6) Lydia Thompson, b. Topsham, Me., Nov. 27, 1805; d. Aug. 28, 1905 (99y., 9m., 1d.); resided Greene, Me.; m. Calvin Mower, b. Greene, Me., May 7, 1800; d. July 22, 1874; farmer; son of John Mower and Elizabeth ———. One wrote of Lydia (Thompson) Mower a few years ago: "Each day finds her busy with her work and taking an active interest in the affairs of the day. During the past year her busy hands have completed ten large bed quilts and more would have followed if the patchwork had held out. Many friends have received gifts of stockings and mittens from her hands, and she has assisted in the housework and the making of clothes for relatives. She said: 'I should be miserable if I did no work, and I spend the greater part of my time in sewing. I had rather do it than anything else.' Her needlework is perfection. Mrs. Mower said: 'My father, Lemuel Thompson, owned the first carriage ever brought into Topsham, Me. It was rather a crude affair, having a high box seat and fender, with straight shafts and wooden springs, yet it was the envy of all. It was greatly admired, though it was a decidedly hard vehicle for riding as compared with the vehicles of the present day. When I was a girl it was rather hard for children to get shoes to wear, and the cost, and the limited amount of money in circulation, cut down our supply so that one pair had to last for a long time. In summer time, to save expense, we walked to school in our bare feet, and except on Sunday to church and to other prominent gatherings, seldom wore our shoes. Churches were not very plenty and the nearest one to my father's was four miles, and we all walked there on Sunday. The older people usually went on horseback. Often in days gone by have I rode on the rump of the horse while I held with one hand to the crupperstrap and with the other to the waist of my mother's dress. When we walked to church we did not put on our shoes and stockings until we came near the place of service, and they were carried in a bundle when we went home. In those early days we used flint instead of matches, and the punk and tow prevailed. We never dared to let the fires on the hearths go out, because it was so hard to light them again with the flint and punk. Sometimes we went to a neighbor's with the tongs and in these bore home a coal of fire. It was hard to make the tallow candles before the moulds for them came into use.

We took pieces of wick and dipped them in the hot tallow, allowing them to drip a bit, and then with each dripping they could be held in the cool of the cellar to harden. This was rather a slow process, but we thus got quite a fair-shaped candle. White bread was somewhat scarce in those days, but afterwards became very common. Bread was made from buttermilk. Soda was not very plenty then, and when we got out of the powder we used a preparation made of corn cobs, which was made by burning the corn and cobs to ashes and then adding water to make a lye, which, after straining, was to all intents and purposes as good to raise a batch of bread as the best soda in the market. Sometimes we used hardwood ashes for liquid soda, but it did not prove so satisfactory as the other kind. Pastry was limited, and cakes and pies were not used much except when company was around. Our cooking was all done over the fireplace, and pork, beans, potatoes, Indian meal pudding and bread, constituted the common bill of fare. The potatoes were boiled in a kettle suspended from a crane over the fire, so that it could be swung in and out as the cook desired. Meat was fried in a long-handled spider or frying pan held over the roaring flames. While the cooking was primitive, I have never been able to find anything which would excel the suet cakes which were cooked by my mother in the old Dutch oven. The children never tired of those cakes, and mother always had some of them ready for us when we came home from school at night."

(7) Susan Eunice Mower, b. Greene, Me., July 5, 1844; resides Greene and 131 First Avenue S., Minneapolis, Minn.; m., 1865, William H. Harris, a lawyer.

(8) Three children, who are married.

(7) Ann Maria Mower, b. Greene, Me., May 4, 1849; resides Lewiston, Me.; m., 1868, Almon Burton Donnell, b. Webster, Me., Oct. 3, 1845; farmer and carpenter; son of Jesse D. Donnell, who d. Feb. 16, 1902, and of Sarah A. Thompson.

(8) Burton Calvin Donnell, b. Greene, Me., Aug. 1, 1869; resides Portland, Me..

(8) Alice Mabel Donnell, b. Greene, Feb. 2, 1872; m., Dec. 30, 1892, George W. Fogg of Auburn, Me.

(9) Elmer Donnell Fogg, b. June 3, 1897.

18

(8) Leslie Mower Donnell, b. Greene, Sept. 28, 1882.

*   *   *   *   *

(6) Oliver Thompson, b. Topsham, Me., May 9, 1808; d. June 1, 1837. "He died on the Mississippi River."

*   *   *   *   *

(6) Lewis Thompson, b. Topsham, Me., Sept. 30, 1810; d. Jan. 12, 1886 (75y., 3m.); he always lived on the Topsham homestead; m., by Rev. Mr. Lord, May 19, 1842, Pauline Barker Sawyer, b Jan. 26, 1817. A noble woman and of great help with these records. She lately wrote: "I have tried for more than 65 years to be a worker in the vineyard of the Lord. I desire to be more faithful. My hope of Heaven grows brighter." The daughter of Joseph Sawyer and Mary Blanchard of Lisbon, Me.

(7) Susan Jane Thompson, b. July 15, 1844; resides Auburn, Me.; m., Feb. 22, 1868, George E. Longley.

(8) Burton Lewis Longley, b. Sept. 18, 1868.

(8) Ada M. Longley, b. Sept. 24, 1873.

(7) Augusta Marilla Thompson; b. June 5, 1846; resides Greene, Me.; m., May 22, 1868, W. E. Longley.

(7) Palmer Curtis Thompson, b. March 8, 1856; resides Boston, Mass.; m., Jan. 1, 1879, Fannie D. Newell.

(8) Ethel M. Thompson, b. Nov. 24, 1880.

(8) Guy Lewis Thompson, b. Dec. 22, 1885.

(8) Melissa Thompson, b. Aug. 7, 1890.

(7) Melissa Thompson; d. May 26, 1861 (10y., 10m., 19d.).

(7) Angeline Thompson, d. May 22, 1864 (11y., 2m., 14d.).

*   *   *   *   *

(6) Rufus Thompson, b. Topsham, Me., Oct. 26, 1812; d. April 21, 1889 (76y., 5m.); farmer in Topsham, Me.; m. Eliza Cole, who d. Feb. 14, 1892.

(7) George Woodbury Thompson. "He lives on his father's farm, being the only male descendant of Lemuel Thompson in Topsham, though six sons settled on farms in that town, and all had one or more sons." M. Gertrude Green.

(8) Gladys Thompson.

(8) Alton Thompson.

*   *   *   *   *

(6) Ezra Thompson, b. March 10, 1815; d. Sept. 18, 1815 (6m.).

APPENDIX.

The Ancestry of Rev. Daniel Parker. Records of Halliday Family and Others Connected with the Parkers.

Much of this is from a pamphlet written by Eben A. Parker, a member of the bar at Indianapolis, Ind. It was read at the semi-centennial anniversary of Clermont Academy. Much of the data was sent by Mrs. S. C. Davis and by Miss Julia P. Cutler of Marietta, Ohio, daughters of Judge Ephraim Cutler.

About 1644 there came to America from Wiltshire, England, five Parker brothers—Abraham, Jacob, James, Joseph and John. They first settled at Woburn, Mass.; they belonged to a family of distinction in England, and bore with them a coat of arms and a crest, evidences of military renown. The coat of arms was kept through four generations and then lost. Heraldic description, "He beareth party perpale, or sable, on a chevron, gules, three bucks' heads between three amulets; the name Parker. The Parker crest is a knight's head, the helmet with the visor closed." The three amulets charged on the shield are marks of distinction conferred on the fifth son.

Abraham and James Parker were farmers. All of these five Parker brothers were men of consideration in that early time, and some held positions of trust and honor. In 1660 James Parker was appointed by the town commissioners to treat with the Indians, and, with others, to set off land adjoining Chelmsford for one of the tribes. In 1663 he was appointed sergeant in a military company for home protection. In 1673, with others, he petitioned the court to lay out and settle a plantation adjoining the town, and to set aside 500 acres of land for the maintenance of an orthodox minister.

(1) Abraham Parker. He was admitted as a freeman in 1645; in 1653, with his brothers, except John Parker, who settled in Andover, Mass., he moved from Woburn, Mass., to Chelmsford, Mass. In Woburn, Mass., Nov. 18, 1644, he m. Rose Whitlock.

(2) Jacob Parker; d. Chelmsford, Mass., 1669; he had nine children; his widow, Sarah, presented an inventory of his estate to the court April 6, 1669. (She m. [second], Aug. 4, 1675, Capt. John Waite of Malden, Mass., a leader in civil and religious life; he represented his town in the House of Deputies for eighteen years; he was speaker of the House in 1664. Sarah d. Jan. 13, 1707 [81y.].)

(3) Jacob Parker, b. Chelmsford, Mass., 1652; d. Malden, Mass., Oct. 31, 1694.

(3) Sarah Parker, b. Chelmsford, Mass., Jan. 14, 1654; d. July 1, 1678. She was the second wife of Nathaniel Howard of Charlestown, Mass.

(3) Thomas Parker, b. Chelmsford, Mass., March 28, 1756; d. Malden, Mass. (79y.). He is said to have built the old Parker mansion on the old homestead where he died. This homestead is one of Malden's historic spots. His widow, Rebecca, d. Dec. 20, 1758 (75y.).

(4) Rebecca Parker, b. Oct. 31, 1705; d. young.

(4) Thomas Parker, b. Oct. 31, 1705; m., April 5, 1731, Mary Upham.

(4) Jacob Parker, b. Jan. 9, 1707.

(4) David Parker, b. May 2, 1710; d. Oct. 5, 1760 (50y.); m., Sept. 5, 1740, Mary Upham, b. 1715; d. Nov. 25, 1794. She was of the fifth Upham generation. (The Upham ancestor was Dea. John Upham, b. England, 1597; settled in Weymouth, Mass.; buried in Malden, Mass., where his gravestone bears the inscription: "Here lies the body of John Upham, age 84 years. He died Feb. 25, 1861. He was the first inhabitant of New England who bore the name of Upham." Lieut. Phineas Upham[2]; d. Oct., 1676, of wounds received at the battle of Canonicus, the Narragansett fort; he m. Ruth Wood; John Upham[3]; Samuel Upham[4], who m. Mary Grover.)

(5) Mary Parker, b. May 26, 1741; d. young.

(5) Rebecca Parker, b. Nov. 18, 1742; d. Oct. 13, 1819.

(5) William Parker, b. June 10, 1745; d. Nov. 26, 1825;
    m., Jan. 28, 1772, Mary Warner[5], b. Feb. 5, 1752; d.
    Feb. 17, 1811. Her Warner ancestry: (1) Will-
    iam Warner, who came from England and settled
    in Ipswich, Mass., 1637, and d. 1648; (2) Elder
    Philemon Warner of Gloucester, Mass., who M.
    Elizabeth Woodward; (3) Daniel Warner; (4)
    Elder Philemon Warner.) This William Parker
    settled in Newburyport, Mass., where he and his
    wife became members of the Presbyterian Church,
    under the ministration of the renowned Jonathan
    Parsons and John Murray. William Parker was a
    man of uprightness and Christian character. A
    cabinet maker by trade, he manufactured furni-
    ture and exported it to the West Indies, where it
    found a profitable market. He thus not only se-
    cured a competency for himself and family but
    had a surplus from which he purchased, in 1787,
    a share of 1,173 acres of land in what was then
    known as the "Ohio Company's Purchase." This
    company was formed of such men as Gen Rufus
    Putnam of Revolutionary renown, with Rev. Ma-
    nassah Cutler, of civic and religious distinction.
    In 1788 William Parker traveled to his posses-
    sions in the West. Truly this was a great strug-
    gle to leave behind the kindred, and the higher
    civilization and refinement which was fast gather-
    ing around them, for the happiness and betterment
    of the young and interesting family. The hard-
    ships and privations which attended their move-
    ments were not so keenly felt upon the journey as
    when, on arriving at western Pennsylvania, no
    habitation could be found to live in except a sheep
    pen which the sturdy pioneer who had preceded
    him permitted him to move his family into, as
    the sheep were driven out, and in which the Par-
    ker family was sick for a month. The Indian
    wars prevented William Parker's forward move-
    ment from this place. He purchased a small farm
    in the forks of the "Yough," where he remained
    until 1800. Then, on a flatboat, he navigated the
    Ohio River to the land he had purchased on Lead-
    ing Creek, in Meigs County, O. On arriving there
    he found the unbroken forest in all its grandeur

and loveliness. The family remained on the flatboat until a cabin was built.

(6) Elizabeth Warner Parker, b. Sept. 21, 1773; d. June 9, 1850; unm.

(6) William Parker, b. Newburyport, Mass., July 4, 1775; d. Pomeroy, O., Dec. 3, 1855 (80y.); m., May 13, 1802, Betsy Wyatt, b. Beverly, Mass., Oct. 2, 1784; d. at Athens, O., Aug. 6, 1889 (85y.); daughter of Joshua Wyatt and Elizabeth Shaw.

 (7) Edwin Warner Parker, b. March 26, 1803; d. Aug. 24, 1839; m., Oct. 11, 1827, Ann Caldwell Stout, b. Oct. 10, 1806; d. Sept. 24, 1837.

 (7) Elizabeth Parker, b. April 7, 1805; d. Feb. 18, 1861; m., April 7, 1822, Samuel Halliday. (See Halliday records.)

 (7) William Parker, b. Feb. 9, 1807; d. Feb. 11, 1880 (73y.); m., Sept. 15, 1831, Lavina Stout, b. Dec. 1, 1812; d. Jan. 16, 1889.

 (7) Daniel Parker, b. Oct. 22, 1809; d. Jan. 19, 1893; m., Nov. 2, 1847, Catherine E. Gillespie, b. Feb. 29, 1823.

 (7) Mary Parker, b. Feb. 19, 1812; d. Feb. 28, 1812.

 (7) Joshua Wyatt Parker, b. Feb. 19, 1812; d. Dubuque, Ia., Feb. 25, 1893; m., Feb. 19, 1834, Eliza McQuigg, b. Spencer, N. Y., Feb. 22, 1812; d. Dubuque, Ia., July 31, 1901.

 (7) John Newton Parker, b. Aug. 14, 1814; d. June 29, 1816.

 (7) Mary Warner Parker, b. Dec. 2, 1816; d. Sept. 20, 1895; m. (first), Sept. 28, 1835, Buckingham J. Cooley, who d. Feb. 7, 1836; m. (second), Jan. 13, 1839, William Drew Bartlett, who d. Dec. 28, 1849 (49y.).

 (7) Silas Parker, b. May 5, 1819; d. April 5, 1878; m., June 16, 1852, Pearley Jane Ward, b. Oct. 2, 1826.

 (7) Sarah Ann Parker, b. Oct. 29, 1823; d. June 30, 1852; m., as his second wife, Dec. 22, 1842, Tobias Avery Plantz, who d. June 19, 1887.

(6) Sally Parker, b. June 6, 1777; d. June 30 1846; m. Ephraim Cutler.

(6) John Parker, b. June 2, 1779; d. 1849; m. Lucy Cotton.

(6) Rev. Daniel Parker, b. Aug. 7, 1781; d. Mount Hygiene, O., March 22, 1861; m. Priscilla (Mulloy) Ring. (See full records.)

(6) Polly Parker, b. May 27, 1783; m. Judge Cushing Shaw.

(6) Nancy Parker, b. March 21, 1785; d. Salem, O., April 4, 1861; m. Stephen Strong; no children.

(6) Susanna Parker, b. March 10, 1787; d. July 5, 1813; m. Dr. Sylvanus Everett.

(6) Fanny Parker, b. March 26, 1789; m. John Fordyce.

(6) Ebenezer Parker, b. Dec. 22, 1792; d. near Cincinnati, O., Sept. 22, 1873; m. Mary Swett, daughter of Benjamin Swett of Newburyport, Mass.

(6) Clarissa Parker, b. May 10, 1795; d. Feb. 24, 1817; m. Peter Shaw.

(5) Jacob Parker, b. Dec. 28, 1748; d. May 25, 1805.

(5) Silas Parker, b. Aug. 6, 1748.

(5) Mary Parker, b. March 12, 1750; d. Nov. 21, 1819.

(5) Phœbe Parker, b. Dec. 7, 1751; d. March 14. 1836.

(5) Nathan Parker, b. Sept. 12, 1752/'53; d. Aug. 28, 1839.

(5) Esther Parker, b. April 30, 1755; d. Feb. 28, 1778.

(5) Huldah Parker, b. June 3, 1757; d. June, 1829.

(5) Ebenezer Parker, b. March 27, 1761; d. Nov. 13, 1823.

(4) John Parker, b. Oct. 28, 1712.

(4) Joanna Parker, b. April 18, 1715; m. Thomas Lynde.

(4) Benjamin Parker, b. April 17, 1817; m. Phœbe Green.

(4) Rebecca Parker, b. May 8, 1719; m. Benjamin Buckman.

(4) Rachel Parker, b. May 8, 1719; m. Jabez Lynde.

(4) Esther Parker, b. Aug. 18, 1721; m. John Harnden.

(3) Tabitha Parker, b. Feb. 28, 1658/'59; m. Stephen Pierce of Chelmsford, Mass.

(3) Rebecca Parker, b. May 29, 1660; m., June 27, 1682, Jonathan Danforth of Billerica, Mass.

(3) Rachel Parker, b. March 8, 1684/'85; m. John Floyd of Malden, Mass.; son of Capt. John Floyd.

(3) Mary Parker, b. Sept. 8, 1687; d. Jan. 8, 1763; m Thomas Waite; son of John Waite of Malden, Mass.

(3) Ebenezer Parker; resided Chelmsford, Mass., 1715.

THE HALLIDAY RECORDS

(1) Alexander Halliday and his wife, Jean Halliday, whose parents were not relatives, lived in Auchencairn, Parish of Kirkmahoe, County of Dumfries, Scotland. Alexander Halliday died in Scotland.

  (2) Samuel Halliday, the second son, b. Scotland, Oct. 17, 1799; d. Aug. 25, 1880; he graduated from the University of Edinburgh, Scotland; he immigrated from Scotland to America, May 19, 1818; Aug. 19, 1818, he stopped in Rutland, Meigs (then Gallia) County, O. His mother, with six other sons, followed two years later and settled in the same county; these sons all married and raised families. In 1906 there were 300 living descendants of the mother, Jean Halliday, scattered in many states west of Ohio. The descendants of Samuel Halliday are ninety. "The Halliday Clan was so numerous in Scotland that the family has not been much traced beyond two generations beyond Alexander Halliday[1]." The coat of arms was copied from one found in the study of Sir Walter Scott. "There are other Hallidays in America, but this family has not traced them to the first ancestors in America, or to a Scotch ancestor." Samuel Halliday m. (first), April 7, 1822, Eliza Parker, b. Rutland, Meigs County, O., April 7, 1805; d. Feb. 18, 1861; daughter of William Parker[6] and Betsy Wyatt; m. (second), April 29, 1866, Mrs. Jeannett Braley, *nee* McKnight, b. New Brunswick, Dec. 9, 1831; d. Galliopolis, O., April 1, 1905.

Children of first wife:

  (3) Alexander Wyatt Halliday, b. Feb. 2, 1825; d. Aug. 24, 1830.

  (3) William Parker Halliday, b. July 21, 1827; d. Sept. 23, 1899; m., at Louisville, Ky., July 13, 1858, Eliza Craig Wright.

  (3) Jane Halliday, b. Jan. 29, 1830; d. April 28, 1885; m., April 17, 1849, Rufus Putnam Robbins.

  (3) Samuel Bennet Halliday, b. July 19, 1832; d. Dec. 1, 1868; m., May 1, 1855, Elizabeth P. Remington, b. Oct. 20, 1836; d. May 10, 1880.

  (3) Edwin Warner Halliday, b. May 11, 1836; resides Cairo, Ill.; m., June 28, 1864, at Macon, Ga., Emma Witherspoon, b. Memphis, Tenn., July 9, 1844.

    (4) Emma Cocke Halliday, b. Nov. 7, 1865; d. July 11, 1866.

(4) Alice Witherspoon Halliday, b. Sept. 26, 1867; graduated Vassar College.

(4) Samuel Halliday, b. Sept. 4, 1869; studied in University of Illinois; m., Feb. 25, 1895, Nellie Barry Gilbert, b. July 22, 1871.

(4) Vesta Halliday, b. Aug. 7, 1870; graduated Vassar College; m., April 15, 1895, Walter H. Wood, b. April 30, 1869.

(4) Edwin Halliday, b. July 20, 1871; d. March 24, 1872.

(4) Edna Halliday, b. Dec. 22, 1872; d. Dec. 22, 1872.

(4) Edwin Halliday, b. Dec. 20, 1873; m., Jan. 18, 1898, Ruth Bristow Hudson, b. April 6, 1874.

(4) Edith Halliday, b. Dec. 9, 1875; m., Dec. 30, 1902, J. J. Jennells.

(4) Emma Halliday, b. Nov. 18, 1877; studied in Chicago University; m., Sept. 8, 1904, Edward L. Gilbert.

(4) Martha Halliday, b. Dec. 19, 1879; studied in Chicago University.

(4) Eliza Halliday, b. March 9, 1882; studied Ascham Hall, Chicago, Ill.

(4) Fred Davis Halliday, b. Sept. 4, 1885; cadet Culver (Ind.) Military Academy.

(3) Daughter, b. Aug. 11, 1838; d. Aug. 14, 1838.

(3) Eliza Shaw Halliday, b. Aug. 2, 1839; d. San Diego, Cal., April 24, 1889; m., Dec. 25, 1862, Charles T. Hinds.

(3) Henry Laing Halliday, b. March 7, 1842; d. Sept. 2, 1895; m., March 7, 1867, Laura Evans, b. July 24, 1846; d. March 12, 1898.

(3) Thomas Wyatt Halliday, b. June 10, 1844; d. Sept. 18, 1892; m., May 1, 1866, Charlotte Josephine Taylor, b. April 3, 1849; d. July 28, 1906.

(3) Mary Caroline Halliday, b. April 2, 1847; resides Atlanta, Ga.

Child of second wife:

(3) Ann Jean Halliday, b. Gallia County, O., Jan. 6, 1868; m., Sept. 17, 1884, John H. Ewing, b. Galliopolis, O., Oct. 27, 1867.

* * * * *

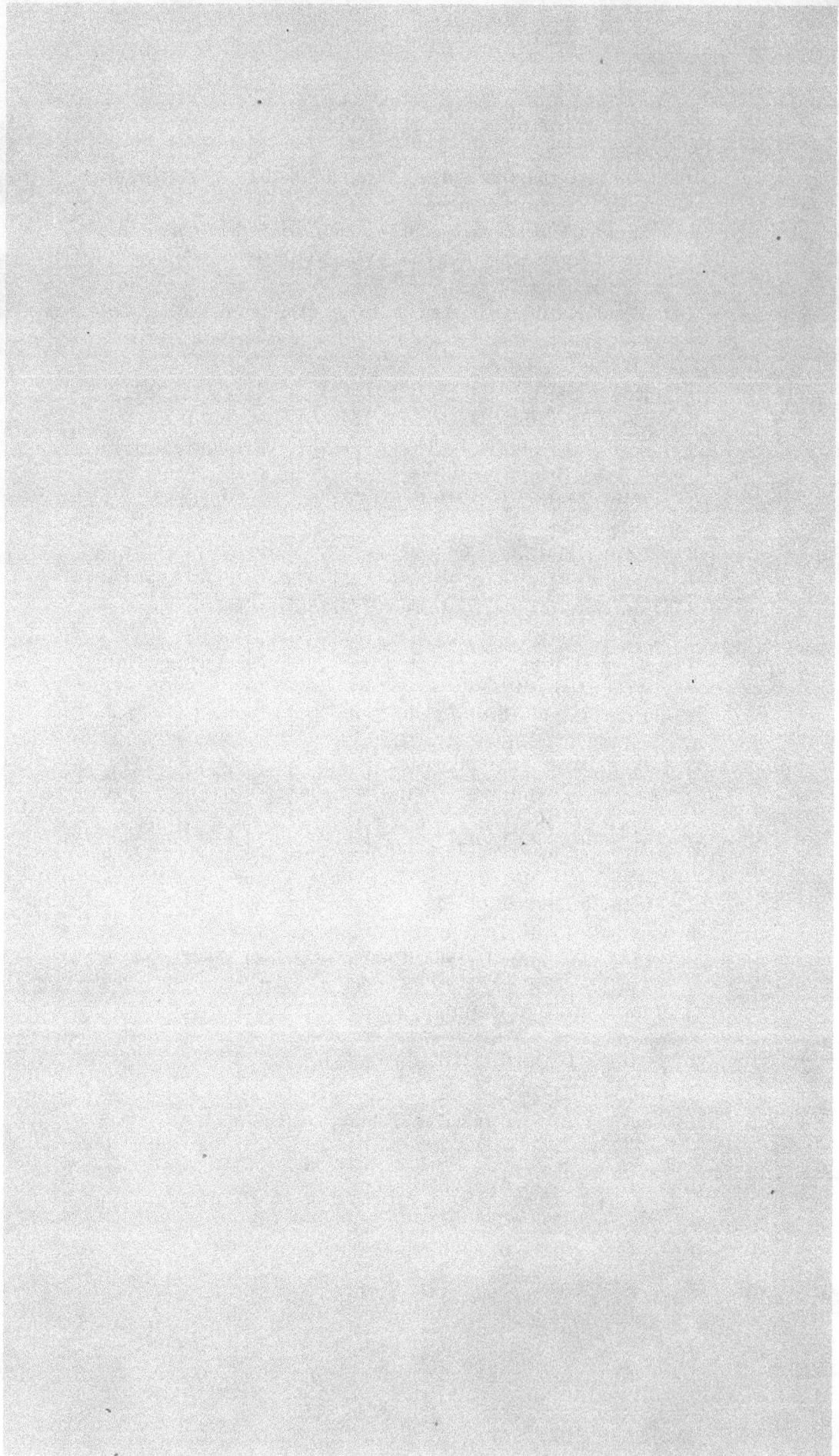

INDEX TO THOMPSON GENEALOGY.

PAGE

Aaron 28, 31, 55, 153
Abbie Esther 271
Abel 8, 81, 119
Abel H..........................140
Abijah 137
Abigail 7, 8, 14, 15, 55, 68, 150, 153
Abijah Harvey 142
Abner Purington 33
Actor Patten 61
Ada E..........................151
Adelbert 256
Adeline Donham 183
Adrian 30
Agnes May 151
Albert 120, 121
Albert T. 42
Albert Trufant 151
Alexander 6, 7, 8, 10, 11
                 13, 156, 248, 261
Alexander Philbrook 168
Alfaretta 264
Alfaretta May 265
Alfred Herrick 68
Alfred Moses 269
Alfred Newton 270
Alfred S. 267
Alice 61
Alice Mildred 127
Alice Quimby 61
Alice Wildes 257
Alonzo 113
Alonzo A. 185
Alonzo Heard 115
Alpheus 119
Alpheus B., Capt................255
Alton 274
Alvah K.........................185
Amos 11, 54, 78, 94, 113
Angeline 274
Anita Mabel 121
Ann Maria 71
Anna 8
Annah 122
Annetta Jane 138
Annie Albretta 267
Annie Eugenia 39
Annie Maud 28
Annie May 270
Arabella 72
Arnold Keith 142
Augusta Marilla 274
Augustine 119
Baker B.........................186
Barbara 41
Barnard Newall 14
Benjamin.........7, 13, 31, 55, 149, 150
                 190, 248, 261, 262
Benjamin Alexander 185
Bertha Marcia 269
Bessie Garfield 271
Betsey 15, 82
Beulah 142
Caleb 13, 14
Caroline 120, 255

PAGE

Caroline M. 127
Caroline Mehitable 62
Caroline Stinson 135
Carylin 121
Catherine McIntosh 70
Celestie Mae 269
C. H...........................27
Chapin Edward 141
Charles 27, 120, 263
Charles Alexander 255, 256
Charles E.......................185
Charles Edgecomb 28
Charles Haynes 117
Charles Holman 74
Charles Lawrence 256
Charles Lewis 262
Charles Sproull 40
Charles Wesley 120
Charles Woodbury 39
Charlotte 68, 163
Charlotte Welsh 181
Chester Ezekiel 75
Chiloa Ann 152
Clara Dunning 263
Clara Sylvia 74
Clarence Fairfield 127
Converse Conkling 185
Cora Mabel 127
Cornelius 11, 16, 44, 46, 62, 70
Cornelius, Capt.................12
Corydon 150
Curtis 8
Cynthia Patten 267
Cyrus 116
Daniel 8
Daniel P........................264
David 13, 14, 156, 271
David Haynes 119
David Lemuel 271
David Otis 271
David Page 14
David, Rev. 162
Dinah 8, 13
Dixey 259
Dixey Wildes 252
Dixey Wildes, Capt..............257
Dodavah Curtis 9, 13
Dora Mollor 41
Dorcas 27
Dwinal Burt 61
Dwinal French, Prof.............61
Ebenezer 8
Edgar 121
Edith 151
Edith Fairfax 41
Edith May 271
Edward Humphrey, Capt...........260
Elbridge 150, 151, 162
Eleanor 118, 263
Elena 255
Elisha Baker 180
Elizabeth...............6, 7, 8, 10, 13
                       14, 15, 18, 28
Elizabeth Allen 7

Elizabeth Dunning 263	Harry Floyd 153
Elizabeth H......................127	Harry Leland....................142
Elizabeth Lois 14	Harry Lewis Brooks..............142
Elizabeth Loring 135	Hattie Irene....................114
Elizabeth Sylvester 62	Helen York......................263
Elmer Ellsworth 115	Henry Franklin..................128
Emery Austin 265	Henry Herrick 62
Emery Austin, Jr...............265	Henry Hersey 41
Emery P........................ 39	Hezekiah Bryant................. 42
Emery Purington 40	Horatio Nelson..............68, 162
Emily 55, 263	Huldah...................9, 13, 156
Emily Amanda 271	Humphrey 27
Emma 269	Humphrey Purington............. 40
Emma Jane......................270	Isaac 7
Esther 8, 9, 13, 135	Isaac, Capt....................264
Ethel Blanchard................139	Isaac Cotton................... 68
Ethel Irene....................270	Isaac Nathaniel................269
Ethel M.......................274	Isaac Newton...................268
Eugene.....................40, 117	Isaac Woodman.................. 68
Eugene, Dr.....................122	Isabella 255
Eunice 7, 47, 123, 250, 270	Isabella Ann K................. 72
Eunice Harding................. 74	Isabella Dunning 41
Eva Laura......................119	Isaiah 31
Everett Andrews................185	James.......3, 6, 7, 8, 9, 10, 14, 16, 27
Ezekiel.......10, 11, 12, 13, 27, 32, 77	28, 31, 44, 78, 149, 190
Ezra........................7, 274	James, Capt............10, 11, 16, 78
Fae 121	James Franklin.................140
Fanny 114	James Smullen.................. 61
Fen B........................... 61	Jane...............13, 150, 162, 248
Flora 121	Jedediah Herrick............... 61
Florence May...................151	Jemima 32
Forest Blake...................127	Jennie 40
Frances E......................256	Jeremiah 163
Frances Ellen..................270	Jerome, Dr.....................121
Francesca Carillo..............255	Jesse 8
Francis 256, 260	Joanna 152
Francis Alexander, Capt........260	Joanna Bryant.................. 43
Frank......................133, 270	Joel........................11, 60
Frank Jones....................269	Joel, Col...................... 55
Frank L........................151	Joel Dwinal.................... 60
Frank Wildes...................256	John A.................6, 8, 9, 12, 252
Franklin 133	John A.........................133
Fred 121	John Albert.................... 28
Fred S.........................267	John Budd, Dr.................. 41
Frederic Eugene................ 75	John Cyrus.....................117
George 162	John Franklin..................141
George Abijah..................141	John Fred......................269
George Kenneth.................142	John Holman.................42, 74
George Knox....................142	John, Sr....................... 5
George Owen.................... 61	Jonathan.........6, 8, 9, 13, 55, 150
George Quincy..................185	Joseph....................8, 10, 12, 14
George Raynard................. 41	Joseph Henry...................140
George Wildes..................255	Joseph, Jr..................... 12
George Woodbury...............274	Josephine Bonaparte............116
Georgianna M...................255	Joshua 14
Gilbert Woodward..............141	Josiah Sanford................. 61
Gladys 274	Judith.............6, 8, 10, 12, 153
Gladys Josephine...............142	Julia Ann...................138, 141
Gladys Teague..................265	Julia Hatch....................152
Gordon Saxton 61	Justin 14
Guy Lewis......................274	Lavina Carr....................263
Hannah..........6, 7, 8, 10, 14, 46, 68	Lavina Rhoda...................139
85, 133, 162, 186, 250	LeGrand Mitchell............... 41
Hannah Curtis..................153	Lemuel.......................7, 261
Hannah Smith................... 69	Leona 270
Harlow 46	Lester Beals...................142
Harmon Coombs.................151	Levi 263
Harold P.......................152	Lewis......................163, 274
Harriet Augusta 68	Lewis Alfred...................264
Harriet M......................127	Lewis William..................267
Harriette 63	Lizzie Jane 141
Harry 27	Lois........................46, 146

Lorena 168
Lorena Anita.........................256
Lucinda Maud.....................185
Lucy 13
Lucy Alice...........................117
Luella May................27, 142
Lydia..........7, 15, 33, 250, 263, 272
Lydia Brown.........................69
Lyman 14
Madaline 151
Mandy Lucy.......................267
Margaret......................13, 255
Maria 46
Maria Ann Goss...................77
Marion Stuart....................263
Martha.........................55, 63
Martha A............................127
Martha Cotton.....................64
Mary......6, 8, 11, 13, 27, 71, 256, 265
Mary Ann......................138, 162
Mary Eleanor.....................115
Mary Elizabeth..................139
Mary Ellen.........................128
Mary Hazen..........................69
Mary Jane..........................126
Mary Louise.......................142
Mary Ruth..........................185
Mary Simpson....................267
Matthew Gardner..............185
Maud 121
Maurice 270
May 7
Mehitable.............13, 15, 55, 88
Melissa.......................120, 274
Mercy.................10, 11, 14, 186
Meribah 8
Minerva E..........................263
Minnie 270
Miriam 13
Moses............................7, 270
Nancy Allen.........................75
Naomi 8
Nathan Webb.....................263
Nathaniel 37
Nathaniel French.................61
Nathaniel Purington, Capt..........139
Nathaniel Thomas Cleveland.......139
Norman Abel.....................141
Olive.......................8, 46, 157
Oliver 274
Oliver Franklin...................270
Origen 162
Orren 168
Otho P...............................185
Otis F.................................263
Palmer Curtis.....................274
Peletiah 263
Peletiah Haley....................264
Penelope 68
Percy Cleveland.................139
Percy E..............................185
Percy F...............................152
Phineas...........11, 55, 62, 77, 125
                        126, 150, 153
Phoebe 68
Polly 14
Priscilla.........8, 42, 55, 153, 156, 190
Priscilla Abbott....................41
Rachel..........27, 30, 43, 70, 126, 168
Rachel Ann.........................140
Rachel Mary.........................75
Rachel Wilson......................62

Ralph Burton........................41
Ralph Lathrop.....................265
Ralph Porter.......................120
Ray 128
Rebecca 27
Reliance...................27, 28, 35
Rhoda.........................68, 146
Richard...............11, 13, 14, 68
Robert..............5, 6, 11, 68, 74
Robert Page..........................14
Roxanna.....................140, 168
Rufus 274
Ruth......13, 27, 31, 43, 68, 71, 72, 117
Sabrina 129
Samuel...................8, 14, 27, 68
Samuel, Brig.-Gen..........18, 27
Samuel, Jr...........................28
Samuel Stowers...................14
Samuel Totman...................142
Sanford Oscar....................151
Sarah.............6, 9, 10, 11, 13, 43
                        62, 63, 150
Sarah A......................9, 28, 40
Sarah Pennell....................262
Sarah Purinton...................257
Seth 15
Shubal 46
Sidney Watson...................151
Simeon Blake.....................127
Sophia 172
Stella 121
Stephen 7
Susan Jane.........................274
Susannah 77
Sybil 147
Tamsin.........................10, 11
Thankful 28
Theodore 14
Theophilus 68
Theophilus Boynton 68
Theophilus Charles............117
Thomas............8, 11, 15, 46, 68
Thomas Cheney....................28
Thomas Curtis....................265
Thomas Roy.......................185
Thomas Wilson, Rev............61
Viola Vincett......................142
Walter Arnold......................74
Weston, Hon......................134
Wildes T., Capt..................256
William........5, 6, 7, 10, 12, 16, 44, 78
                        149, 162, 190, 248, 261
William A...........................185
William Amos.....................117
William Converse...............185
William Curtis....................151
William, Dr........................121
William H., Jr.....................267
William Henry............141, 267
William Lee........................139
William Lester....................270
William Putnam..................257
William R...........................185
William Reed......................162
William Wilson....................61
Willie P..............................259
Winifred Alice....................270
Woodward 138
Wooster 126
Unia Ellis...........................141
Upham 14

OTHER NAMES THAN THOMPSON.

PAGE

Adams, Mary A.....................187
  Mary F.........................114
Allard, Horatio C..............:... 87
  William H...................... 87
Allen, Daniel P. and family........160
  Ezekiel 82–85
  Jessie 70
  Joseph and family.............. 46
  Joseph D. and family......... 47
  Mary Ann...................80–82
  Mehitable 68
Alley, Margaret.................... 61
  Rose 61
Alexander, Cyrus and family.......118
  Hattie 40
  James 145
  John and family...............118
  Lewis P.......................146
  Mary and family...............121
  Minerva 139
Anderson, Carrie M................243
  Nels S........................243
  William and family........157–158
Andonaegui, Marie and family......256
Andrews, Christopher..............246
  Greenleaf 166
  Capt. Greenleaf and family....166
  Kate Sophia and family.......166
  Otis and family............168–172
Archibald, John...................139
  Rebecca 139
Atchley, Charles..................240
Aultman, Bernice..................242
  Cassius M.....................241
  Daniel 240, 241
  Eben Lee......................243
  Jennie 240
  William Boggers...............241
Aumond, Sarah Maria...............222
Austin, —— 11
Baker, Capt. Elisha...............157
  Hannah 157
  James O.......................218
  Sarah Preston.................218
Baldwin, Charles B................244
  P. L..........................244
Banghart, William T. and family...247
Bannon, John T....................84
Barker, Caleb and family.......135–137
Barkley, John Spencer and family..221
  Rebecca 229
Barnes, James..................... 86
Barter, Harriet...................151
  Henry 151
Bates, Hosea......................150
Beck, Callie Ellen................ 85
  William Nelson................185
Bennion, Hattie...................259
Benson, William and family........151
Bibber, Eugene Coffin and family...160
Bickford, Hosea and family........ 86
Billings, Ella Belle..............246
  Lydia 92

PAGE

Black, Garfield T.................. 92
  Dr. Herbert A.................170
Blaisdell, Walter and family...204–206
Blake, Catherine..................126
  Jemima 126
  Simeon 126
Blossom, Matthias. ancestry and descendants 186–189
Boone, Louisa C...................117
  William C.....................117
Bowler, W. O. and family 193
Boynton, Barnard and family...139–140
  Edith M.......................139
  Henry 139
Bradford, William.................143
Bradley, Andrew and family........162
  Foster 129
  Mary L........................129
Bragdon, Jonathan and family..179–180
Branch, Sarah..................... 70
Briggs, George.................267–268
Brigham, Capt. Bertrand B. and family 153
Brookman, Albert and family...... 93
Brooks, Carrie L..................142
  Nelson 142
  Robert and family.............231
Brown, Lieut. Benjamin............ 28
  Gertrude Rogers............... 75
  Moses 75
  Willie 75
Bryan, James T....................121
Bryant, Benjamin R. and family.... 31
Buchans, Robert B.................223
Buck, Eugene......................223
Bundy, W. J...................232–233
Buker, Edward..................... 87
  Emma J........................ 87
  Timothy 87
  William G..................... 87
Burdakin, James...................129
  Walter 129
Burke, Elizabeth A. C.............239
  William 239
Burrows, Annie.................... 74
Burt, Mary Lena................... 61
  Solomon 61
Buss, Katherine................... 84
Byrne, Mary.......................207
Camillo, Francesca................255
Carlton, Charles.................. 76
  Emma Ella..................... 76
Carmichael, Daniel K.............. 84
  Irene 84
  May Bessie.................... 84
Carr, Charles Edwin and family...232
  James 136
  John and family...............138
  Joseph 138
  Dr. Lancelot..............232–234
  Lizzie 232
  Martha Ellen..................233
  Mary 136

Carr, Nannie and family.............233
Carroll, Edward F..................251
    James N......................251
    William S....................251
Carson, Alexander...................137
Case, David F.......................173
    Elizabeth Katherine and family.165
Chamberlain, Dr. DeWitt and fam-
    ily.............................128
    Dr. George....................128
Chase, Addie Frances................ 75
    Thomas and family............158
Charles, Delilah Alexandria Amer-
    ica.............................119
    Irene Moore and family....113-118
    Levin 113
Chatman, James..................... 71
    Inez.......................... 71
    Mildred 71
Chick, Augusta D. and family.......171
    Levi..........................171
    Orra D........................171
Christy, Mary...................... 83
Clark, Abbie....................... 61
    Harriet E..................... 73
    Howard R. and family......... 73
    Medora Frances............... 73
    Nathaniel, Jr..............73-74
    Zillah 71
Coburn, James Edward...............267
Coffin, Caro.......................265
    Caroline 74
    Jeremiah and family.......157-162
Cole, Daniel and family............ 74
    Eliza.........................274
Collins, Mary L. and family........127
Colson, David and family...........193
Colvin, Nannie.....................231
Connor, Charity and family.....142-145
    Simeon 145
Converse, Constant and family..160-161
Cook, Samuel M. and family...183-185
Coombs, Ebenezer and family...153-156
    George L......................126
    Harmon 152
    Lidia 142
    Rhoda and family..........161-162
    Samuel 152
Corbett, Charlotte................. 68
    Horace, Esq., and family.....64-65
    Otis.......................... 68
Cornish, Catherine A...............145
    Elbridge G....................145
    Helen T. and family..........159
Cotton, Isaac...................... 62
    Lois.......................... 65
    Martha 55
    Sarah 62
    Rev. Thomas................... 55
Coulter, Al....................... 91
    Susan 91
Courtney, Elizabeth................ 84
    Peter......................... 84
Cousens, George....................131
    Joshua L. and family.........131
Cox, Cyrus Bede.................... 63
    Isaac......................56, 63
    Maria Ella.................... 86
Crane, Oliver......................241
    Phoebe Ann H.................241
Cranston, Bishop Earl.........228-229
Crawford, James....................156

Crebs, David.......................219
    John A........................219
Cromwell, Ashley...................129
    Bernard 129
Crosby, Charles and family......167-168
    Nathaniel 163
    Nathaniel D. and family.......163
Crosier, Catherine H...............234
Cummings, Birdie L................. 74
Cunningham, Edward................. 72
Currier, Bertha V..................219
    Rev. Charles Warren and fam-
        ily....................218-219
    Edith H.......................219
    Helen J.......................219
Cushing, Alonzo.................... 69
    John 69
Cushman, Rhoda Ann.................269
Cutler, Reuben and family.......... 58
Dakin, George S.................... 65
Danks, Henrietta R.................269
Davis, David...................... 72
    Capt. John....................163
    Mary and family...........163-166
    Stephen 8
    William and family........... 68
    William E. and family........194
Dawson, Albert.....................245
    Claude S......................246
    Jesse and family.............245
    Joseph 245
    Joseph Alva and family.......246
    Martha E. and family.........245
    Osia M........................246
    Susannah 246
Day, Henry H. and family...........183
    Sarah E.......................185
Denman, Ann.......................222
Diggles, James K...................132
    Samuel A......................132
Dill, Abigail H....................271
Dixon, Mary J..................... 83
Dodson, Drusilla and family........171
    George 171
Dolph, Anna S......................116
    John 116
Donaldson, Christian...............221
    Elvira Herrick................221
    Emily H.......................220
    Howard Gay....................221
    Jessie 222
    Parker 222
    Thomas and family.........220-222
Donnell, Almon B. and family..273-274
    Charles 72
    Nathaniel 153
Douglas, Andrew S. and family....164
Duffett, Emma Stewart and family..263
Duncan, Julia..................... 91
Dunnells, Fred T..............76, 77
    Harold Alfred................. 76
    Herbert Ernest................ 76
    Idella M...................... 75
    Irving Clarence............... 76
    John Wesley and family......75-77
Dunning, Clarissa and family...262-263
Dutch, Marshall H................. 60
Dwinal, Aaron..................... 60
    Luther and family............ 36
    Ruth 60
Eames, Emma.....................65-67
    Horace Hayden................. 65

Eames, Ithamar Bellows............. 65
    Joshua 64
      Lucy Curtis................ .. 67
    Capt. Nathaniel.............. 64
Early, Etty and family.........93–94
Eastman, Levi.................152
    Wilbur A. and family........152
Eckerman, George W............ 89
Eddy, Ralph Lewis and family......233
Edgecombe, Aaron..............146
    Arthur 146
    James and family.........28–30
Edson, Lena................. 62
Edwards, George D. and family..176–177
    John W. and family..........270
Ellis, H. and family..........235
Emery, Jacob................. 9
Endicott, Alice............... 89
Ennis, Elizabeth.............. 84
    Henry 84
Estes, Desire...............63, 86
Everett, Prof. Charles Carroll and
    family 36
Fairbanks, Alexander.............251
    Calvin, ancestry and descend-
      ants 250–252
    John Calvin and family........252
    Lydia and family............163
Fairfield, Albert A.............175
    Bartson W. S. and family..173–174
    Charles R. and family........175
    Cyrus and family.............173
    Evan B. and family...........174
    Josiah, ancestry and descend-
      ants 172–180
    Lorenzo Dow and family....173–174
    Rev. Oliver J. and family...175–176
    Otho P.....................174
    Samuel R. and family......175–176
    W. Grant...................175
Farnum, Stephen................ 71
Ferrin, David.................147
    Mary Jane..................147
Fields, James and family............179
Finley, Dr. George W. and family...179
Fletcher, Maud.........................130
    Walter 130
    Walter V. and family..........130
    Warren 130
Fogg, George W.....................273
Foot, Elizabeth.................... 84
Foss, Charles and family.......267–268
Found, J. E. and family............. 90
Fox, Hannah Josephine.............265
Frank, Elizabeth M.................184
Fraser, Alfred and family............238
Frazier, Louisa J. and family...159–160
French, Harriet Newell............. 60
    Nathaniel 61
Freeman, Mrs. Abbie M............139
Frisell, Kate................. 91
Frost, Cora B...................269
Frye family....................9–15
    Adrian 9
    Elizabeth 9
Fuller, Raymond August.............174
Furbush, Everett W. and family....267
Gibson, Eliza Jane................. 72
    George 176
Gilhurley, Sara and family.........177
Gillette, Frederick K.............221
Given, Ella.................... 71

Golden, Sarah................. 63
Gooding, Abraham..............122
    Althea J...................122
Goodwin, Charles W............170
    Sarah 126
Gorman, George Albert and family.. 76
Gowell, Hiram.................271
    Wyman and family........144–145
Graham, Eva................. 71
Grant, Daniel and family........ 68
Green, Eleanor S..............188
    Gertrude 274
Gregory, Christine..............232
    Idella 232
Griffin, Ella..................241
    Jesse R...................241
Grover, Ezekiel............... 85
    James and family....... 85–88
Grows, Joseph Ross............ 74
    Margaret Oaks............ 74
Gullick, George H. and family.......136
    James 136
Haines, Lyman................ 86
Haley, Peletiah, ancestry and fam-
    ily 261–264
    Susannah 7, 261–274
Hall, Elijah and family........ 46
Halliday, Frank................115
    Genealogy of family, appendix.
                   280–281
Ham, Abner L................. 71
    Charles A................70–71
    Cornelius F. and family........ 71
    Daniel H................... 70
    Eva Jane................... 71
    Frank E. and family........... 71
    Hiram H.................... 70
    James, Jr................. 70
    Joel M....................269
    John 32, 70
    John C. and family...........171
    Lena B.................... 76
    Lucy G.................... 71
    Mary Luella................ 71
    Rhoda 31
    Ruth A.................... 71
    Walter C.................. 71
Hamilton, David S..............121
    James Andrew..............121
Hamlin, Gen. Charles and family
                   257–259
Harmon, Hannah................ 61
    Littleton D................ 93
Harris, Dr. James M. and family....205
    William A.................273
Harrison, Theophilus, ancestry and
    descendants 115–116
Harsh, Barbara A...............182
    Daniel 182
Hart, Tillie Florence..............236
Hathaway, Meribah............. 63
Hathorn, Alexander S...........121
    Frederick G...............129
    Luella 121
Hayden, Emma................. 65
    George 65
    John 65
    Capt. William.............. 65
Hayford, Rose................. 62
Haynes, David and family..........122
    Dwinal 123
    James 123

Haynes, Lyman.........................'86
  Mary, ancestry and descend-
    ants 81–122
  Capt. Stephen S...........122, 142
Healey, Capt. Abraham............. 63
  Carl Ernest and family........ 64
  David 63
  Hattie Alice.................. 64
  Joseph 63
  Virgil Theron................. 64
Heinzleman, John................117
  Ondaletta 117
Heltman, Charles................. 24
  Pamelia, ...241
Herrick, Hon. Anson............203
  Anson 204
  Carleton Moses..............203
  Carlton Tremper.............208
  Hon. Ebenezer and family...202–208
  Eli 186
  Henry and family.........64–68
  Hugh Mulloy.............206–208
  Gen. Jedediah and family...55–64
  John 202
  Joseph 64
  Mary Gove...............204–205
  Capt. Oliver and family......34–35
  Richard C. and family.........208
  Samuel and family........193–202
Herron, Joseph.................228
  Lucy E.....................228
Higgins, Mary.................18, 90
  Robert 90
  Sally 75
  Sarah 72
Hill, Dr. C. H.................. 68
  Cyrus E. and family........120
  Ethel 68
  Florence 68
  Dr. Henry M.................120
  John Henry and family........120
  Joshua and family........... 60
Hilton, Thomas J. and family.... 60
Hinkley, Atkins L. and family..132–133
  Mary 12
  Mehitable 46
  Phoebe 46
  Reliance 17
  Dea. Samuel.................12, 17
  Theophilus 43
  Thomas 46
Hitch, Abbie C.................194
  Annie Sherwin..............236
  Arthur E....................236
  Chilcarra S.................235
  James, Narlbro O'Neal.........236
  Robert H. and family.....234–237
  Susan Jane..................235
  Thomas T....................235
  William Shakespeare..........234
Hodge, Elizabeth, ancestry and de-
  scendants 164–165
Hoenstine, Leah May.............246
  Zeigler 246
Hoffman, Mark and family........ 89
Hogan, W. and family............143
Holbert, Anna B.,...............118
  Charles 118
Holbrook, Isabella A. and family....152
  John 72
  Capt. John and family........72–74
  John Quincy A................. 72

Holbrook, Samuel H..............152
  Samuel S. and family...........147
Holcomb, John................... 83
  Mary Ann.................... 82
Hood, Elisha...................136
  John H. A. and family.....136–137
Hooker, Walter O. and family...169–170
Horton, George.................244
  Harriet M..................244
House, Mary J..................268
Houston, Charles M. and family.....237
  James W....................237
  Leona Priscilla and family......238
  Martha Pepper..............238
  Nancy Ann..................237
  Nellie M...................238
  Robert M. and family......237–238
  Thomas C. and family......237–238
  Walter A...................237
Howard, Addie.................. 93
  Alonzo and family.......... 93
  Hiram and family........... 93
  Josephine 93
  Louis and family............. 93
  Marcellus M. and family....... 93
  Nellie 71
  Rose Lee................... 93
  Thomas F. and family......... 93
Hubler, John Henry and family......247
Huckins, Frank.................251
  Rufus 251
Humphreys, Rev. Evan W. and fam-
  ily 177–179
Hunt, Charlie O................263
Huston, Sarah S................ 90
Hyde, Huldah Crawford and family..271
Inloes, Sophia.................228
Ivens, Emma E.................182
Jackson, John W................172
  Susannah 151
  Walter 172
Jameson, Eliza and family.........270
Jeffries, Blair and family...........173
  Tabitha and family.........173–174
Jewell, ——.................55, 68, 150
  Annie 150
  Lydia 151–153
Johnson, Frederick W. and family...116
  Israel 68
Jones, Alexander B................ 92
  Mrs. Annie Elizabeth (Heard)..114
  Betsy J. and family............269
  Elston A. and family.......... 63
  Rev. Josiah Hayden............. 57
Jordan, Robert.................148
  Rosannah 62
  William M..................257
Junkins, Daniel................. 9
  Capt. John................. 8
  Olive 8
  Philip 10, 11
  Sarah 9
Keith, Clara E.................142
Kell, Bertha...................120
Kellett, Estelle................143
Kelley, Annie J................267
Kendrick, Frank S..............145
Kenyon, Martha Ann............208
Kidder, Camilius and family......59–60
King, D. Webster and family...249–250
Klemme, Nellie R...............228
Knight, Henry E. and family.......207

Knight, Lendall E....................271
Kohler, Andrew and family.........161
Lacey, John........................255
    Thomas Jefferson and family....255
Lakin, Sarah Maria................224
    William P.....................224
Lane, Eliza Davis................. 58
    Mary Ann...................... 58
Larrabee, Hannah..................267
Lawrence, George N. and family....170
Lee, Cushman...................... 62
Leeds, Moses......................173
Lemont, Charles W.................128
Lewis, George, ancestry and family
                              129-132
    Nathaniel 9
    Ray T......................130-131
Libby, Cora.......................268
Liecester, Sir Peter..............249
Lindley, Edward P. and family.....114
Linscott, Abijah..................148
    Albert J. and family..........148
    Jeremiah 8
Littlefield, Abner................ 7
    Isaac 15
    Jonathan 14
Lockridge, Andrew L...............116
Long, Charles L. and family.......130
Longley, George E. and family.....274
Lovering, John.................... 6
    Mary 6
Lunt, Judah.......................158
    Mary 158
Machan, Dr. George S. and family... 41
Maddox, Elizabeth................. 13
    John 13
Mallett, John..................... 27
    Samuel T..................... 27
Mariner, Elizabeth and family.....139
    Gustavus 141
    John 139
    John and family..............146
    Unite and family.........147-148
    William B....................141
Mark, John A......................244
    Milton Ashley................243
Marshall, Rev. Charles K. and
    family 205
    Harry Sandford...............234
Marston, Martha R................. 61
Maxwell, Elsie M. and family.....171
Maynard, Anne May................. 59
    Hon. Horace................... 60
Mayo, Albert A.................... 58
McCall, ————......................194
McCullough, Samuel and family.....204
McDonald, Sarah Emeline...........227
McGiff, Francis B. and family.....182
McGohan, Augustus E...............185
McIntosh, Ann..................... 70
    Capt. John.................... 70
McKenney, Susan................... 70
McManus, Priscilla................249
    Robert 249
McMurchy, William and family..181-182
    William C....................184
McNair, Archibald and family...204-205
Merrill, Isaac Cotton and family.... 65
    John 65
Metcalf, Mary.....................126
Middleton, Joseph B...............240
    Walter Guy...................239

Middleton, William H..............239
Miller, Alexander................. 91
    Isaac Rudolph................223
    Miranda J.................... 91
Minnick, Jessie Elizabeth and family.178
Mooers, Althea A.................. 76
Moore, Clara G....................268
    Ella 177
    Jonathan 113
Moreton, Susannah.................239
Moseley, Orlando P. and family....145
    Phineas T....................145
    William and family...........142
Moulton, Marietta................. 61
Mower, Calvin and family......272-274
Mulloy, Abigail...................193
    Alvah Milton.................240
    Catherine 193
    Charles Moreton..............240
    Charles William..............244
    David and family..192-193, 239-240
    Edwin M. and family..........243
    Elizabeth Priscilla and family
                              245-247
    Elvira Herrick and family.....246
    Frank and family.............240
    Hugh 156, 240
    Hugh, ancestry and descend-
        ants 190-249
    Hugh C.......................244
    Isaac and family.............237
    James 202
    James Guston and family..243-244
    John Rogers and family,
                         240-243, 244
    Lettie Kate..................241
    Lida Luella..................241
    Martha 230-238
    Moreton 240-241
    Nannie 243-244
    Priscilla 208-230
    Susan Elizabeth 244
    Susannah and family.......241-242
    Thomas 234-237
    Thomas Benton................240
    William and family...........241
    William T....................241
Murray, Jane......................260
    Capt. William................260
Mustard, Capt. Charles............262
    Mary and family..........252-255
Myers, George Lawrence and family.236
Nason, Prof. Arthur Huntington.... 69
    Charles Henry,............... 69
    Edwin Francis................ 70
    Joseph Frost, ancestry and
        descendants 69
Needham, Earle H..................177
    Harry E......................177
Nelson, Lot P. and family.........262
Nevers, Dr. John.................. 10
Newell, Fannie D..................274
Nichols, Edna True................229
    George B.....................229
    Mary Childs.................. 58
Norris, John......................243
    Dr. Lewis E.................. 57
    Mary Eliza...................243
Northcutt, Minnie A...............237
    Uriah 237
Oatley, Fannie M..................236
    Luther 237

Ogden, George and family............206
Page, Abigail.......................... 14
    Col. David.......................... 14
Paine, Elmer E. and family..........178
Parker, Anna M......................223
    Barkley 229
    Dr. Charles Coleman........223–226
    Charles Lucius....................227
    Charlotte Frances..............218
    Rev. Daniel and family.....213–230
    Daniel Mason.....................227
    Daniel Mulloy.....................228
    Eben Armstrong.................229
    Eva 220
    Frederick Donaldson.............222
    Dr. James Kennedy.............220
    John 267–268
    Josephine 215
    Lucie M.....................228–229
    Mary Priscilla....................229
    Mason D...........................228
    Mason Doane.....................228
    Mattie M..........................229
    Sarah Belle........................229
    Susanna Evarts.............220–222
    Wilhelmina M.....................223
    Dr. William Tell..............222
Parker Genealogy, appendix.....275–279
Parrish, Alice E.....................247
    Alonzo 246
    Maud Leona.......................247
    Musetta Iduma and family.246–247
    Raymond Hugh.................247
Parsons, Martin...................... 90
Patton, Catherine Fulton...........249
    George F.........................249
Paul, Alice L.......................151
Pease, Capt. Martin.................173
    Mary and family................173
Pendleton, Rev. A. B.............250
    Charles A.........................250
    Theodosia 250
Pennell, Hannah....................262
    Stephen 262
    Thomas 262
Perkins, Daniel....................... 7
    Lydia 14
Philbrook, Abigail........13, 55, 149–189
Phillips, Alonzo and family......... 88
    Amos and family................. 90
    Daniel T. and family........... 88
    David 88
    Guy F............................. 92
    Harris W......................... 92
    Jerome and family............. 91
    Mary Elizabeth.................. 92
    Mary F........................... 88
    Matabell 92
    Nellie P........................... 92
    Sarah Haseltine.................219
    Samuel and family.........88–94
    Wylie H. and family............ 92
Pinkham, H. E.......................263
Plunkett, Rollin A. and ancestry....176
Podfield, W. R......................118
Porter, George E... 138
    Nathaniel C...................... 138
    Rufus King......................167
Potter, James and family..........127
    Jesse 127
Pratt, Levi H. and family..........147
Preble, Josiah H. and family........ 38

Preble, Mehitable and family...126–135
Preston, Penicy.......................119
Pribble, John M. and family.......238
Prince, George J.....................271
Pritchard, Frances E. and family...223
Purdin, C. W. and family........... 88
Purington, Abel.................123–124
    Abizer, ancestry and descend-
      ants 123–124
    Abner 124
    Betsy 125
    Cornelius 125
    Daniel T..........................125
    Elisha 123
    Emma 124
    Esther 124
    Fanny D..........................124
    Humphrey 75–78
    Mary Etta........................ 75
    Miles S......................... 75
    Sarah Abbie...................... 75
    Simeon 75
Purinton, Abial..................... 27
    Ann Emery...................... 39
    Daniel T. and family...........147
    Dea. Humphrey................. 27
    Priscilla 32, 33
    Sarah E. and family.......257–260
    Woodbury Bryand and family,
                     249–250
Putnam, Israel.....................256
    Octavia 256
Quick, Susan.......................137
Randall, Archella H................157
    Daniel F. and family...........161
    David F. and family.......160–161
    Eliza 62
    Capt. George B...................157
    Capt. George W.................157
    Martha 62
    William 62
Read, Rev. Andrew and family.....220
Redmond, Nora D...................235
Reed, Mary and family.............162
Rettinghouse, Charles A............. 91
    Elsa 136
    Isaac 90
    John and family.................137
    Zadie 136
Richard, Marguerite..............136
Richardson, Aaron.................. 49
    Abijah, ancestry and descend-
      ants 47–54
    Almira 50
    Ambrose 50
    Amos and family................. 48
    Atwell 53
    Augustine 48
    Celia A........................... 49
    Clarissa 50
    Columbus 48
    Correctus 49
    David 48
    Dora A........................... 53
    Edith M........................... 54
    Edward P......................... 53
    Emily 50
    Emma and family............... 46
    Emma T.......................... 45
    Eunice 50
    Eunice C......................... 50
    Frederick S....................... 53

Richardson, George C.................... 54
    Guy Carlton..................... 50
    Hannah Smith.................... 51
    Harriet 50
    Henry Coombs................... 49
    Hester Ann R.................52-53
    Jedediah 48
    Jennie 48
    Jesse and family............48-49
    John 260
    Kirkwood 49
    Laura 49
    Lois 49
    Lyman 48
    Martha 49
    Mary Baker 48
    Mary P......................... 53
    Max F.......................... 49
    Nancy Ann...................... 49
    Orrin 50
    Patty 48
    Phineas 51, 52
    Prince W....................... 49
    Prudence May................... 52
    Rachel 54
    Robert 50
    Rolla T........................ 54
    Sally 48
    Sarah 260
    Sarah Maria.................... 52
    Sarah S........................ 48
    Wesley 48
    William B...................... 54
    William H...................... 54
    William M...................... 49
Ricker, Elizabeth..............46, 68
Ridley, Capt. Isaac N. and family...152
Ring, Benjamin.................211-212
Roach, Katie.......................... 93
Roberts, Emma Jane...................269
    Sarah Hannah...............85, 87
Robinson, Caleb C.................... 49
    Charles 168
    Daniel 49
    Hannah 49
    Levi and family.............49-50
    Lorenzo 49
    Margaret 50
    Mary 49
    Mary and family...........175-176
    Mattie 49
    Nahum 50
    Sarah Ann...................... 50
    Seth 49
    Wealthy 256
Rogers, John.........................239
    Susannah 239
Rose, Walter E.................268-269
Rounds, Lydia........................ 61
Rush, Daniel.........................237
    Margaret Elizabeth.............237
Sawyer, John and family............. 47
    Louise 259
    Pauline B......................274
Saunders, George W. and family.... 89
    Harriet Ann.................... 25
    William 251
Schubert, George H. and family.....238
Scott, Henry and family.............148
Seykora, Edward J. and family..242-243
Shannon, Kitty Ann..................154
Sharp, Walter.......................232

Sharp, William A. and family.......119
Shearer, Walter S.................... 90
Sheldon, Sadie......................232
Sherwin, Abigail Charlotte and fam-
    ily 234-237
    Hugh E. and family.............238
    James L. C. and family....230-232
    Nancy Thompson and family
                               232-234
    Susan P. and family......237-238
    William Bacon and family..230-239
    William T......................234
Schrinkel, Benner F. and family.... 84
Simmons, Mary H.....................236
Sinnett, George W. and family.......153
    William Henry and family.....152
Skolfield, Jacob....................133
    William S......................133
Small, Maj. A. H. and family........ 73
    Granville M.................... 86
    Mander 87
    Sarah H........................270
Smith, Alphonso W. and family....123
    Clara A. and family............180
    Cora L.........................121
    Darling and family............. 90
    Enos and family.........172-173
    Hannah..........7, 14, 45, 150, 171
    Isaac......................231-232
    John P. and family.............231
    Mary 14
    Martha C....................... 86
    Melville and family............140
Snow, Harriet.......................271
    Rebecca 42
    Samuel 42
South, Capt. Thomas W...............222
Spencer, Isabel and family..........168
Spitz, Conrad....................... 83
    Mary Katherine................. 83
Sproull, Annie Matilda Stag and
    family 40
    John J......................... 40
Stackpole, Rev. Dr. E. S., 5, 6, 13, 45, 69
    James 12
Stafford, Ann....................... 68
Stanley, Laura...................... 70
Staples, Eleanor M.................. 8
Stetson, Reuben H. and family...... 57
Stevens, Herbert A.................. 68
    Levi W. and family.............141
Stewart, Richard....................235
Stickney, Alan Kent.................220
    David H........................219
Stinson, David......................134
    Sarah Dow......................134
Stockin, Abner C. and family...188-189
    Annie 189
    Arthur and family..............189
    Edwin and family..........188-189
Story, Julian W..................... 66
    William W...................... 66
Stover, Fidelia.....................263
Stowers, Elizabeth.................. 14
Stuntz, Conrad...................... 82
    George O. and family........... 83
    Capt. John..................... 82
    Lucius Dow..................... 82
    Lucius D., Jr.................. 83
Sullivan, Eleanor...................266
    Malvina Fitzlan and family.234-235
Swett, Nancy Parker.................252

Swett, Hon. Woodbury..............252
Sylvester, Abigail................. 62
    Boynton 62
    Elizabeth 62
    William 62
Taber, Gustavus................... 60
    Matilda C..................... 60
Taggart, Benjamin D...............122
    Kate Mary.....................122
Tallman, Edgar I. and family...207-208
Tate, D. M........................ 88
    Martha 88-90
    Patten and family.............128
Tebbetts, Isaac and family.......35-37
    Paul C. and family............ 42
    Samuel 153
    William 250
Tedford, Jonathan E...............145
Terrell, Arthur D................. 84
    Edward A...................... 84
    Edward D...................... 84
    Hannah A...................... 84
    James Earle 84
    James Jeremiah................ 84
    Jeremiah 83
    Martha Jane................... 84
    Mary Elizabeth 83
    William Ennis................. 84
Thomas, J. F...................... 74
Thorne, John......................127
    John F........................127
Tichnor, Walter E. and family.....133
Totman, Lorenzo and family........270
Townsend, Carrie L................131
    James 131
Tremper, Louisa M.................207
Troynham, Rebecca F...............237
Truett, John D. and family........116
Trufant, Addie G..................152
    Albert T......................152
    William 151
Truman, Violet....................227
Turner, Ezekiel E. and family..181-183
    Hon. L. D..................... 94
Truslow, John and family.......... 59
Tyler, Melissa.................... 61
Ullen, Maj. Benjamin L............ 59
    Mary Ellen....................185
Ulrey, Malinda....................184
    Olive 185
    Samuel 185
Varner, Abraham................... 83
    Mary J........................ 83
Varney, Linwood E. and family..159-160
Vavra, Adolph.....................245
    Lucile 245
Vickers, G. B. and family......... 89
Vinal, Ellen L....................130
    Harry A.......................130
Visonhaler, Jacob.................114
    Mary 114
Wakefield, Julia and family....... 140
Walker, Anna...................... 7
    Caroline 250
    Caroline Sears................249
    Catherine P...................249
    Elizabeth J. and family....249-250
    Georgianna 249
    Lucinda and family............172
    Rev. Obed B...................172
    Maj. Nathaniel.............248-250
    Sylvia 74

Walker, Wilder P..................249
Ward, Cora S......................242
    Luke 242
Warden, Edward and family.........249
Watson, Lydia Florence and family..151
    Robert 151
Watt, Anna C..................242-243
Way, Benjamin F...................141
    Nancy M.......................141
Weed, Daniel and family........... 18
Welch, Daniel..................... 69
    Edward and descendants....163-168
    Mary 8
    Mary Thompson................. 69
    Samuel 69
Wells, Amos R. and family.....204-205
    John B........................245
    John Levi and family..........245
Wentworth, Maj. Jesse and family.. 58
Weymouth, Daniel................31, 65
    Eva J......................... 65
    Francis Purington............. 65
Wheeler, Hiram and family.....168-171
    Sylva J....................... 86
Whitcomb, Frank J. and family.....251
    Henry F.......................251
White, Harold J...................233
    Henry 233
    John 5
    Nellie Maud...................233
Whitmore, Francis.................128
    Martha Elizabeth..............128
Whitney, Jane Hunter.............. 39
    Joseph and family.............271
    Maj. Warren L................. 62
Wible, Olive and family...........180
Wildes, Lydia.....................248
Wilcox, Helen E...................143
    John W........................143
Wildman, Albert E. and family.....120
    George 120
Willard, Randilla................. 52
Williams, Ethel................... 61
Wilson, Abizer C..................140
    Frances A..................... 76
    George L......................263
    Horace G...................... 76
    Col. John and family..........250
    John 27
    Mary 27
    Samuel Alva...................229
Wingate, Alice May................ 91
    Stanley J..................... 91
Wise, William.................... 28
Wood, Alonzo and family.......182-183
    Henry Ellis and family........133
    James S.......................133
    Mary 203
Woodward, Eben....................140
    Gilbert and family............140
    Rachel and family.............138
    Rev. Samuel 138
    Samuel and family.............147
Wooster, Hannah....54, 78, 81, 122, 123
    125, 135, 137, 142, 146, 147
Wright, Benjamin F. and family...169
    Harold B. and family..........169
    James E...................169-170
    Linwood P. and family.....169-170
Wyer, Jane E. and family.......264-270
Youngman, David T. and family....173

www.ingramcontent.com/pod-product-compliance
Lightning Source LLC
Chambersburg PA
CBHW080326270326
41927CB00014B/3113